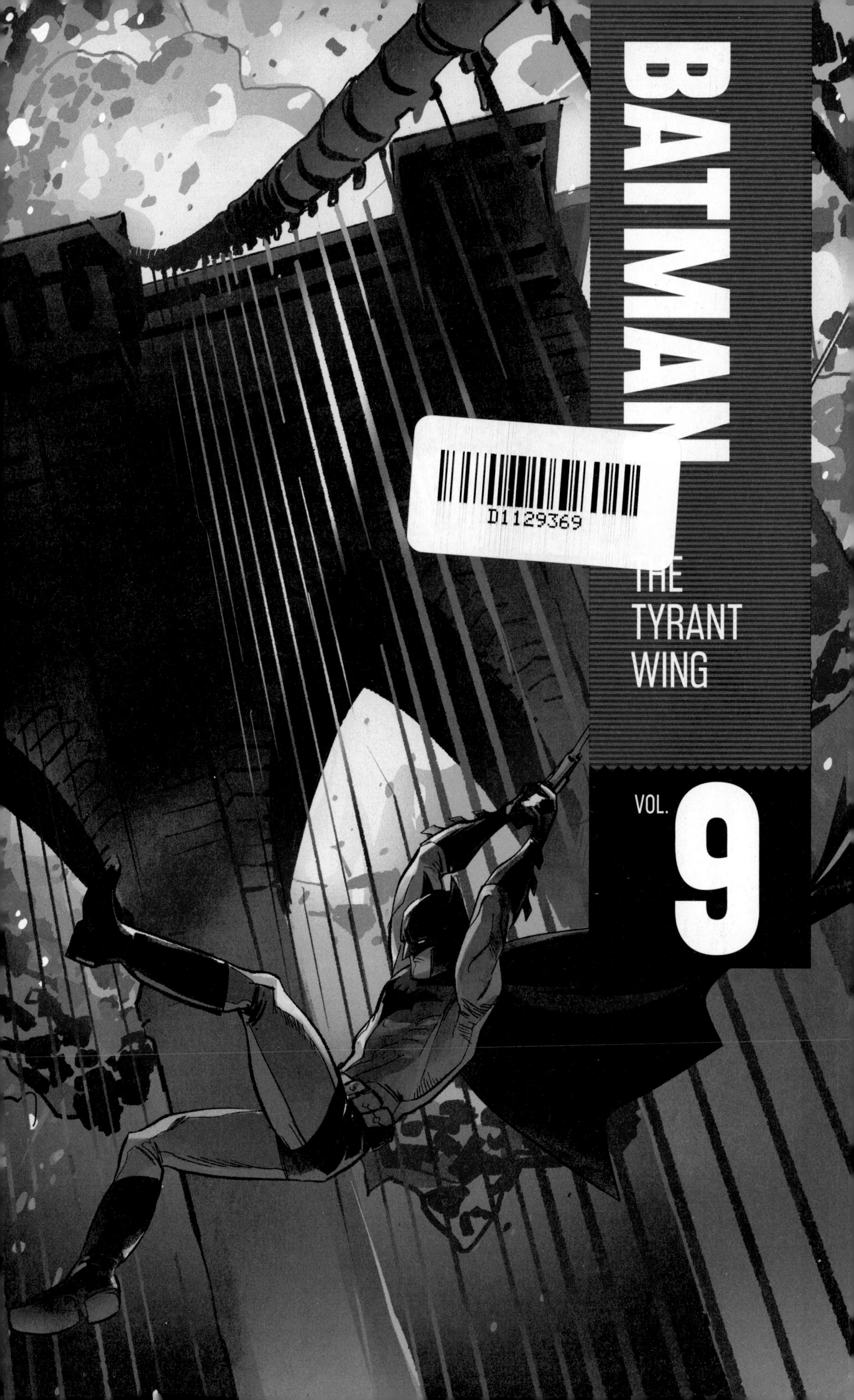

BATMAN

THE TYRANT WING

VOL. 9

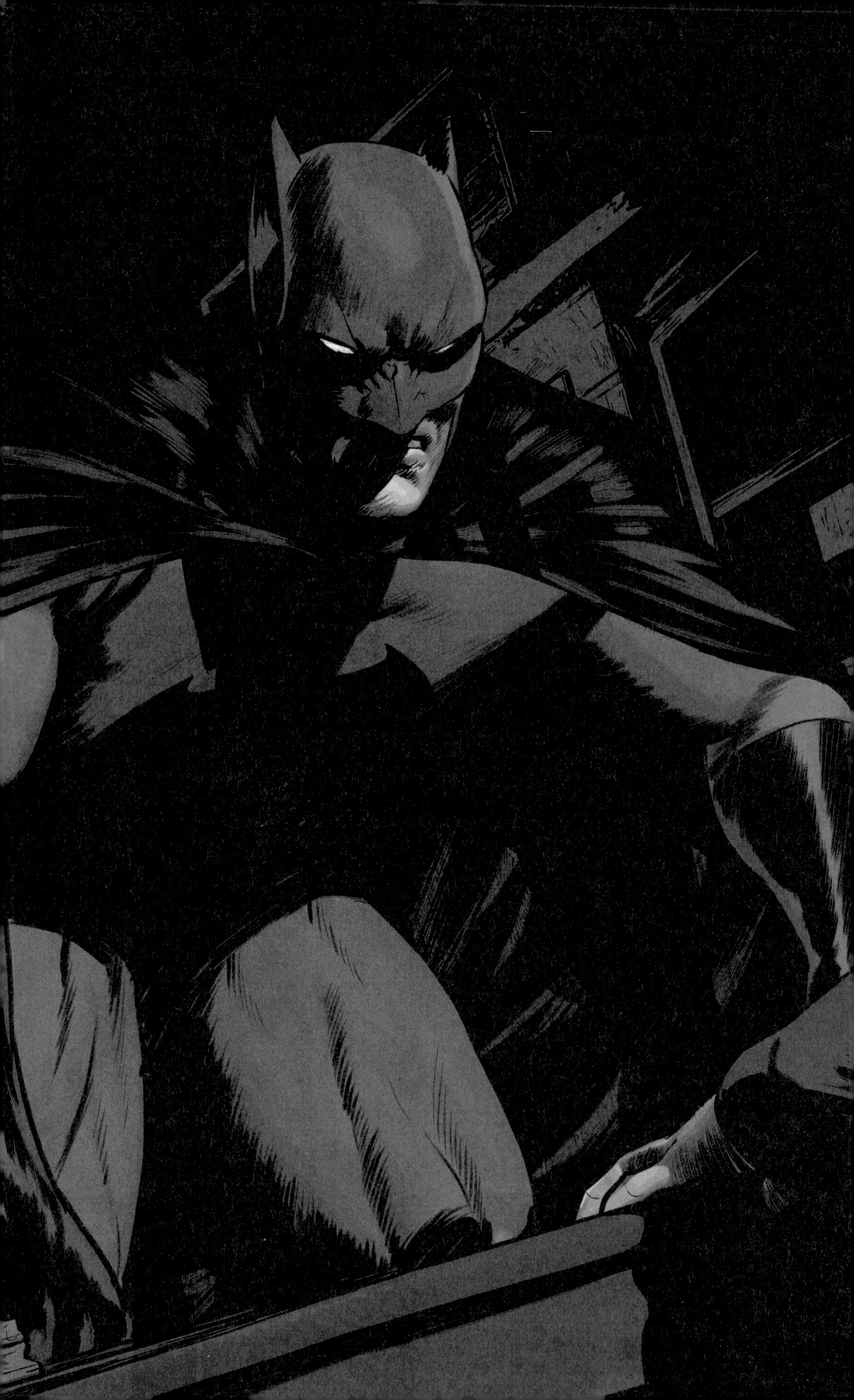

BATMAN
THE TYRANT WING

writers

TOM KING
TOM TAYLOR
RAM V
CHERYL LYNN EATON
JORDIE BELLAIRE

artists

MIKEL JANÍN
OTTO SCHMIDT
JORGE FORNES
ELENA CASAGRANDE
JILL THOMPSON
BRAD WALKER
ANDREW HENNESSY

colorists

JORDIE BELLAIRE
MATT WILSON
TRISH MULVIHILL
OTTO SCHMIDT

letterers

CLAYTON COWLES
STEVE WANDS
DERON BENNETT
TOM NAPOLITANO
A LARGER WORLD'S TROY PETERI

collection cover artist

MIKEL JANÍN

VOL.
9

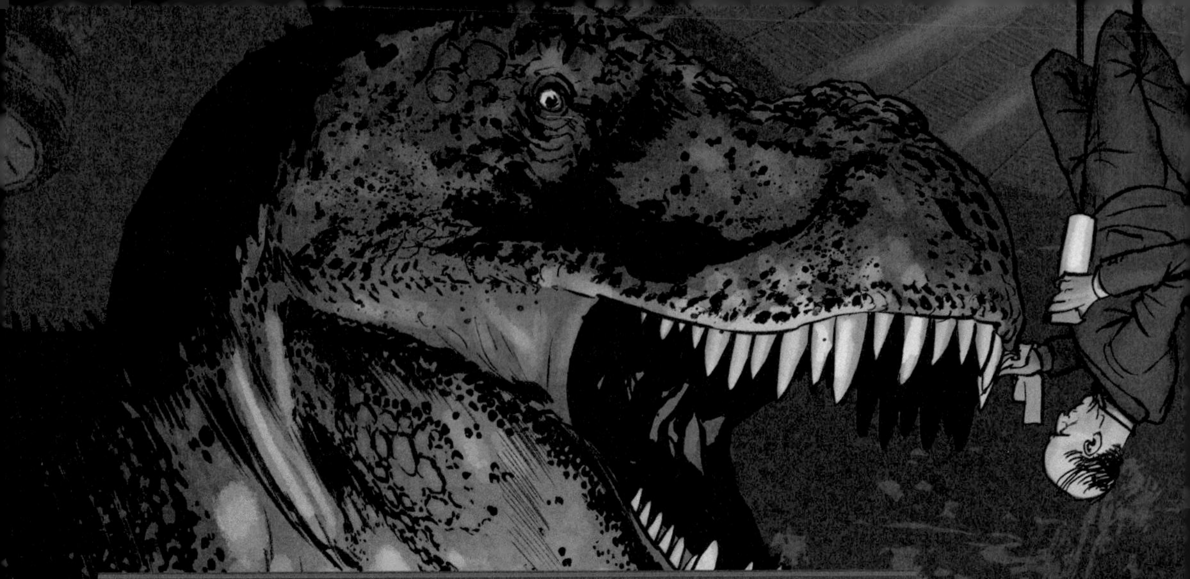

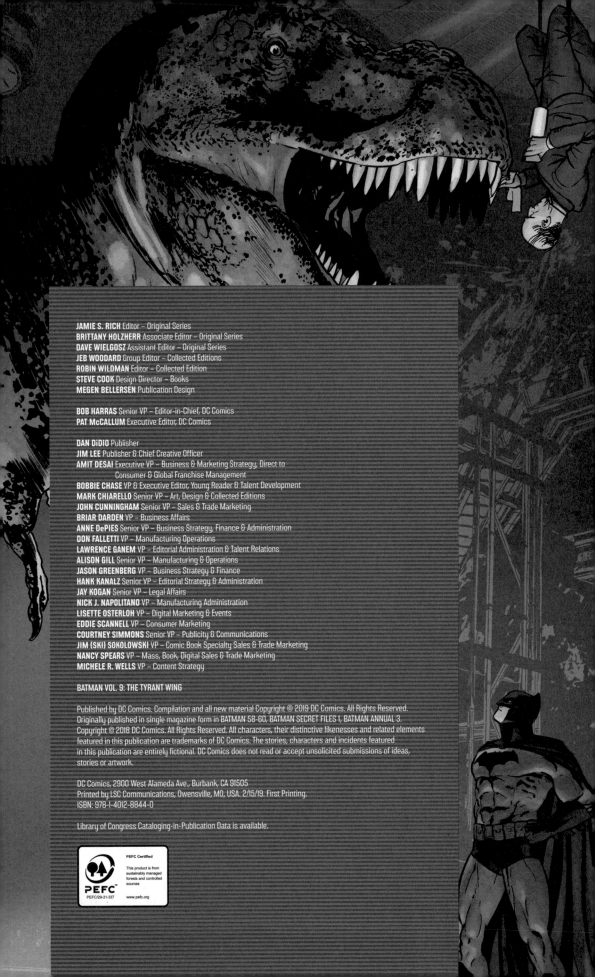

JAMIE S. RICH Editor – Original Series
BRITTANY HOLZHERR Associate Editor – Original Series
DAVE WIELGOSZ Assistant Editor – Original Series
JEB WOODARD Group Editor – Collected Editions
ROBIN WILDMAN Editor – Collected Edition
STEVE COOK Design Director – Books
MEGEN BELLERSEN Publication Design

BOB HARRAS Senior VP – Editor-in-Chief, DC Comics
PAT McCALLUM Executive Editor, DC Comics

DAN DiDIO Publisher
JIM LEE Publisher & Chief Creative Officer
AMIT DESAI Executive VP – Business & Marketing Strategy, Direct to Consumer & Global Franchise Management
BOBBIE CHASE VP & Executive Editor, Young Reader & Talent Development
MARK CHIARELLO Senior VP – Art, Design & Collected Editions
JOHN CUNNINGHAM Senior VP – Sales & Trade Marketing
BRIAR DARDEN VP – Business Affairs
ANNE DePIES Senior VP – Business Strategy, Finance & Administration
DON FALLETTI VP – Manufacturing Operations
LAWRENCE GANEM VP – Editorial Administration & Talent Relations
ALISON GILL Senior VP – Manufacturing & Operations
JASON GREENBERG VP – Business Strategy & Finance
HANK KANALZ Senior VP – Editorial Strategy & Administration
JAY KOGAN Senior VP – Legal Affairs
NICK J. NAPOLITANO VP – Manufacturing Administration
LISETTE OSTERLOH VP – Digital Marketing & Events
EDDIE SCANNELL VP – Consumer Marketing
COURTNEY SIMMONS Senior VP – Publicity & Communications
JIM (SKI) SOKOLOWSKI VP – Comic Book Specialty Sales & Trade Marketing
NANCY SPEARS VP – Mass, Book, Digital Sales & Trade Marketing
MICHELE R. WELLS VP – Content Strategy

BATMAN VOL. 9: THE TYRANT WING

DC Comics, 2900 West Alameda Ave., Burbank, CA 91505
Printed by LSC Communications, Owensville, MO, USA. 2/15/19. First Printing.
ISBN: 978-1-4012-8844-0

Library of Congress Cataloging-in-Publication Data is available.

PEFC Certified
This product is from sustainably managed forests and controlled sources
PEFC
PEFC/29-31-337
www.pefc.org

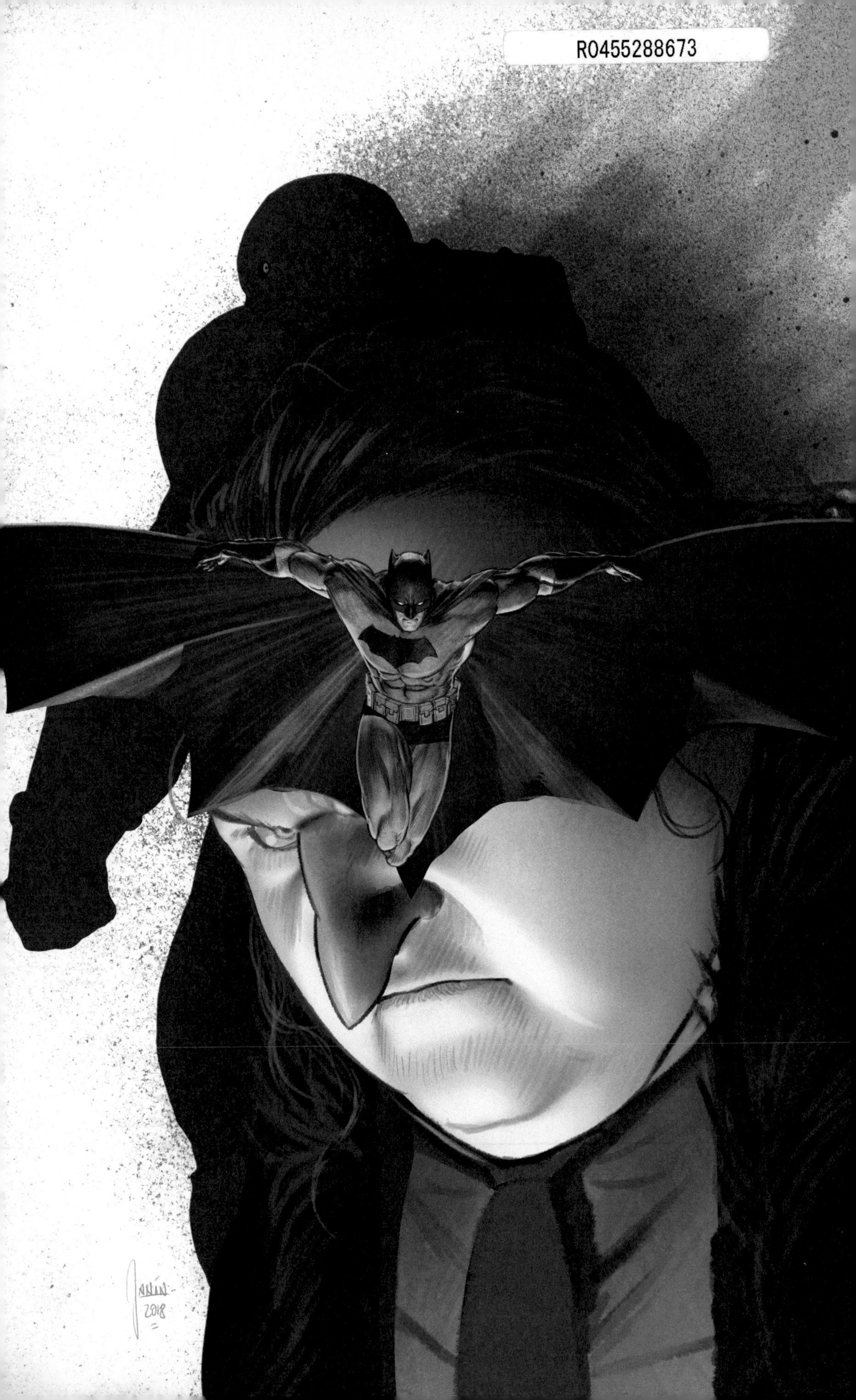

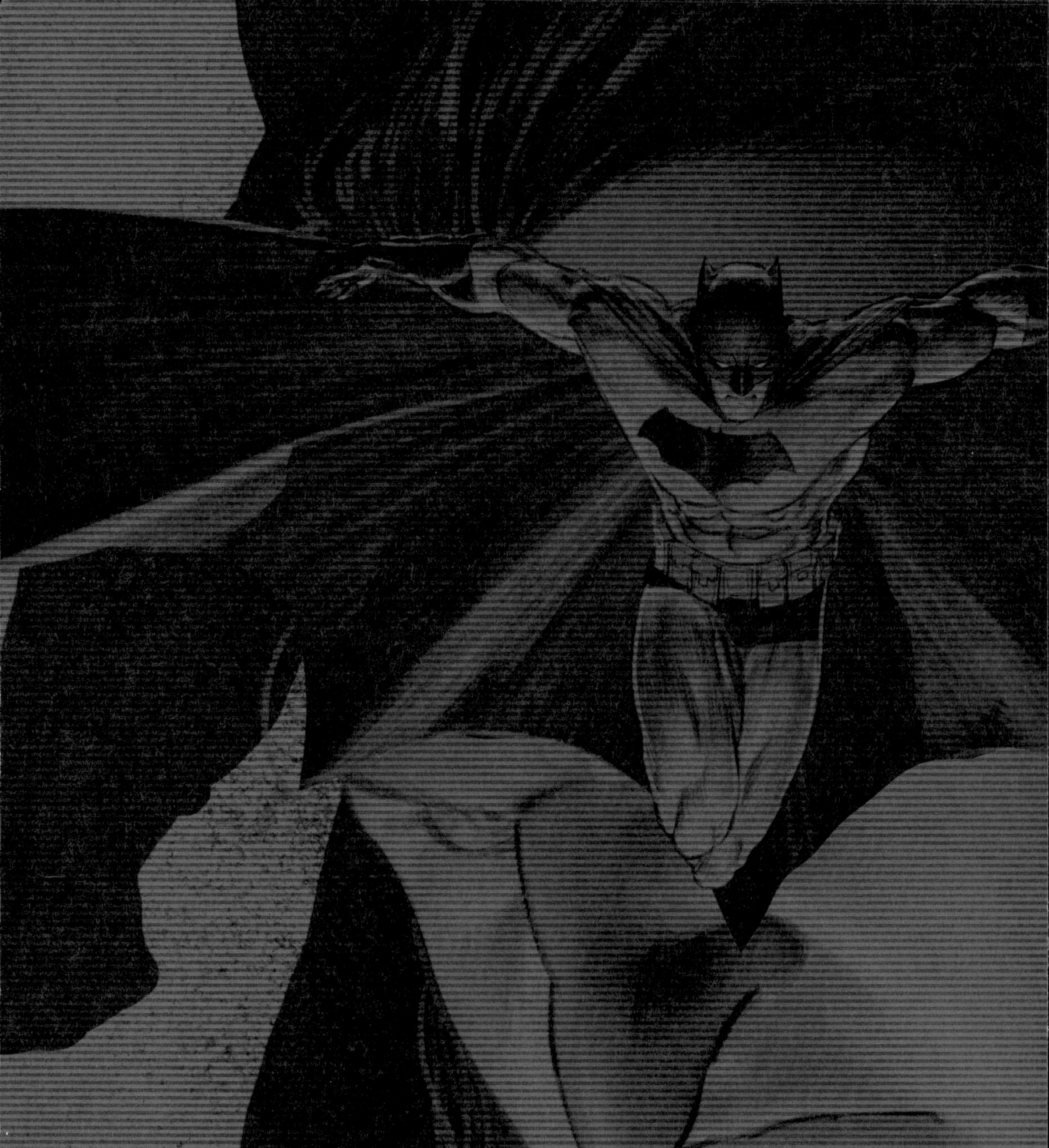

BATMAN
#58

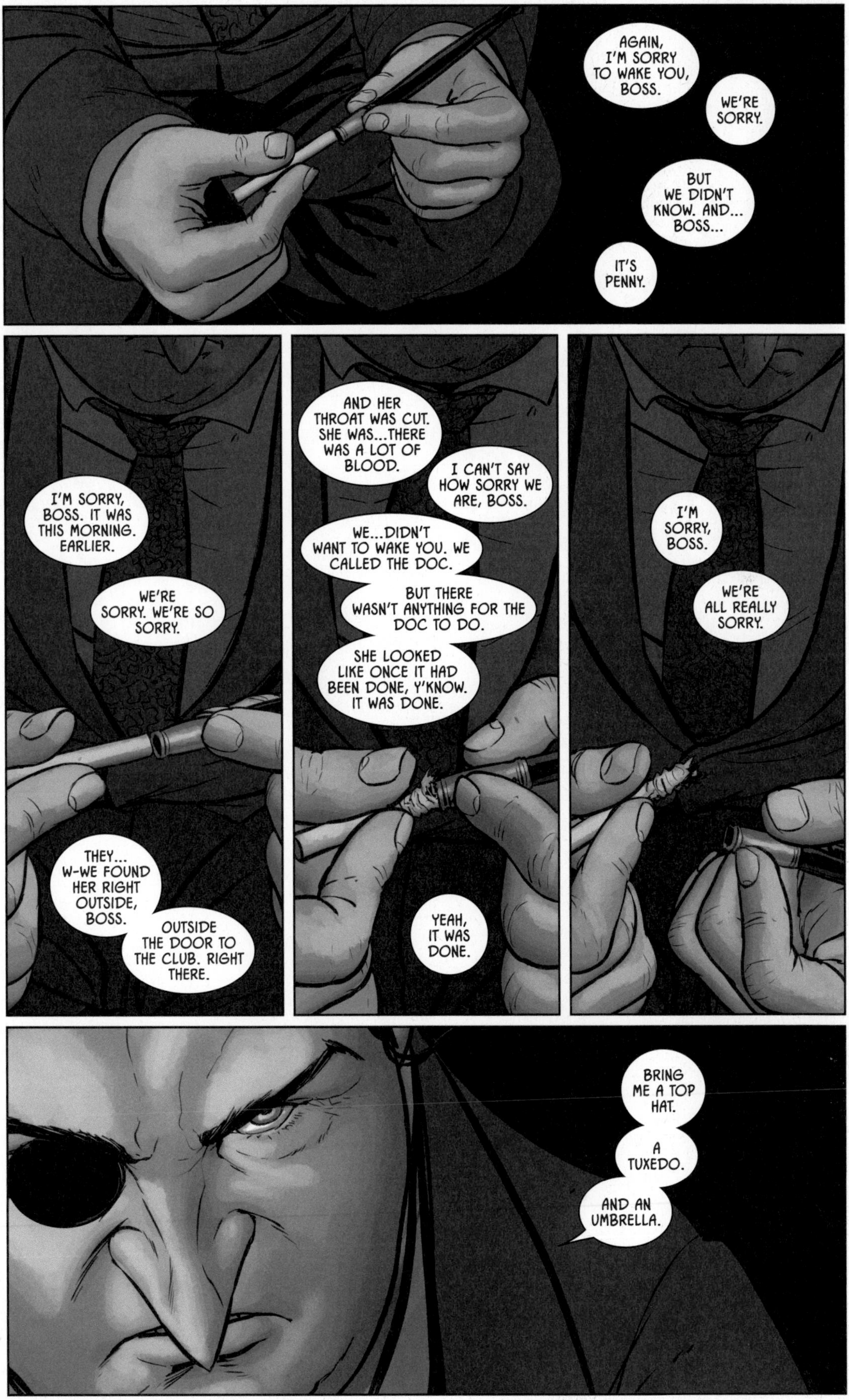
AGAIN, I'M SORRY TO WAKE YOU, BOSS.
WE'RE SORRY.
BUT WE DIDN'T KNOW. AND... BOSS...
IT'S PENNY.
I'M SORRY, BOSS. IT WAS THIS MORNING. EARLIER.
WE'RE SORRY. WE'RE SO SORRY.
THEY... W-WE FOUND HER RIGHT OUTSIDE, BOSS.
OUTSIDE THE DOOR TO THE CLUB. RIGHT THERE.
AND HER THROAT WAS CUT. SHE WAS...THERE WAS A LOT OF BLOOD.
I CAN'T SAY HOW SORRY WE ARE, BOSS.
WE...DIDN'T WANT TO WAKE YOU. WE CALLED THE DOC.
BUT THERE WASN'T ANYTHING FOR THE DOC TO DO.
SHE LOOKED LIKE ONCE IT HAD BEEN DONE, Y'KNOW. IT WAS DONE.
YEAH, IT WAS DONE.
I'M SORRY, BOSS.
WE'RE ALL REALLY SORRY.
BRING ME A TOP HAT.
A TUXEDO.
AND AN UMBRELLA.

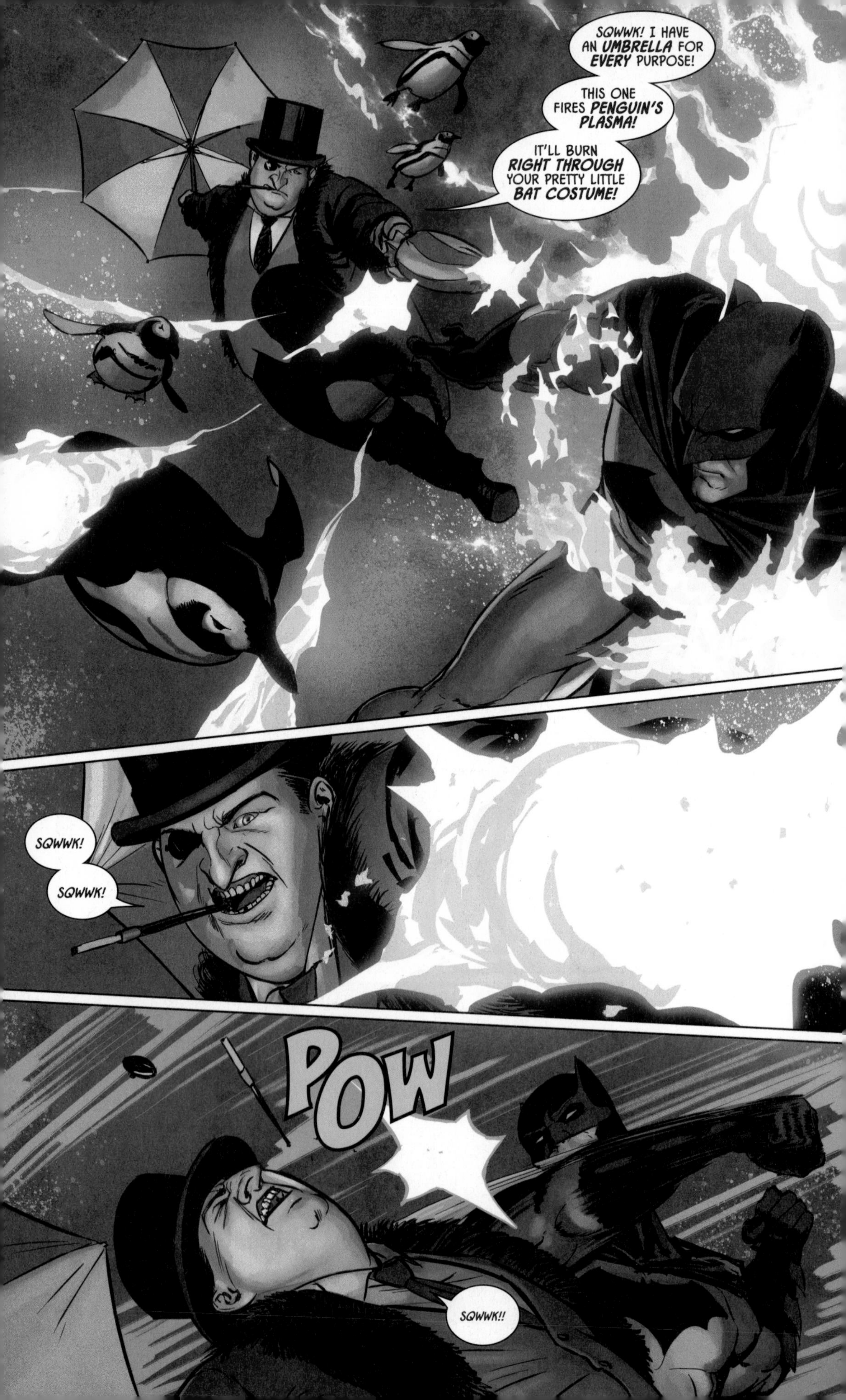
SQWWK! I HAVE AN UMBRELLA FOR EVERY PURPOSE!
THIS ONE FIRES PENGUIN'S PLASMA!
IT'LL BURN RIGHT THROUGH YOUR PRETTY LITTLE BAT COSTUME!
SQWWK!
SQWWK!
POW
SQWWK!!

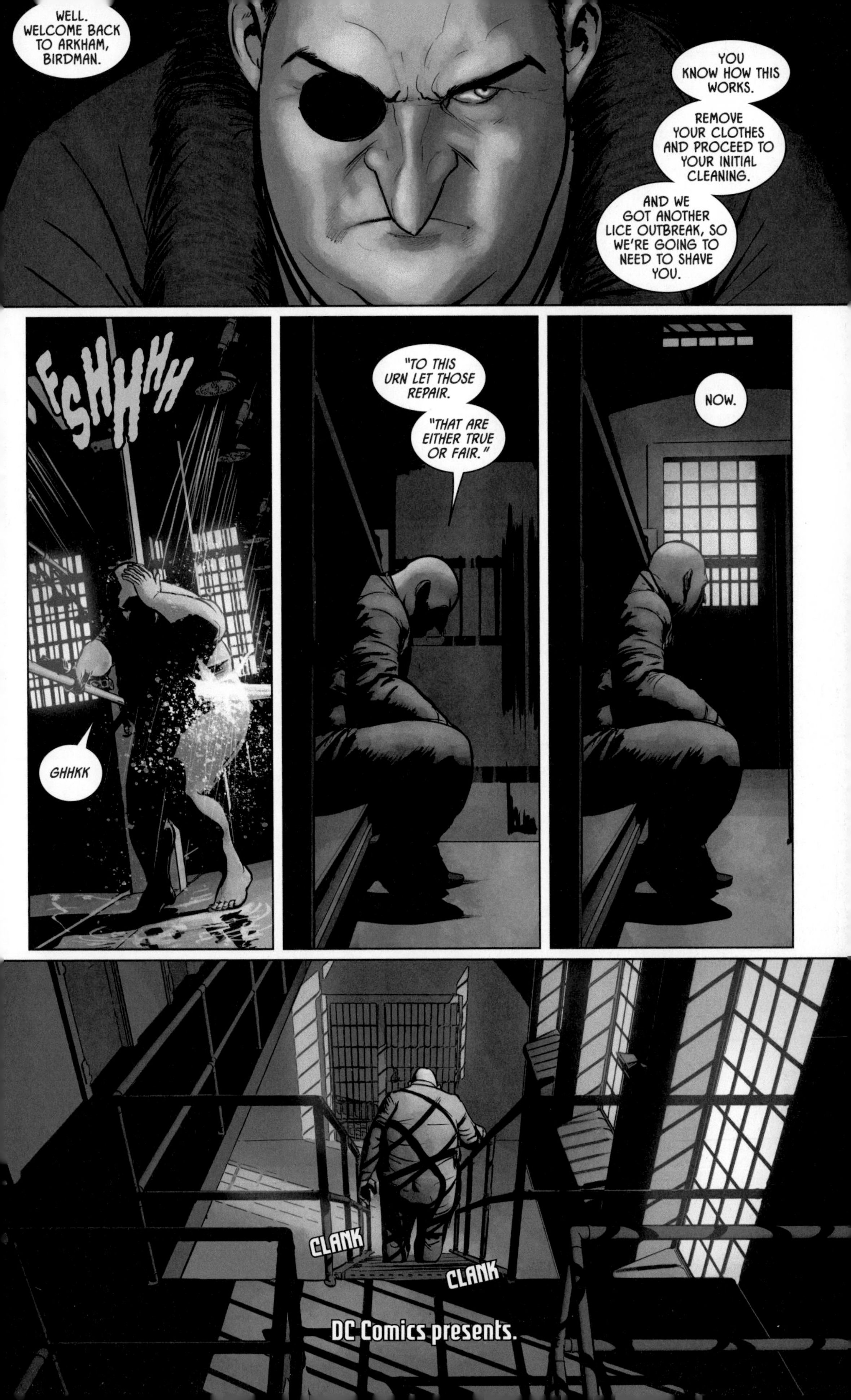
WELL. WELCOME BACK TO ARKHAM, BIRDMAN.
YOU KNOW HOW THIS WORKS.
REMOVE YOUR CLOTHES AND PROCEED TO YOUR INITIAL CLEANING.
AND WE GOT ANOTHER LICE OUTBREAK, SO WE'RE GOING TO NEED TO SHAVE YOU.
FSHHHH
GHHKK
"TO THIS URN LET THOSE REPAIR.
"THAT ARE EITHER TRUE OR FAIR."
NOW.
CLANK
CLANK
DC Comics presents.

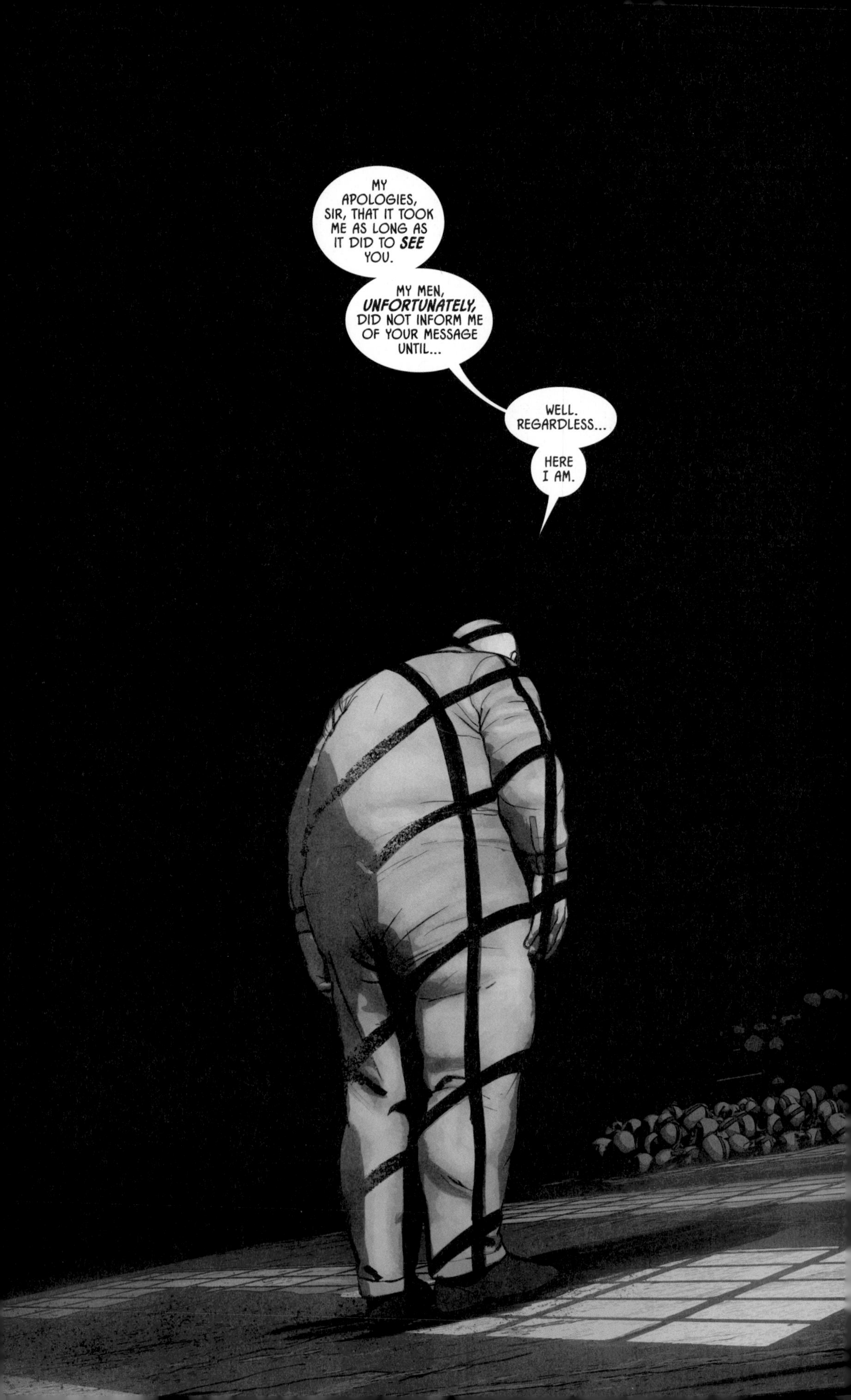
MY APOLOGIES, SIR, THAT IT TOOK ME AS LONG AS IT DID TO **SEE** YOU.
MY MEN, ***UNFORTUNATELY,*** DID NOT INFORM ME OF YOUR MESSAGE UNTIL...
WELL. REGARDLESS...
HERE I AM.

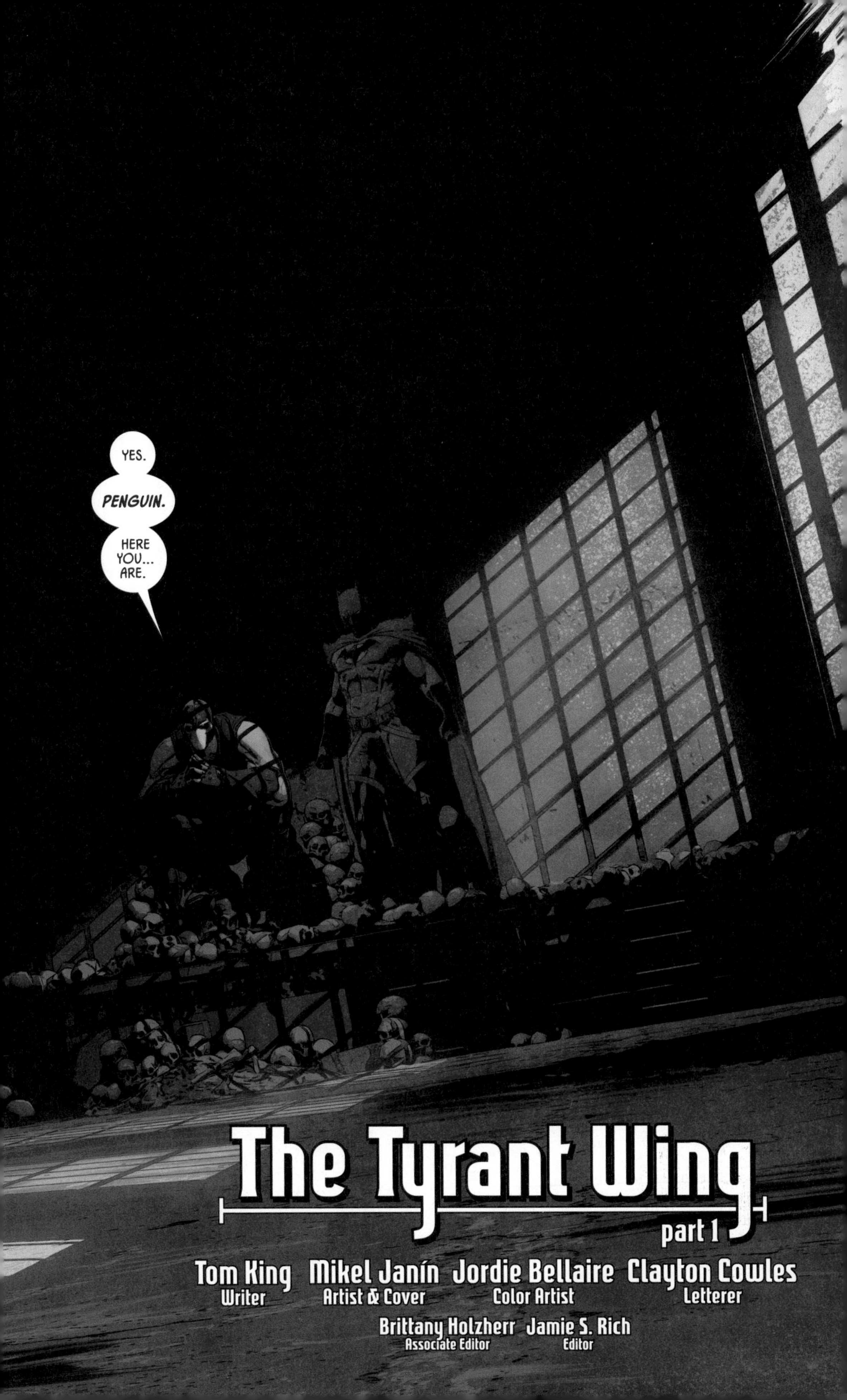
YES.
PENGUIN.
HERE YOU... ARE.
The Tyrant Wing
part 1
Tom King Writer
Mikel Janín Artist & Cover
Jordie Bellaire Color Artist
Clayton Cowles Letterer
Brittany Holzherr Associate Editor
Jamie S. Rich Editor

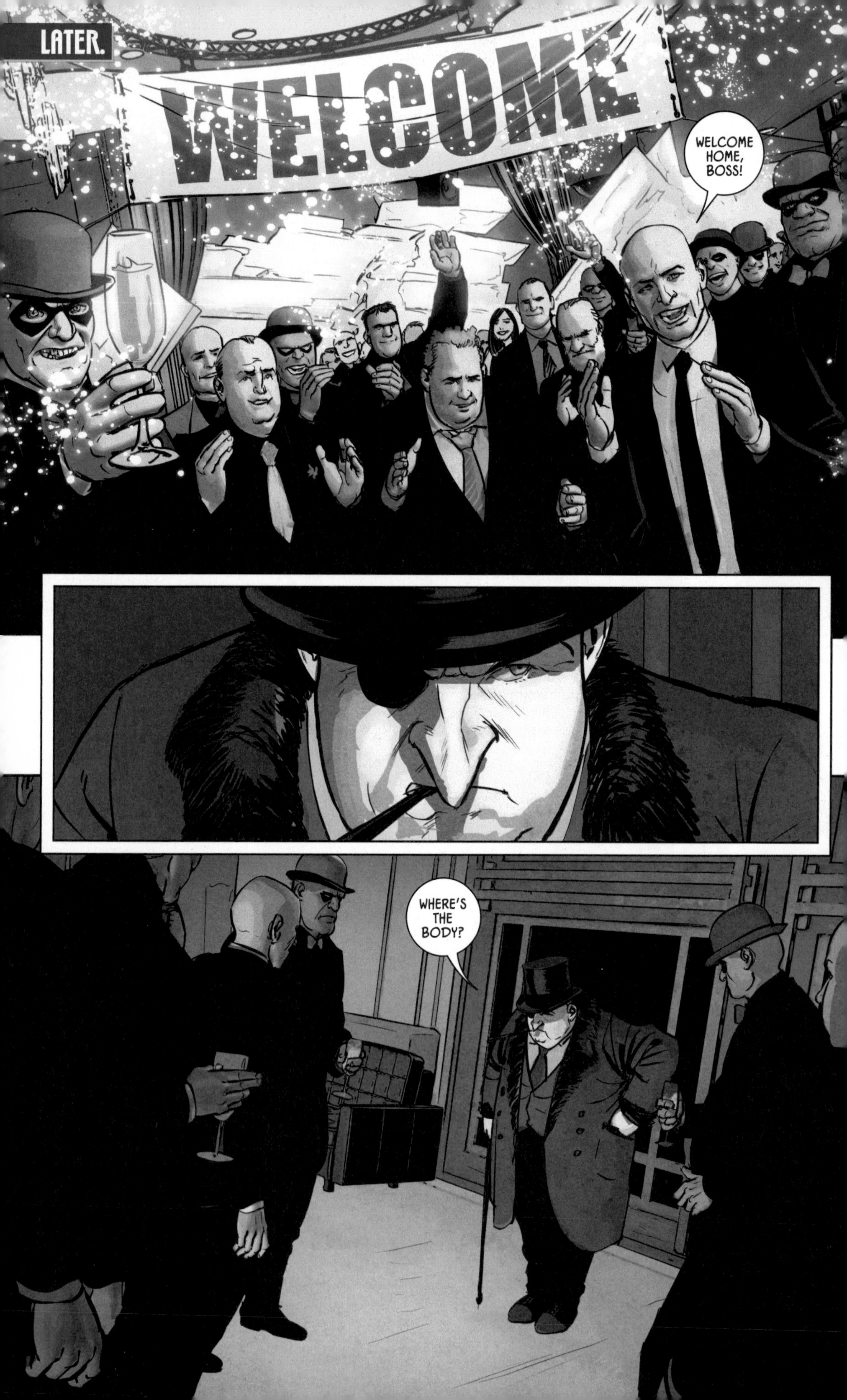
LATER.
WELCOME
WELCOME HOME, BOSS!
WHERE'S THE BODY?

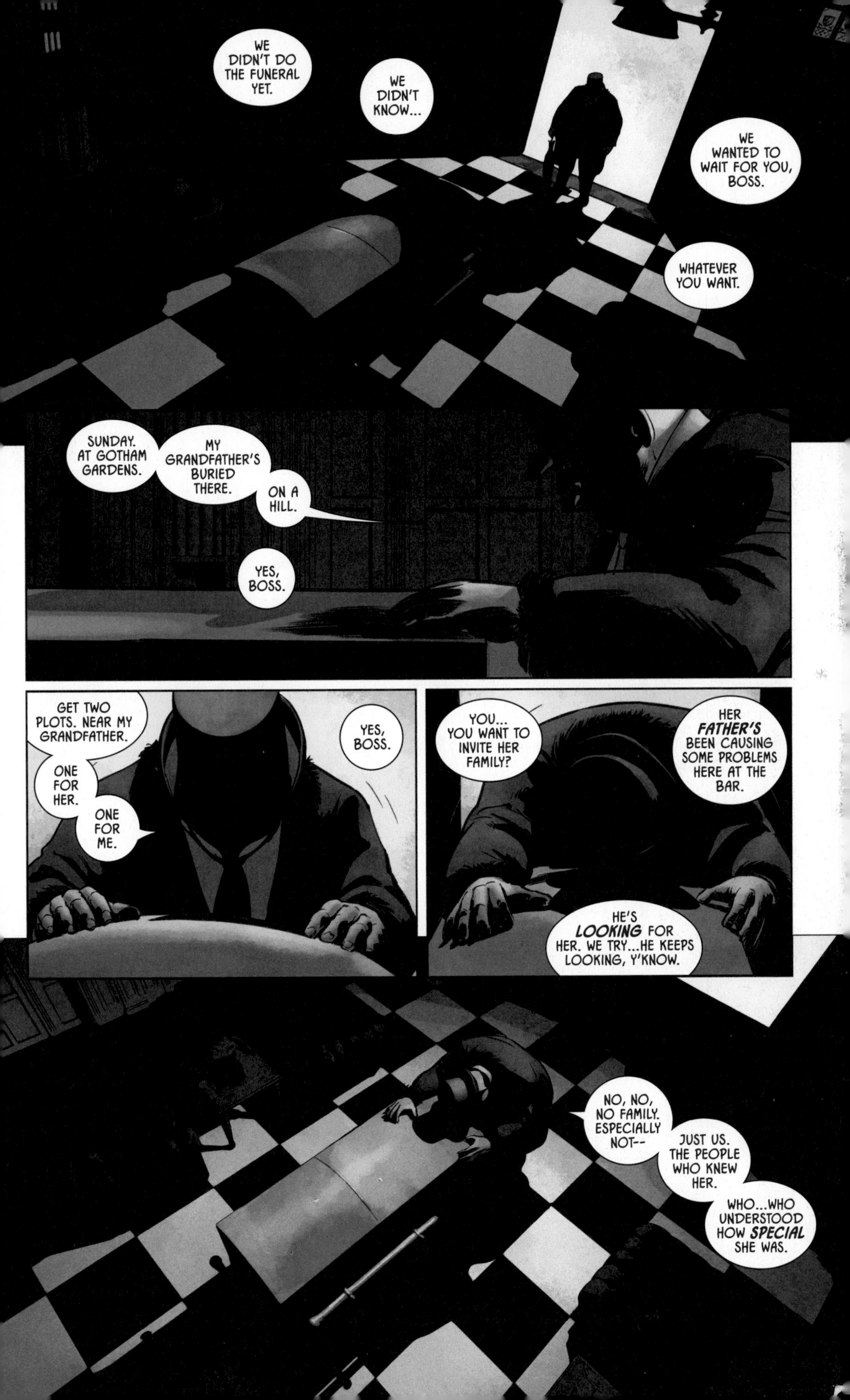

WE DIDN'T DO THE FUNERAL YET.
WE DIDN'T KNOW...
WE WANTED TO WAIT FOR YOU, BOSS.
WHATEVER YOU WANT.
SUNDAY. AT GOTHAM GARDENS.
MY GRANDFATHER'S BURIED THERE.
ON A HILL.
YES, BOSS.
GET TWO PLOTS. NEAR MY GRANDFATHER.
ONE FOR HER.
ONE FOR ME.
YES, BOSS.
YOU... YOU WANT TO INVITE HER FAMILY?
HER **FATHER'S** BEEN CAUSING SOME PROBLEMS HERE AT THE BAR.
HE'S **LOOKING** FOR HER. WE TRY...HE KEEPS LOOKING, Y'KNOW.
NO, NO, NO FAMILY. ESPECIALLY NOT--
JUST US. THE PEOPLE WHO KNEW HER.
WHO...WHO UNDERSTOOD HOW **SPECIAL** SHE WAS.

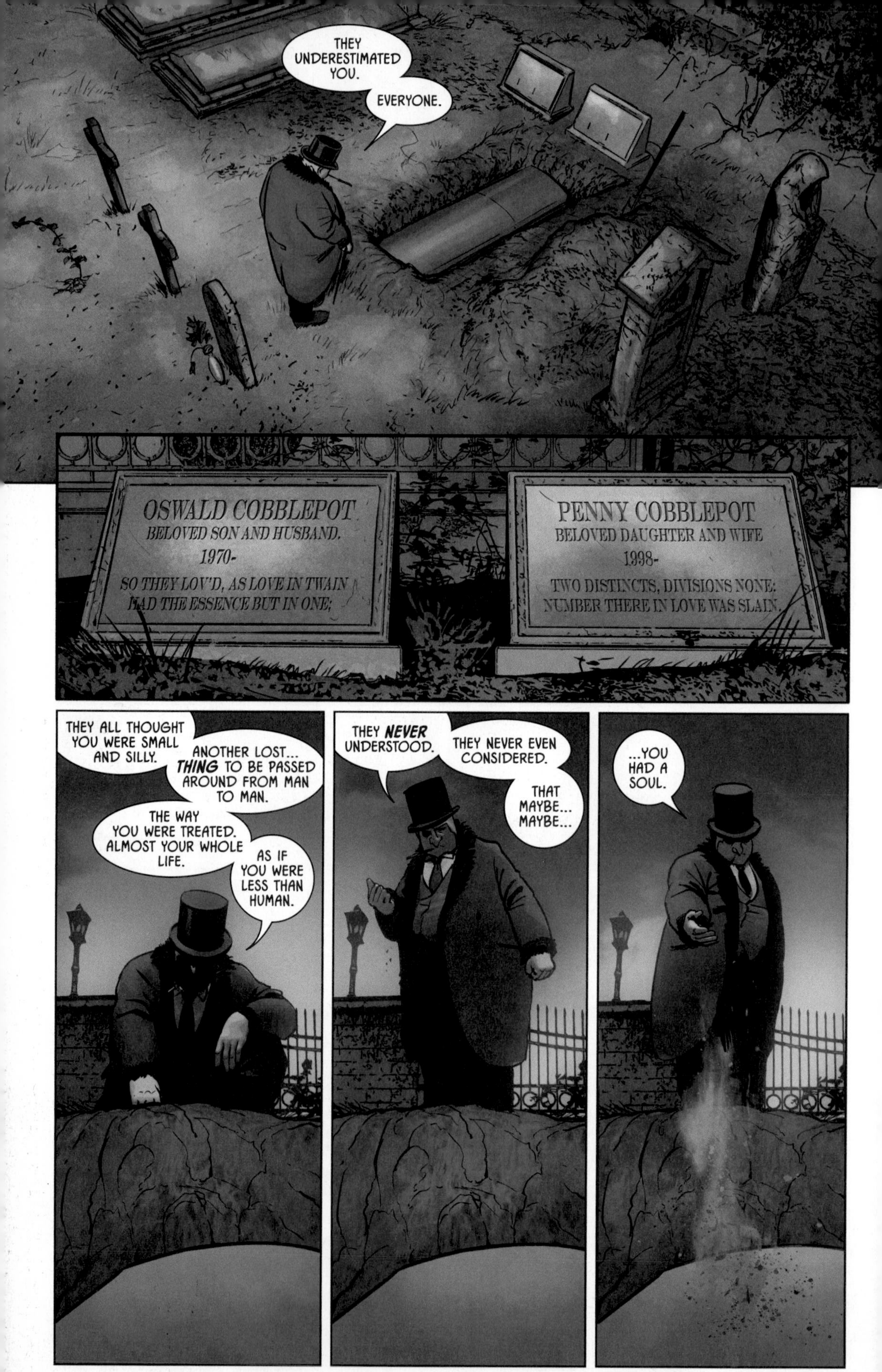
THEY UNDERESTIMATED YOU.
EVERYONE.
OSWALD COBBLEPOT
BELOVED SON AND HUSBAND.
1970-
SO THEY LOV'D, AS LOVE IN TWAIN
HAD THE ESSENCE BUT IN ONE;
PENNY COBBLEPOT
BELOVED DAUGHTER AND WIFE
1998-
TWO DISTINCTS, DIVISIONS NONE:
NUMBER THERE IN LOVE WAS SLAIN.
THEY ALL THOUGHT YOU WERE SMALL AND SILLY.
ANOTHER LOST... THING TO BE PASSED AROUND FROM MAN TO MAN.
THE WAY YOU WERE TREATED. ALMOST YOUR WHOLE LIFE.
AS IF YOU WERE LESS THAN HUMAN.
THEY NEVER UNDERSTOOD.
THEY NEVER EVEN CONSIDERED.
THAT MAYBE... MAYBE...
...YOU HAD A SOUL.

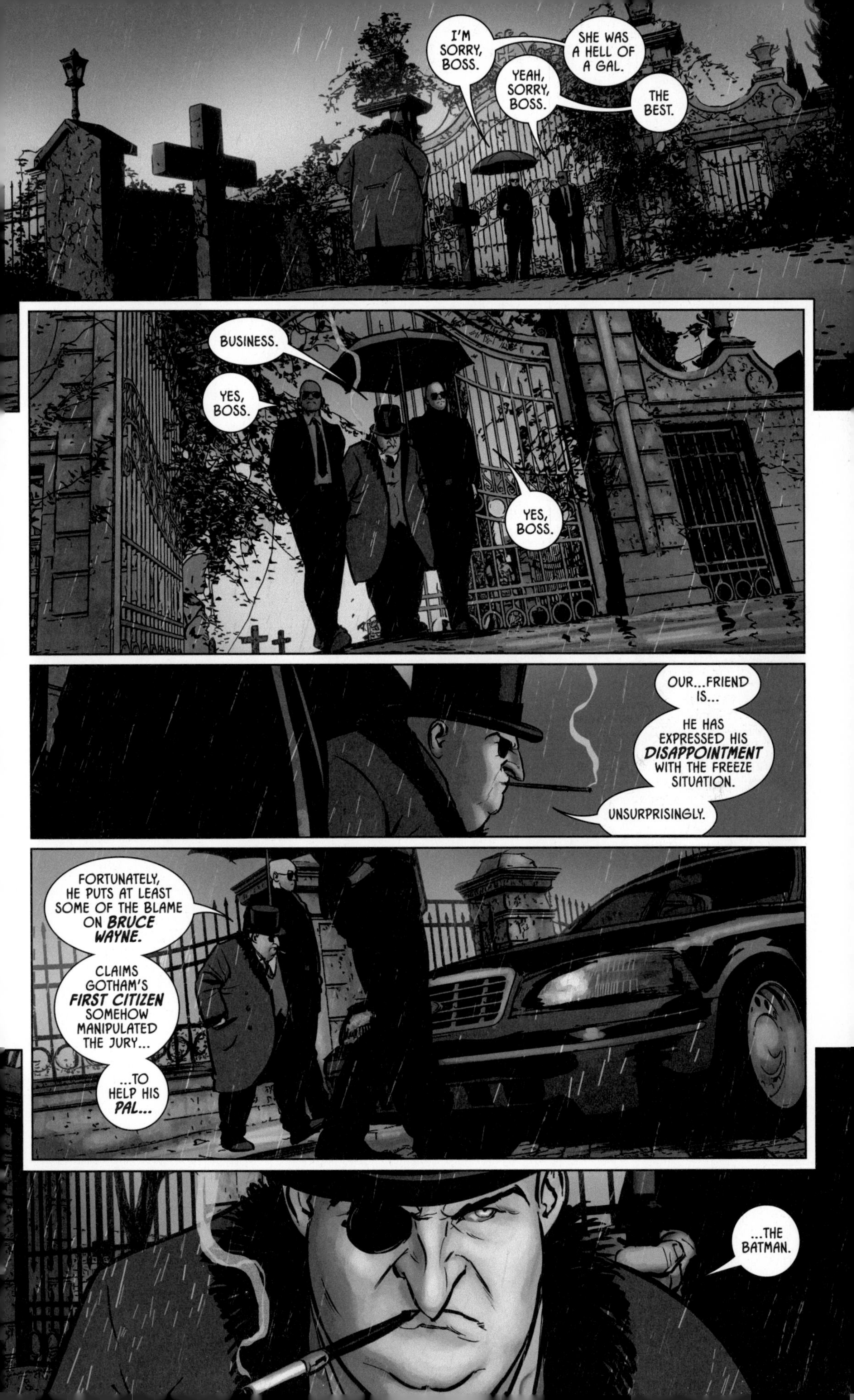
I'M SORRY, BOSS.
SHE WAS A HELL OF A GAL.
YEAH, SORRY, BOSS.
THE BEST.
BUSINESS.
YES, BOSS.
YES, BOSS.
OUR...FRIEND IS...
HE HAS EXPRESSED HIS DISAPPOINTMENT WITH THE FREEZE SITUATION.
UNSURPRISINGLY.
FORTUNATELY, HE PUTS AT LEAST SOME OF THE BLAME ON BRUCE WAYNE.
CLAIMS GOTHAM'S FIRST CITIZEN SOMEHOW MANIPULATED THE JURY...
...TO HELP HIS PAL...
...THE BATMAN.

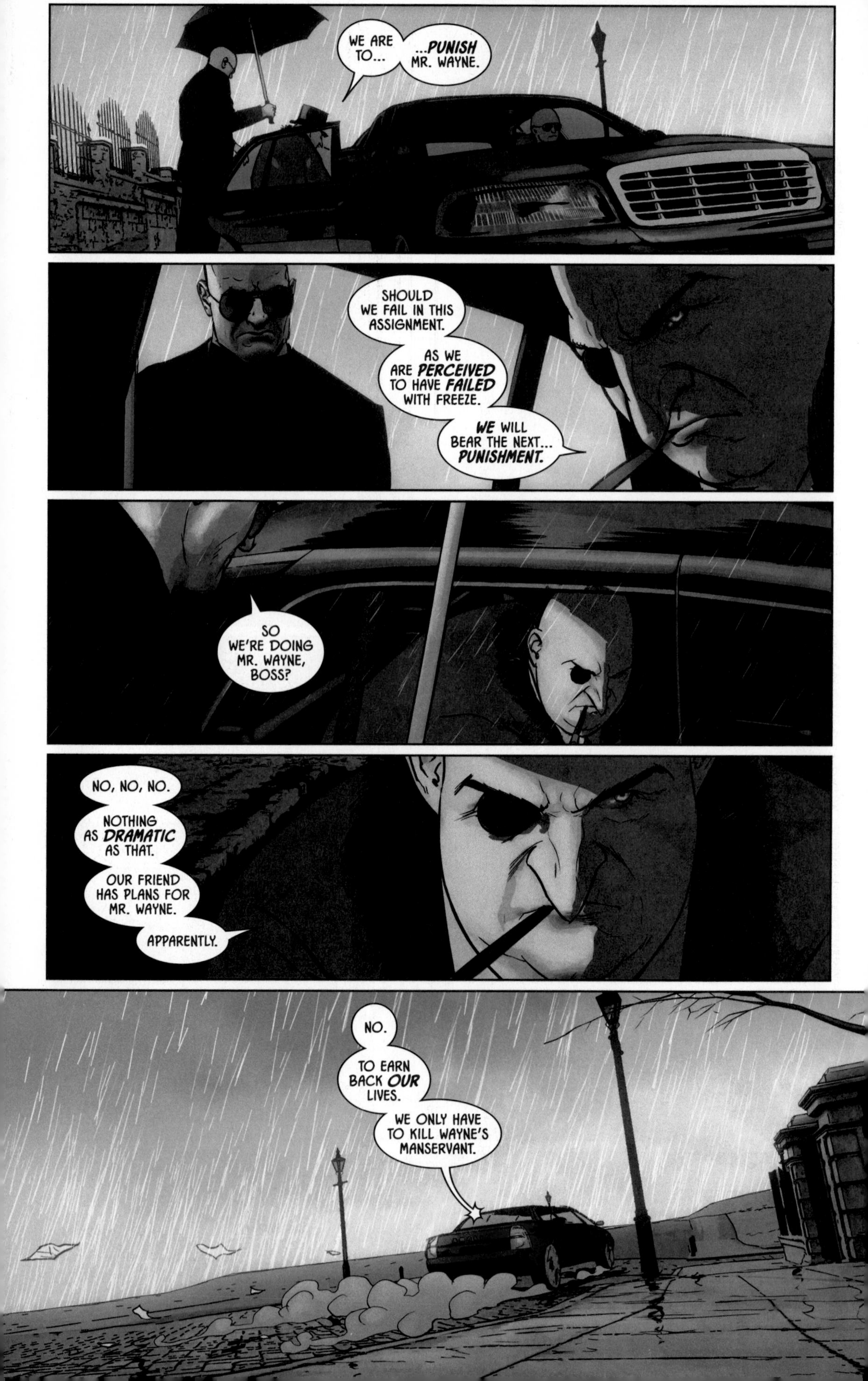
WE ARE TO...
...PUNISH MR. WAYNE.
SHOULD WE FAIL IN THIS ASSIGNMENT.
AS WE ARE PERCEIVED TO HAVE FAILED WITH FREEZE.
WE WILL BEAR THE NEXT... PUNISHMENT.
SO WE'RE DOING MR. WAYNE, BOSS?
NO, NO, NO.
NOTHING AS DRAMATIC AS THAT.
OUR FRIEND HAS PLANS FOR MR. WAYNE.
APPARENTLY.
NO.
TO EARN BACK OUR LIVES.
WE ONLY HAVE TO KILL WAYNE'S MANSERVANT.

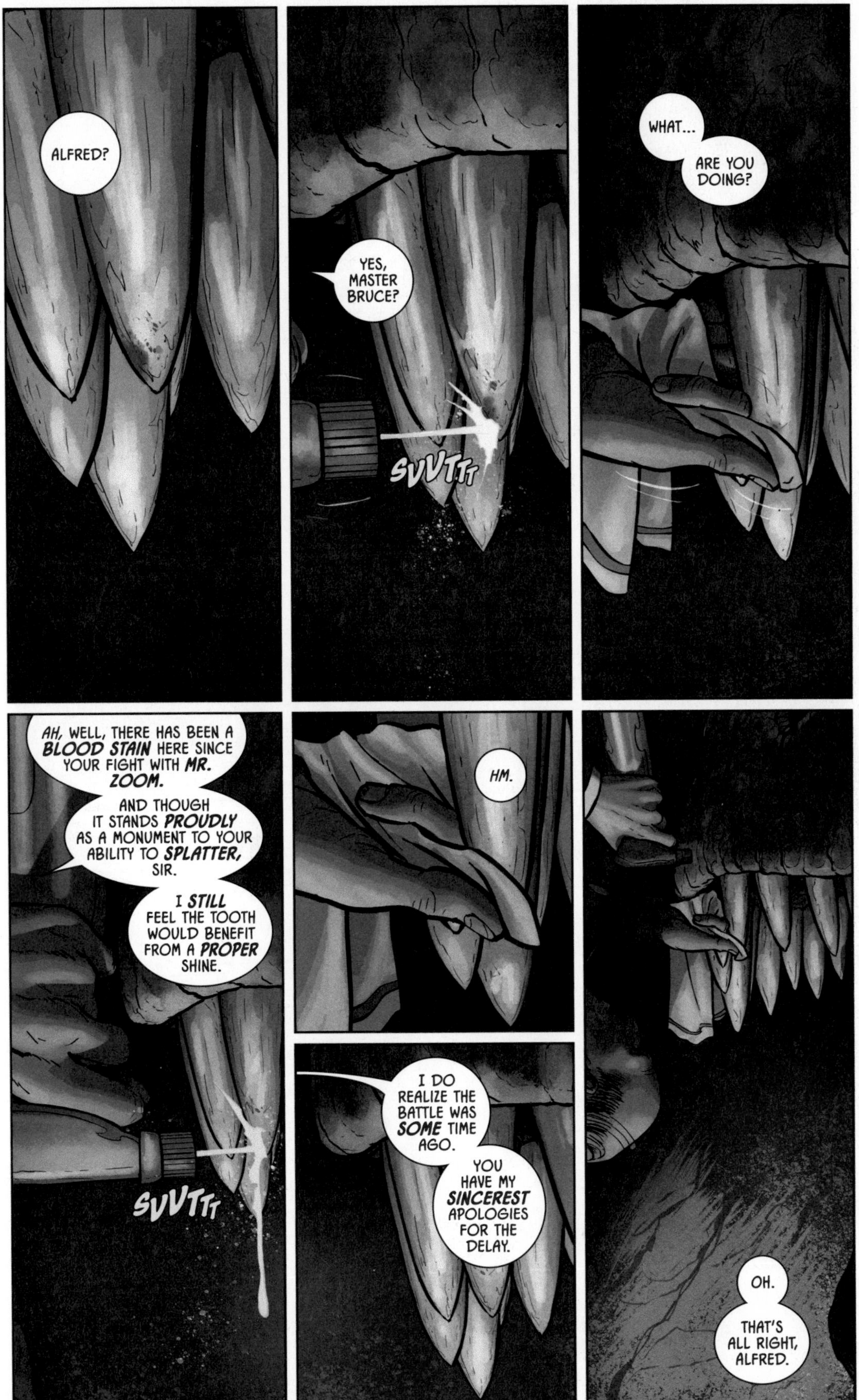
ALFRED?
YES, MASTER BRUCE?
SVUTTT
WHAT...
ARE YOU DOING?
AH, WELL, THERE HAS BEEN A BLOOD STAIN HERE SINCE YOUR FIGHT WITH MR. ZOOM.
AND THOUGH IT STANDS PROUDLY AS A MONUMENT TO YOUR ABILITY TO SPLATTER, SIR.
I STILL FEEL THE TOOTH WOULD BENEFIT FROM A PROPER SHINE.
SVUTTT
HM.
I DO REALIZE THE BATTLE WAS SOME TIME AGO.
YOU HAVE MY SINCEREST APOLOGIES FOR THE DELAY.
OH.
THAT'S ALL RIGHT, ALFRED.

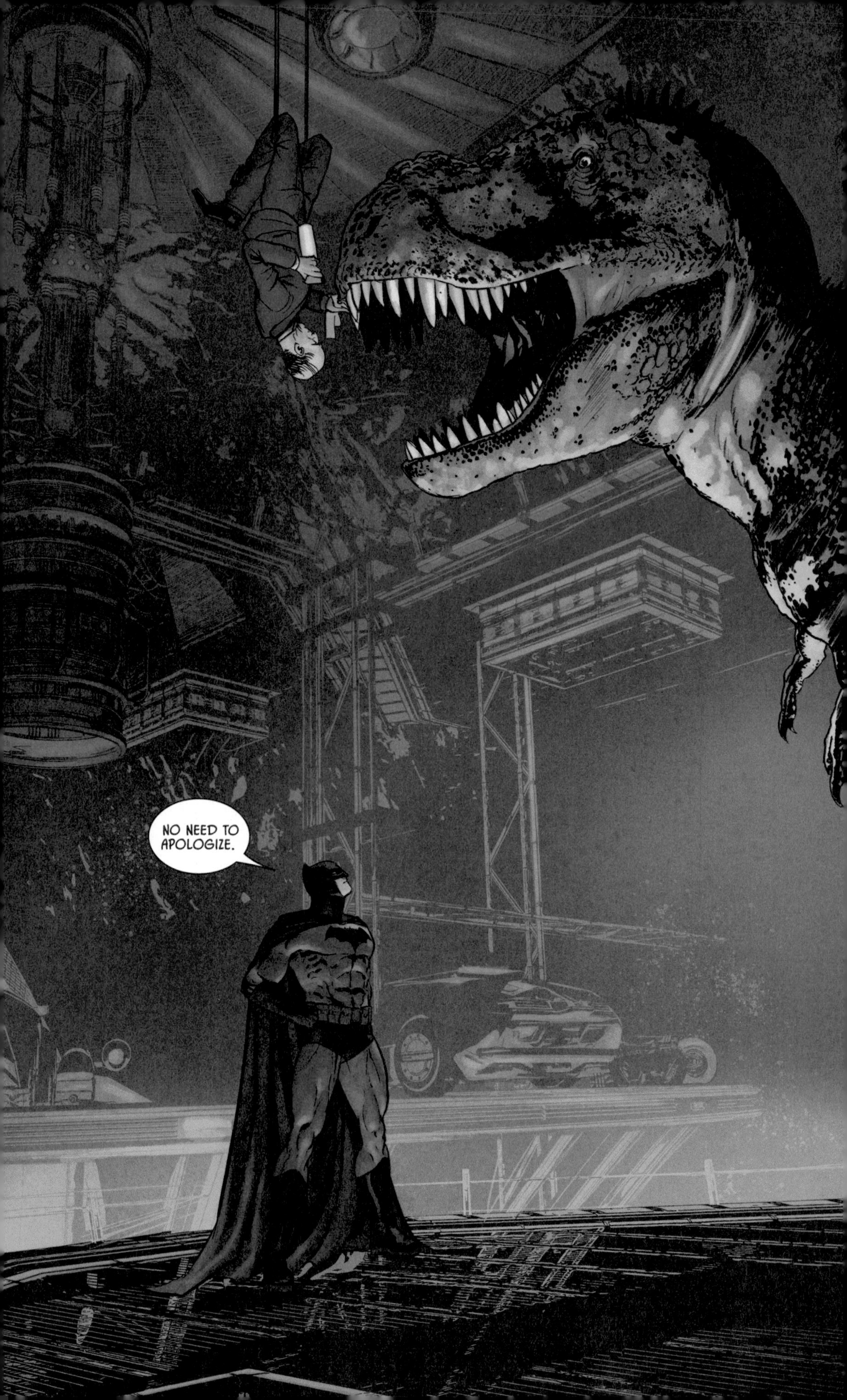
NO NEED TO
APOLOGIZE.

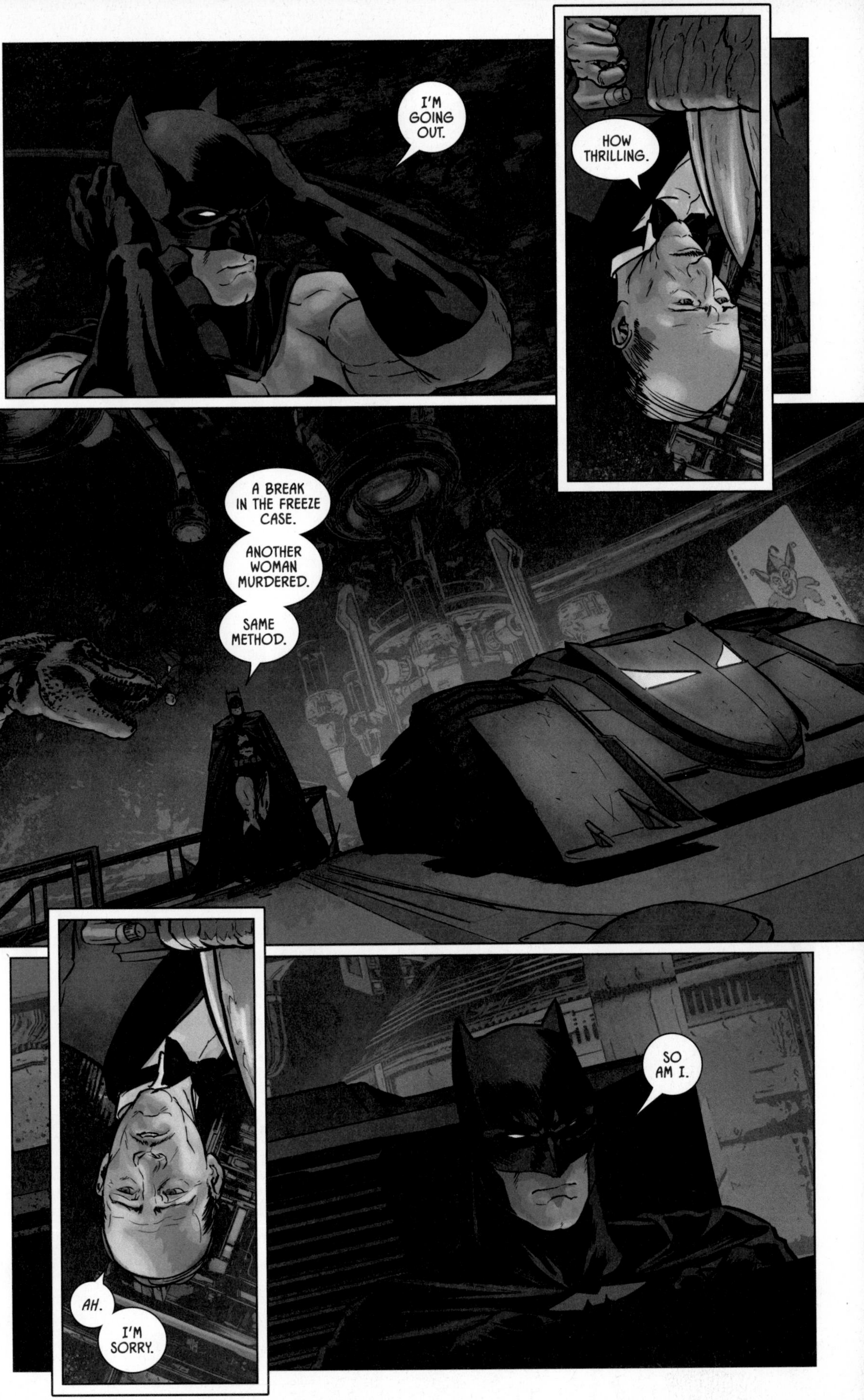

I'M GOING OUT.
HOW THRILLING.
A BREAK IN THE FREEZE CASE.
ANOTHER WOMAN MURDERED.
SAME METHOD.
AH.
I'M SORRY.
SO AM I.

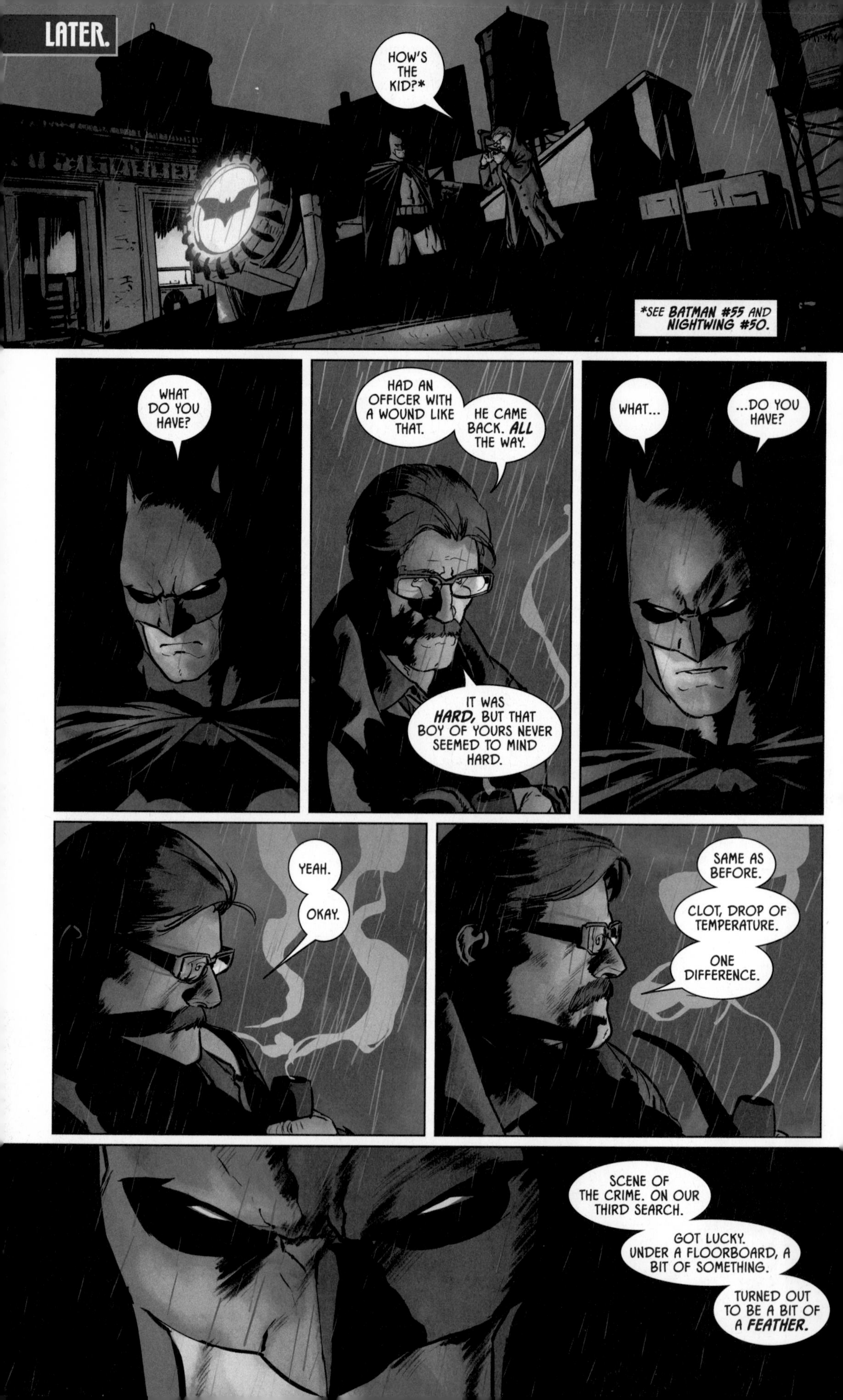
LATER.
HOW'S THE KID?*
*SEE BATMAN #55 AND NIGHTWING #50.
WHAT DO YOU HAVE?
HAD AN OFFICER WITH A WOUND LIKE THAT.
HE CAME BACK. ALL THE WAY.
IT WAS HARD, BUT THAT BOY OF YOURS NEVER SEEMED TO MIND HARD.
WHAT...
...DO YOU HAVE?
YEAH.
OKAY.
SAME AS BEFORE.
CLOT, DROP OF TEMPERATURE.
ONE DIFFERENCE.
SCENE OF THE CRIME. ON OUR THIRD SEARCH.
GOT LUCKY. UNDER A FLOORBOARD, A BIT OF SOMETHING.
TURNED OUT TO BE A BIT OF A FEATHER.

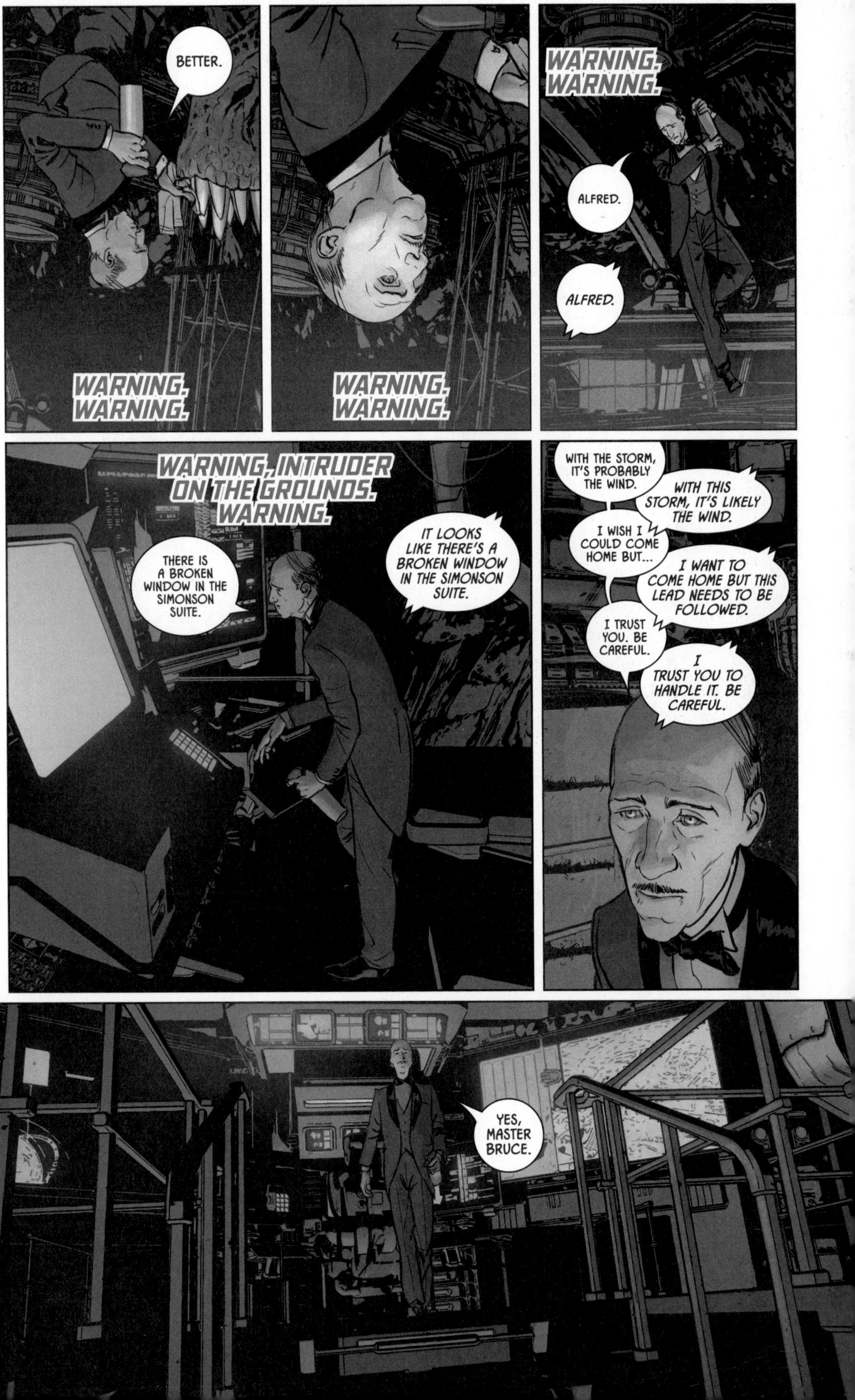

BETTER.
WARNING. WARNING.
WARNING. WARNING.
WARNING. WARNING.
ALFRED.
ALFRED.
WARNING. INTRUDER ON THE GROUNDS. WARNING.
THERE IS A BROKEN WINDOW IN THE SIMONSON SUITE.
IT LOOKS LIKE THERE'S A BROKEN WINDOW IN THE SIMONSON SUITE.
WITH THE STORM, IT'S PROBABLY THE WIND.
WITH THIS STORM, IT'S LIKELY THE WIND.
I WISH I COULD COME HOME BUT...
I WANT TO COME HOME BUT THIS LEAD NEEDS TO BE FOLLOWED.
I TRUST YOU. BE CAREFUL.
I TRUST YOU TO HANDLE IT. BE CAREFUL.
YES, MASTER BRUCE.

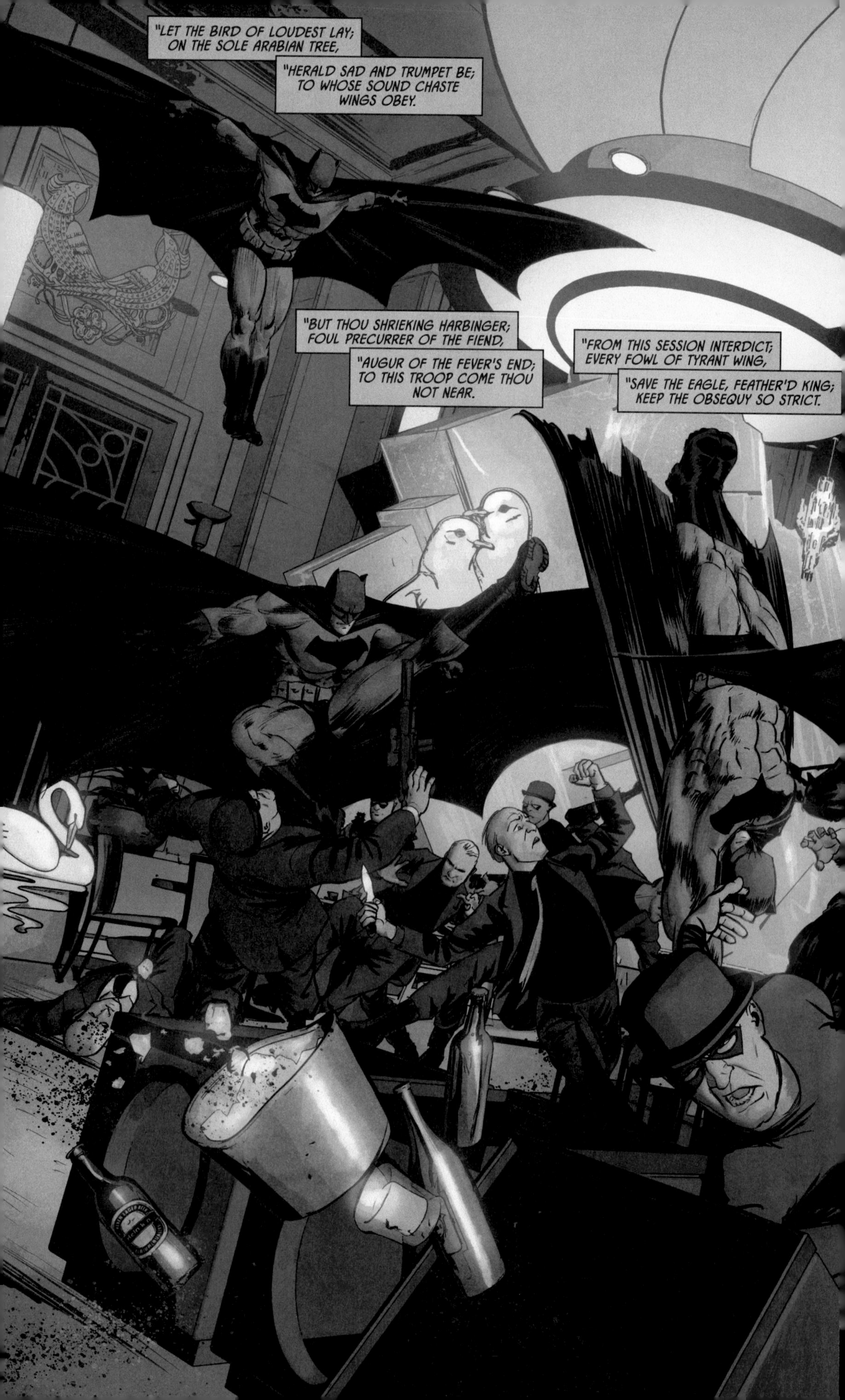
"LET THE BIRD OF LOUDEST LAY; ON THE SOLE ARABIAN TREE,
"HERALD SAD AND TRUMPET BE; TO WHOSE SOUND CHASTE WINGS OBEY.
"BUT THOU SHRIEKING HARBINGER; FOUL PRECURRER OF THE FIEND,
"AUGUR OF THE FEVER'S END; TO THIS TROOP COME THOU NOT NEAR.
"FROM THIS SESSION INTERDICT; EVERY FOWL OF TYRANT WING,
"SAVE THE EAGLE, FEATHER'D KING; KEEP THE OBSEQUY SO STRICT.

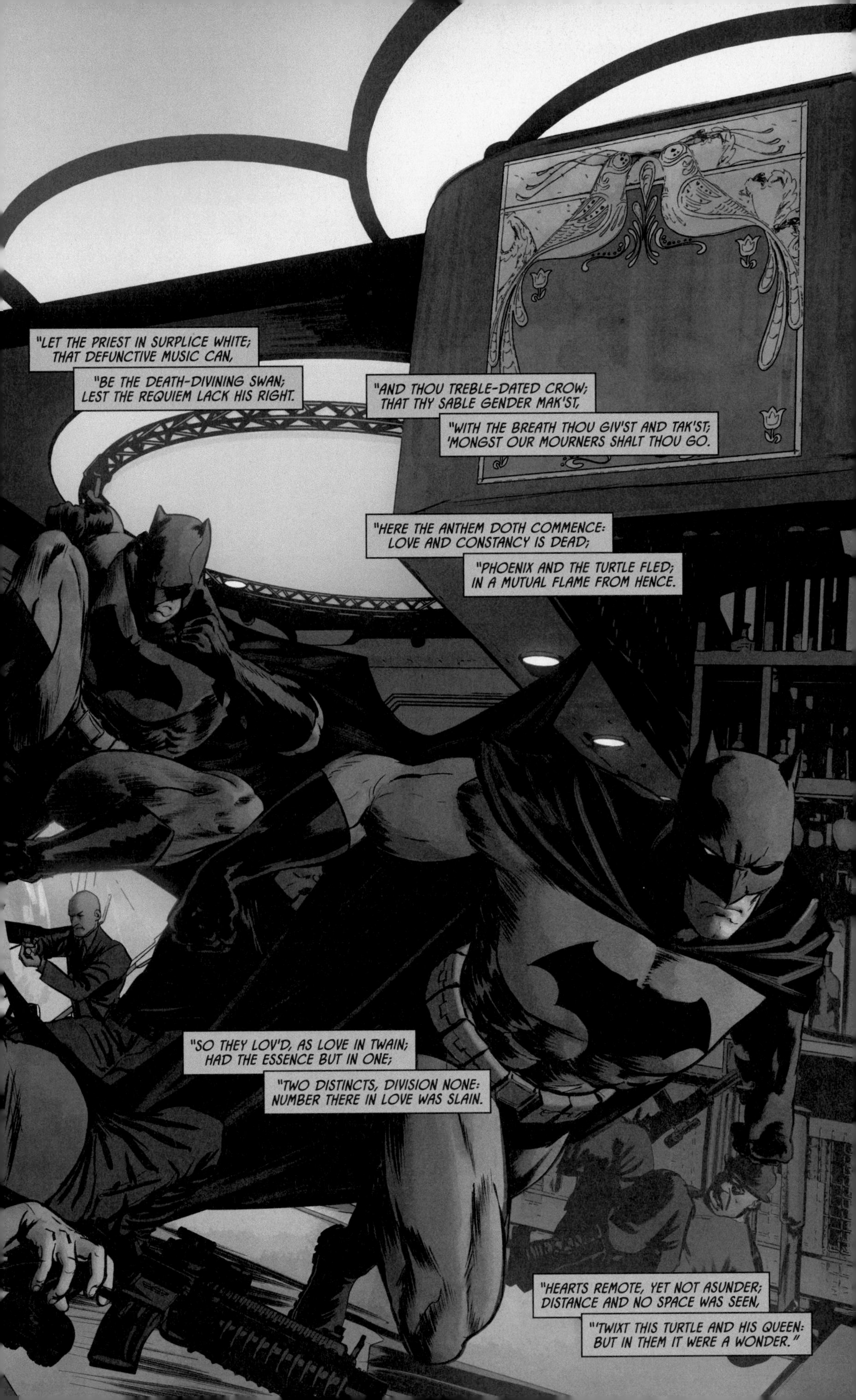
"LET THE PRIEST IN SURPLICE WHITE; THAT DEFUNCTIVE MUSIC CAN,
"BE THE DEATH-DIVINING SWAN; LEST THE REQUIEM LACK HIS RIGHT.
"AND THOU TREBLE-DATED CROW; THAT THY SABLE GENDER MAK'ST,
"WITH THE BREATH THOU GIV'ST AND TAK'ST; 'MONGST OUR MOURNERS SHALT THOU GO.
"HERE THE ANTHEM DOTH COMMENCE: LOVE AND CONSTANCY IS DEAD;
"PHOENIX AND THE TURTLE FLED; IN A MUTUAL FLAME FROM HENCE.
"SO THEY LOV'D, AS LOVE IN TWAIN; HAD THE ESSENCE BUT IN ONE;
"TWO DISTINCTS, DIVISION NONE: NUMBER THERE IN LOVE WAS SLAIN.
"HEARTS REMOTE, YET NOT ASUNDER; DISTANCE AND NO SPACE WAS SEEN,
"'TWIXT THIS TURTLE AND HIS QUEEN: BUT IN THEM IT WERE A WONDER."

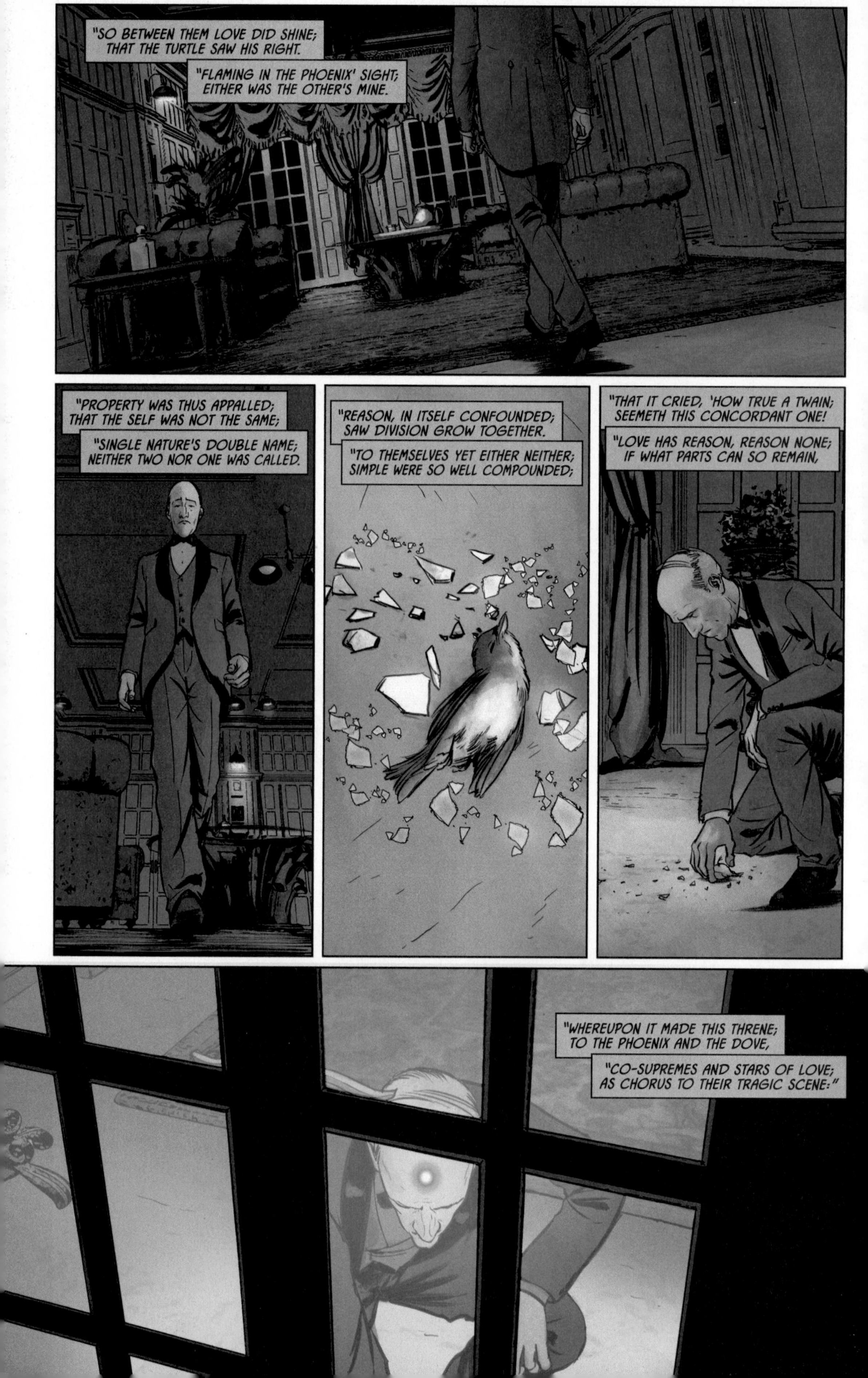
"SO BETWEEN THEM LOVE DID SHINE; THAT THE TURTLE SAW HIS RIGHT.
"FLAMING IN THE PHOENIX' SIGHT; EITHER WAS THE OTHER'S MINE.
"PROPERTY WAS THUS APPALLED; THAT THE SELF WAS NOT THE SAME;
"SINGLE NATURE'S DOUBLE NAME; NEITHER TWO NOR ONE WAS CALLED.
"REASON, IN ITSELF CONFOUNDED; SAW DIVISION GROW TOGETHER.
"TO THEMSELVES YET EITHER NEITHER; SIMPLE WERE SO WELL COMPOUNDED;
"THAT IT CRIED, 'HOW TRUE A TWAIN; SEEMETH THIS CONCORDANT ONE!
"LOVE HAS REASON, REASON NONE; IF WHAT PARTS CAN SO REMAIN,
"WHEREUPON IT MADE THIS THRENE; TO THE PHOENIX AND THE DOVE,
"CO-SUPREMES AND STARS OF LOVE; AS CHORUS TO THEIR TRAGIC SCENE:"

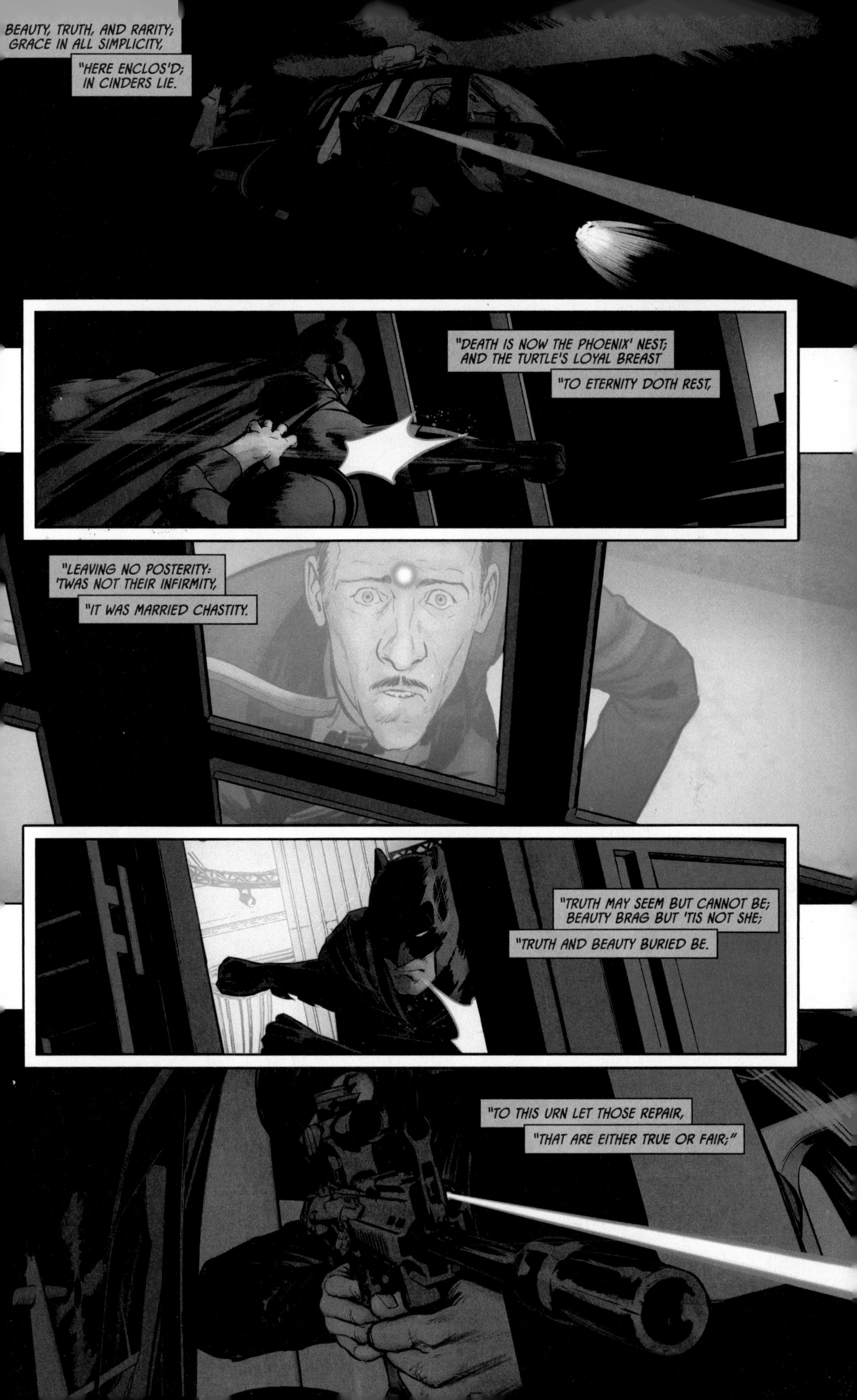

BEAUTY, TRUTH, AND RARITY; GRACE IN ALL SIMPLICITY,
"HERE ENCLOS'D; IN CINDERS LIE.
"DEATH IS NOW THE PHOENIX' NEST; AND THE TURTLE'S LOYAL BREAST
"TO ETERNITY DOTH REST,
"LEAVING NO POSTERITY: 'TWAS NOT THEIR INFIRMITY,
"IT WAS MARRIED CHASTITY.
"TRUTH MAY SEEM BUT CANNOT BE; BEAUTY BRAG BUT 'TIS NOT SHE;
"TRUTH AND BEAUTY BURIED BE.
"TO THIS URN LET THOSE REPAIR,
"THAT ARE EITHER TRUE OR FAIR;"

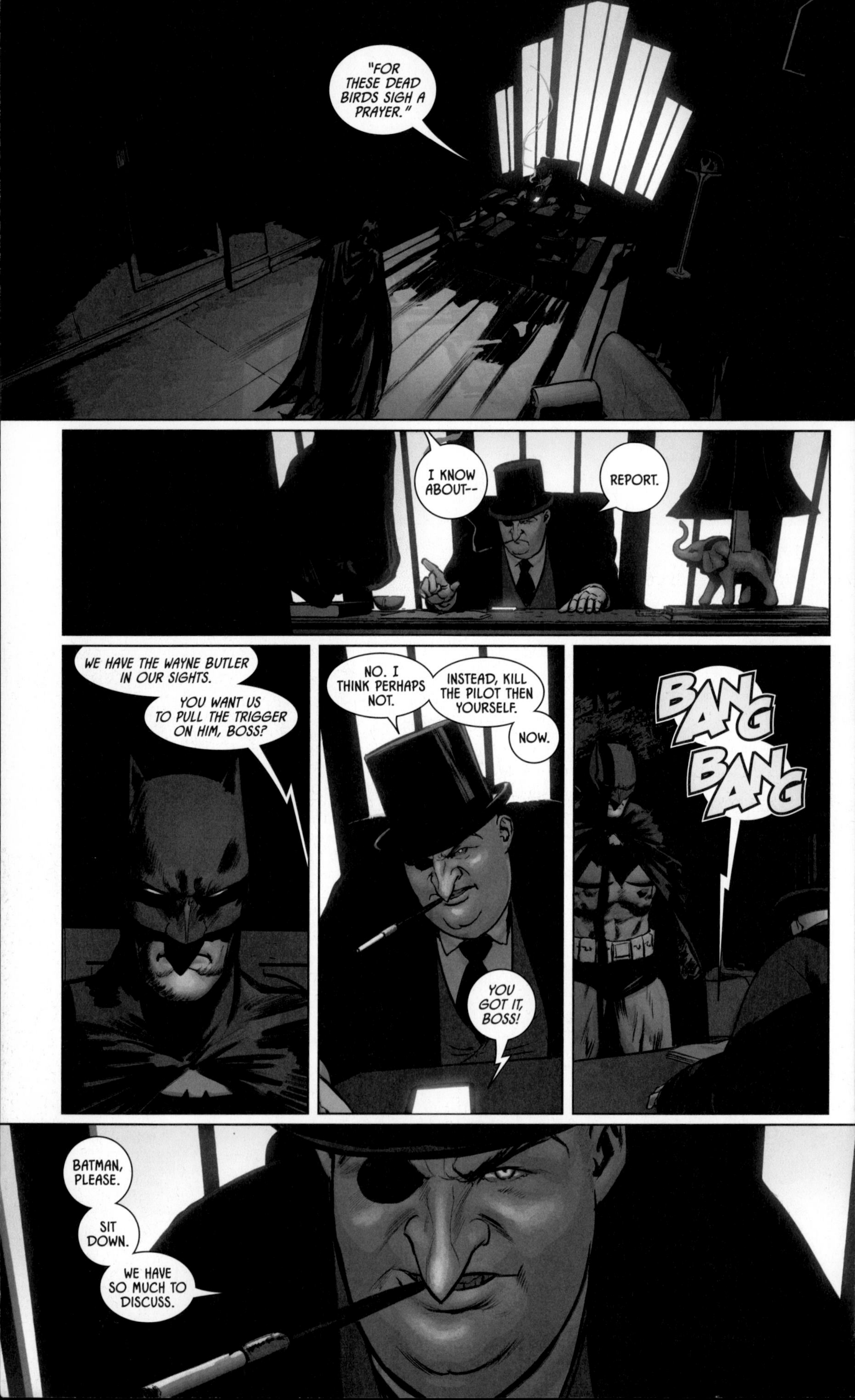
"FOR THESE DEAD BIRDS SIGH A PRAYER."
I KNOW ABOUT--
REPORT.
WE HAVE THE WAYNE BUTLER IN OUR SIGHTS.
YOU WANT US TO PULL THE TRIGGER ON HIM, BOSS?
NO. I THINK PERHAPS NOT.
INSTEAD, KILL THE PILOT THEN YOURSELF.
NOW.
YOU GOT IT, BOSS!
BANG BANG
BATMAN, PLEASE.
SIT DOWN.
WE HAVE SO MUCH TO DISCUSS.

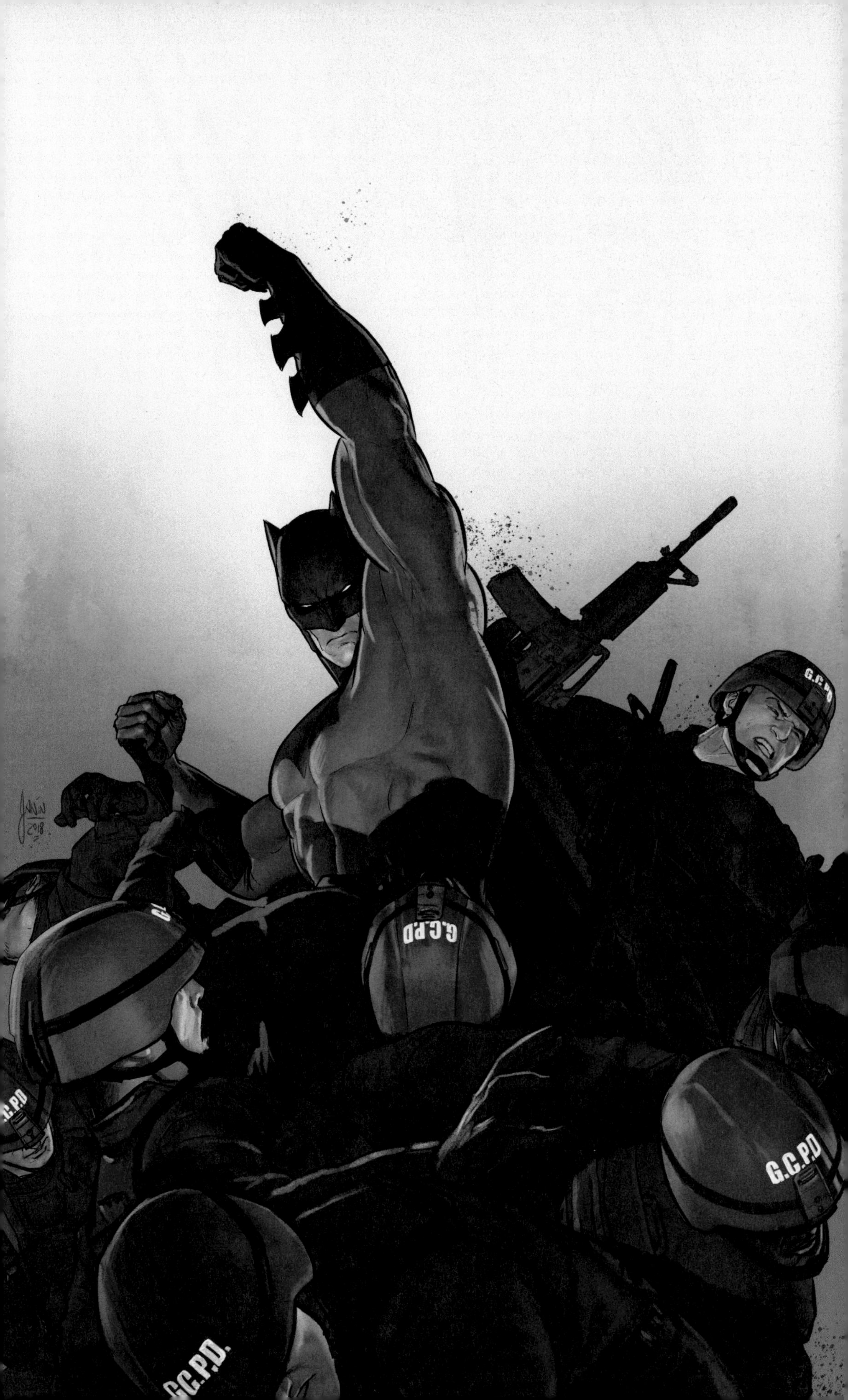
G.C.P.D
G.C.P.D
G.C.P.D
G.C.P.D.

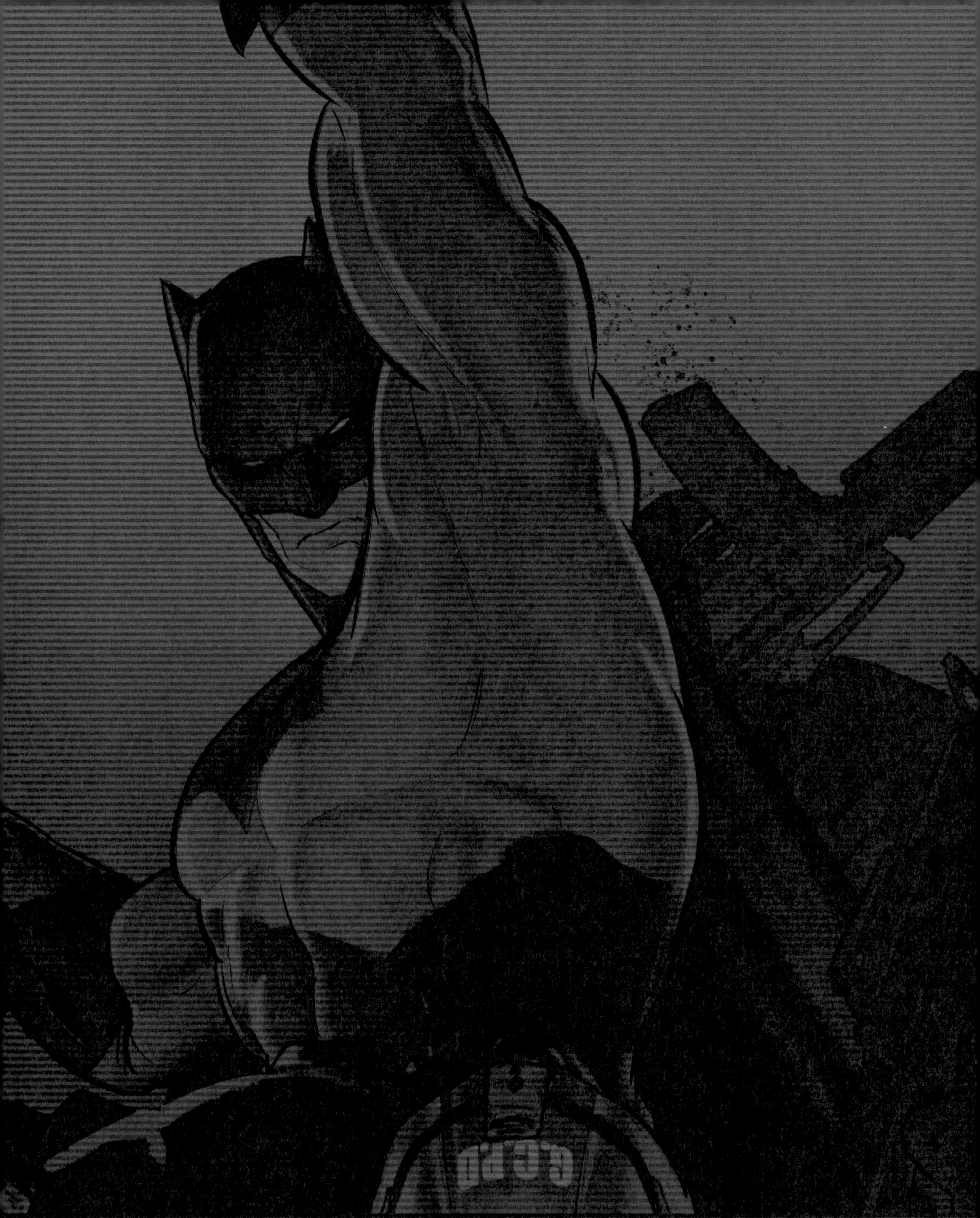

BATMAN
#59

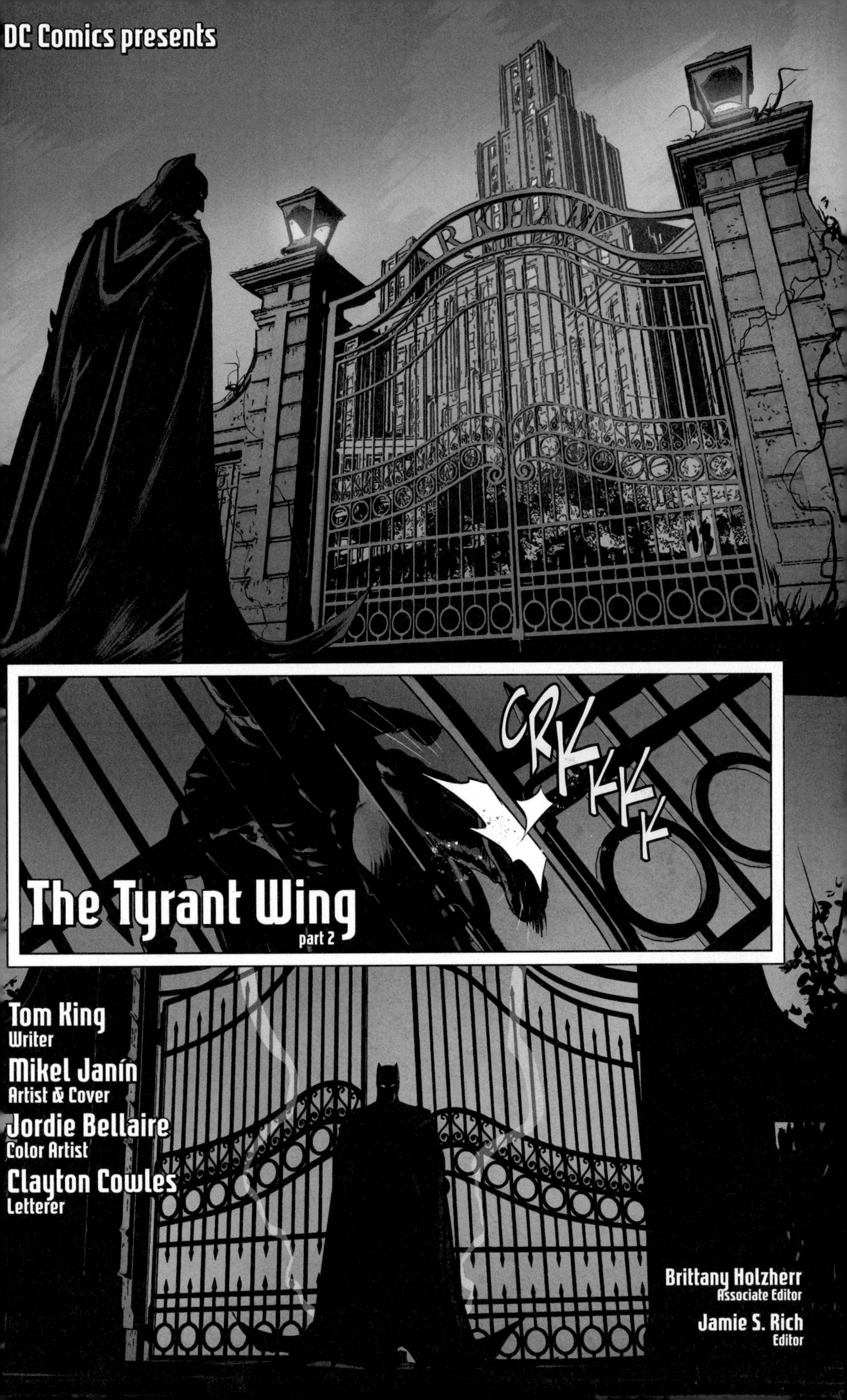
DC Comics presents
CRKKKK
The Tyrant Wing
part 2
Tom King
Writer
Mikel Janín
Artist & Cover
Jordie Bellaire
Color Artist
Clayton Cowles
Letterer
Brittany Holzherr
Associate Editor
Jamie S. Rich
Editor

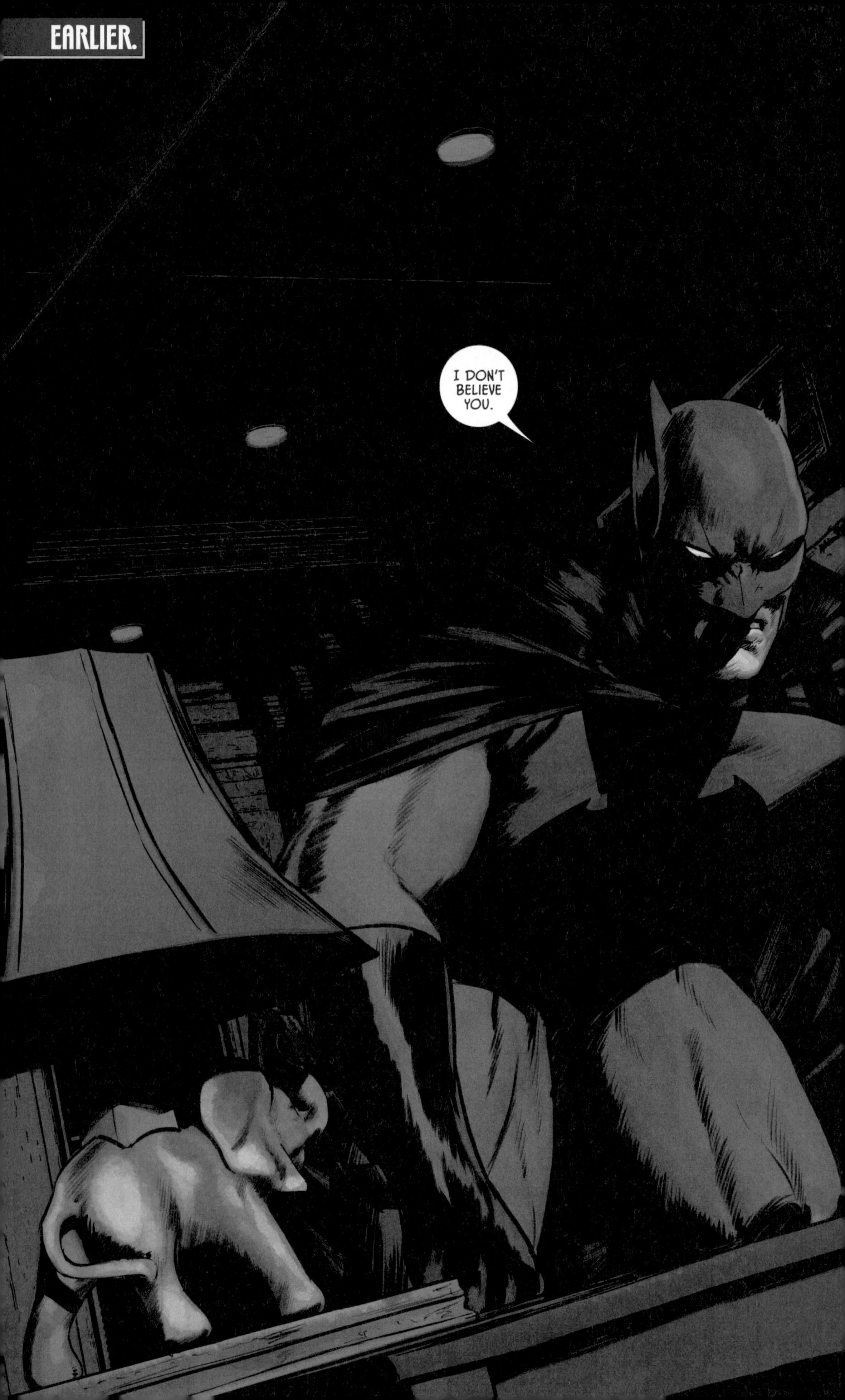
EARLIER.
I DON'T BELIEVE YOU.

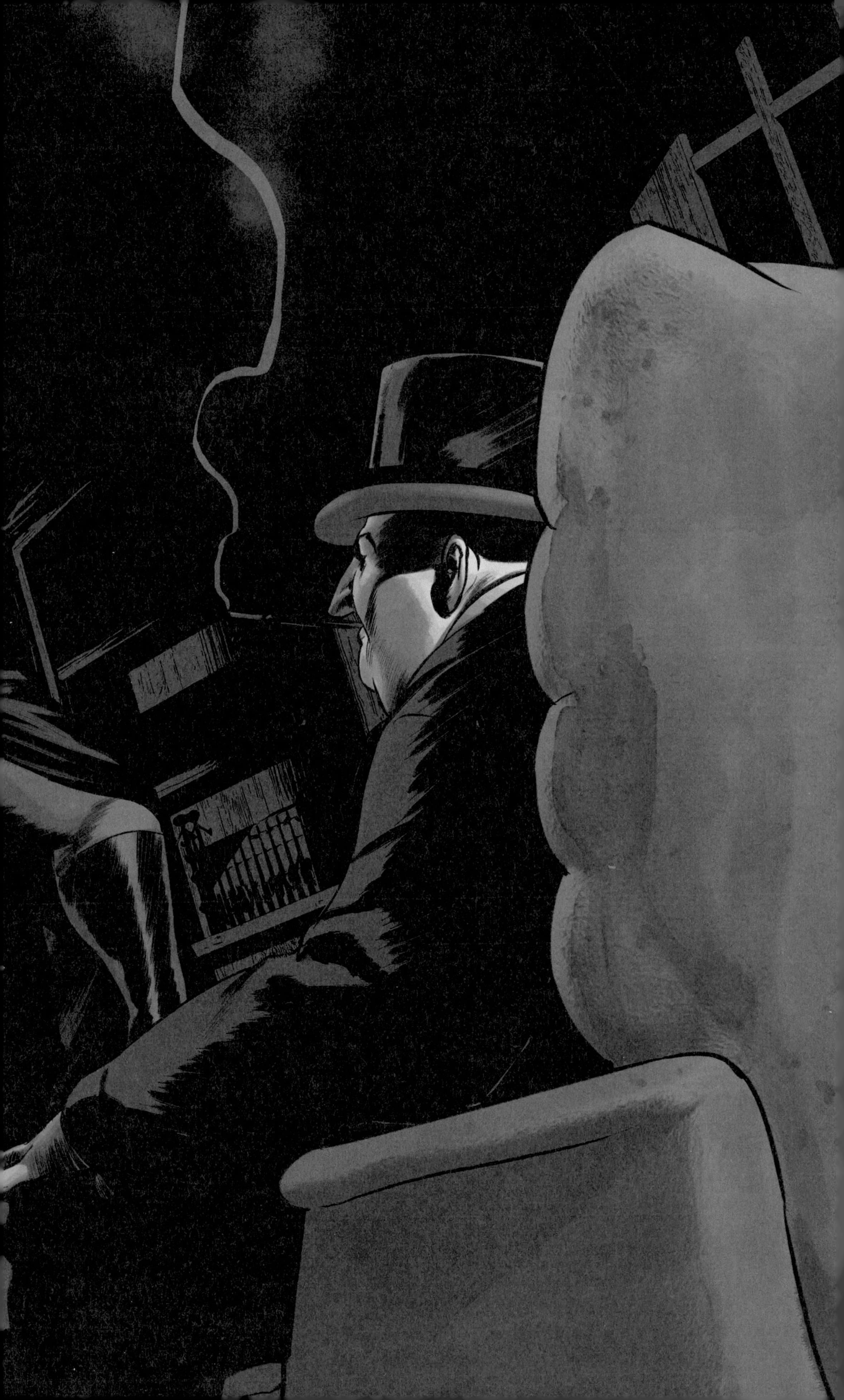

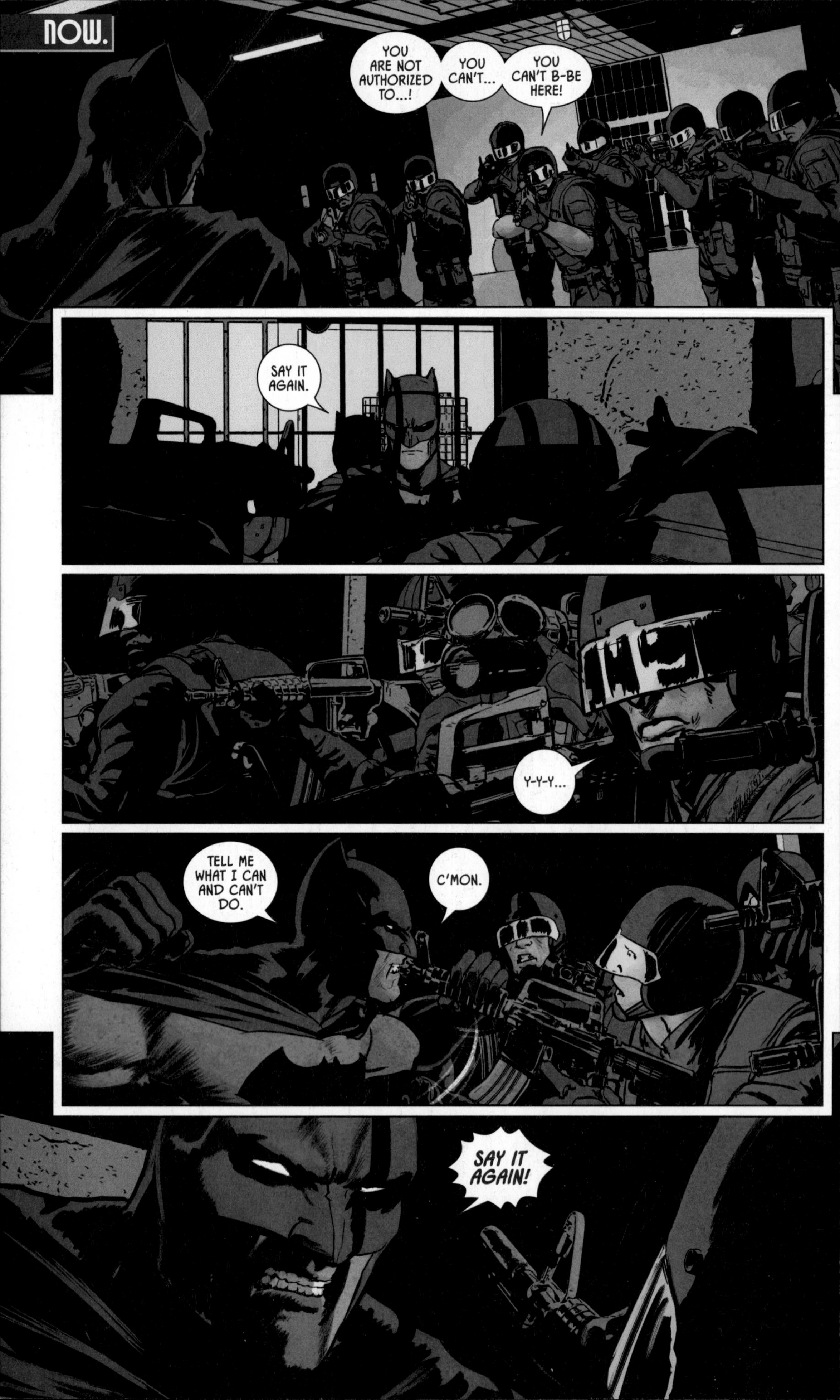
NOW.
YOU ARE NOT AUTHORIZED TO...!
YOU CAN'T...
YOU CAN'T B-BE HERE!
SAY IT AGAIN.
Y-Y-Y...
TELL ME WHAT I CAN AND CAN'T DO.
C'MON.
SAY IT AGAIN!

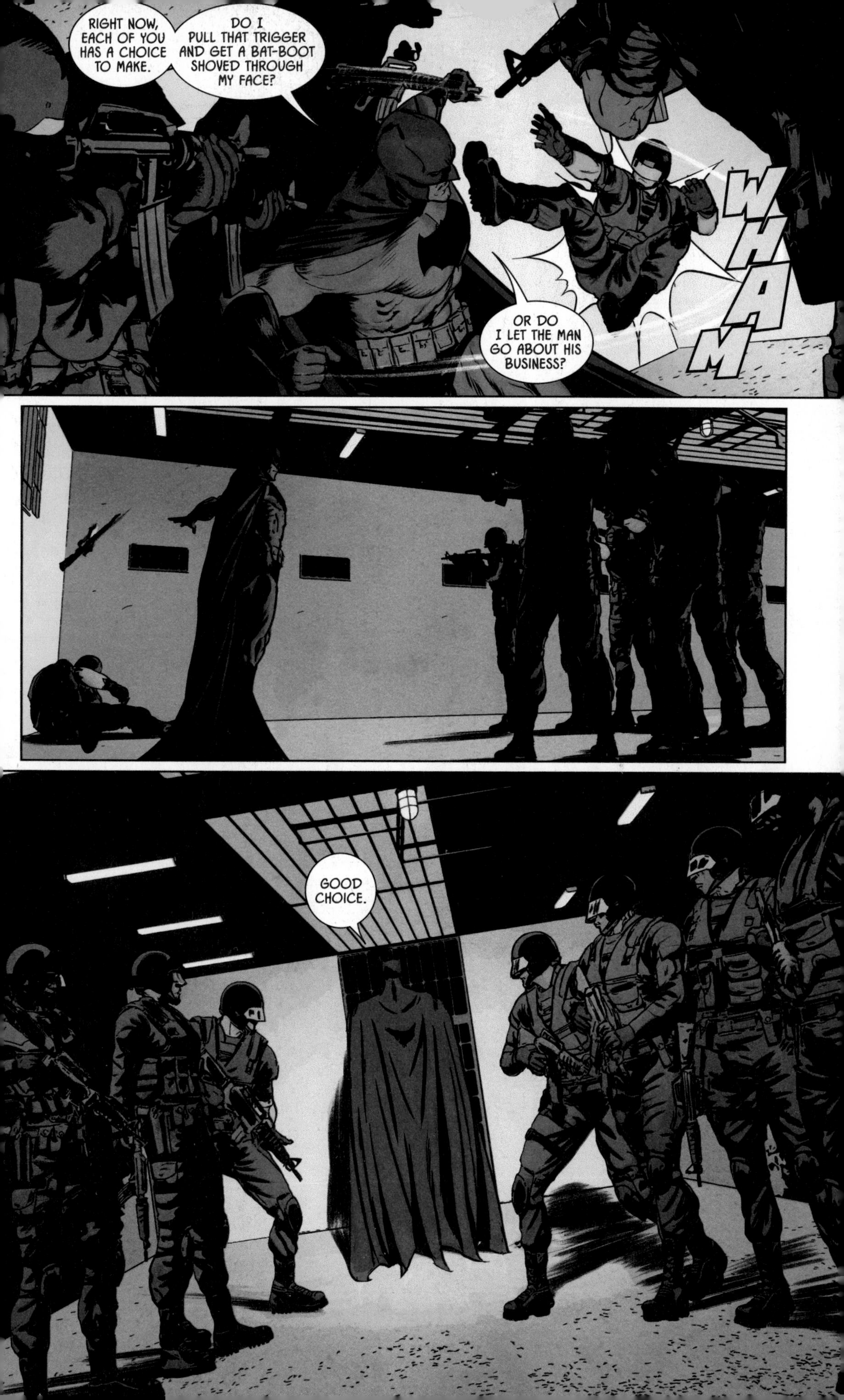
RIGHT NOW, EACH OF YOU HAS A CHOICE TO MAKE.
DO I PULL THAT TRIGGER AND GET A BAT-BOOT SHOVED THROUGH MY FACE?
OR DO I LET THE MAN GO ABOUT HIS BUSINESS?
WHAM
GOOD CHOICE.

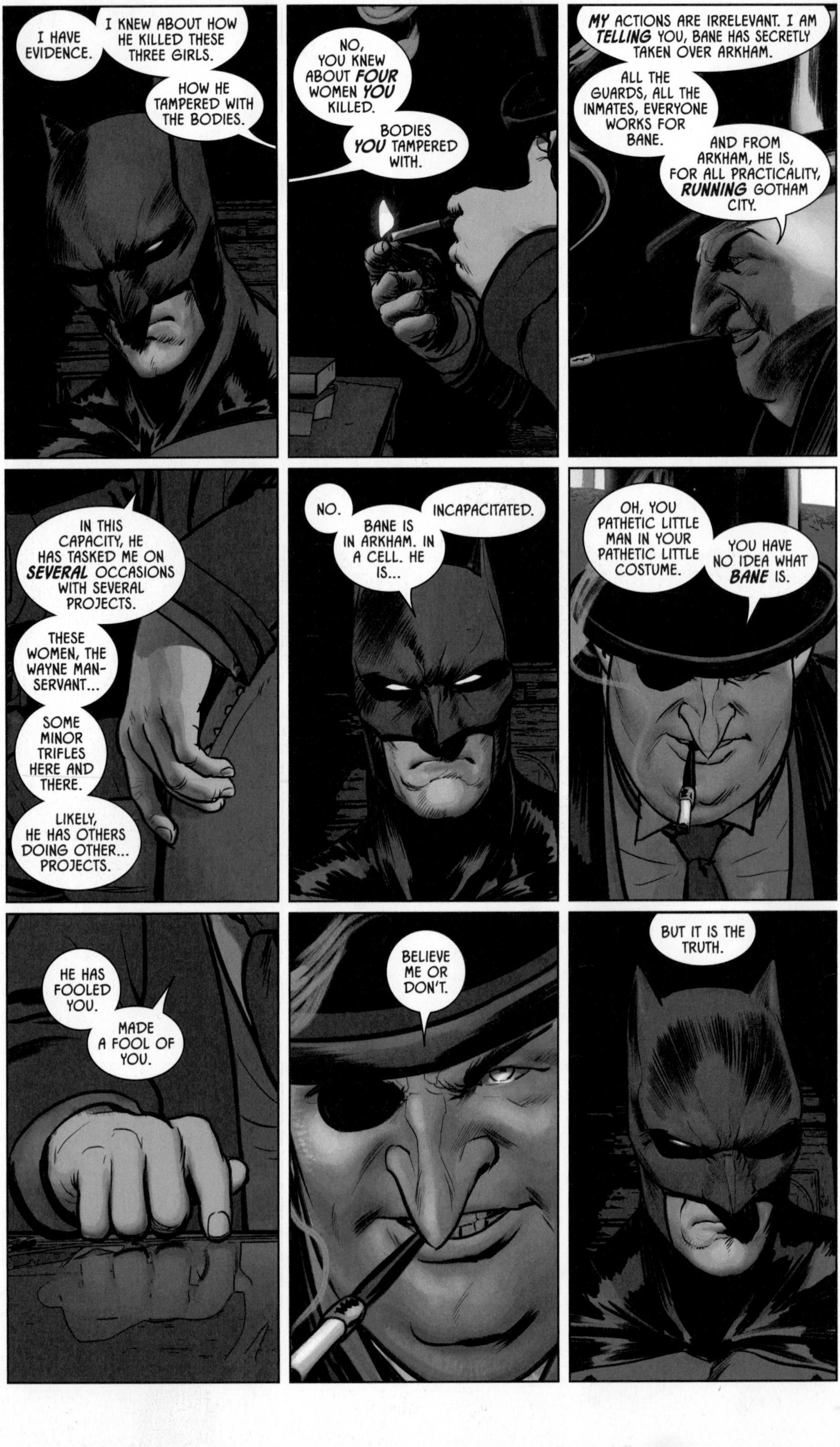
I HAVE EVIDENCE.
I KNEW ABOUT HOW HE KILLED THESE THREE GIRLS.
HOW HE TAMPERED WITH THE BODIES.
NO, YOU KNEW ABOUT FOUR WOMEN YOU KILLED.
BODIES YOU TAMPERED WITH.
MY ACTIONS ARE IRRELEVANT. I AM TELLING YOU, BANE HAS SECRETLY TAKEN OVER ARKHAM.
ALL THE GUARDS, ALL THE INMATES, EVERYONE WORKS FOR BANE.
AND FROM ARKHAM, HE IS, FOR ALL PRACTICALITY, RUNNING GOTHAM CITY.
IN THIS CAPACITY, HE HAS TASKED ME ON SEVERAL OCCASIONS WITH SEVERAL PROJECTS.
THESE WOMEN, THE WAYNE MAN-SERVANT...
SOME MINOR TRIFLES HERE AND THERE.
LIKELY, HE HAS OTHERS DOING OTHER... PROJECTS.
NO.
BANE IS IN ARKHAM. IN A CELL. HE IS...
INCAPACITATED.
OH, YOU PATHETIC LITTLE MAN IN YOUR PATHETIC LITTLE COSTUME.
YOU HAVE NO IDEA WHAT BANE IS.
HE HAS FOOLED YOU.
MADE A FOOL OF YOU.
BELIEVE ME OR DON'T.
BUT IT IS THE TRUTH.

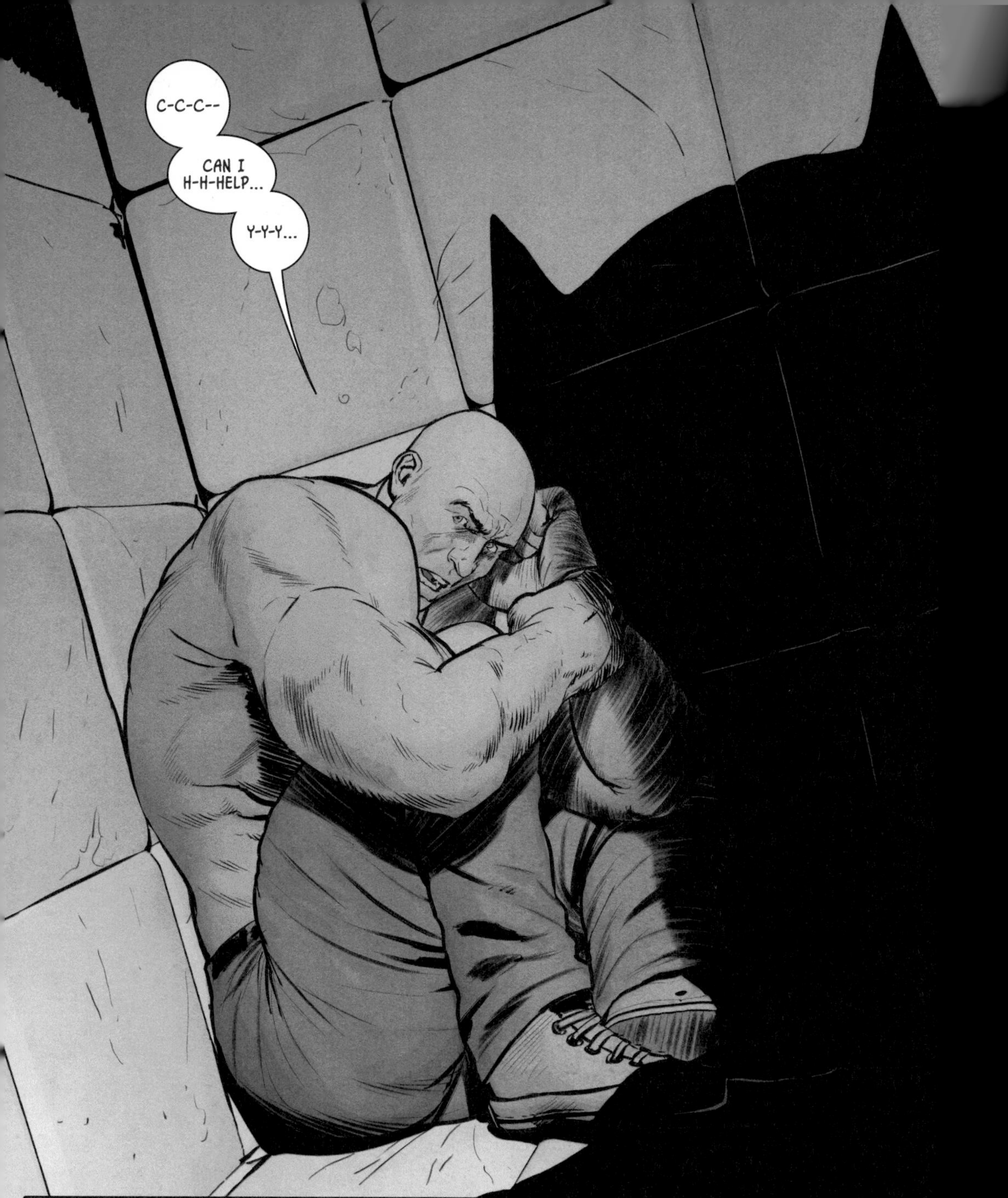
C-C-C--
CAN I H-H-HELP...
Y-Y-Y...
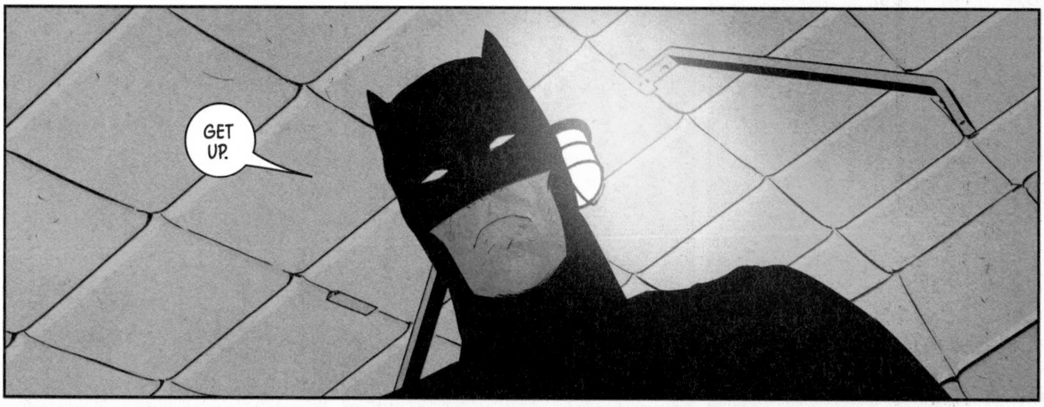
GET UP.

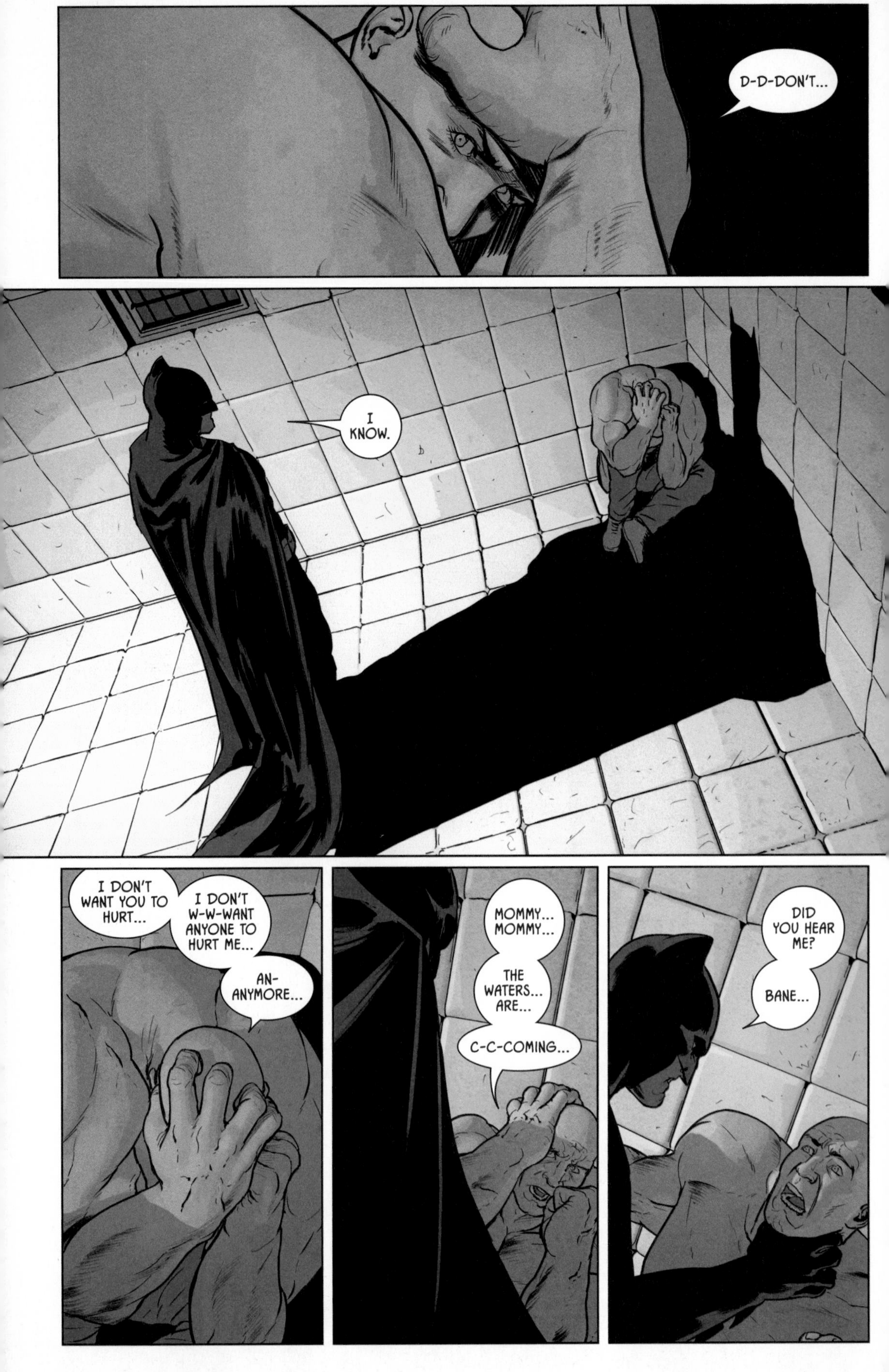

D-D-DON'T...
I KNOW.
I DON'T WANT YOU TO HURT...
I DON'T W-W-WANT ANYONE TO HURT ME...
AN- ANYMORE...
MOMMY... MOMMY...
THE WATERS... ARE...
C-C-COMING...
DID YOU HEAR ME?
BANE...

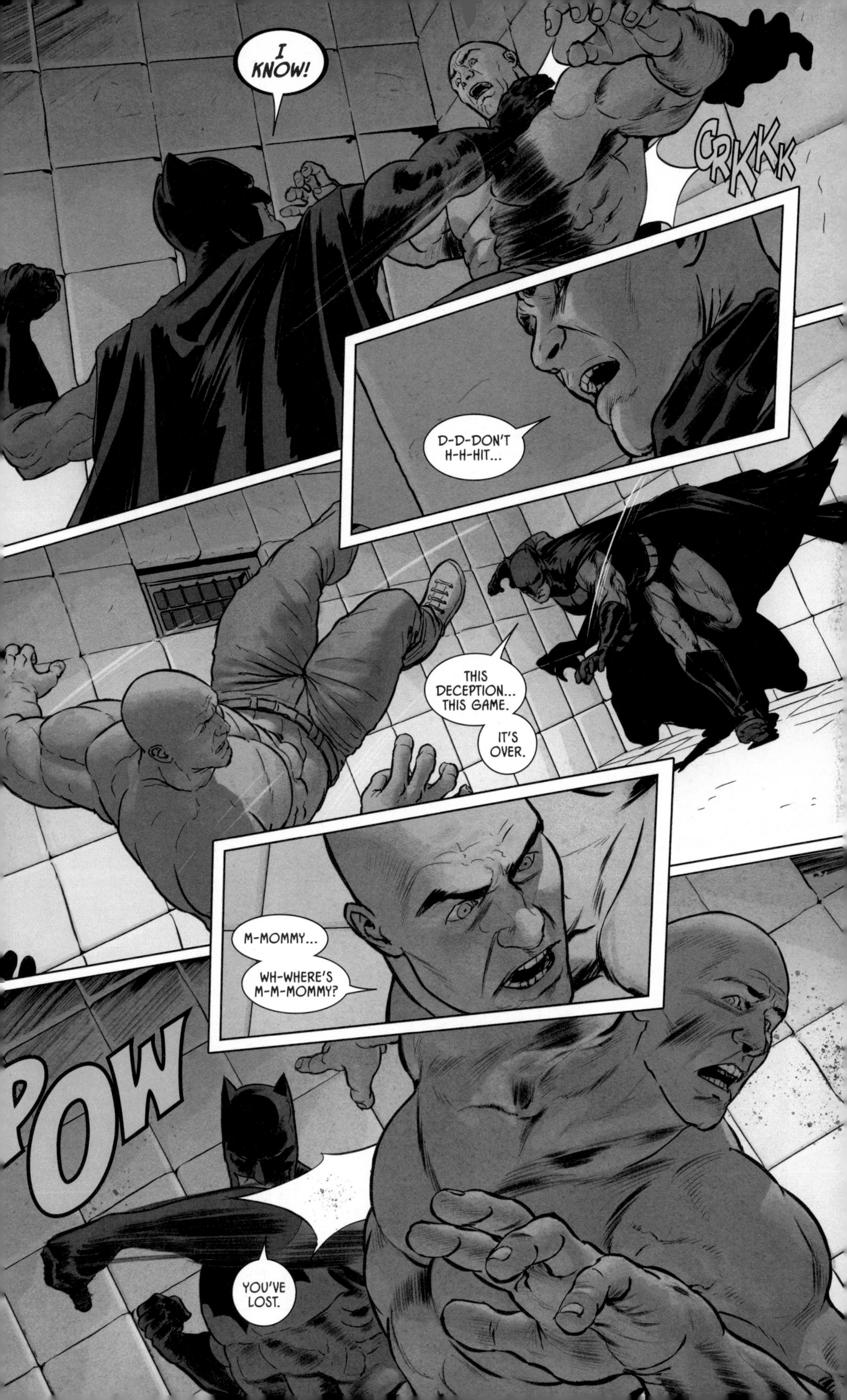
I KNOW!
CRKKK
D-D-DON'T H-H-HIT...
THIS DECEPTION... THIS GAME.
IT'S OVER.
M-MOMMY...
WH-WHERE'S M-M-MOMMY?
POW
YOU'VE LOST.

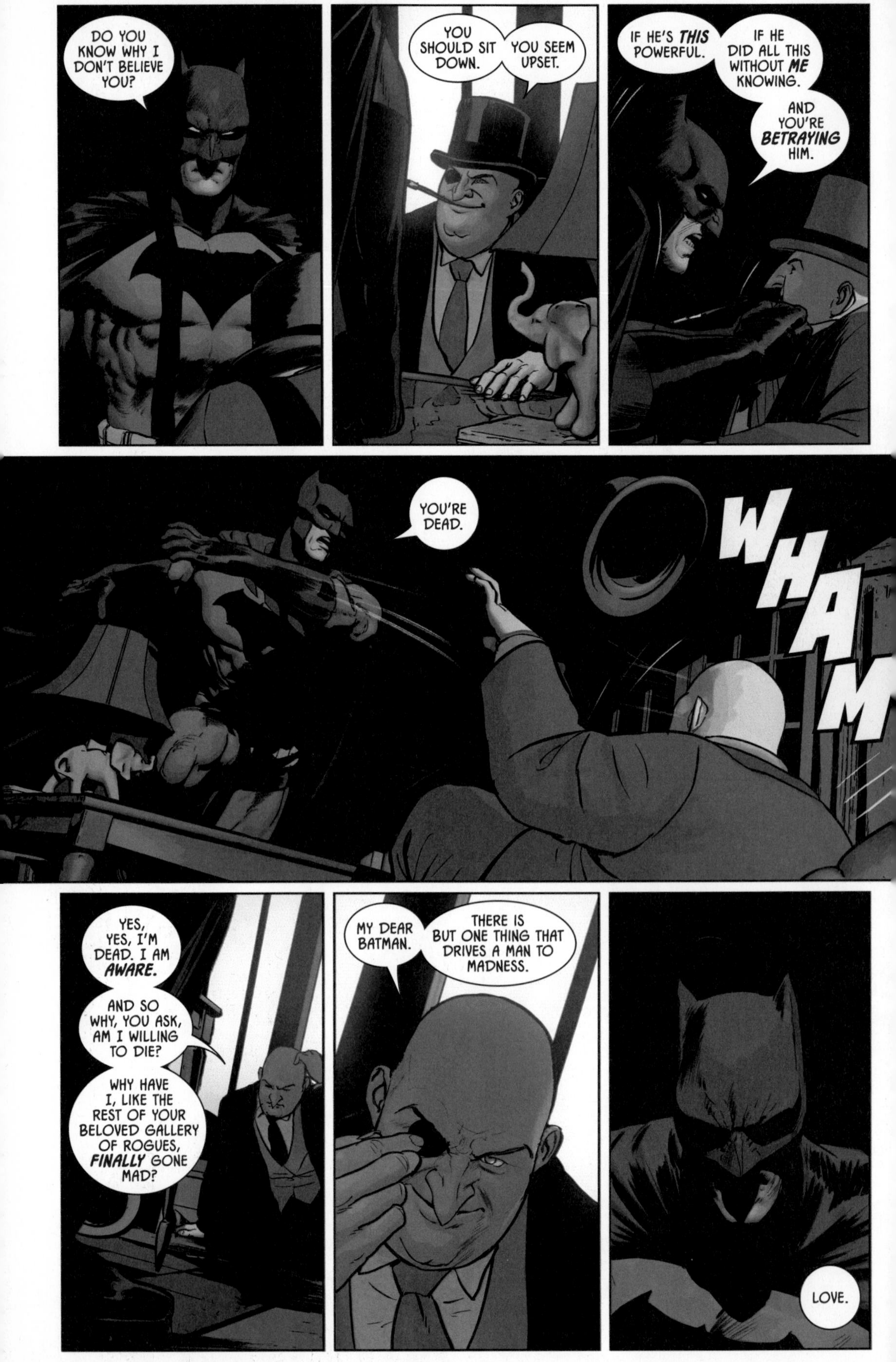
DO YOU KNOW WHY I DON'T BELIEVE YOU?
YOU SHOULD SIT DOWN.
YOU SEEM UPSET.
IF HE'S THIS POWERFUL.
IF HE DID ALL THIS WITHOUT ME KNOWING.
AND YOU'RE BETRAYING HIM.
YOU'RE DEAD.
WHAM
YES, YES, I'M DEAD. I AM AWARE.
AND SO WHY, YOU ASK, AM I WILLING TO DIE?
WHY HAVE I, LIKE THE REST OF YOUR BELOVED GALLERY OF ROGUES, FINALLY GONE MAD?
MY DEAR BATMAN.
THERE IS BUT ONE THING THAT DRIVES A MAN TO MADNESS.
LOVE.

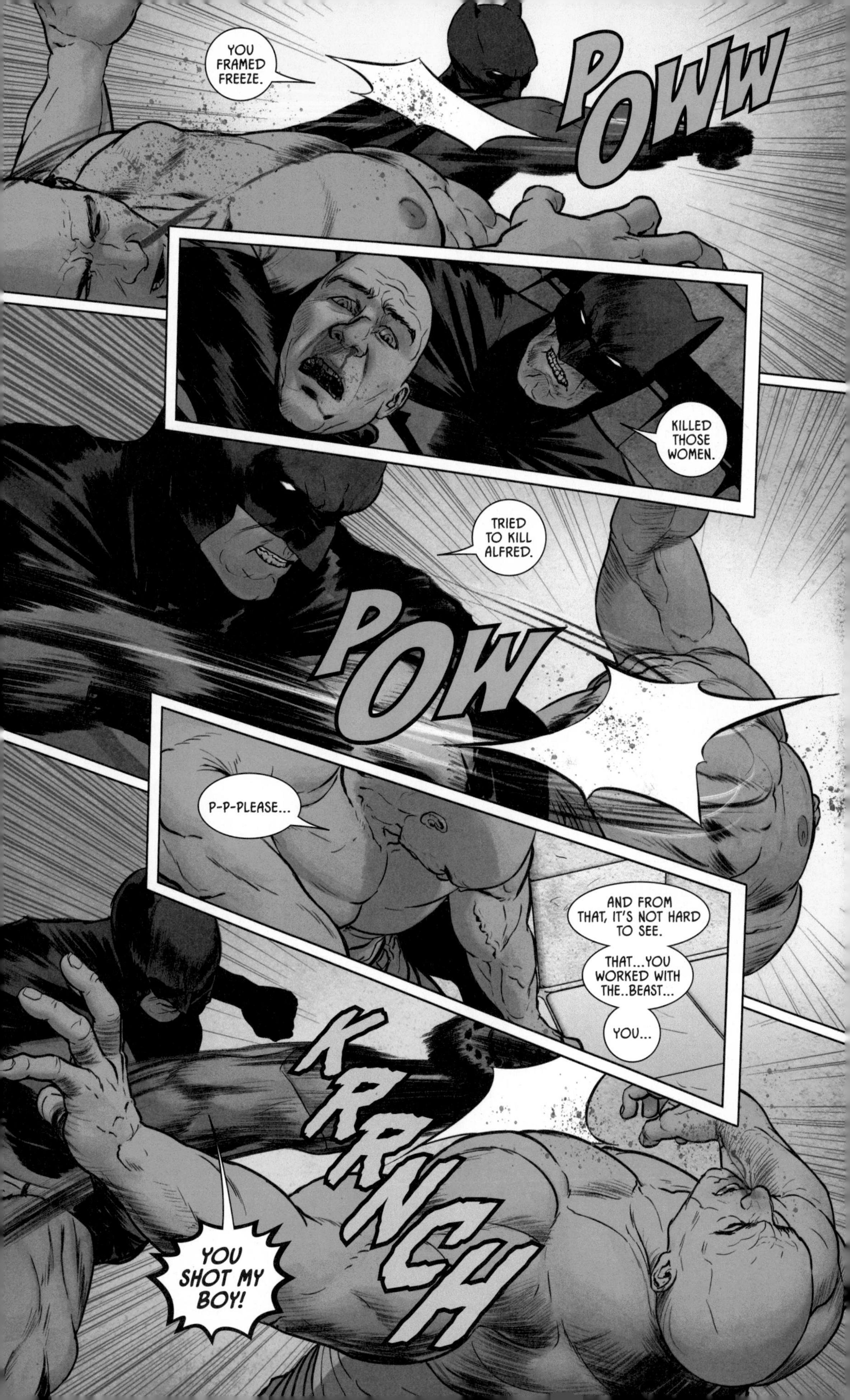
YOU FRAMED FREEZE.
POWW
KILLED THOSE WOMEN.
TRIED TO KILL ALFRED.
POW
P-P-PLEASE...
AND FROM THAT, IT'S NOT HARD TO SEE.
THAT...YOU WORKED WITH THE..BEAST...
YOU...
KRRNCH
YOU SHOT MY BOY!

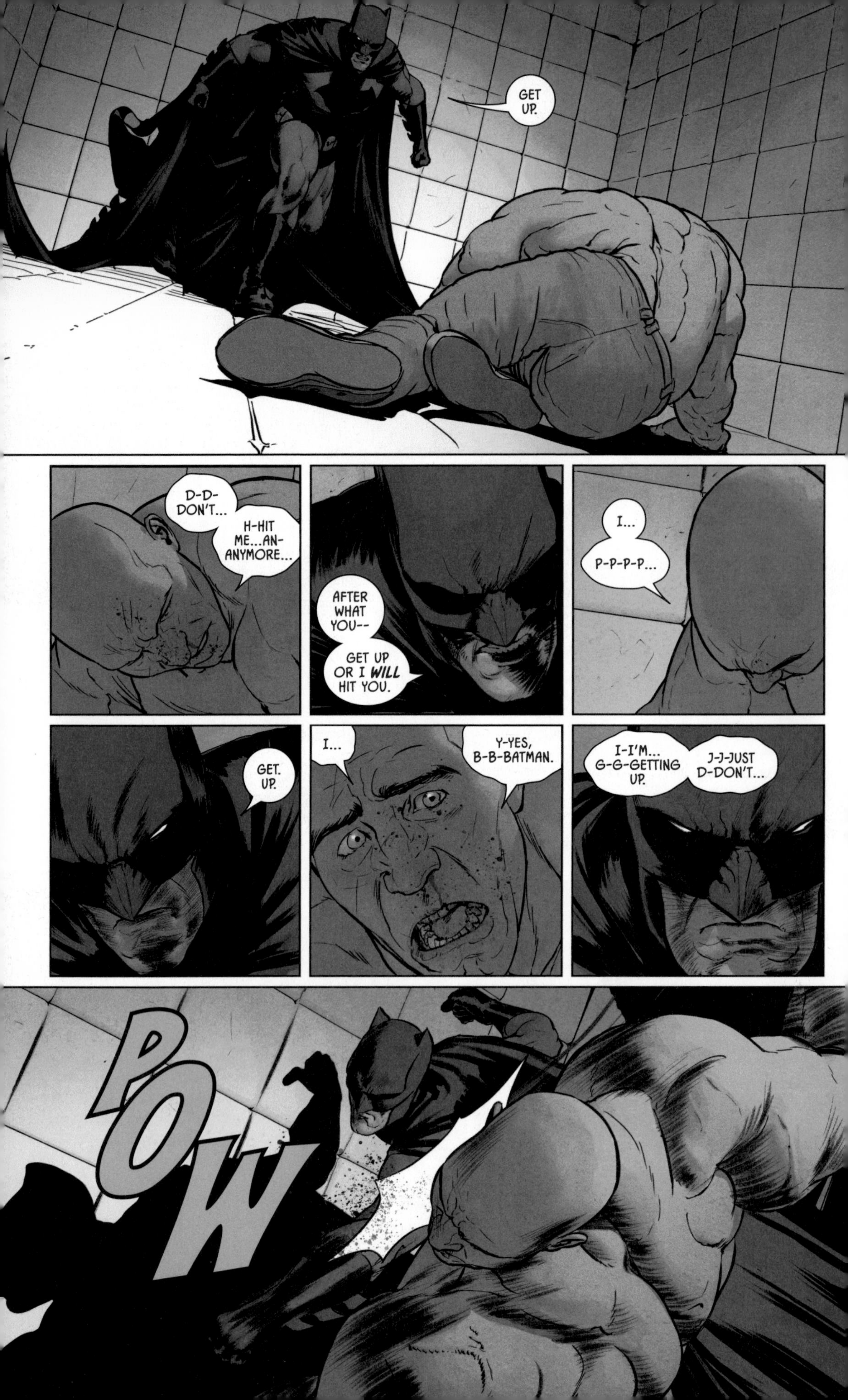
GET UP.
D-D-DON'T...
H-HIT ME...AN-ANYMORE...
AFTER WHAT YOU--
GET UP OR I WILL HIT YOU.
I...
P-P-P-P...
GET. UP.
I...
Y-YES, B-B-BATMAN.
I-I'M... G-G-GETTING UP.
J-J-JUST D-DON'T...
POW

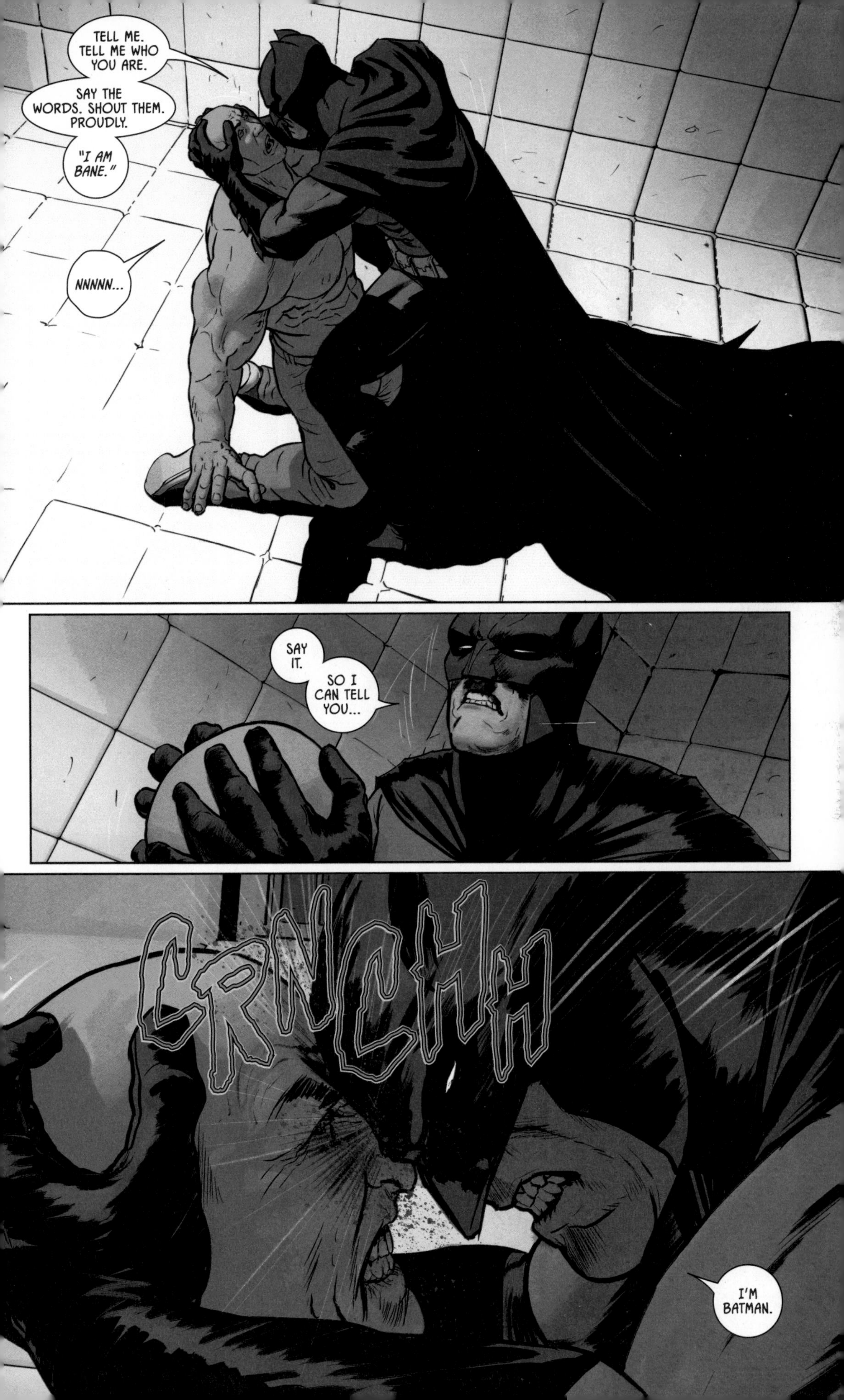
TELL ME. TELL ME WHO YOU ARE.
SAY THE WORDS. SHOUT THEM. PROUDLY.
"I AM BANE."
NNNNN...
SAY IT.
SO I CAN TELL YOU...
CRNCHH
I'M BATMAN.

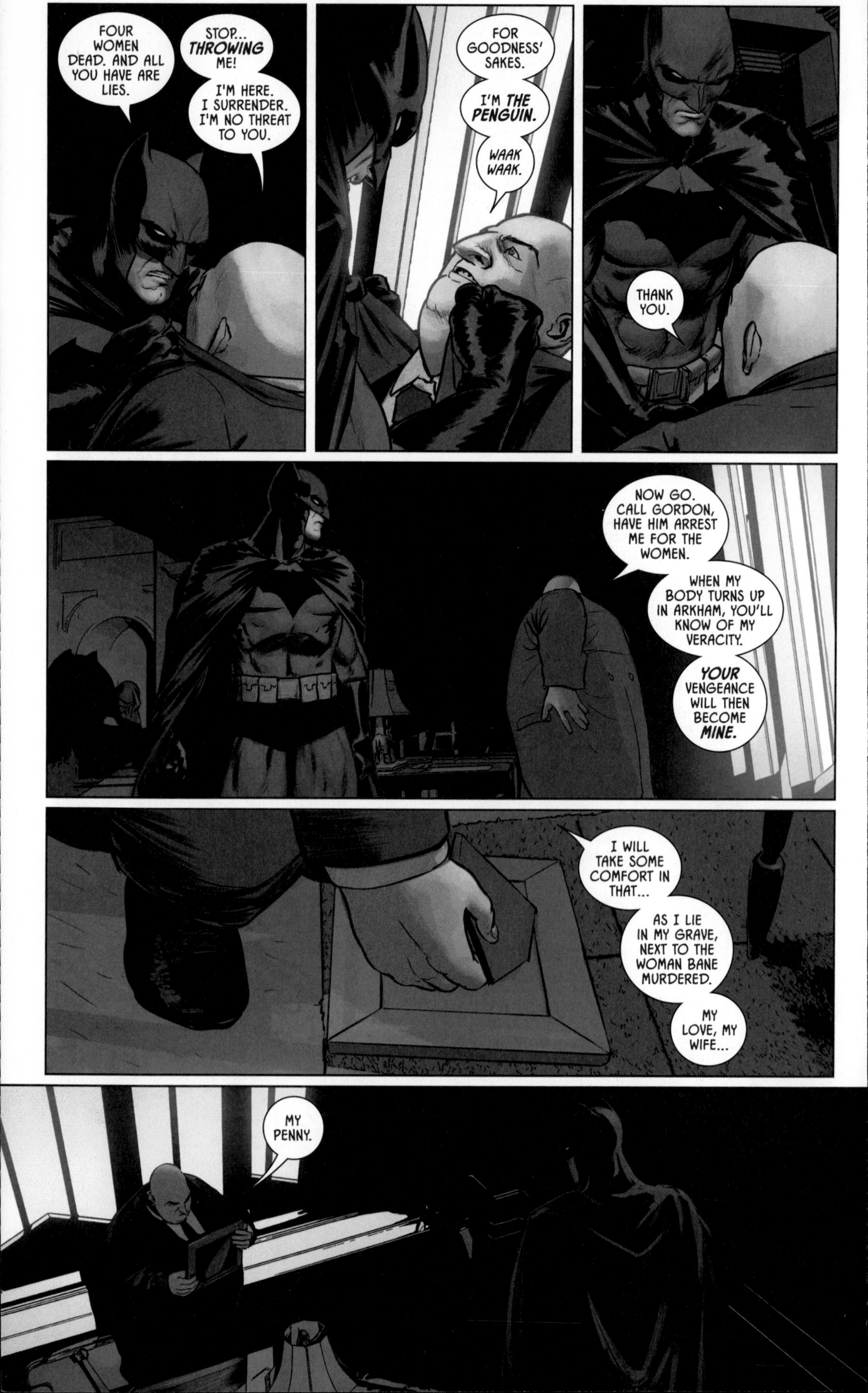
FOUR WOMEN DEAD. AND ALL YOU HAVE ARE LIES.
STOP... THROWING ME!
I'M HERE. I SURRENDER. I'M NO THREAT TO YOU.
FOR GOODNESS' SAKES.
I'M THE PENGUIN.
WAAK WAAK.
THANK YOU.
NOW GO. CALL GORDON, HAVE HIM ARREST ME FOR THE WOMEN.
WHEN MY BODY TURNS UP IN ARKHAM, YOU'LL KNOW OF MY VERACITY.
YOUR VENGEANCE WILL THEN BECOME MINE.
I WILL TAKE SOME COMFORT IN THAT...
AS I LIE IN MY GRAVE, NEXT TO THE WOMAN BANE MURDERED.
MY LOVE, MY WIFE...
MY PENNY.

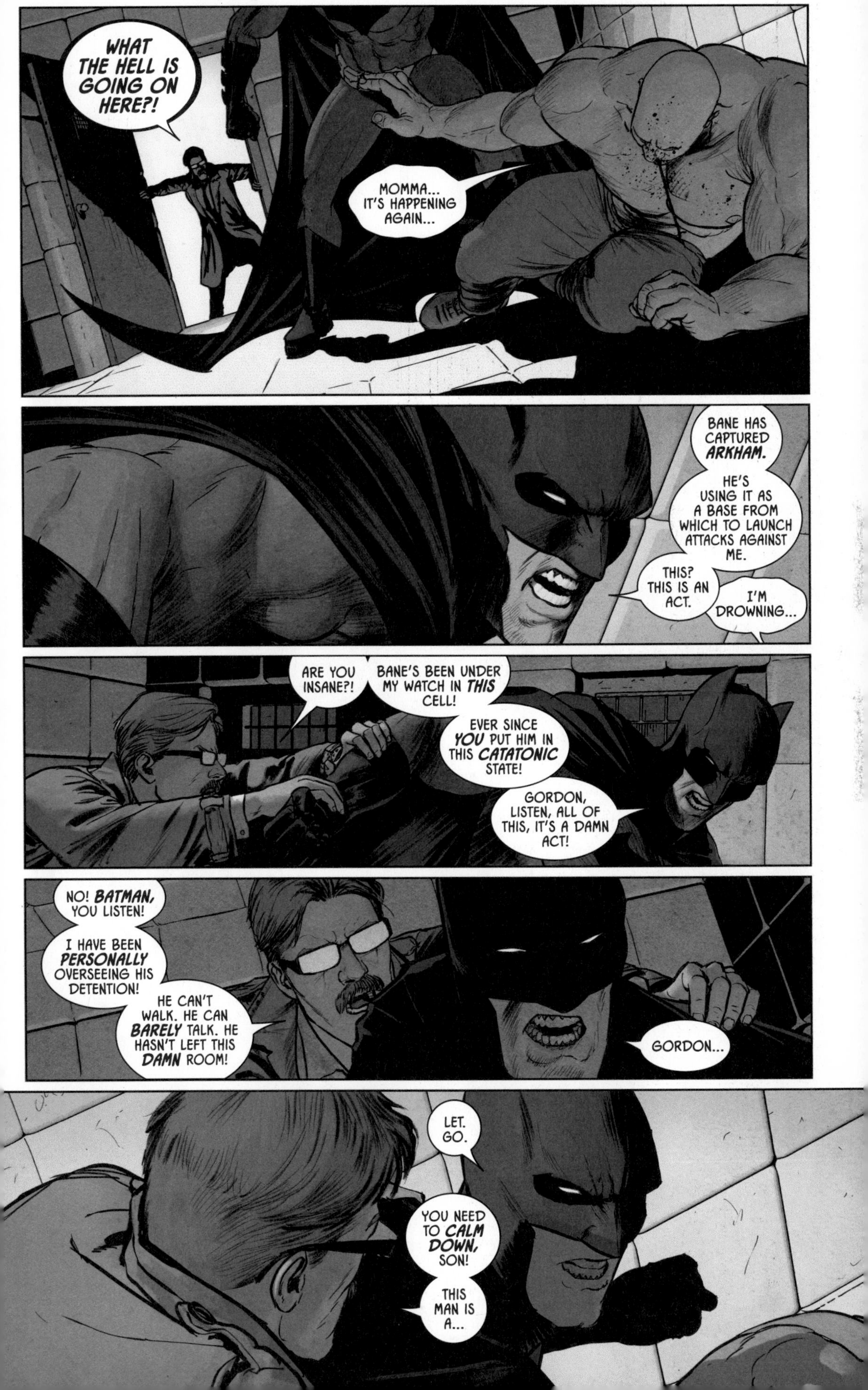
WHAT THE HELL IS GOING ON HERE?!
MOMMA... IT'S HAPPENING AGAIN...
BANE HAS CAPTURED ARKHAM.
HE'S USING IT AS A BASE FROM WHICH TO LAUNCH ATTACKS AGAINST ME.
THIS? THIS IS AN ACT.
I'M DROWNING...
ARE YOU INSANE?!
BANE'S BEEN UNDER MY WATCH IN THIS CELL!
EVER SINCE YOU PUT HIM IN THIS CATATONIC STATE!
GORDON, LISTEN, ALL OF THIS, IT'S A DAMN ACT!
NO! BATMAN, YOU LISTEN!
I HAVE BEEN PERSONALLY OVERSEEING HIS DETENTION!
HE CAN'T WALK. HE CAN BARELY TALK. HE HASN'T LEFT THIS DAMN ROOM!
GORDON...
LET. GO.
YOU NEED TO CALM DOWN, SON!
THIS MAN IS A...

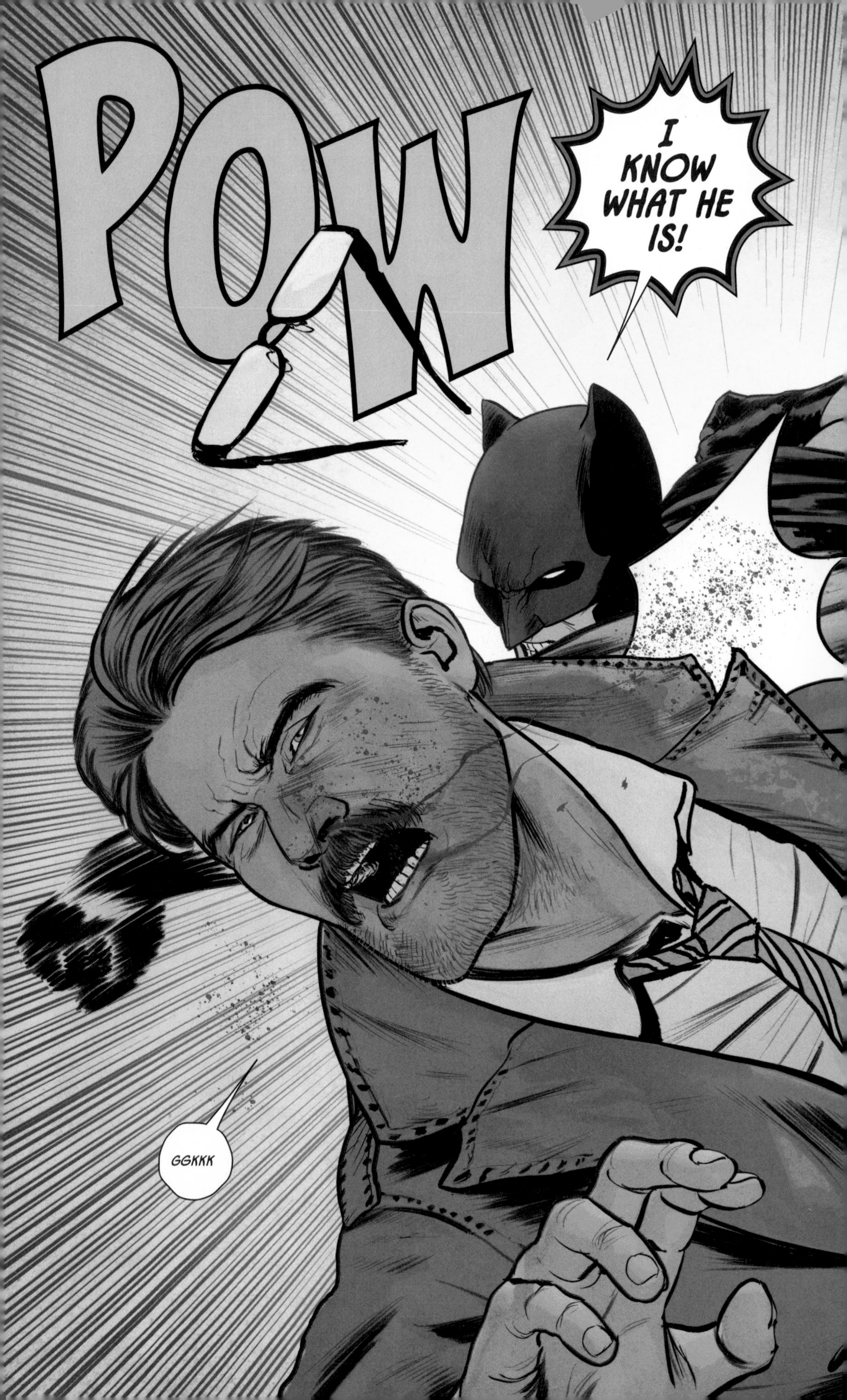
POW
I KNOW WHAT HE IS!
GGKKK

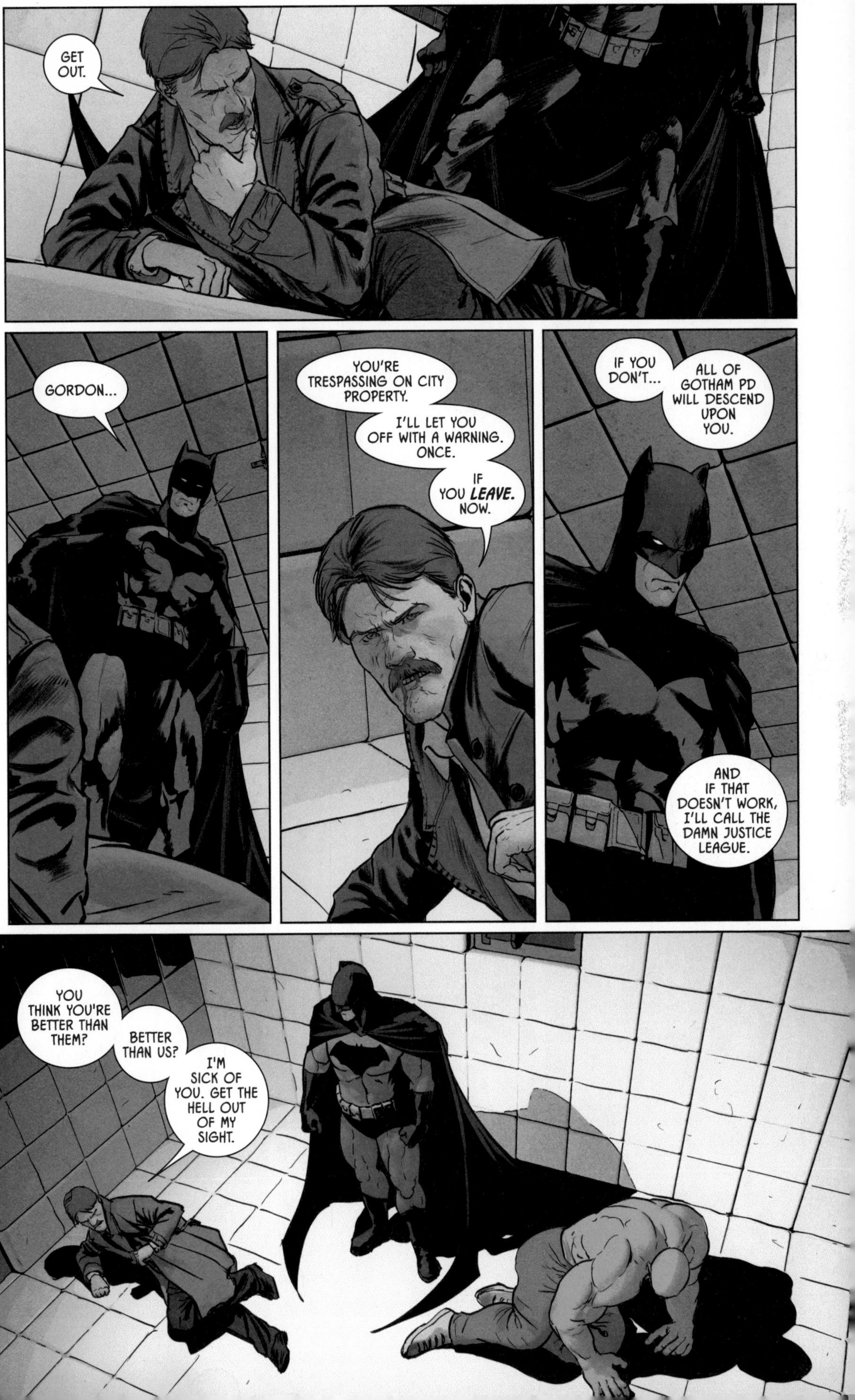
GET OUT.
GORDON...
YOU'RE TRESPASSING ON CITY PROPERTY.
I'LL LET YOU OFF WITH A WARNING. ONCE.
IF YOU **LEAVE.** NOW.
IF YOU DON'T...
ALL OF GOTHAM PD WILL DESCEND UPON YOU.
AND IF THAT DOESN'T WORK, I'LL CALL THE DAMN JUSTICE LEAGUE.
YOU THINK YOU'RE BETTER THAN THEM?
BETTER THAN US?
I'M SICK OF YOU. GET THE HELL OUT OF MY SIGHT.

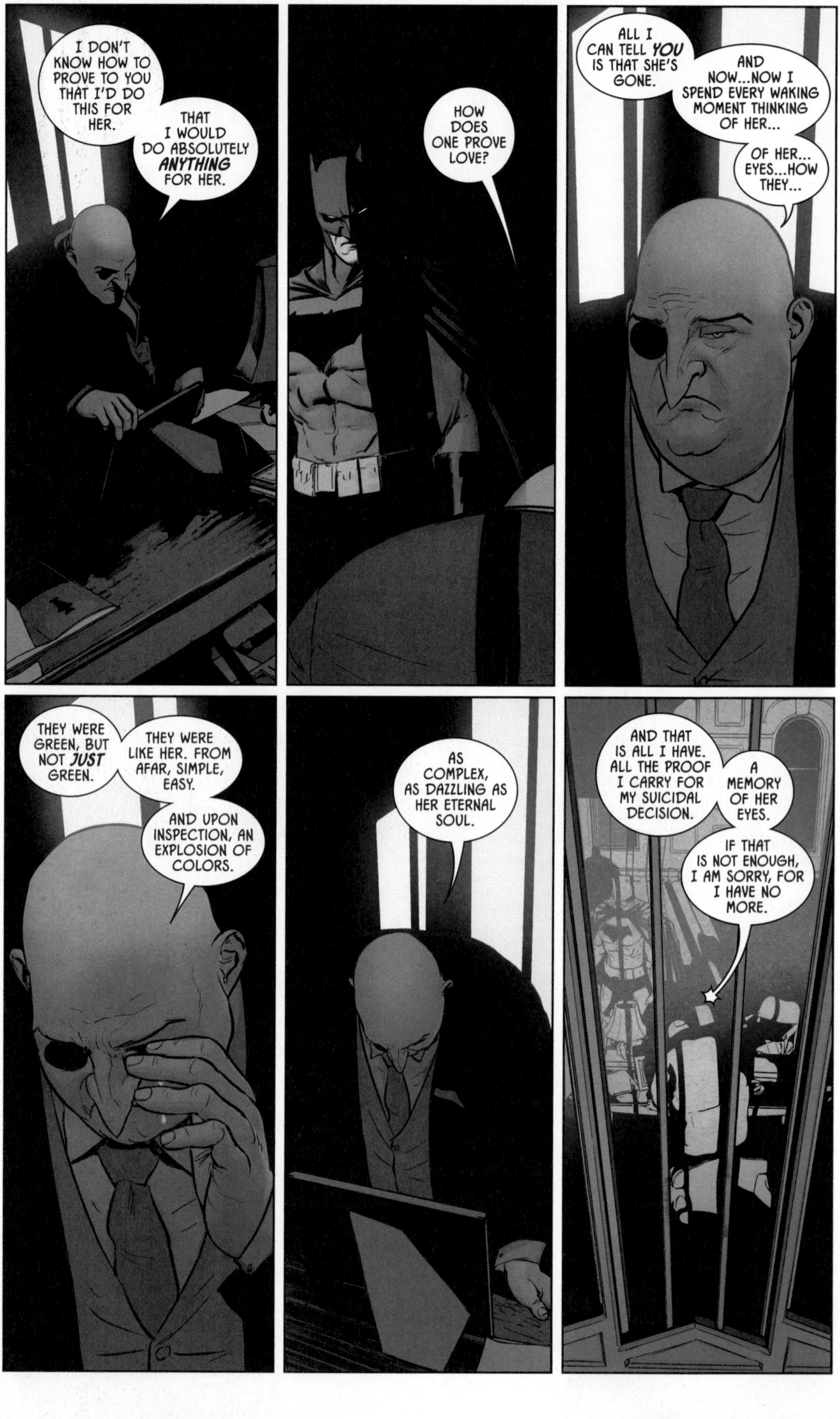
I DON'T KNOW HOW TO PROVE TO YOU THAT I'D DO THIS FOR HER.
THAT I WOULD DO ABSOLUTELY *ANYTHING* FOR HER.
HOW DOES ONE PROVE LOVE?
ALL I CAN TELL *YOU* IS THAT SHE'S GONE.
AND NOW...NOW I SPEND EVERY WAKING MOMENT THINKING OF HER...
OF HER... EYES...HOW THEY...
THEY WERE GREEN, BUT NOT *JUST* GREEN.
THEY WERE LIKE HER. FROM AFAR, SIMPLE, EASY.
AND UPON INSPECTION, AN EXPLOSION OF COLORS.
AS COMPLEX, AS DAZZLING AS HER ETERNAL SOUL.
AND THAT IS ALL I HAVE. ALL THE PROOF I CARRY FOR MY SUICIDAL DECISION.
A MEMORY OF HER EYES.
IF THAT IS NOT ENOUGH, I AM SORRY, FOR I HAVE NO MORE.

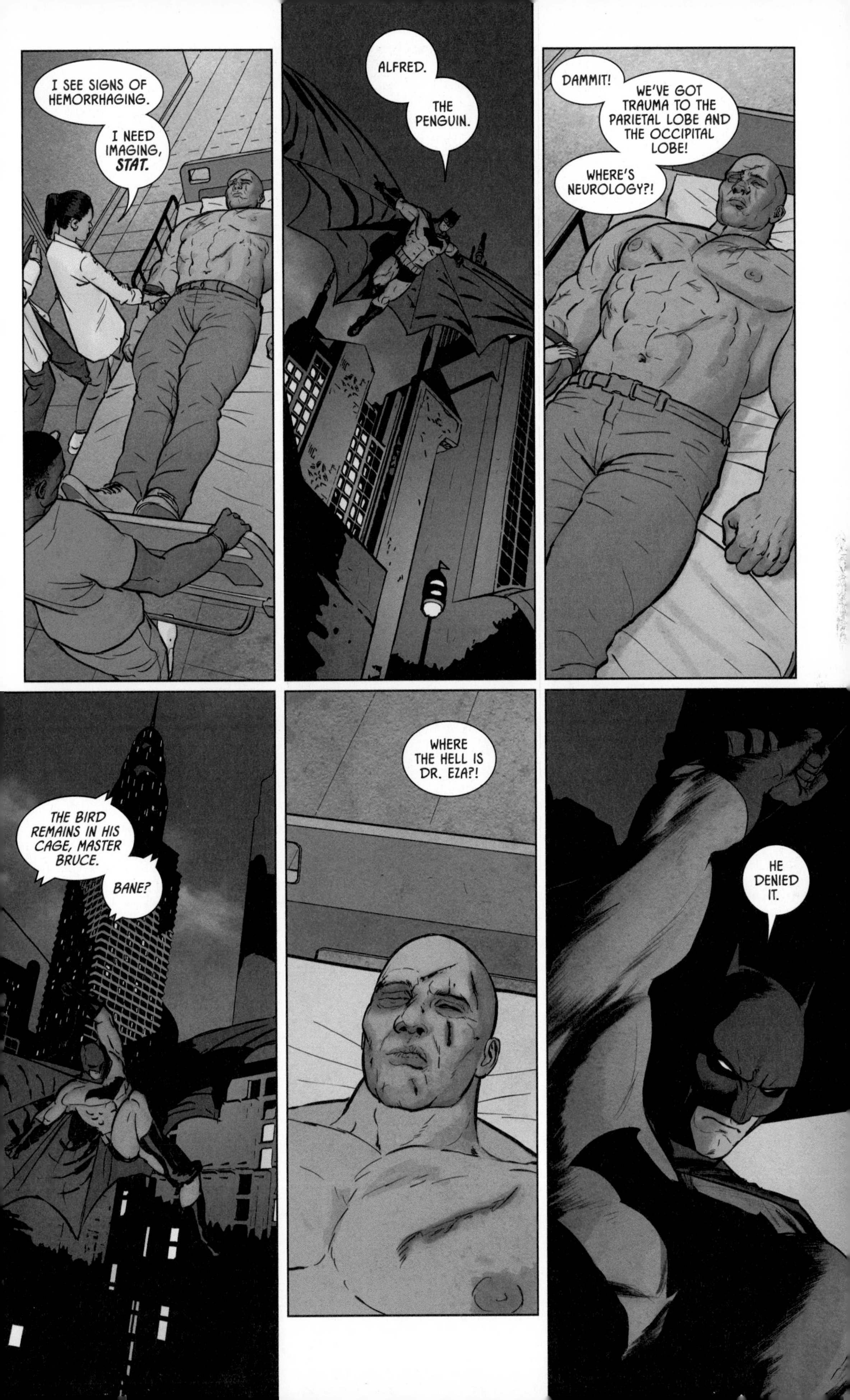
I SEE SIGNS OF HEMORRHAGING.
I NEED IMAGING, STAT.
ALFRED.
THE PENGUIN.
DAMMIT!
WE'VE GOT TRAUMA TO THE PARIETAL LOBE AND THE OCCIPITAL LOBE!
WHERE'S NEUROLOGY?!
THE BIRD REMAINS IN HIS CAGE, MASTER BRUCE.
BANE?
WHERE THE HELL IS DR. EZA?!
HE DENIED IT.

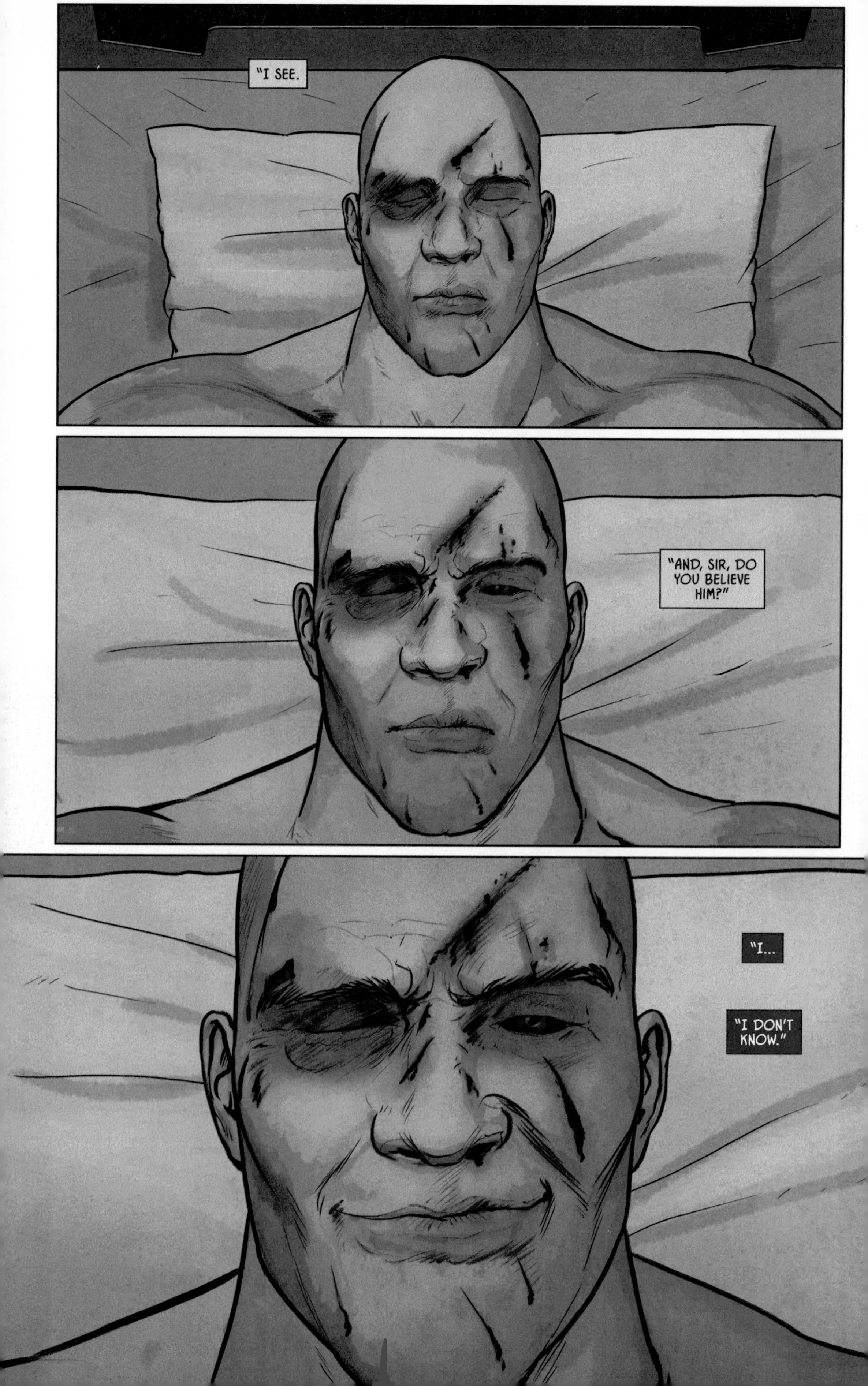
"I SEE.
"AND, SIR, DO YOU BELIEVE HIM?"
"I...
"I DON'T KNOW."

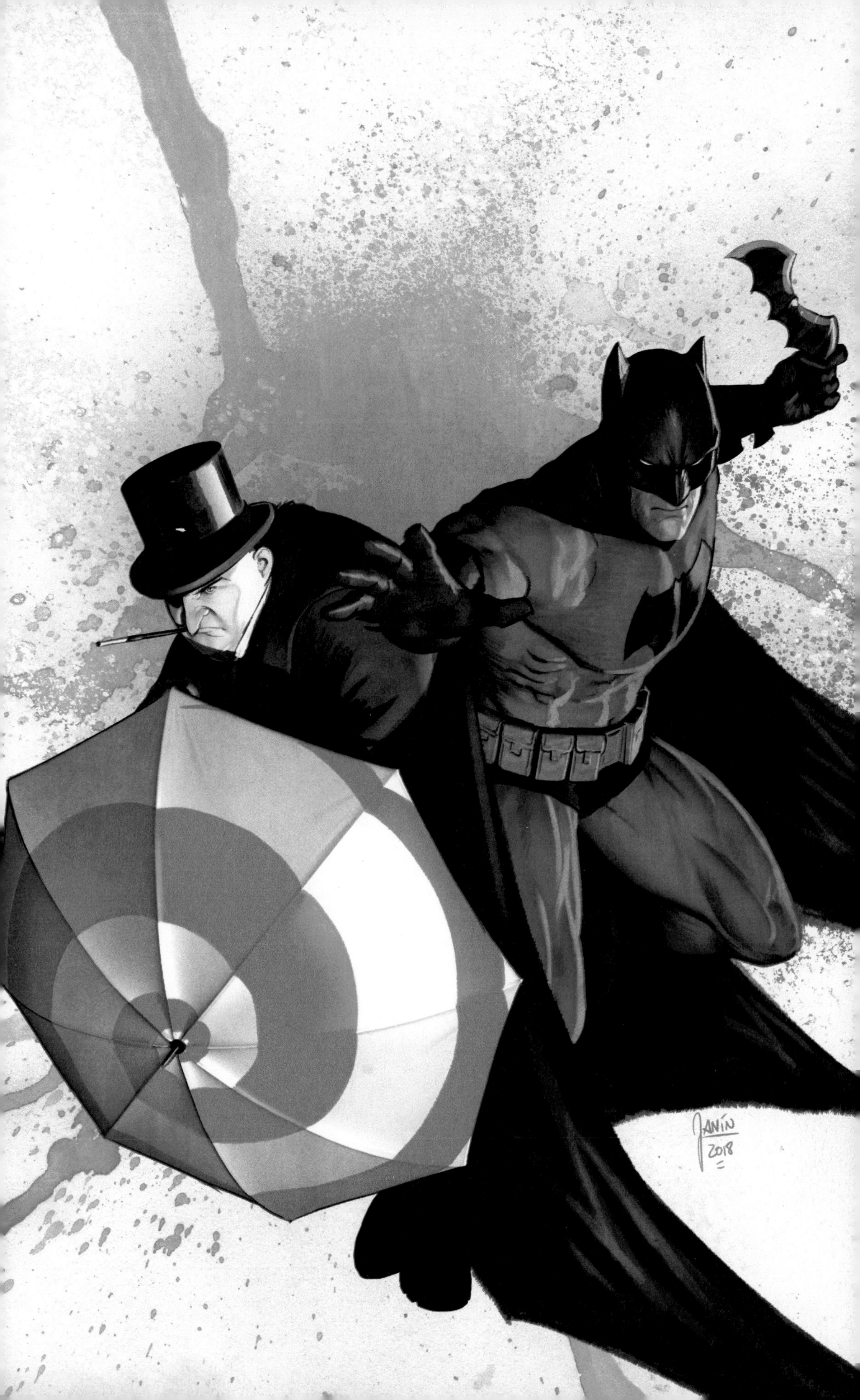
JANÍN
2018

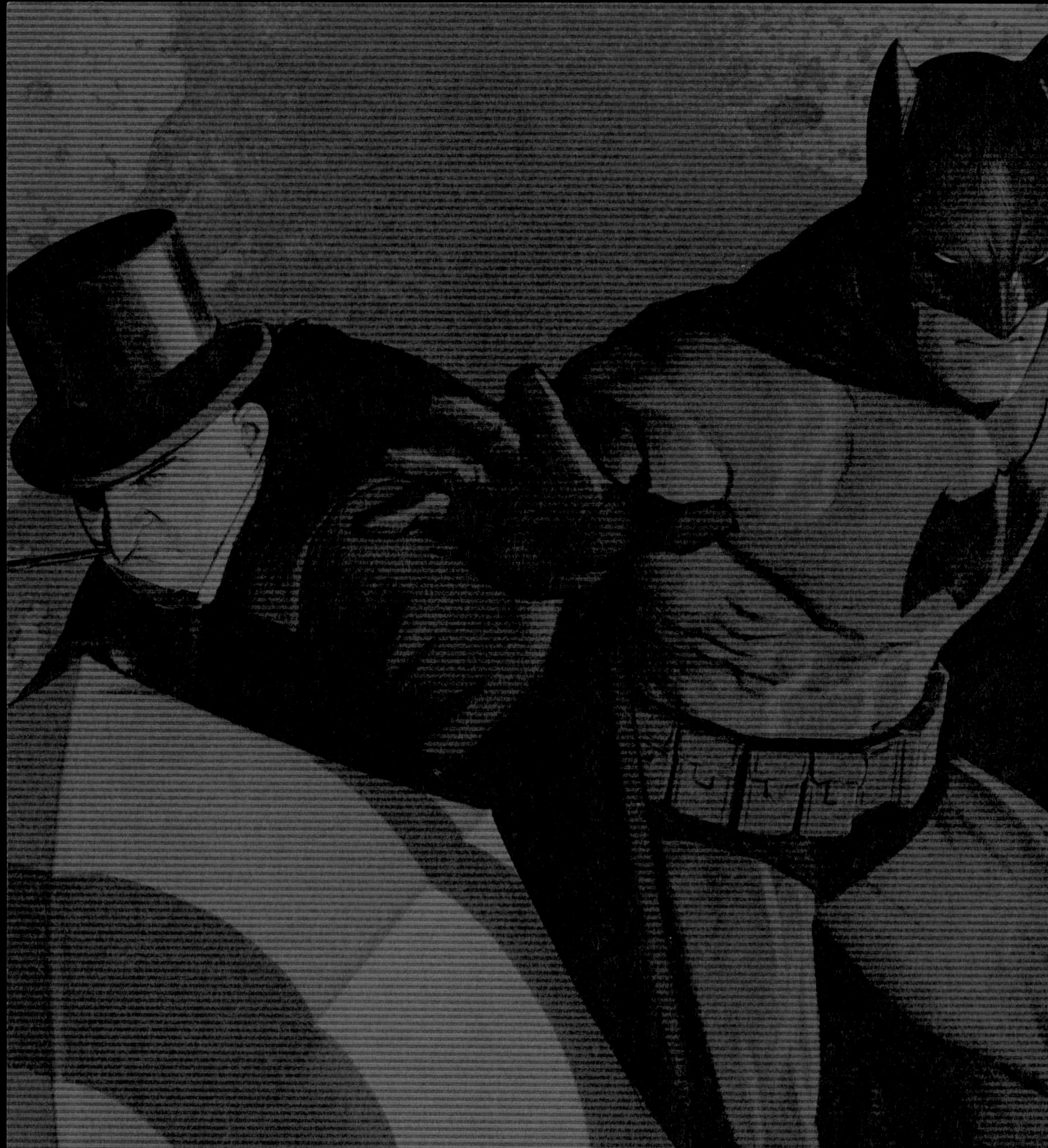

BATMAN
#60

beeeep
beeeep
beeeeep

AM 5:00 PM

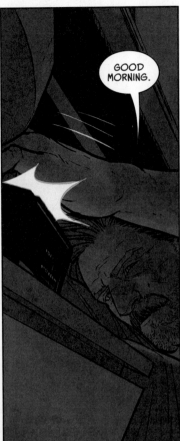

GOOD MORNING.

EXPECT RAIN ALL DAY AND NIGHT WITH TEMPERATURES FALLING LATER.

WE MIGHT HAVE SOME SLEET BEFORE THE DAY'S THROUGH.

OH, HEY, COMMISSIONER.

SERGEANT.

ssioner Gordon

PAT, CAN YOU GET HARVEY IN HERE? TELL HIM I WANT TO TALK THE FREEZE CASE.

RECENT ONE. PLEASE.

THE ONE WHERE *BATMAN* JUST KEPT HITTING HIM.

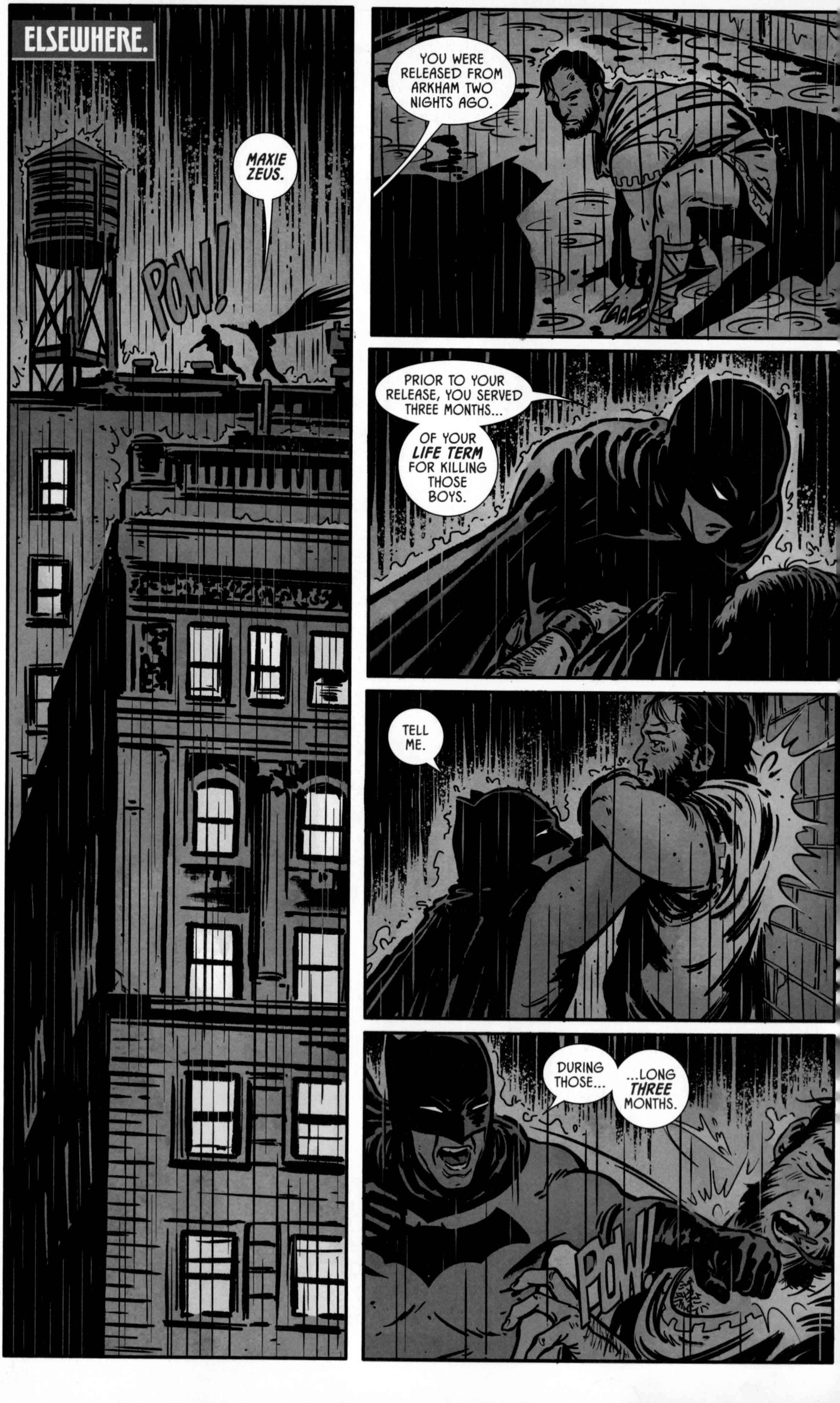
ELSEWHERE.
MAXIE ZEUS.
POW!
YOU WERE RELEASED FROM ARKHAM TWO NIGHTS AGO.
PRIOR TO YOUR RELEASE, YOU SERVED THREE MONTHS...
OF YOUR LIFE TERM FOR KILLING THOSE BOYS.
TELL ME.
DURING THOSE...
...LONG THREE MONTHS.
POW!

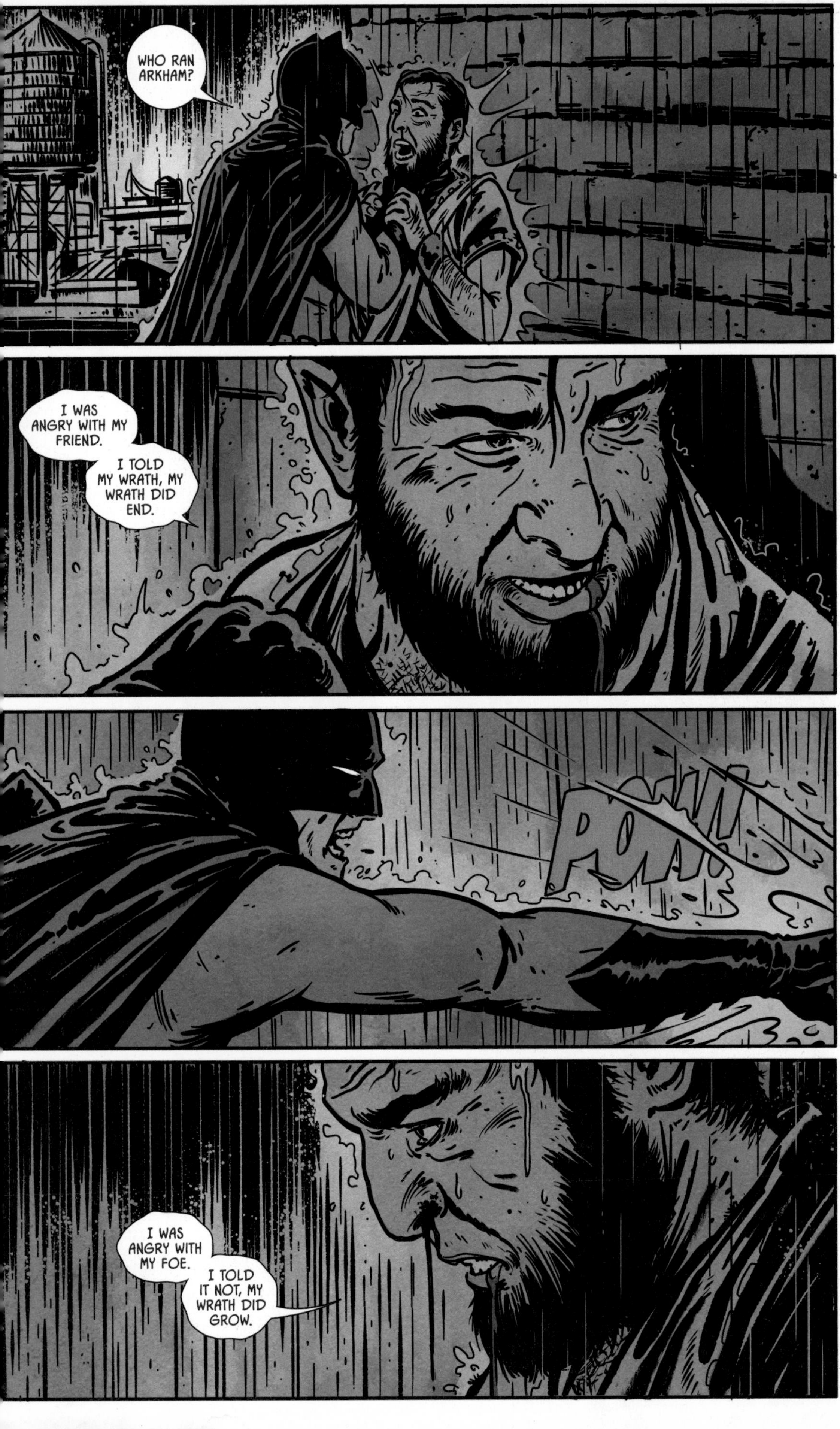

WHO RAN ARKHAM?
I WAS ANGRY WITH MY FRIEND.
I TOLD MY WRATH, MY WRATH DID END.
POW!
I WAS ANGRY WITH MY FOE.
I TOLD IT NOT, MY WRATH DID GROW.

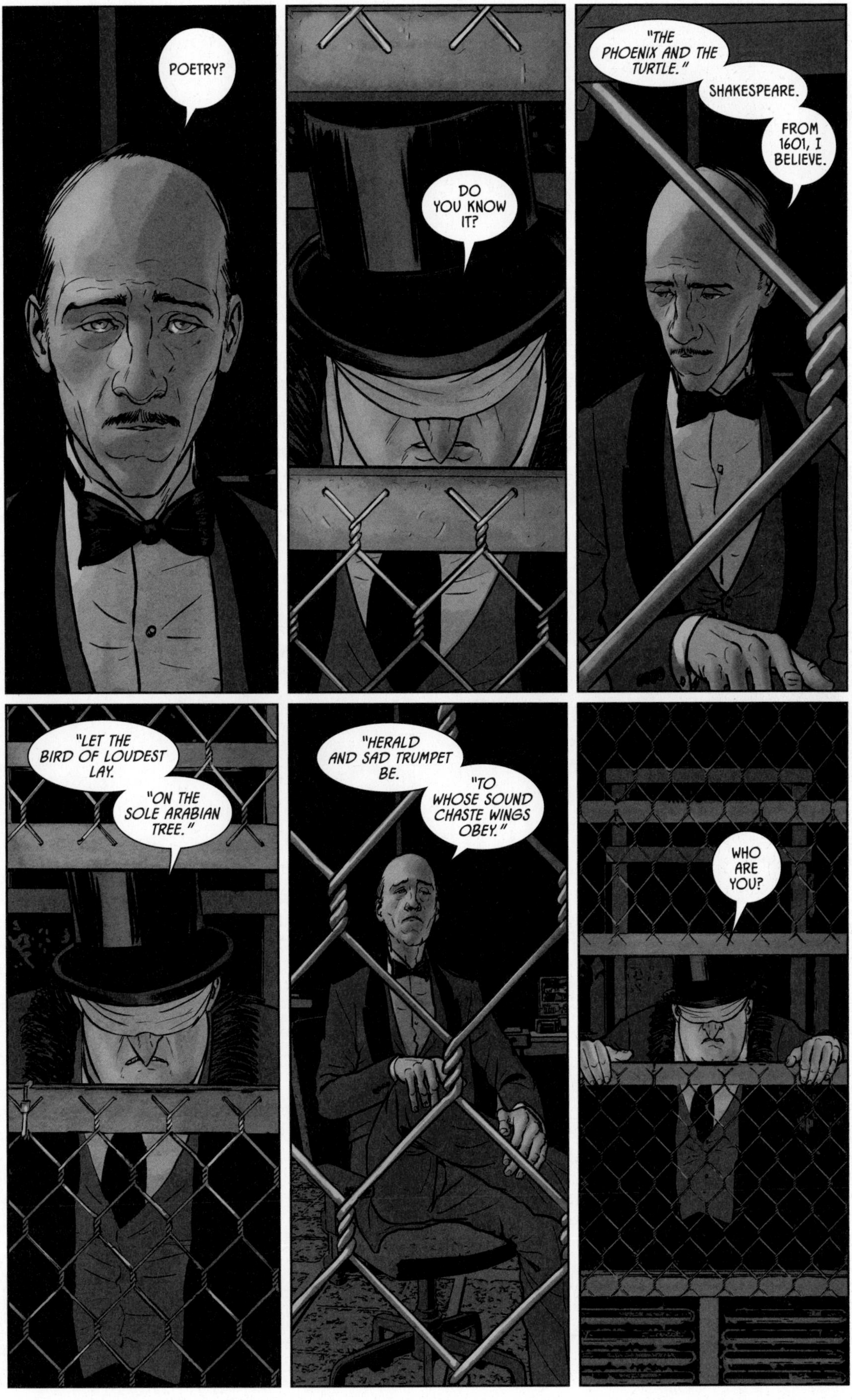
POETRY?
DO YOU KNOW IT?
"THE PHOENIX AND THE TURTLE."
SHAKESPEARE.
FROM 1601, I BELIEVE.
"LET THE BIRD OF LOUDEST LAY.
"ON THE SOLE ARABIAN TREE."
"HERALD AND SAD TRUMPET BE.
"TO WHOSE SOUND CHASTE WINGS OBEY."
WHO ARE YOU?

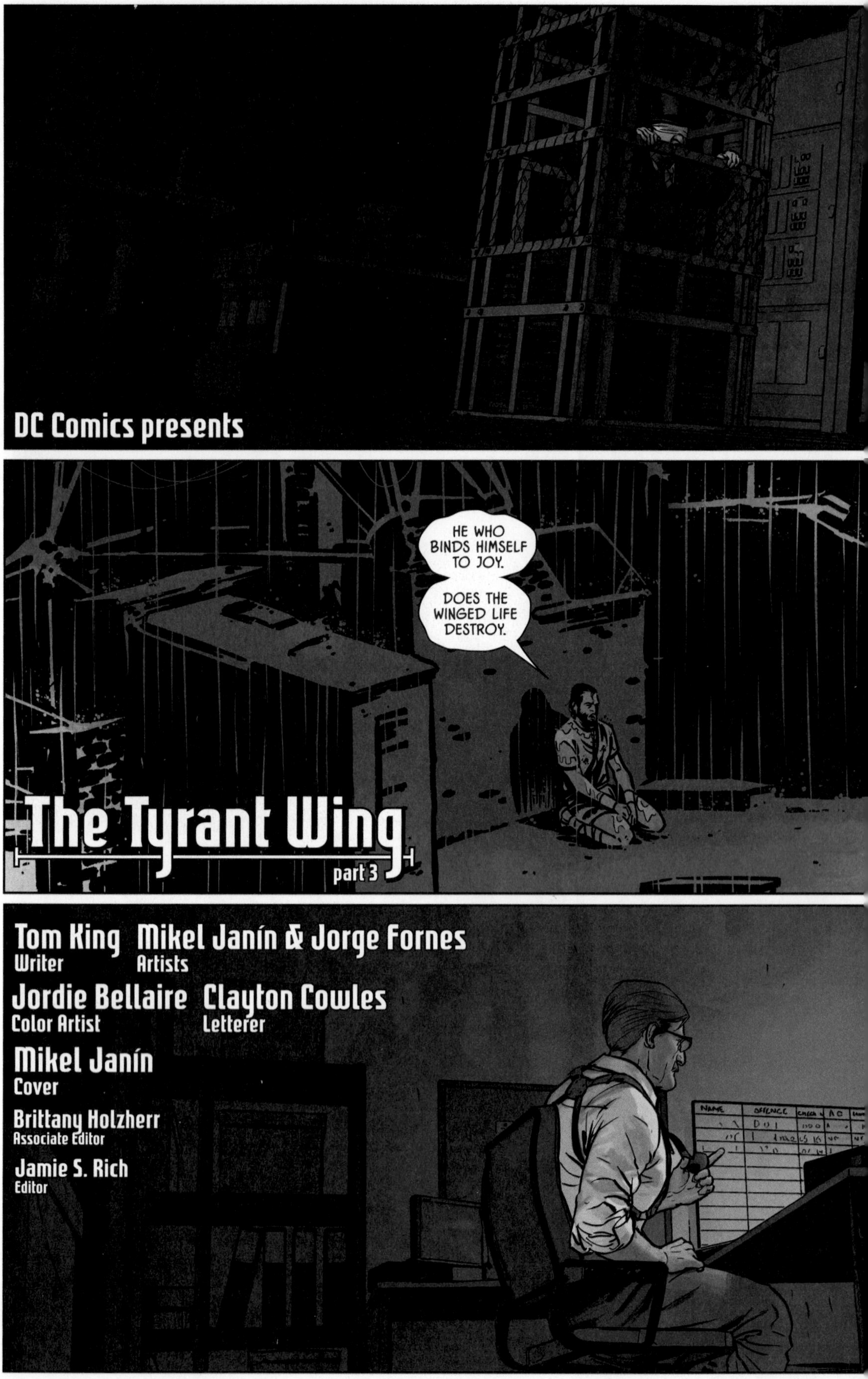
DC Comics presents
HE WHO BINDS HIMSELF TO JOY.
DOES THE WINGED LIFE DESTROY.
The Tyrant Wing
part 3
Tom King
Writer
Mikel Janín & Jorge Fornes
Artists
Jordie Bellaire
Color Artist
Clayton Cowles
Letterer
Mikel Janín
Cover
Brittany Holzherr
Associate Editor
Jamie S. Rich
Editor

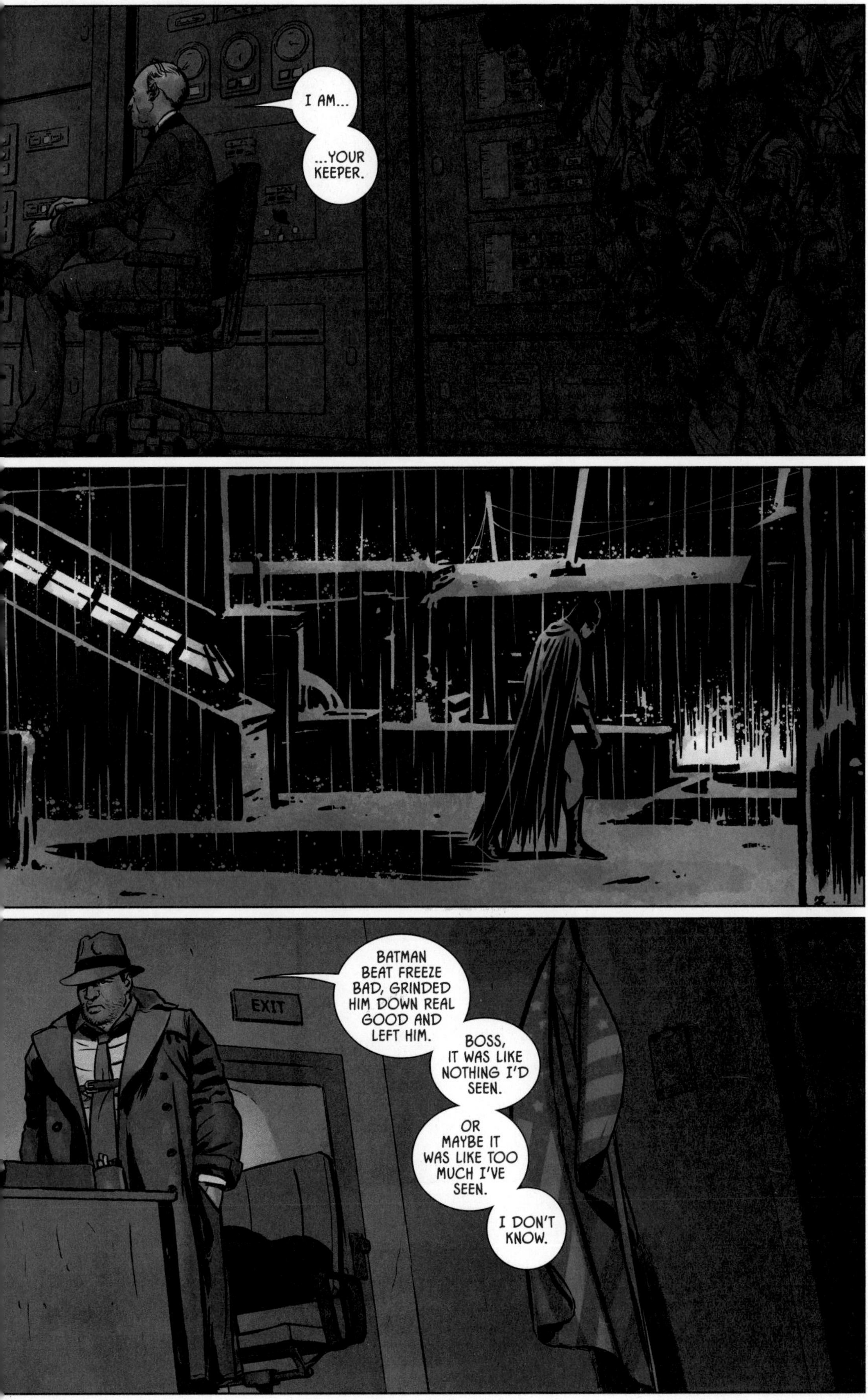
I AM...
...YOUR KEEPER.
BATMAN BEAT FREEZE BAD, GRINDED HIM DOWN REAL GOOD AND LEFT HIM.
BOSS, IT WAS LIKE NOTHING I'D SEEN.
OR MAYBE IT WAS LIKE TOO MUCH I'VE SEEN.
I DON'T KNOW.
EXIT

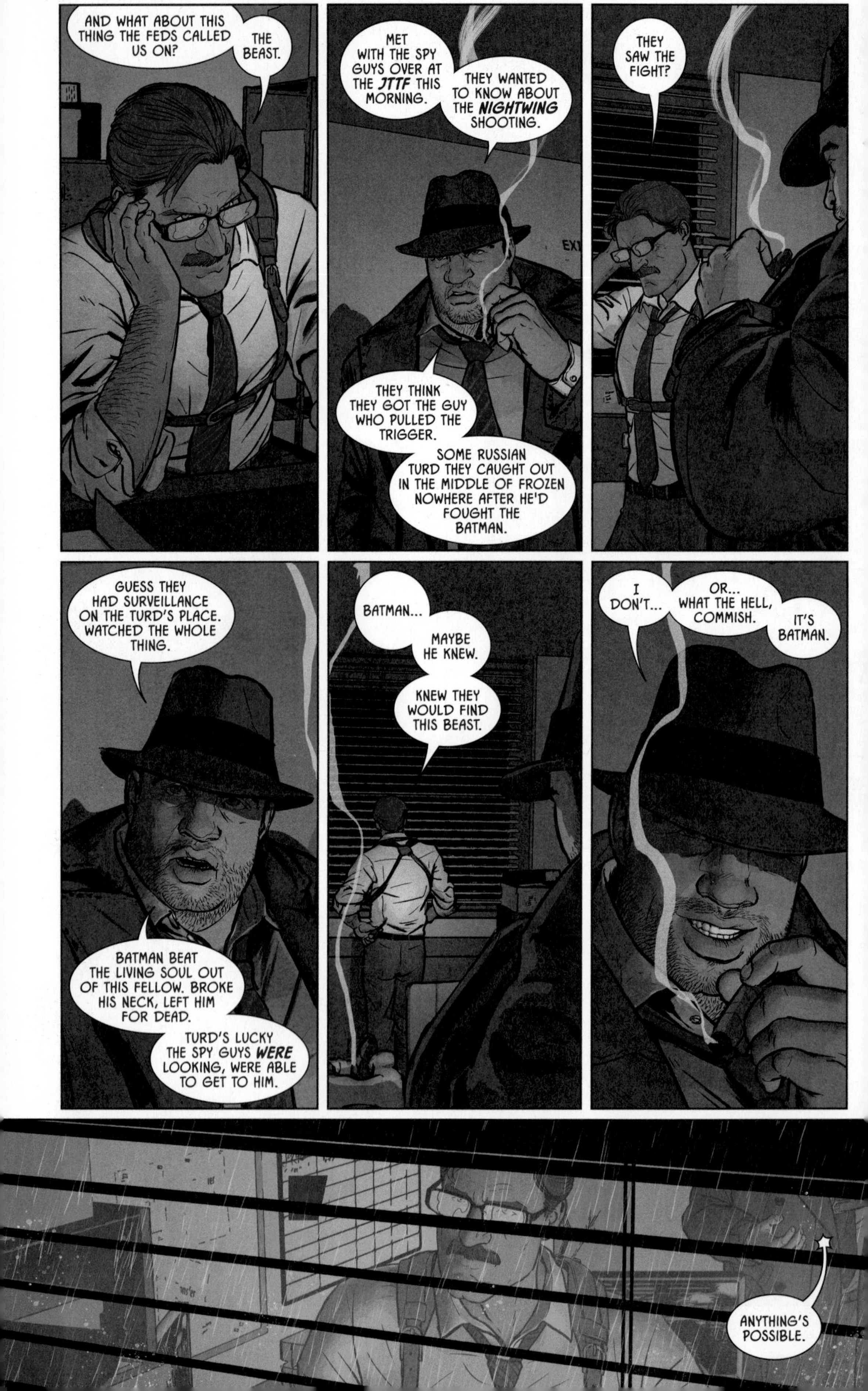

AND WHAT ABOUT THIS THING THE FEDS CALLED US ON?
THE BEAST.
MET WITH THE SPY GUYS OVER AT THE JTTF THIS MORNING.
THEY WANTED TO KNOW ABOUT THE NIGHTWING SHOOTING.
THEY THINK THEY GOT THE GUY WHO PULLED THE TRIGGER.
SOME RUSSIAN TURD THEY CAUGHT OUT IN THE MIDDLE OF FROZEN NOWHERE AFTER HE'D FOUGHT THE BATMAN.
THEY SAW THE FIGHT?
GUESS THEY HAD SURVEILLANCE ON THE TURD'S PLACE. WATCHED THE WHOLE THING.
BATMAN BEAT THE LIVING SOUL OUT OF THIS FELLOW. BROKE HIS NECK, LEFT HIM FOR DEAD.
TURD'S LUCKY THE SPY GUYS WERE LOOKING, WERE ABLE TO GET TO HIM.
BATMAN...
MAYBE HE KNEW.
KNEW THEY WOULD FIND THIS BEAST.
I DON'T...
OR... WHAT THE HELL, COMMISH.
IT'S BATMAN.
ANYTHING'S POSSIBLE.

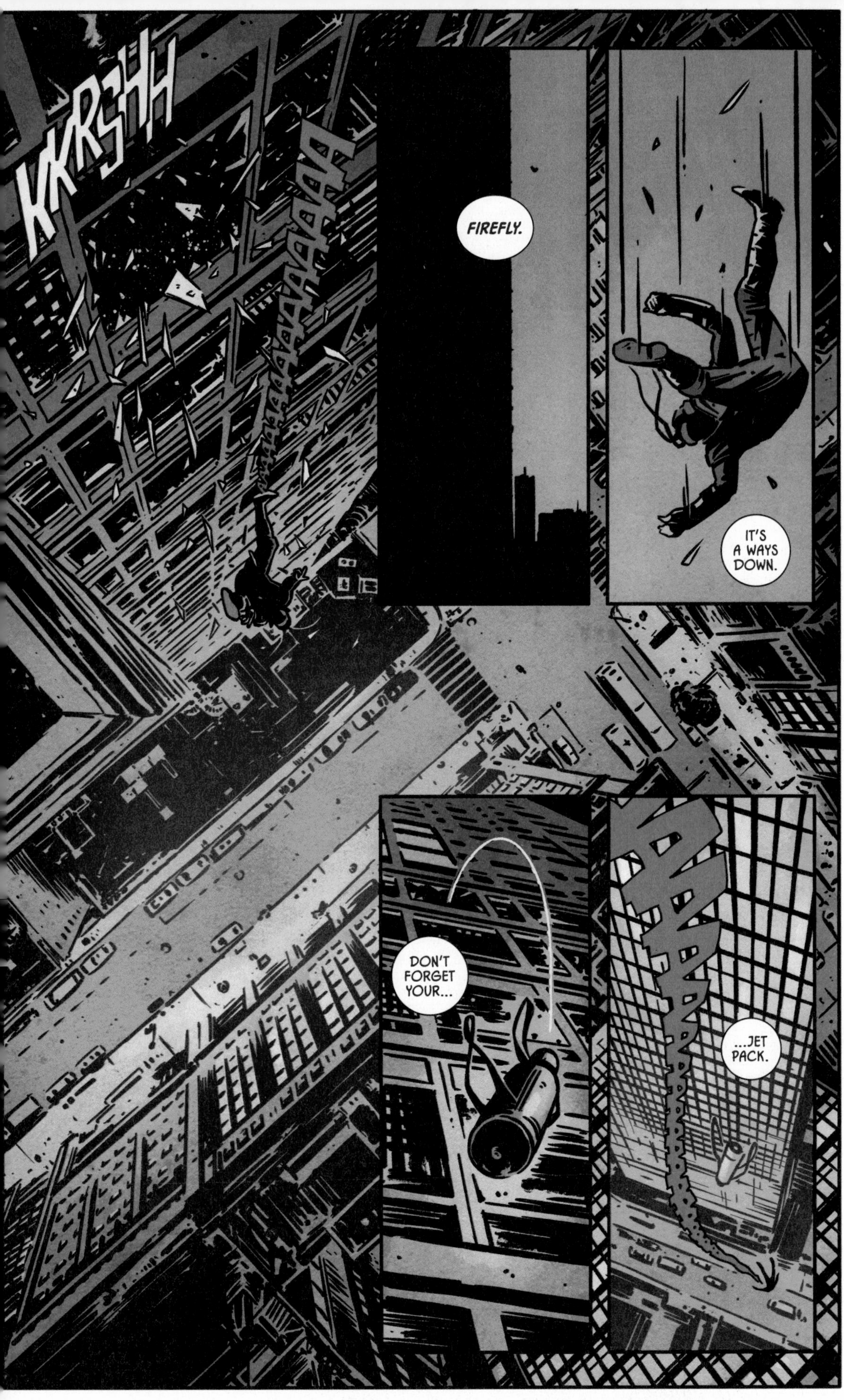
KKRSHH
FIREFLY.
IT'S A WAYS DOWN.
DON'T FORGET YOUR...
...JET PACK.

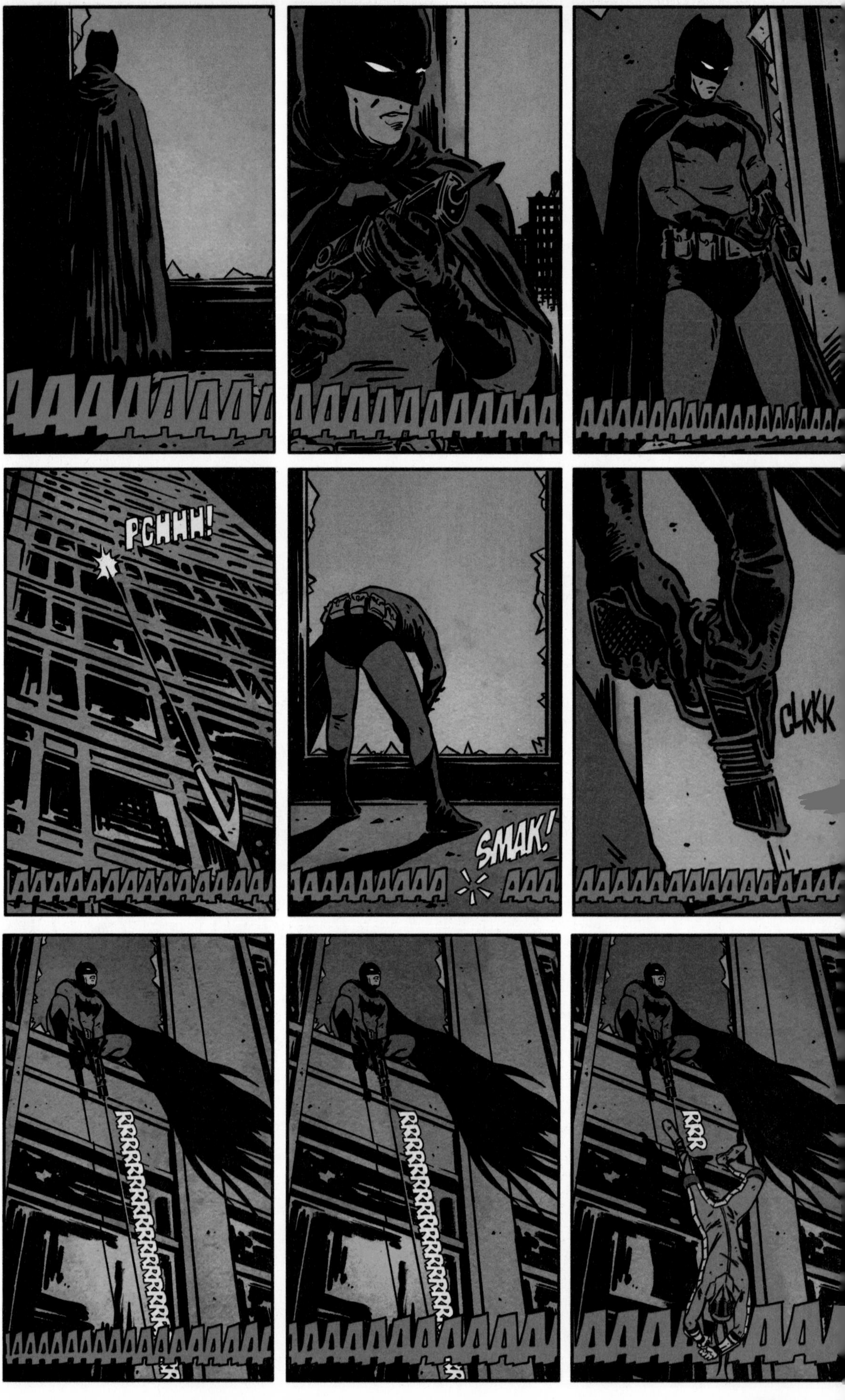
AAAAAAAAA
AAAAAAAAAAAAA
AAAAAAAAAAAAAAAAAA
PCHHH!
AAAAAAAAAAAAAAAAAA
SMAK!
AAAAAAAAA
AAA
CLKKK
AAAAAAAAAAAAAAAAAA
RRRRRRRRRRRRRRRRRRRR
AAAAAAAAAAAAAAAAA
RRRRRRRRRRRRRRRRRRRRR
AAAAAAAAAAAAAAAAA
RRR
AAAA
AAA

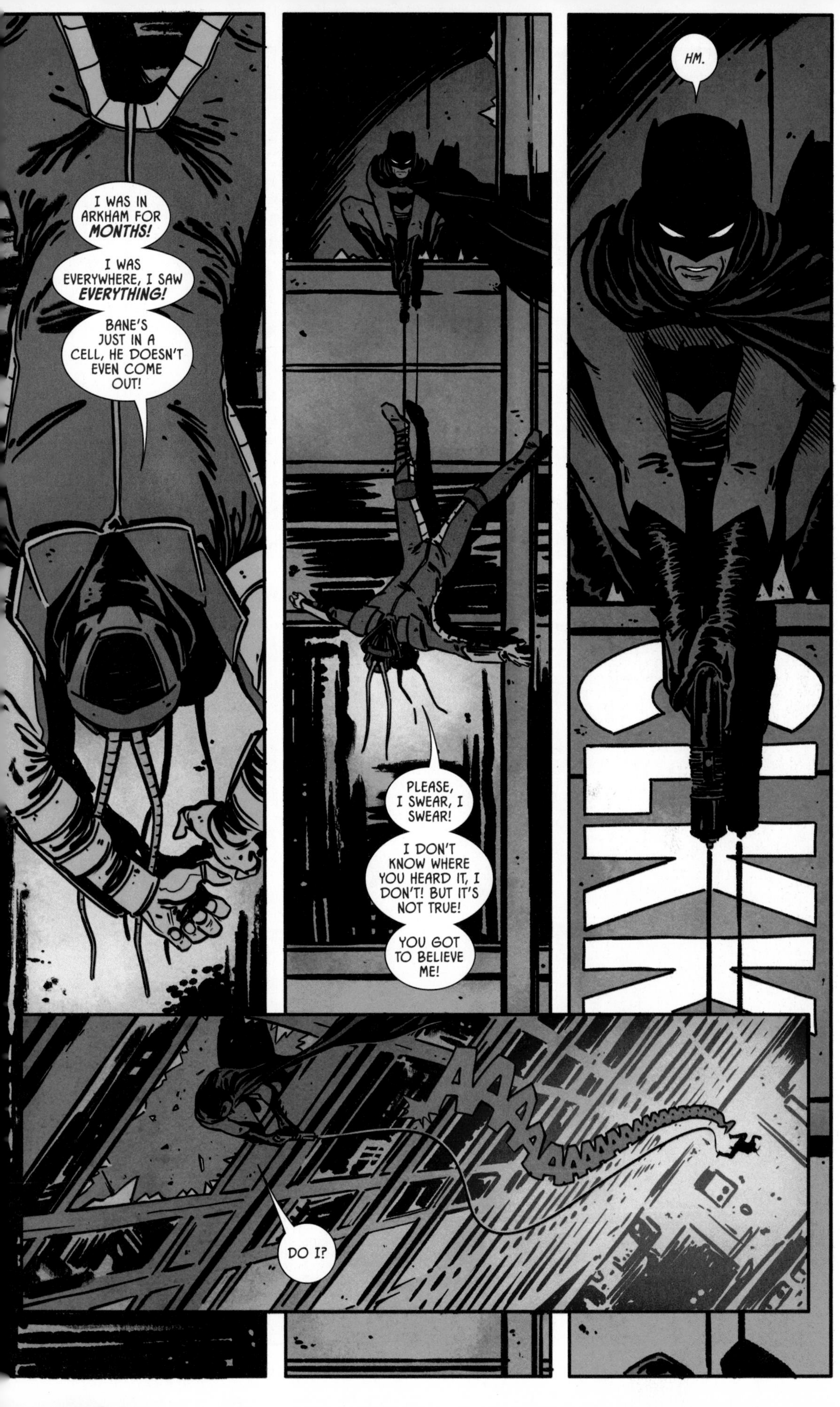
I WAS IN ARKHAM FOR MONTHS!
I WAS EVERYWHERE, I SAW EVERYTHING!
BANE'S JUST IN A CELL, HE DOESN'T EVEN COME OUT!
PLEASE, I SWEAR, I SWEAR!
I DON'T KNOW WHERE YOU HEARD IT, I DON'T! BUT IT'S NOT TRUE!
YOU GOT TO BELIEVE ME!
HM.
DO I?

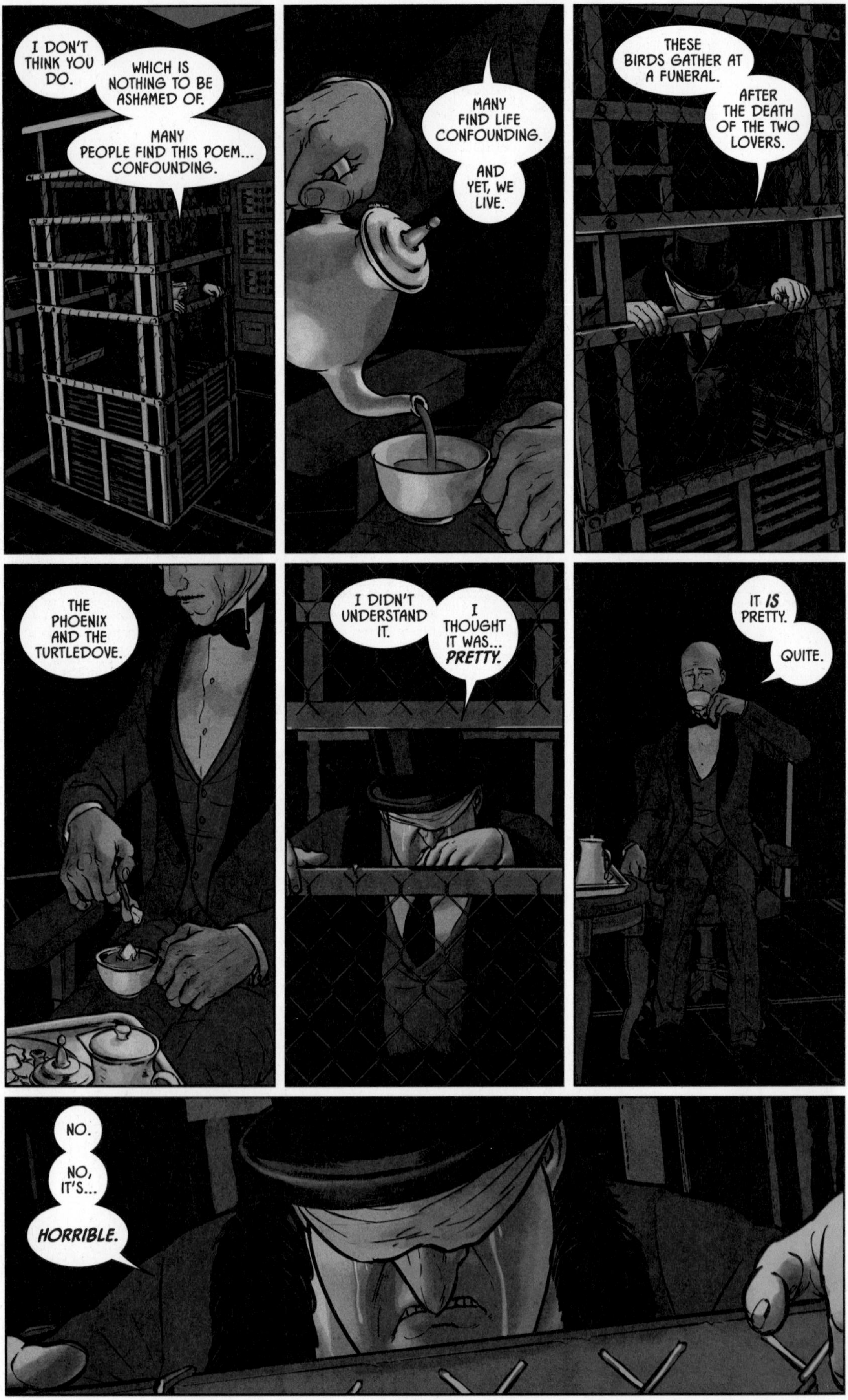
I DON'T THINK YOU DO.
WHICH IS NOTHING TO BE ASHAMED OF.
MANY PEOPLE FIND THIS POEM... CONFOUNDING.
MANY FIND LIFE CONFOUNDING.
AND YET, WE LIVE.
THESE BIRDS GATHER AT A FUNERAL.
AFTER THE DEATH OF THE TWO LOVERS.
THE PHOENIX AND THE TURTLEDOVE.
I DIDN'T UNDERSTAND IT.
I THOUGHT IT WAS... *PRETTY.*
IT *IS* PRETTY.
QUITE.
NO.
NO, IT'S...
HORRIBLE.

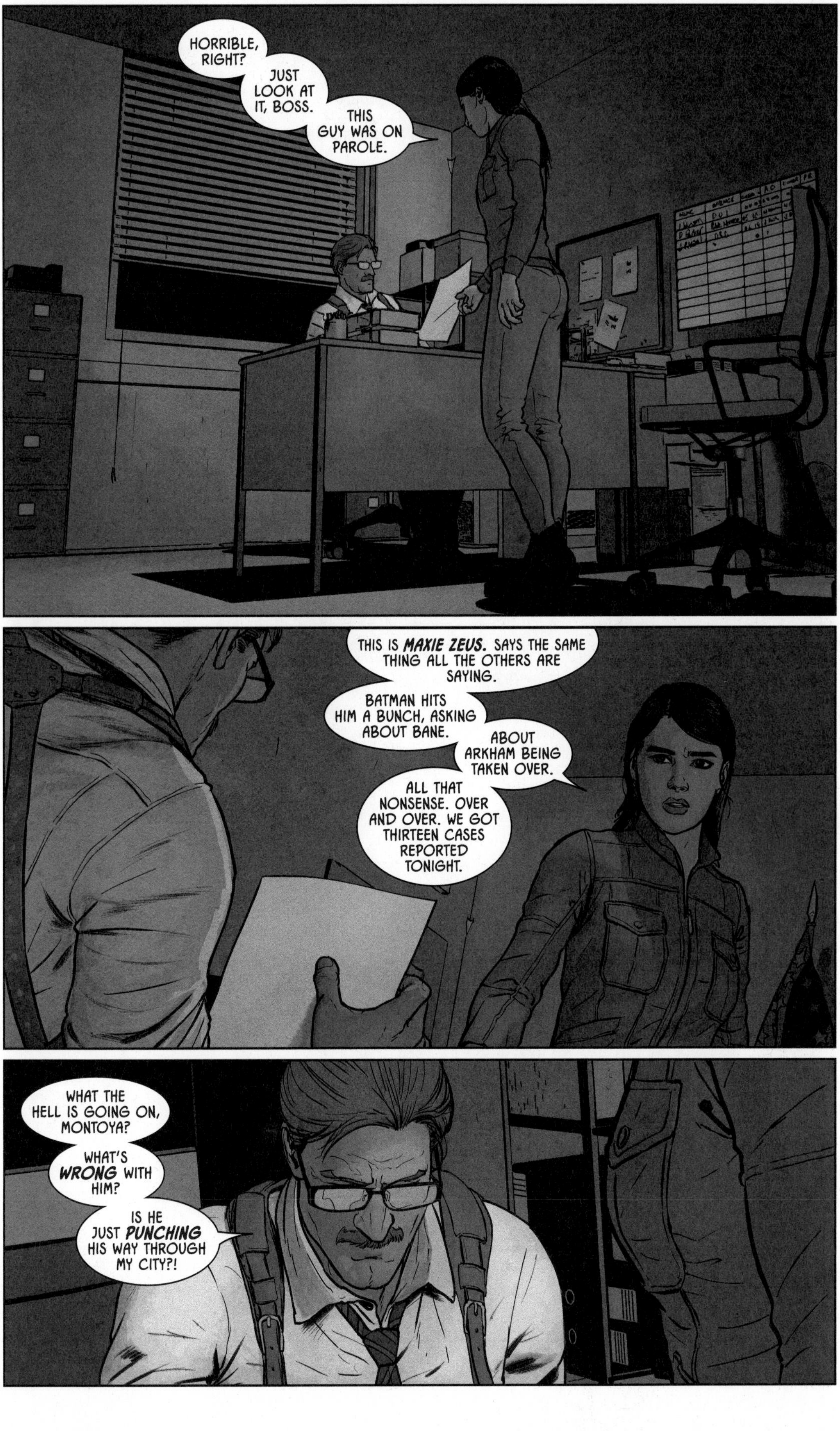
HORRIBLE, RIGHT?
JUST LOOK AT IT, BOSS.
THIS GUY WAS ON PAROLE.
THIS IS MAXIE ZEUS. SAYS THE SAME THING ALL THE OTHERS ARE SAYING.
BATMAN HITS HIM A BUNCH, ASKING ABOUT BANE.
ABOUT ARKHAM BEING TAKEN OVER.
ALL THAT NONSENSE. OVER AND OVER. WE GOT THIRTEEN CASES REPORTED TONIGHT.
WHAT THE HELL IS GOING ON, MONTOYA?
WHAT'S WRONG WITH HIM?
IS HE JUST PUNCHING HIS WAY THROUGH MY CITY?!

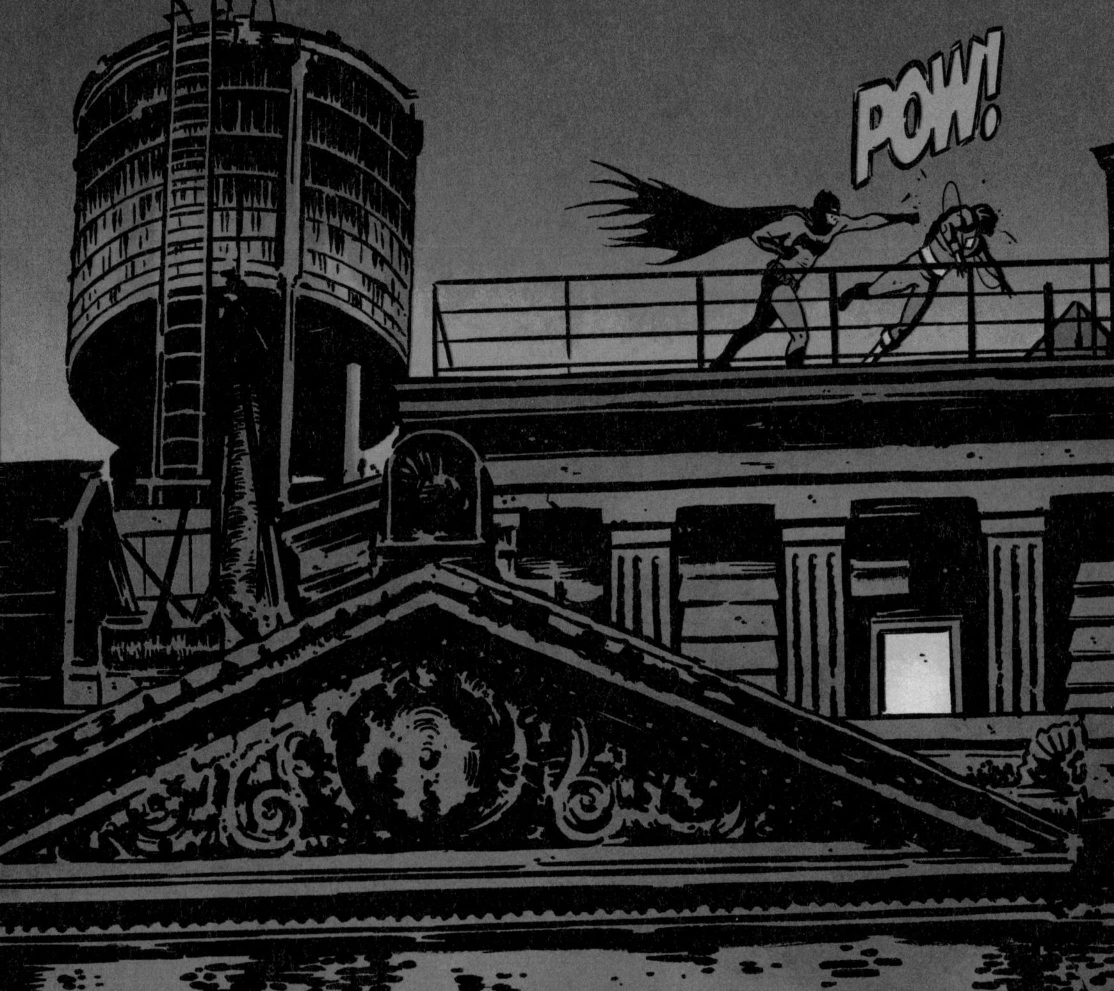
POW!

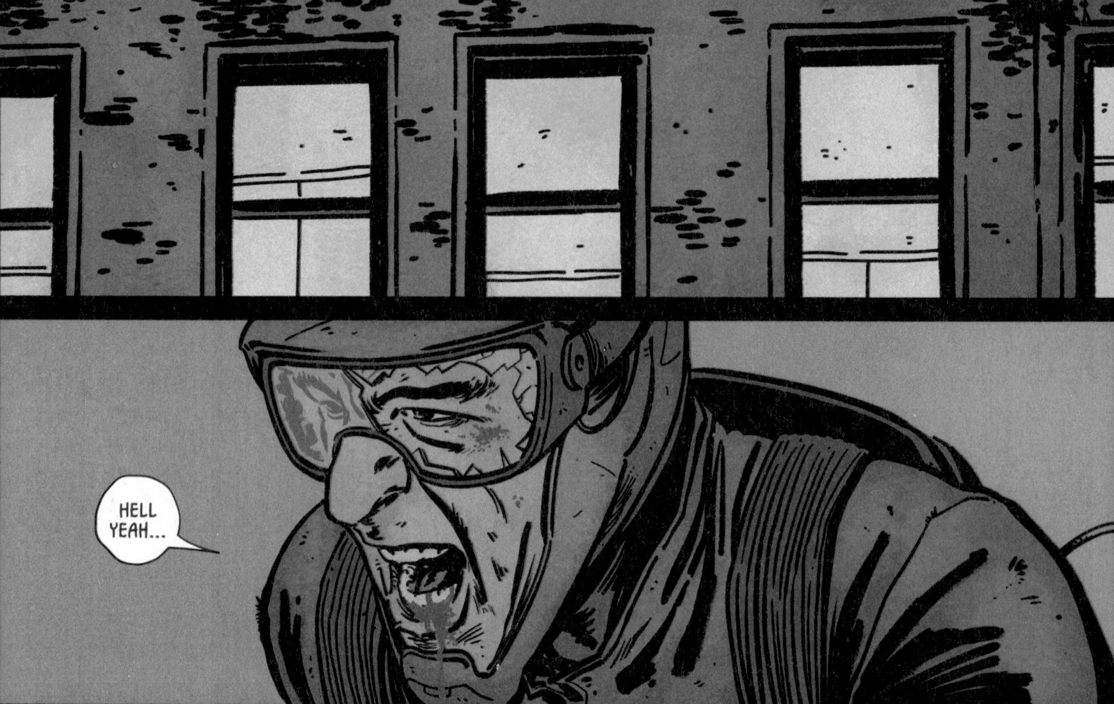
HELL YEAH...

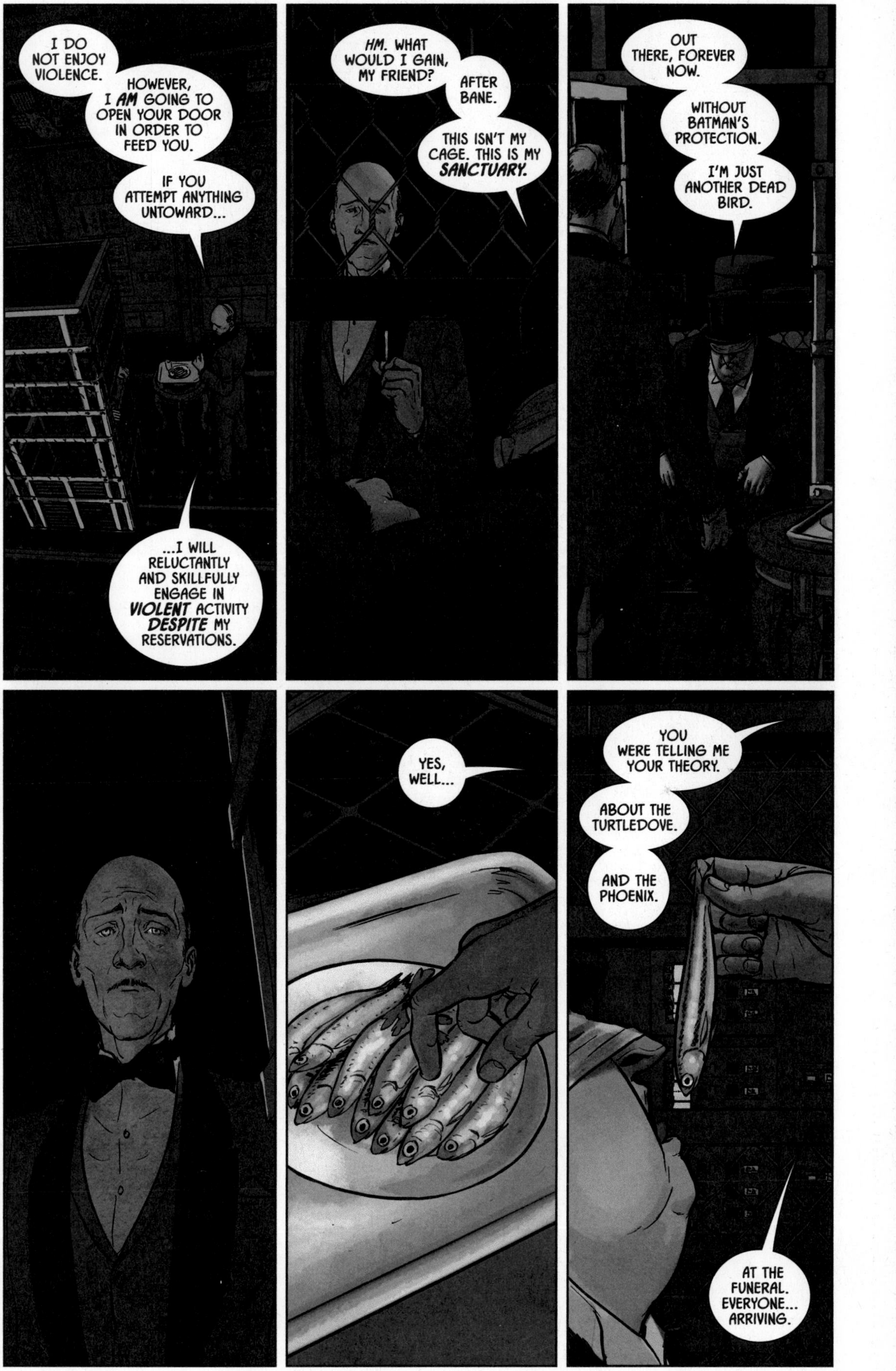
I DO NOT ENJOY VIOLENCE.
HOWEVER, I *AM* GOING TO OPEN YOUR DOOR IN ORDER TO FEED YOU.
IF YOU ATTEMPT ANYTHING UNTOWARD...
...I WILL RELUCTANTLY AND SKILLFULLY ENGAGE IN *VIOLENT* ACTIVITY *DESPITE* MY RESERVATIONS.
HM. WHAT WOULD I GAIN, MY FRIEND?
AFTER BANE.
THIS ISN'T MY CAGE. THIS IS MY *SANCTUARY.*
OUT THERE, FOREVER NOW.
WITHOUT BATMAN'S PROTECTION.
I'M JUST ANOTHER DEAD BIRD.
YES, WELL...
YOU WERE TELLING ME YOUR THEORY.
ABOUT THE TURTLEDOVE.
AND THE PHOENIX.
AT THE FUNERAL. EVERYONE... ARRIVING.

COME IN! IT'S OPEN!

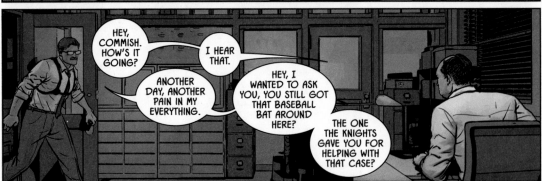

HEY, COMMISH. HOW'S IT GOING?

I HEAR THAT.

ANOTHER DAY, ANOTHER PAIN IN MY EVERYTHING.

HEY, I WANTED TO ASK YOU, YOU STILL GOT THAT BASEBALL BAT AROUND HERE?

THE ONE THE KNIGHTS GAVE YOU FOR HELPING WITH THAT CASE?

SURE, OVER THERE, BY THE WINDOW.

GOT IT SIGNED BY THE WHOLE TEAM.

THAT'S MY RETIREMENT POLICY THERE.

I NEED TO BORROW IT, JUST FOR A SECOND, OKAY?

WHATEVER YOU WANT, BOSS.

JUST...Y'KNOW, IN CASE IT'S WORTH SOMETHING...

I'LL BRING IT BACK.

HEY, YEAH, I KNOW I CAN TRUST YOU.

LOOK AT YOU, RIGHT? GOT TO TRUST YOU.

NOW YOU'RE, OFFICIALLY, THE *BATMAN*.

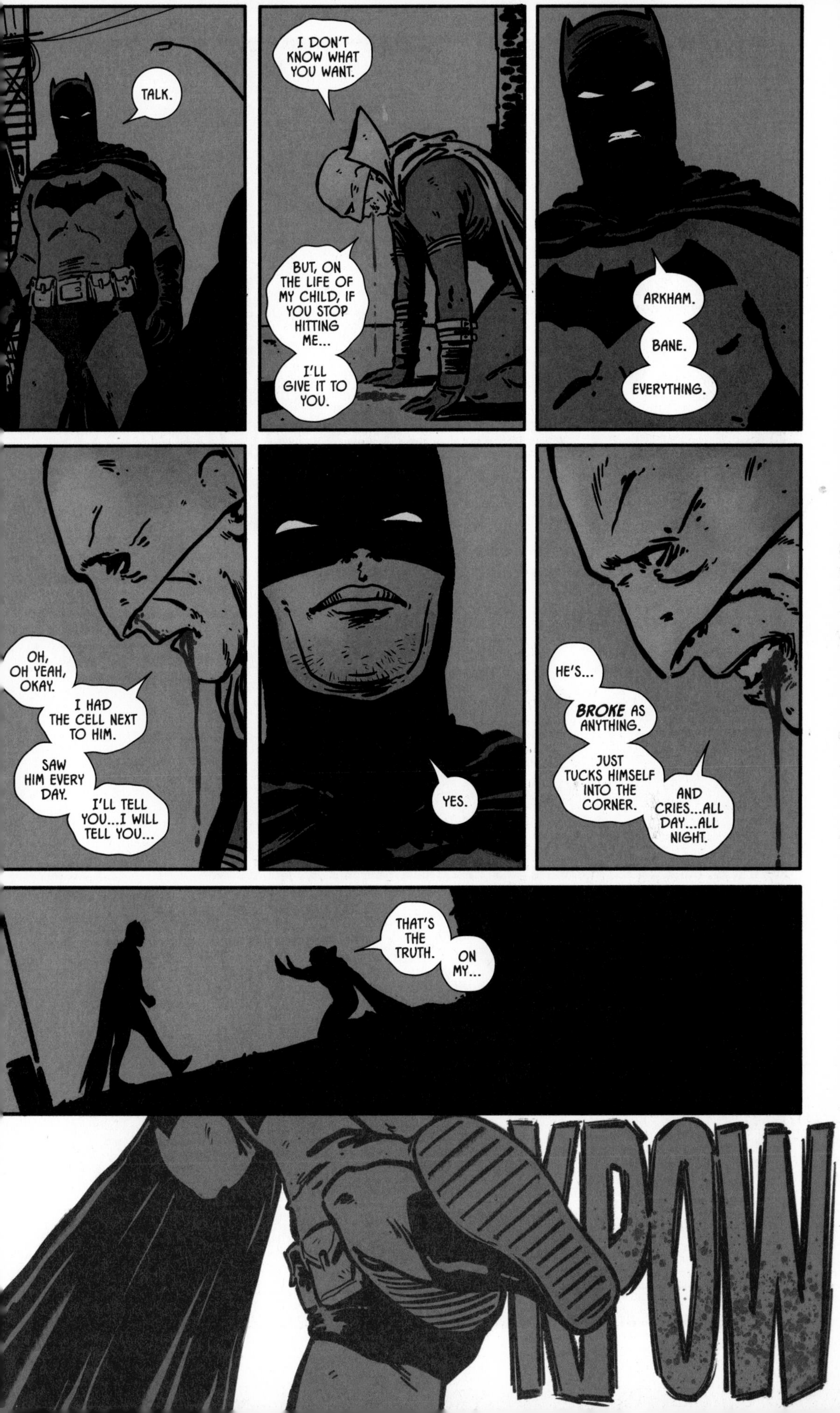
TALK.
I DON'T KNOW WHAT YOU WANT.
BUT, ON THE LIFE OF MY CHILD, IF YOU STOP HITTING ME...
I'LL GIVE IT TO YOU.
ARKHAM.
BANE.
EVERYTHING.
OH, OH YEAH, OKAY.
I HAD THE CELL NEXT TO HIM.
SAW HIM EVERY DAY.
I'LL TELL YOU...I WILL TELL YOU...
YES.
HE'S...
BROKE AS ANYTHING.
JUST TUCKS HIMSELF INTO THE CORNER.
AND CRIES...ALL DAY...ALL NIGHT.
THAT'S THE TRUTH.
ON MY...
KPOW

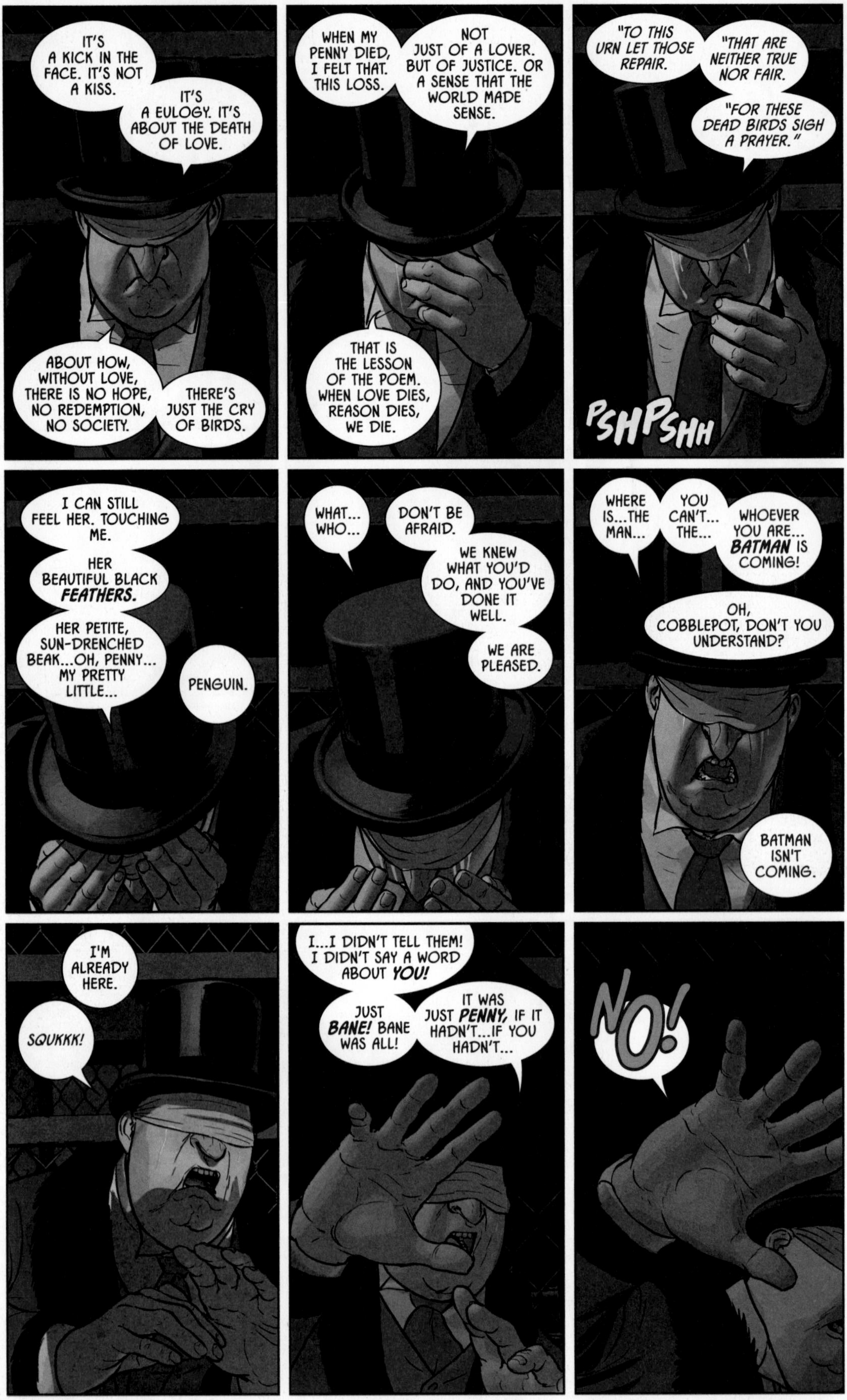
IT'S A KICK IN THE FACE. IT'S NOT A KISS.
IT'S A EULOGY. IT'S ABOUT THE DEATH OF LOVE.
ABOUT HOW, WITHOUT LOVE, THERE IS NO HOPE, NO REDEMPTION, NO SOCIETY.
THERE'S JUST THE CRY OF BIRDS.
WHEN MY PENNY DIED, I FELT THAT. THIS LOSS.
NOT JUST OF A LOVER. BUT OF JUSTICE. OR A SENSE THAT THE WORLD MADE SENSE.
THAT IS THE LESSON OF THE POEM. WHEN LOVE DIES, REASON DIES, WE DIE.
"TO THIS URN LET THOSE REPAIR.
"THAT ARE NEITHER TRUE NOR FAIR.
"FOR THESE DEAD BIRDS SIGH A PRAYER."
PSHPSHH
I CAN STILL FEEL HER. TOUCHING ME.
HER BEAUTIFUL BLACK FEATHERS.
HER PETITE, SUN-DRENCHED BEAK...OH, PENNY... MY PRETTY LITTLE...
PENGUIN.
WHAT... WHO...
DON'T BE AFRAID.
WE KNEW WHAT YOU'D DO, AND YOU'VE DONE IT WELL.
WE ARE PLEASED.
WHERE IS...THE MAN...
YOU CAN'T... THE...
WHOEVER YOU ARE... BATMAN IS COMING!
OH, COBBLEPOT, DON'T YOU UNDERSTAND?
BATMAN ISN'T COMING.
I'M ALREADY HERE.
SQUKKK!
I...I DIDN'T TELL THEM! I DIDN'T SAY A WORD ABOUT YOU!
JUST BANE! BANE WAS ALL!
IT WAS JUST PENNY, IF IT HADN'T...IF YOU HADN'T...
NO!

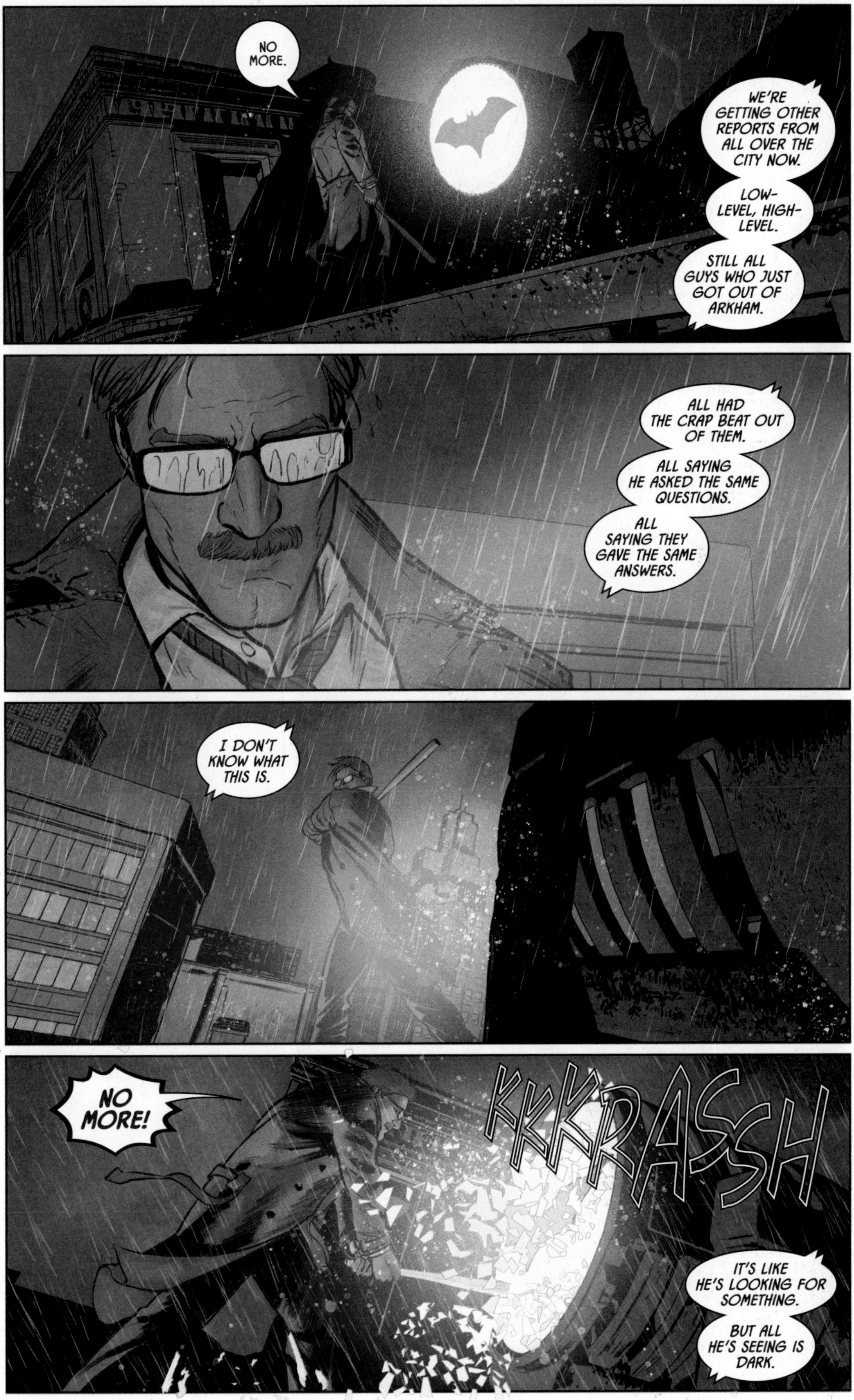
NO MORE.
WE'RE GETTING OTHER REPORTS FROM ALL OVER THE CITY NOW.
LOW-LEVEL, HIGH-LEVEL.
STILL ALL GUYS WHO JUST GOT OUT OF ARKHAM.
ALL HAD THE CRAP BEAT OUT OF THEM.
ALL SAYING HE ASKED THE SAME QUESTIONS.
ALL SAYING THEY GAVE THE SAME ANSWERS.
I DON'T KNOW WHAT THIS IS.
NO MORE!
KKKRASSH
IT'S LIKE HE'S LOOKING FOR SOMETHING.
BUT ALL HE'S SEEING IS DARK.

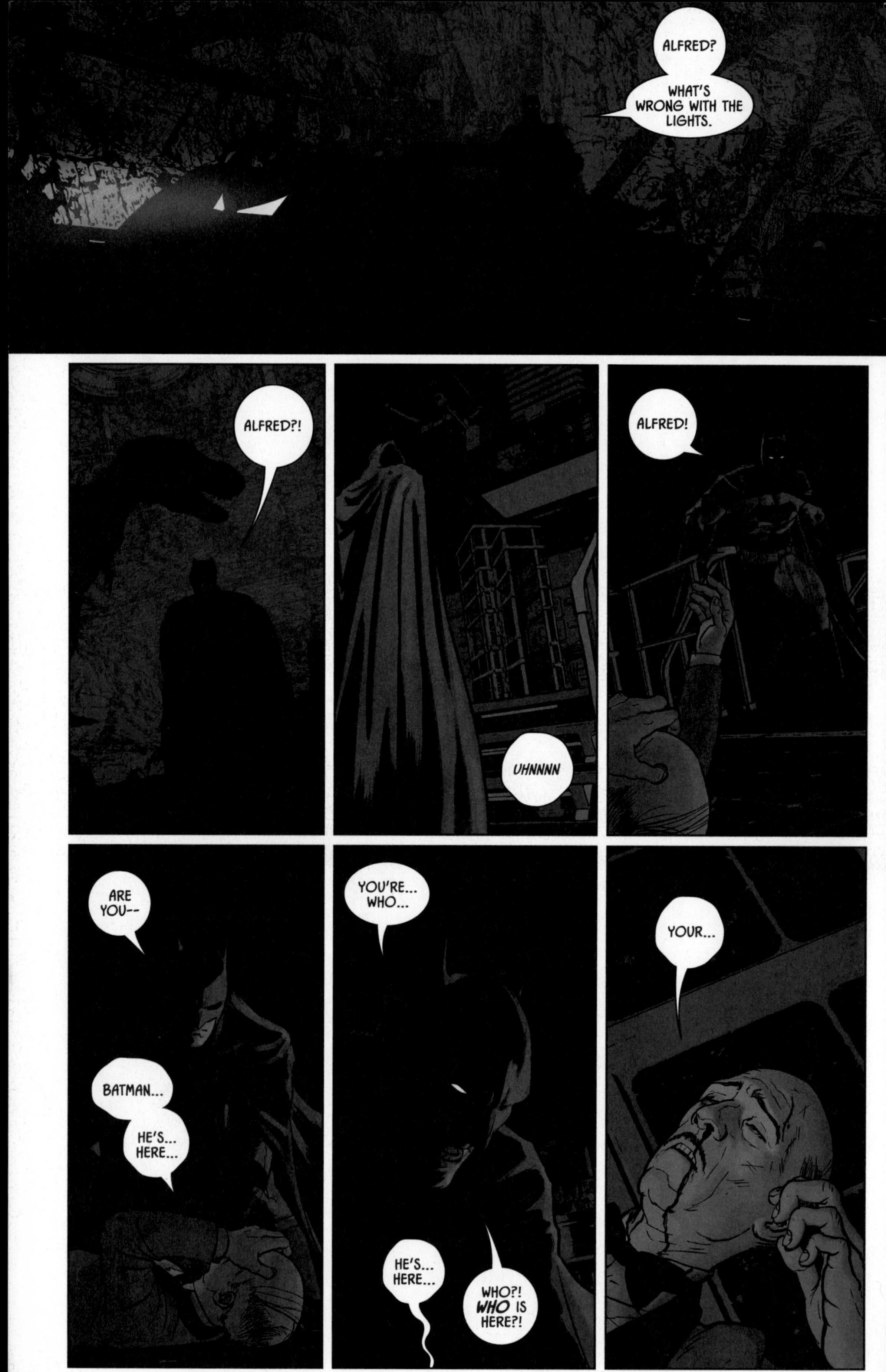
ALFRED?
WHAT'S WRONG WITH THE LIGHTS.
ALFRED?!
UHNNNN
ALFRED!
ARE YOU--
BATMAN...
HE'S... HERE...
YOU'RE... WHO...
HE'S... HERE...
WHO?! WHO IS HERE?!
YOUR...

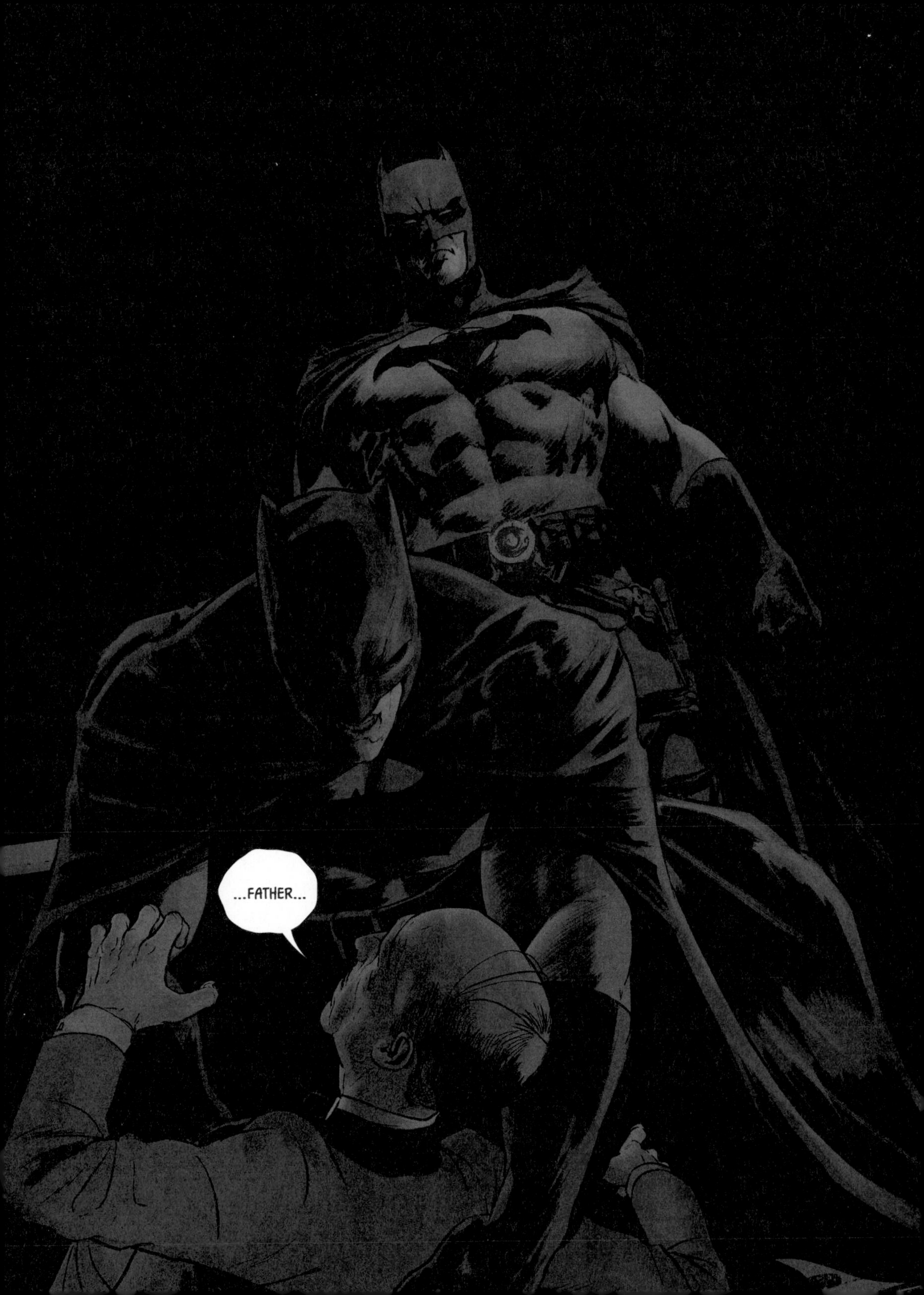
...FATHER...

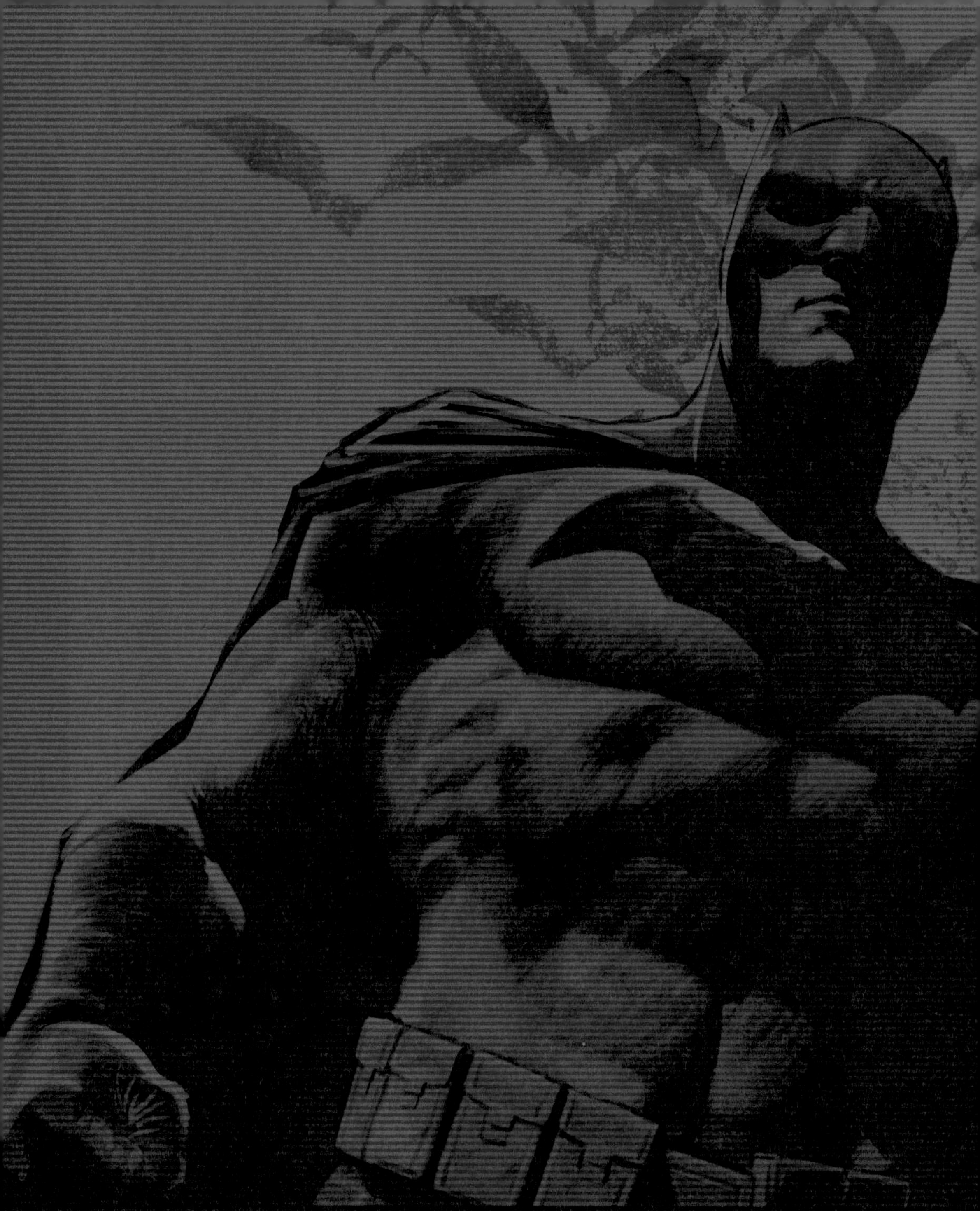

BATMAN
SECRET FILES #1

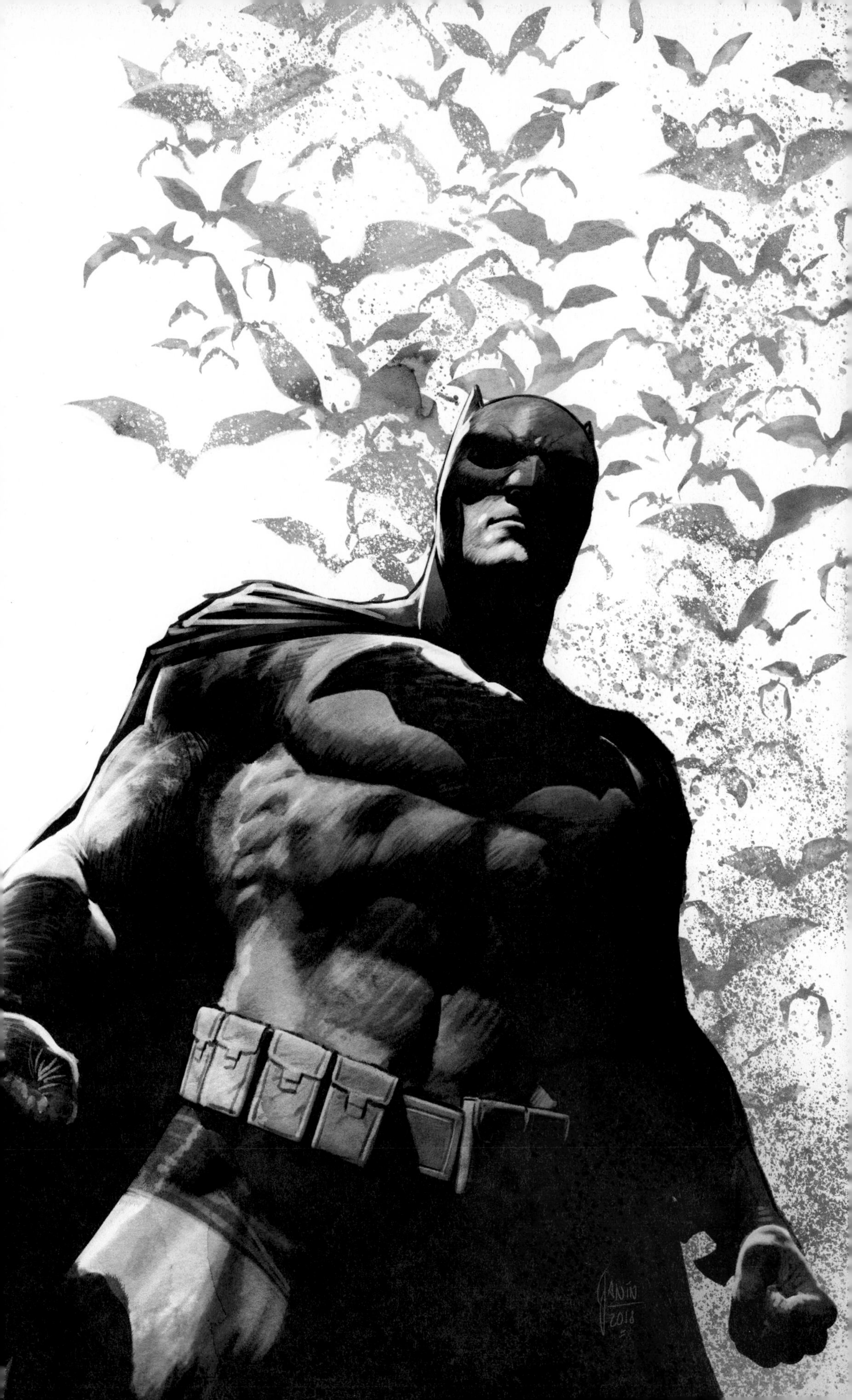
JANIN
2018

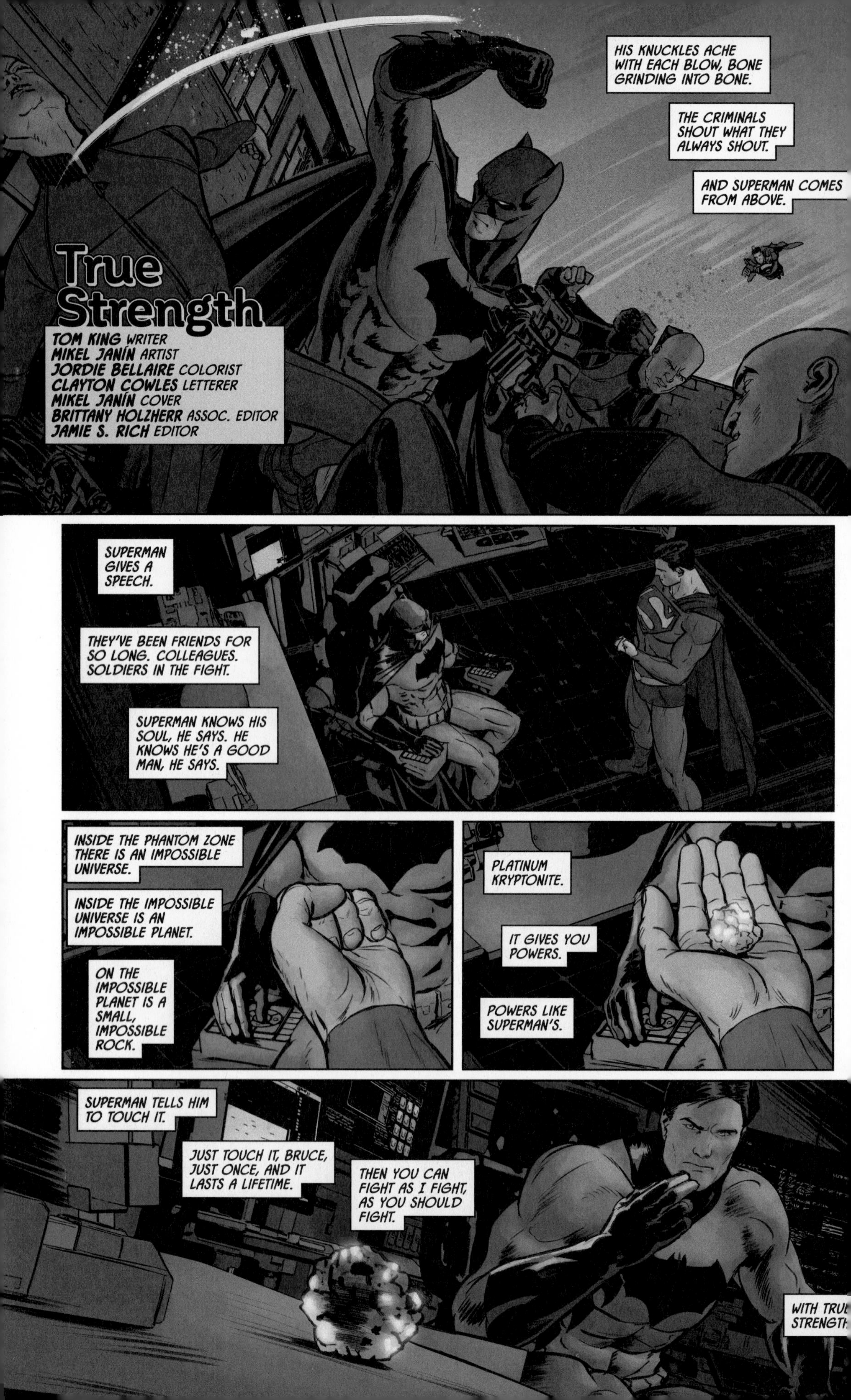
True Strength
TOM KING WRITER
MIKEL JANÍN ARTIST
JORDIE BELLAIRE COLORIST
CLAYTON COWLES LETTERER
MIKEL JANÍN COVER
BRITTANY HOLZHERR ASSOC. EDITOR
JAMIE S. RICH EDITOR
HIS KNUCKLES ACHE WITH EACH BLOW, BONE GRINDING INTO BONE.
THE CRIMINALS SHOUT WHAT THEY ALWAYS SHOUT.
AND SUPERMAN COMES FROM ABOVE.
SUPERMAN GIVES A SPEECH.
THEY'VE BEEN FRIENDS FOR SO LONG. COLLEAGUES. SOLDIERS IN THE FIGHT.
SUPERMAN KNOWS HIS SOUL, HE SAYS. HE KNOWS HE'S A GOOD MAN, HE SAYS.
INSIDE THE PHANTOM ZONE THERE IS AN IMPOSSIBLE UNIVERSE.
INSIDE THE IMPOSSIBLE UNIVERSE IS AN IMPOSSIBLE PLANET.
ON THE IMPOSSIBLE PLANET IS A SMALL, IMPOSSIBLE ROCK.
PLATINUM KRYPTONITE.
IT GIVES YOU POWERS.
POWERS LIKE SUPERMAN'S.
SUPERMAN TELLS HIM TO TOUCH IT.
JUST TOUCH IT, BRUCE, JUST ONCE, AND IT LASTS A LIFETIME.
THEN YOU CAN FIGHT AS I FIGHT, AS YOU SHOULD FIGHT.

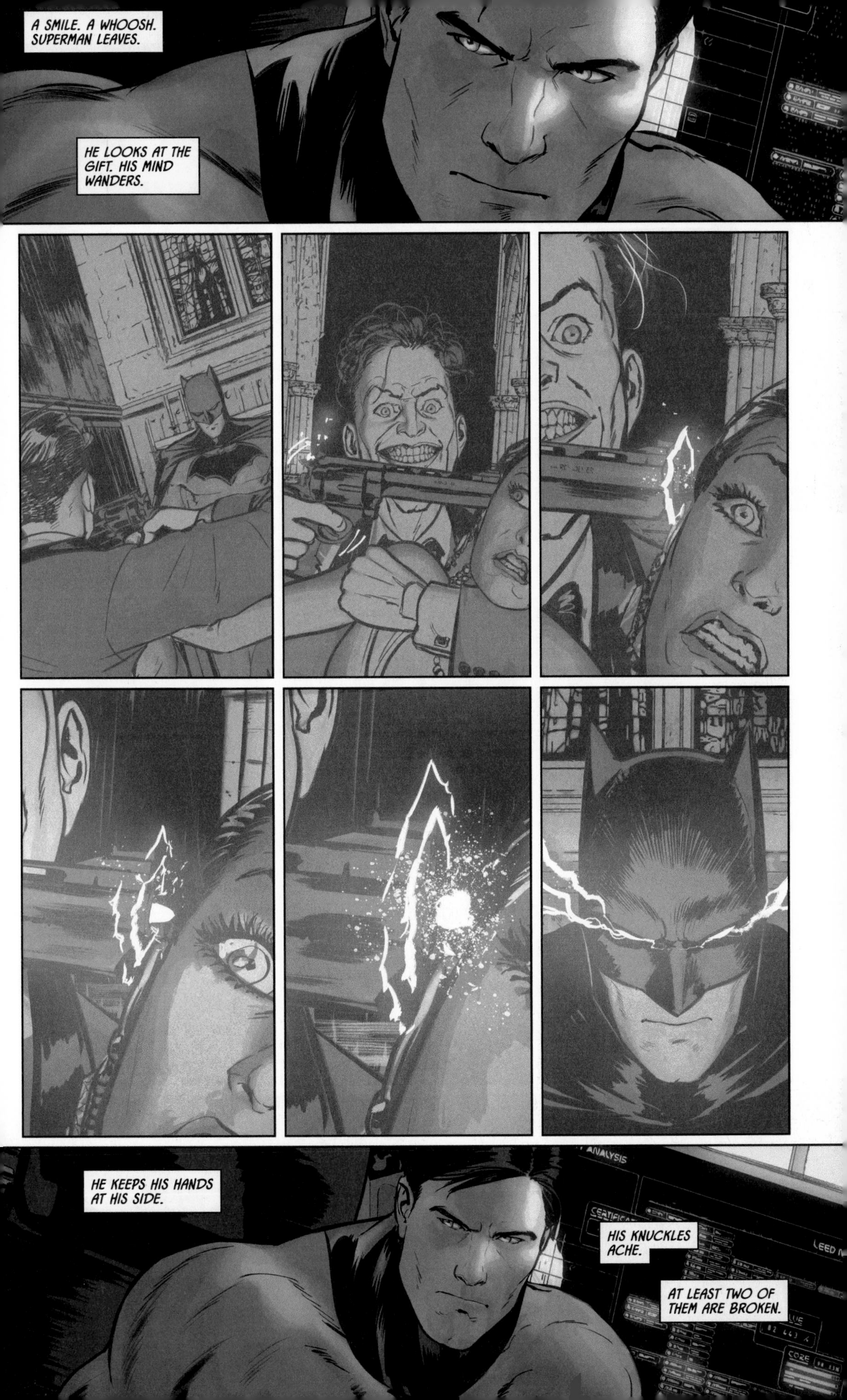
A SMILE. A WHOOSH. SUPERMAN LEAVES.
HE LOOKS AT THE GIFT. HIS MIND WANDERS.
HE KEEPS HIS HANDS AT HIS SIDE.
HIS KNUCKLES ACHE.
AT LEAST TWO OF THEM ARE BROKEN.

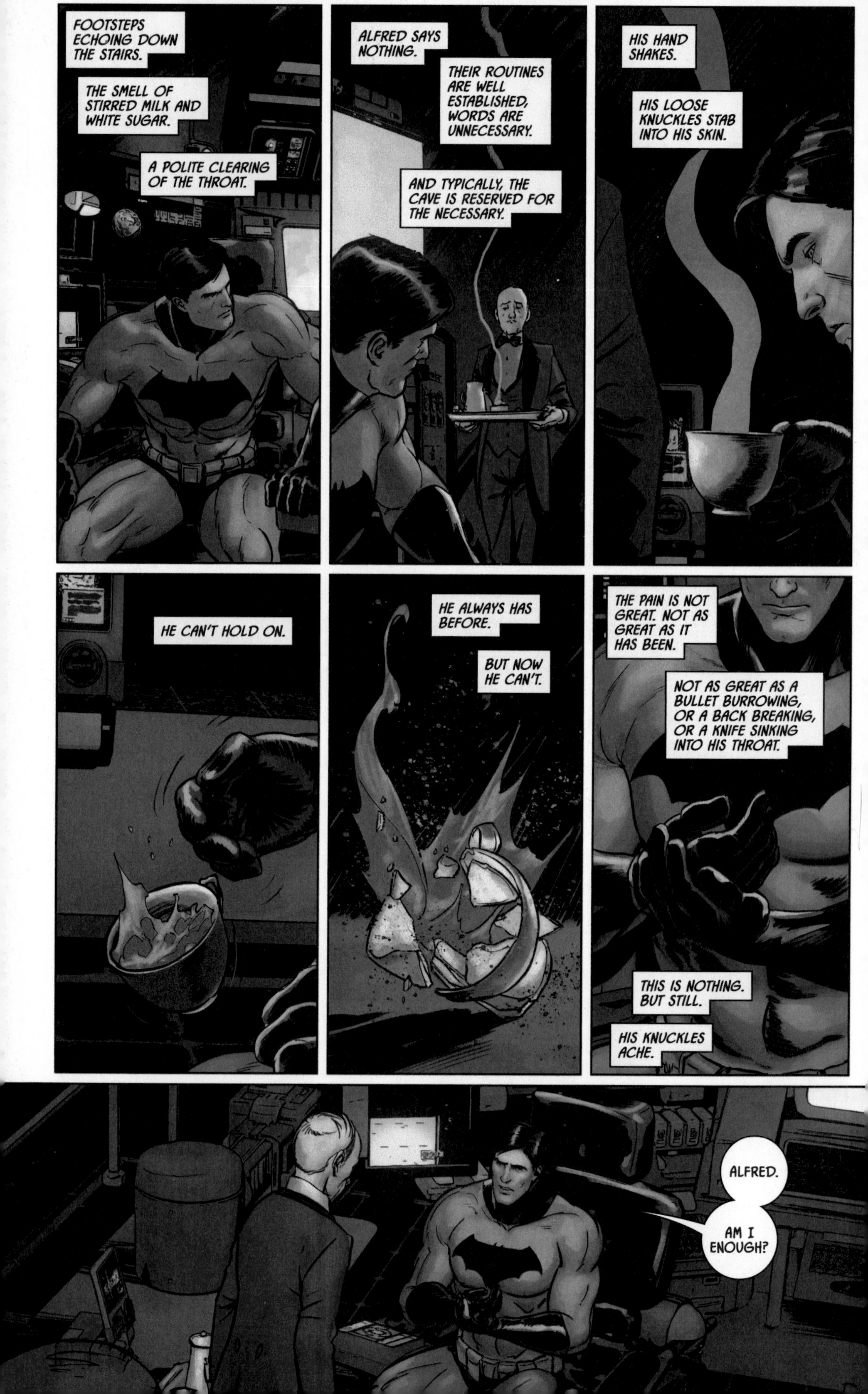
FOOTSTEPS ECHOING DOWN THE STAIRS.
THE SMELL OF STIRRED MILK AND WHITE SUGAR.
A POLITE CLEARING OF THE THROAT.
ALFRED SAYS NOTHING.
THEIR ROUTINES ARE WELL ESTABLISHED, WORDS ARE UNNECESSARY.
AND TYPICALLY, THE CAVE IS RESERVED FOR THE NECESSARY.
HIS HAND SHAKES.
HIS LOOSE KNUCKLES STAB INTO HIS SKIN.
HE CAN'T HOLD ON.
HE ALWAYS HAS BEFORE.
BUT NOW HE CAN'T.
THE PAIN IS NOT GREAT. NOT AS GREAT AS IT HAS BEEN.
NOT AS GREAT AS A BULLET BURROWING, OR A BACK BREAKING, OR A KNIFE SINKING INTO HIS THROAT.
THIS IS NOTHING. BUT STILL.
HIS KNUCKLES ACHE.
ALFRED.
AM I ENOUGH?

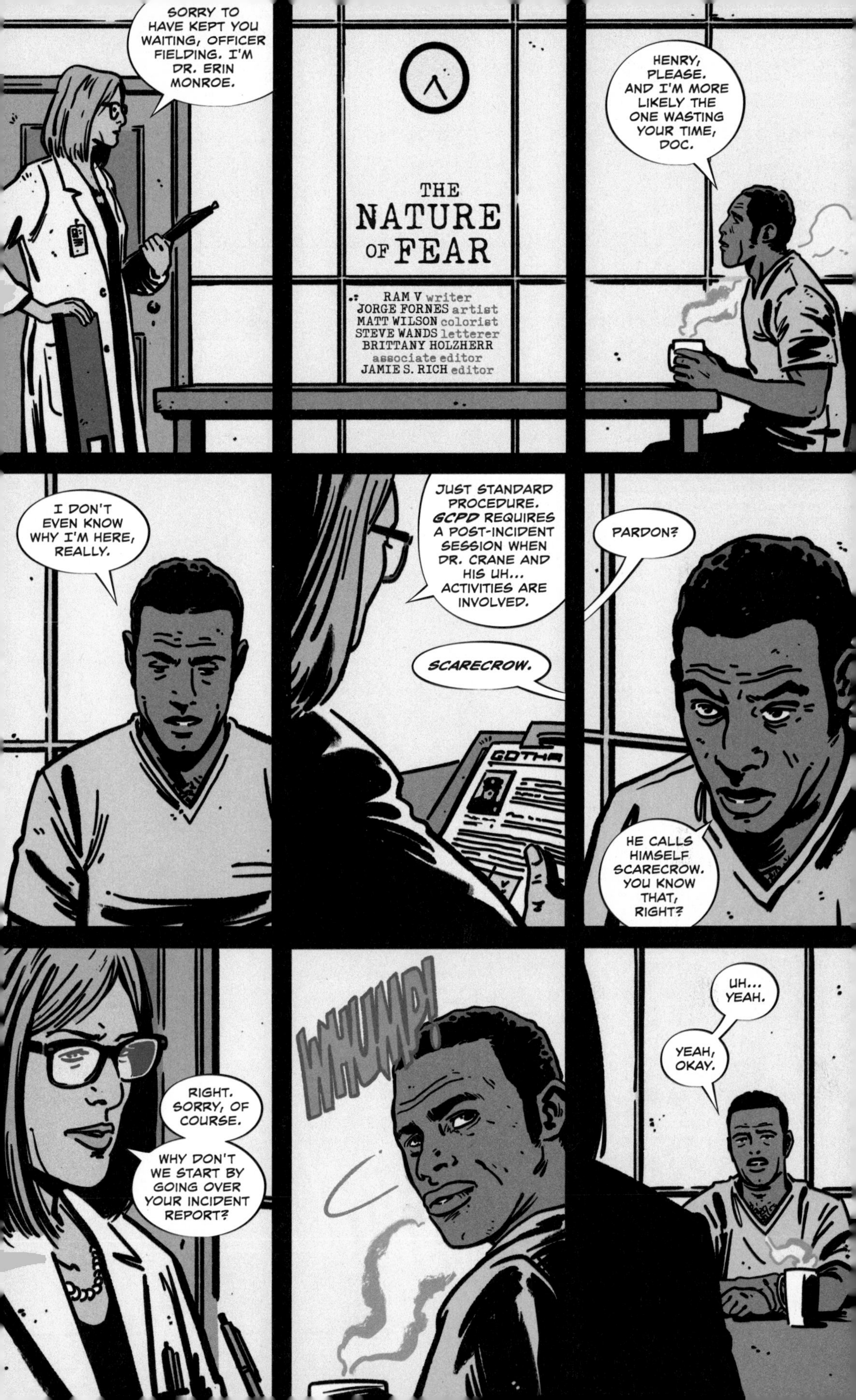
SORRY TO HAVE KEPT YOU WAITING, OFFICER FIELDING. I'M DR. ERIN MONROE.
THE NATURE OF FEAR
RAM V writer
JORGE FORNES artist
MATT WILSON colorist
STEVE WANDS letterer
BRITTANY HOLZHERR associate editor
JAMIE S. RICH editor
HENRY, PLEASE. AND I'M MORE LIKELY THE ONE WASTING YOUR TIME, DOC.
I DON'T EVEN KNOW WHY I'M HERE, REALLY.
JUST STANDARD PROCEDURE. GCPD REQUIRES A POST-INCIDENT SESSION WHEN DR. CRANE AND HIS UH... ACTIVITIES ARE INVOLVED.
PARDON?
SCARECROW.
HE CALLS HIMSELF SCARECROW. YOU KNOW THAT, RIGHT?
RIGHT. SORRY, OF COURSE.
WHY DON'T WE START BY GOING OVER YOUR INCIDENT REPORT?
WHUMP!
UH... YEAH.
YEAH, OKAY.

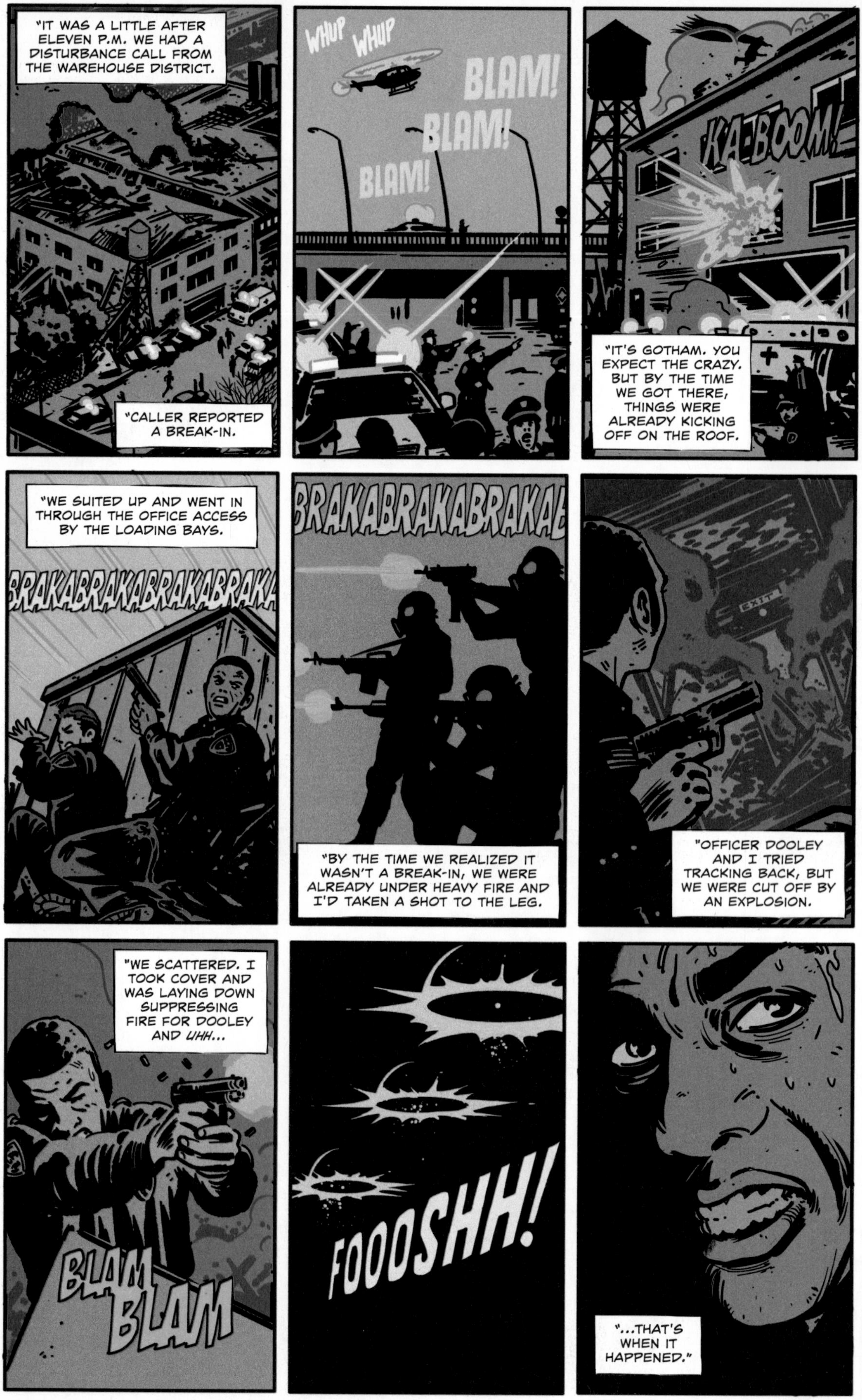
"IT WAS A LITTLE AFTER ELEVEN P.M. WE HAD A DISTURBANCE CALL FROM THE WAREHOUSE DISTRICT.
"CALLER REPORTED A BREAK-IN.
WHUP WHUP
BLAM!
BLAM!
BLAM!
KA-BOOM!
"IT'S GOTHAM. YOU EXPECT THE CRAZY. BUT BY THE TIME WE GOT THERE, THINGS WERE ALREADY KICKING OFF ON THE ROOF.
"WE SUITED UP AND WENT IN THROUGH THE OFFICE ACCESS BY THE LOADING BAYS.
BRAKABRAKABRAKABRAKA
BRAKABRAKABRAKA
"BY THE TIME WE REALIZED IT WASN'T A BREAK-IN, WE WERE ALREADY UNDER HEAVY FIRE AND I'D TAKEN A SHOT TO THE LEG.
EXIT
"OFFICER DOOLEY AND I TRIED TRACKING BACK, BUT WE WERE CUT OFF BY AN EXPLOSION.
"WE SCATTERED. I TOOK COVER AND WAS LAYING DOWN SUPPRESSING FIRE FOR DOOLEY AND *UHH*...
BLAM
BLAM
FOOOSHH!
"...THAT'S WHEN IT HAPPENED."

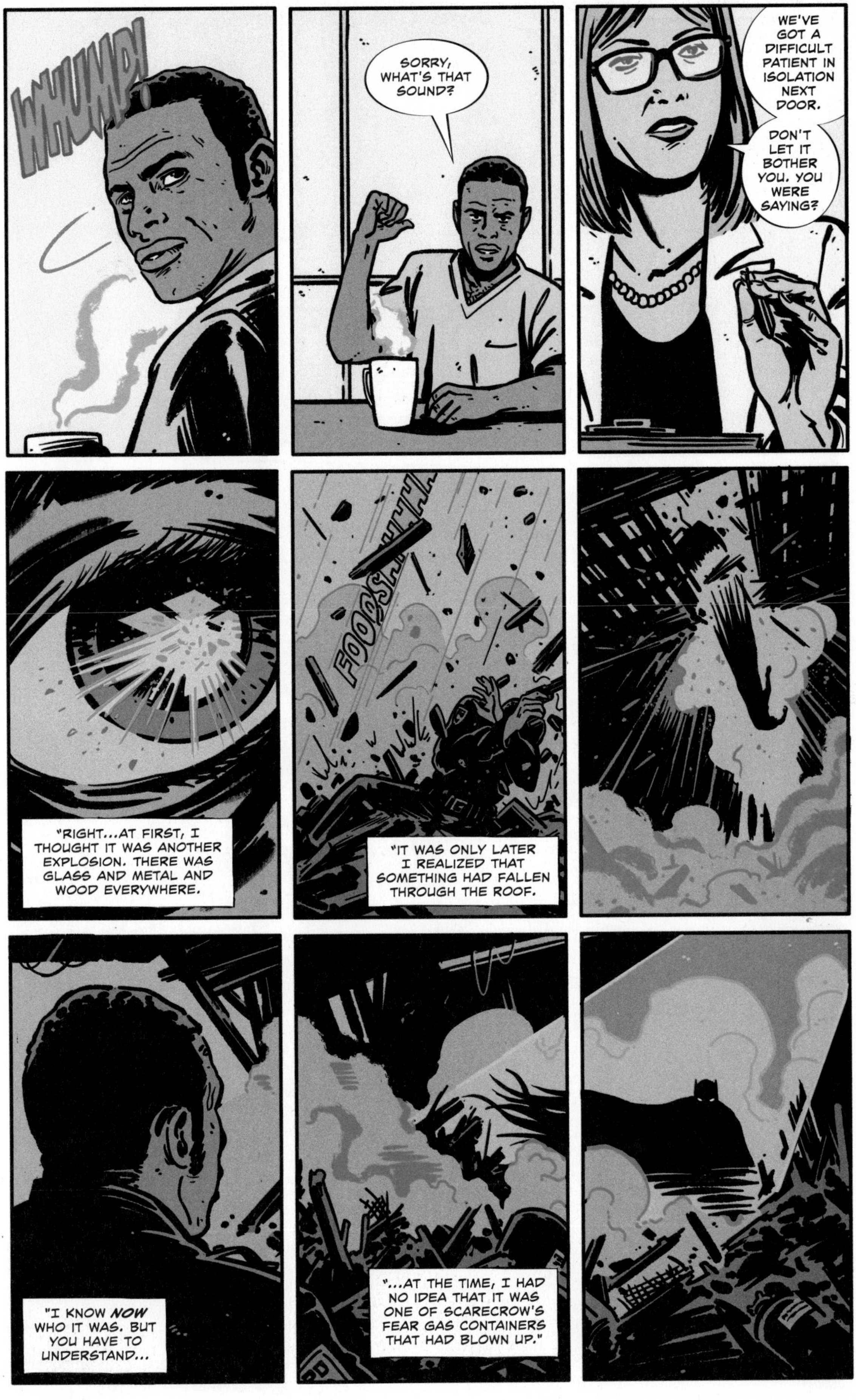
WHUMP!
SORRY, WHAT'S THAT SOUND?
WE'VE GOT A DIFFICULT PATIENT IN ISOLATION NEXT DOOR.
DON'T LET IT BOTHER YOU. YOU WERE SAYING?
"RIGHT...AT FIRST, I THOUGHT IT WAS ANOTHER EXPLOSION. THERE WAS GLASS AND METAL AND WOOD EVERYWHERE.
FOOOSHHH
"IT WAS ONLY LATER I REALIZED THAT SOMETHING HAD FALLEN THROUGH THE ROOF.
"I KNOW *NOW* WHO IT WAS. BUT YOU HAVE TO UNDERSTAND...
"...AT THE TIME, I HAD NO IDEA THAT IT WAS ONE OF SCARECROW'S FEAR GAS CONTAINERS THAT HAD BLOWN UP."

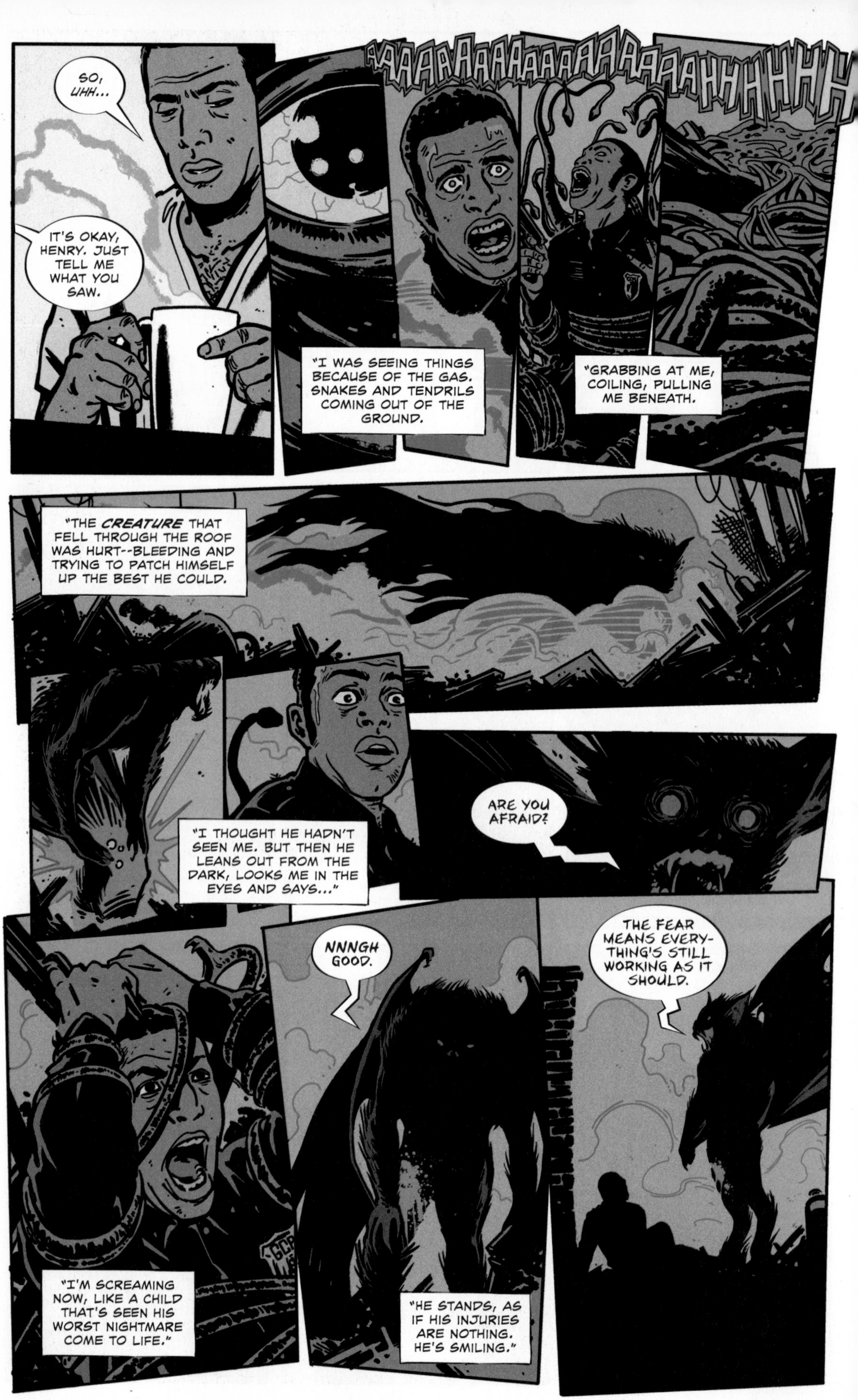
AAAAAAAAAAAAAAAAAAAHHHHHH
SO, UHH...
IT'S OKAY, HENRY. JUST TELL ME WHAT YOU SAW.
"I WAS SEEING THINGS BECAUSE OF THE GAS. SNAKES AND TENDRILS COMING OUT OF THE GROUND.
"GRABBING AT ME, COILING, PULLING ME BENEATH.
"THE CREATURE THAT FELL THROUGH THE ROOF WAS HURT--BLEEDING AND TRYING TO PATCH HIMSELF UP THE BEST HE COULD.
"I THOUGHT HE HADN'T SEEN ME. BUT THEN HE LEANS OUT FROM THE DARK, LOOKS ME IN THE EYES AND SAYS..."
ARE YOU AFRAID?
"I'M SCREAMING NOW, LIKE A CHILD THAT'S SEEN HIS WORST NIGHTMARE COME TO LIFE."
NNNGH GOOD.
"HE STANDS, AS IF HIS INJURIES ARE NOTHING. HE'S SMILING."
THE FEAR MEANS EVERY-THING'S STILL WORKING AS IT SHOULD.

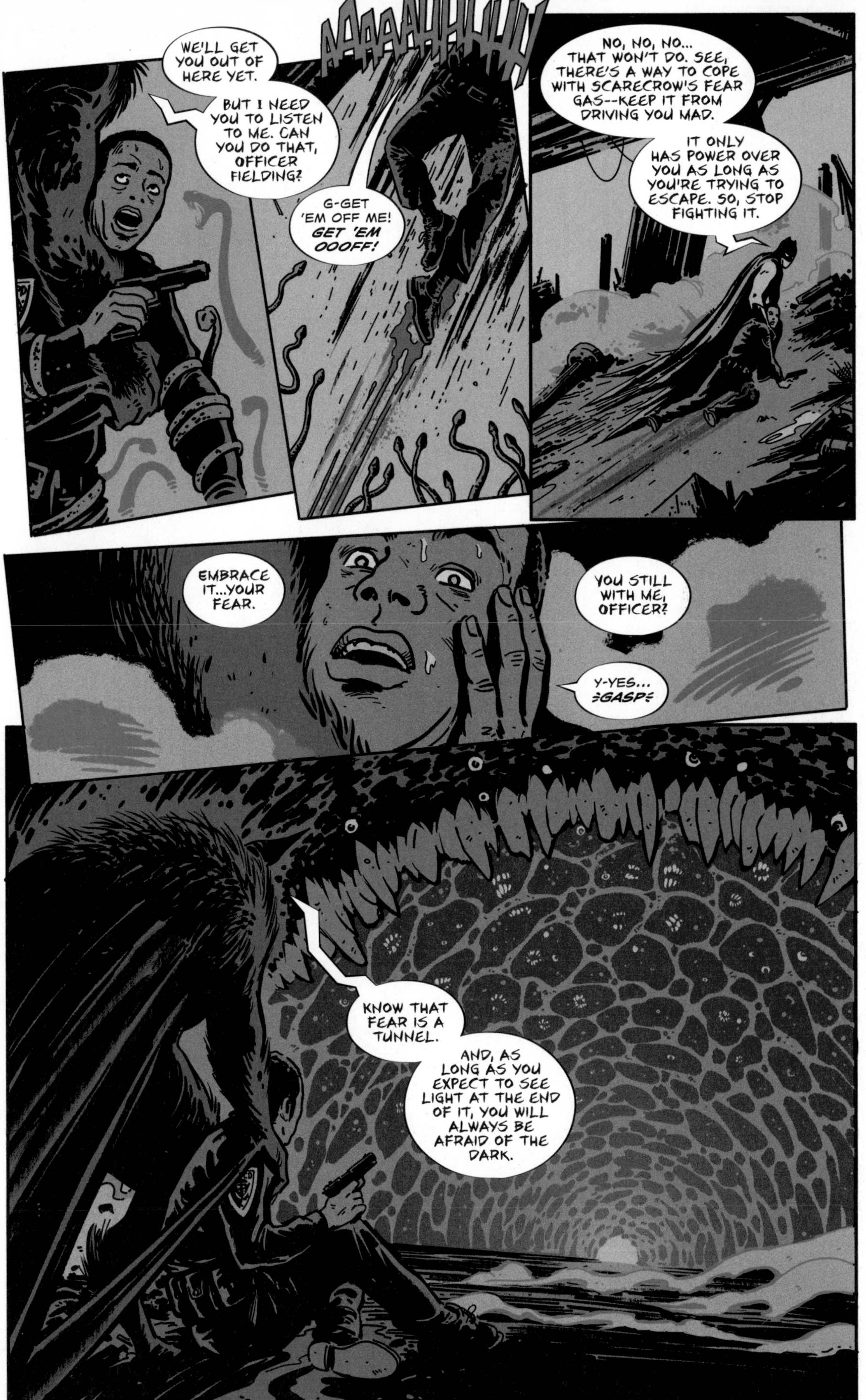
WE'LL GET YOU OUT OF HERE YET.
BUT I NEED YOU TO LISTEN TO ME. CAN YOU DO THAT, OFFICER FIELDING?
AAAAAHHHHH
G-GET 'EM OFF ME! GET 'EM OOOFF!
NO, NO, NO... THAT WON'T DO. SEE, THERE'S A WAY TO COPE WITH SCARECROW'S FEAR GAS--KEEP IT FROM DRIVING YOU MAD.
IT ONLY HAS POWER OVER YOU AS LONG AS YOU'RE TRYING TO ESCAPE. SO, STOP FIGHTING IT.
EMBRACE IT...YOUR FEAR.
YOU STILL WITH ME, OFFICER?
Y-YES... GASP
KNOW THAT FEAR IS A TUNNEL.
AND, AS LONG AS YOU EXPECT TO SEE LIGHT AT THE END OF IT, YOU WILL ALWAYS BE AFRAID OF THE DARK.

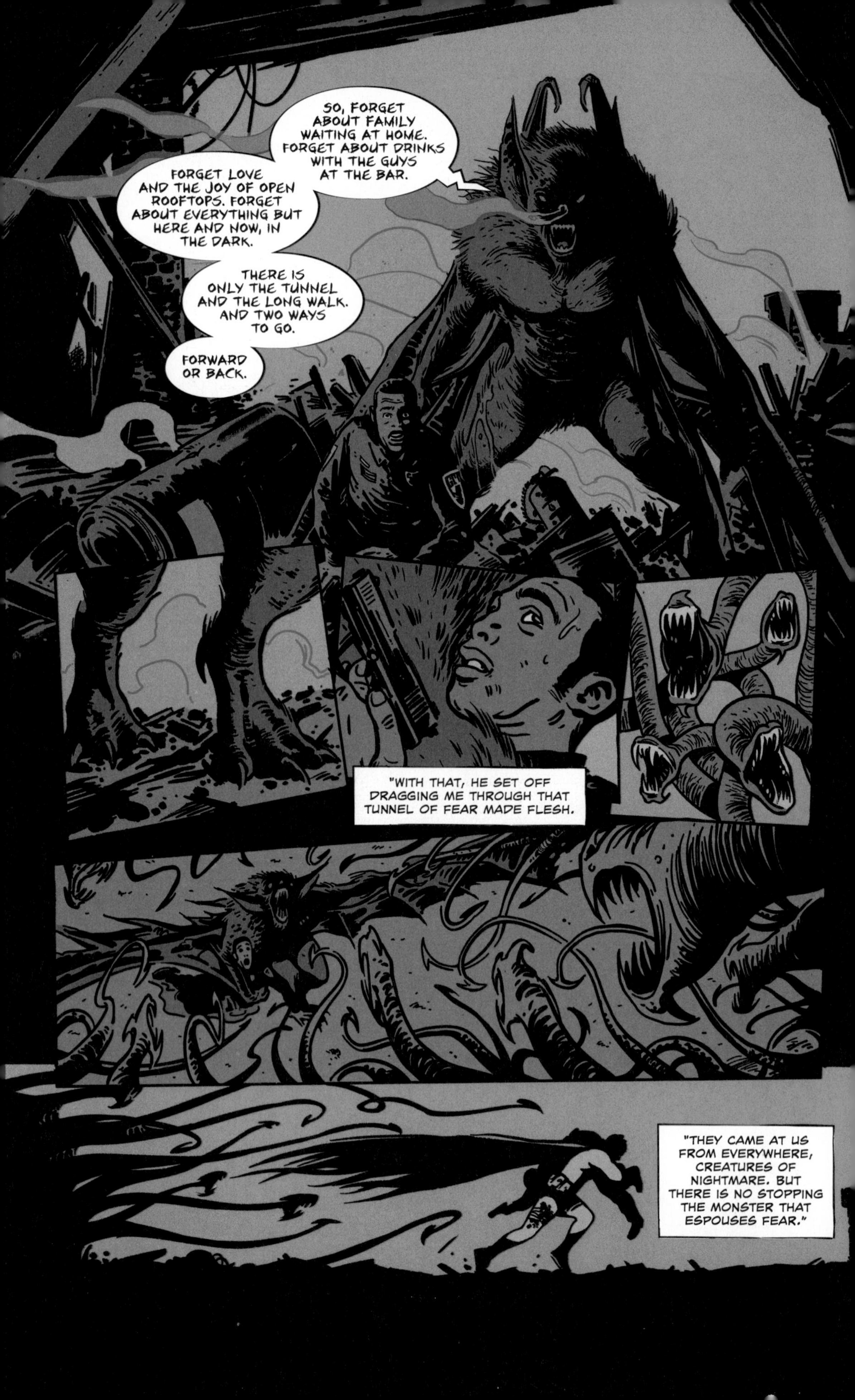
SO, FORGET ABOUT FAMILY WAITING AT HOME. FORGET ABOUT DRINKS WITH THE GUYS AT THE BAR.
FORGET LOVE AND THE JOY OF OPEN ROOFTOPS. FORGET ABOUT EVERYTHING BUT HERE AND NOW, IN THE DARK.
THERE IS ONLY THE TUNNEL AND THE LONG WALK. AND TWO WAYS TO GO.
FORWARD OR BACK.
"WITH THAT, HE SET OFF DRAGGING ME THROUGH THAT TUNNEL OF FEAR MADE FLESH.
"THEY CAME AT US FROM EVERYWHERE, CREATURES OF NIGHTMARE. BUT THERE IS NO STOPPING THE MONSTER THAT ESPOUSES FEAR."

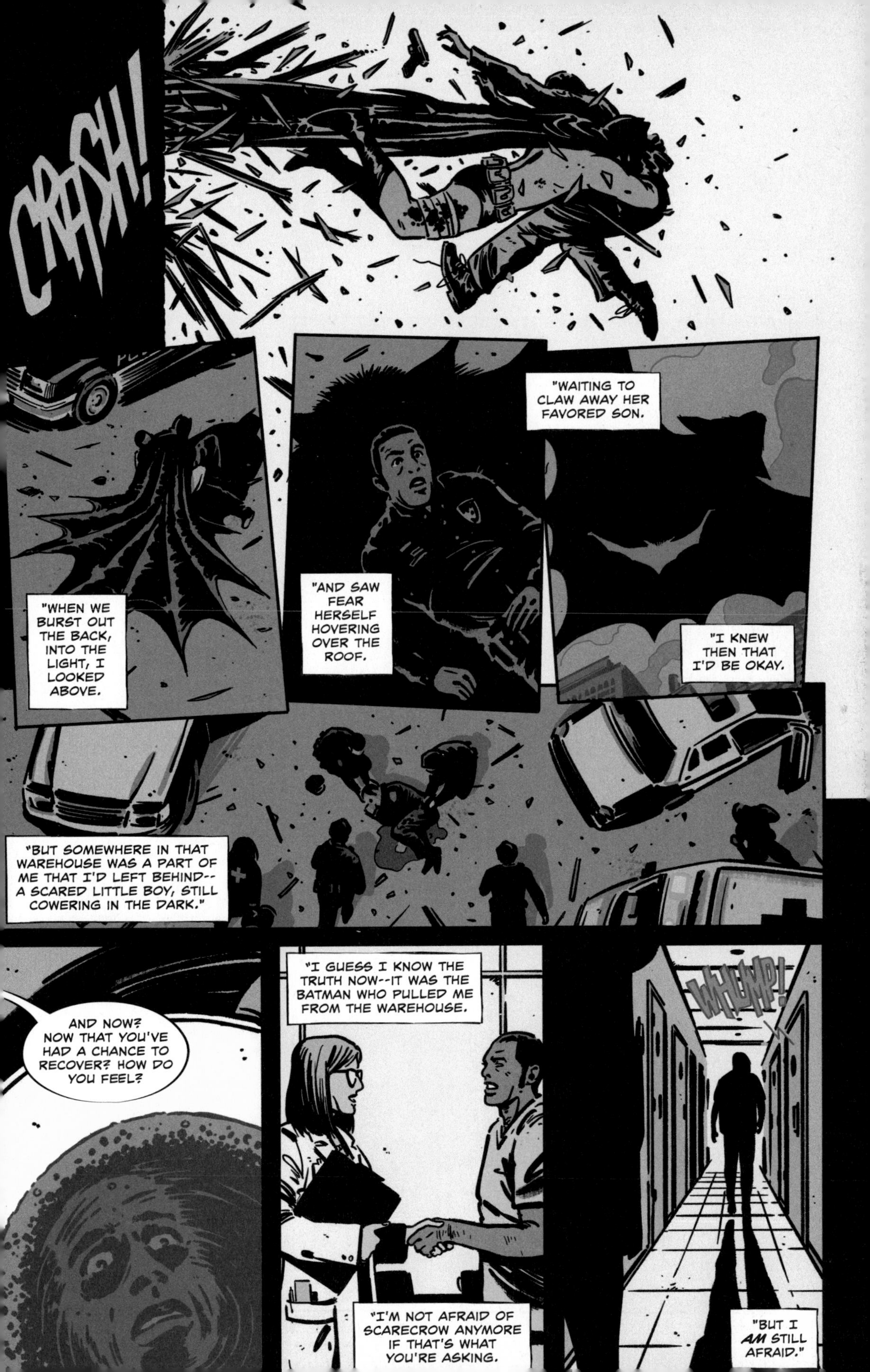
CRASH!
"WHEN WE BURST OUT THE BACK, INTO THE LIGHT, I LOOKED ABOVE.
"AND SAW FEAR HERSELF HOVERING OVER THE ROOF.
"WAITING TO CLAW AWAY HER FAVORED SON.
"I KNEW THEN THAT I'D BE OKAY.
"BUT SOMEWHERE IN THAT WAREHOUSE WAS A PART OF ME THAT I'D LEFT BEHIND-- A SCARED LITTLE BOY, STILL COWERING IN THE DARK."
AND NOW? NOW THAT YOU'VE HAD A CHANCE TO RECOVER? HOW DO YOU FEEL?
"I GUESS I KNOW THE TRUTH NOW--IT WAS THE BATMAN WHO PULLED ME FROM THE WAREHOUSE.
"I'M NOT AFRAID OF SCARECROW ANYMORE IF THAT'S WHAT YOU'RE ASKING.
WHUMP!
"BUT I AM STILL AFRAID."

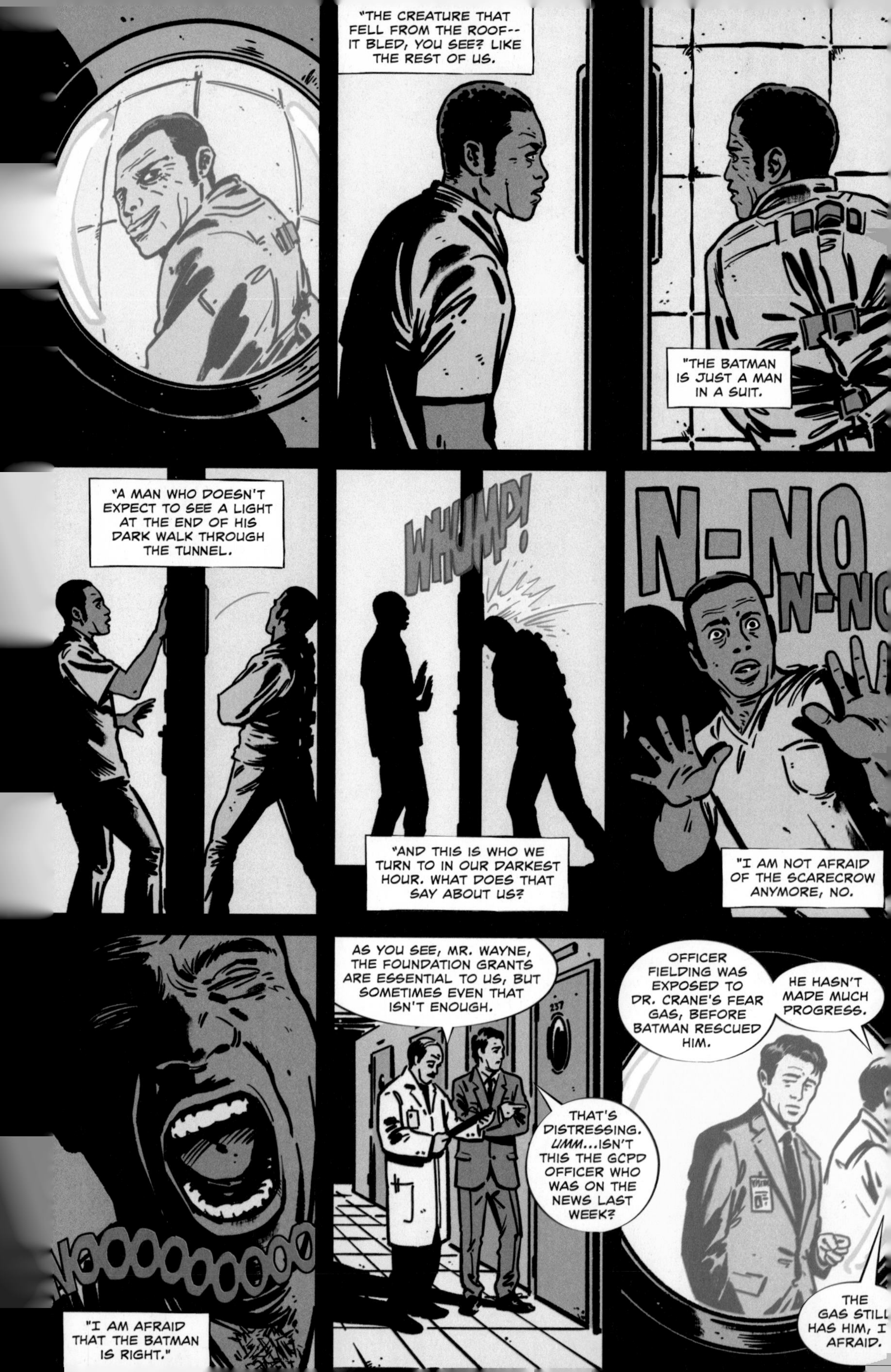
"THE CREATURE THAT FELL FROM THE ROOF-- IT BLED, YOU SEE? LIKE THE REST OF US.
"THE BATMAN IS JUST A MAN IN A SUIT.
"A MAN WHO DOESN'T EXPECT TO SEE A LIGHT AT THE END OF HIS DARK WALK THROUGH THE TUNNEL.
WHUMP!
"AND THIS IS WHO WE TURN TO IN OUR DARKEST HOUR. WHAT DOES THAT SAY ABOUT US?
N-NO
N-NO
"I AM NOT AFRAID OF THE SCARECROW ANYMORE, NO.
NOOOOOOOOOO
"I AM AFRAID THAT THE BATMAN IS RIGHT."
AS YOU SEE, MR. WAYNE, THE FOUNDATION GRANTS ARE ESSENTIAL TO US, BUT SOMETIMES EVEN THAT ISN'T ENOUGH.
THAT'S DISTRESSING. *UMM*...ISN'T THIS THE GCPD OFFICER WHO WAS ON THE NEWS LAST WEEK?
OFFICER FIELDING WAS EXPOSED TO DR. CRANE'S FEAR GAS, BEFORE BATMAN RESCUED HIM.
HE HASN'T MADE MUCH PROGRESS.
THE GAS STILL HAS HIM, I AFRAID.

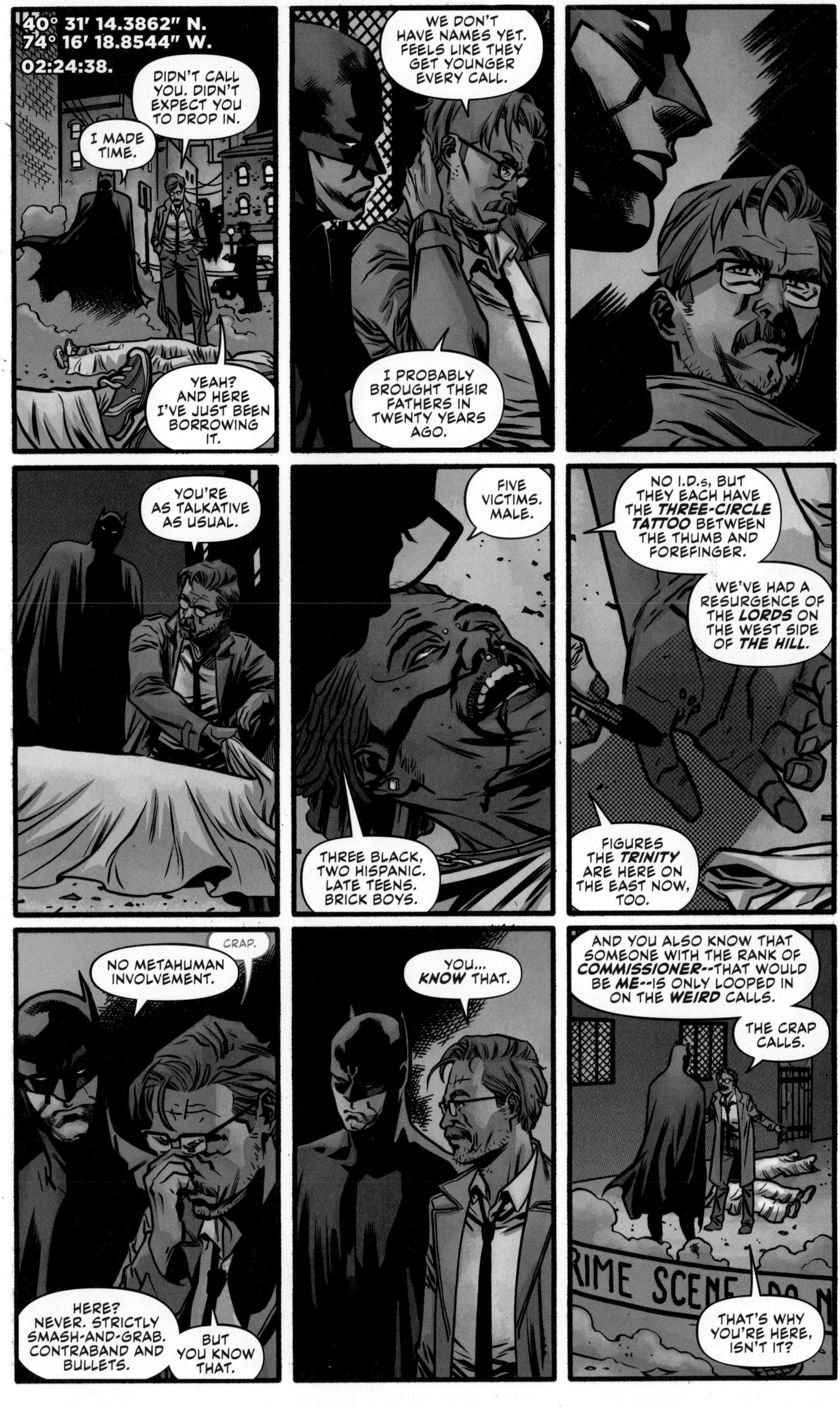
40° 31′ 14.3862″ N.
74° 16′ 18.8544″ W.
02:24:38.
DIDN'T CALL YOU. DIDN'T EXPECT YOU TO DROP IN.
I MADE TIME.
YEAH? AND HERE I'VE JUST BEEN BORROWING IT.
WE DON'T HAVE NAMES YET. FEELS LIKE THEY GET YOUNGER EVERY CALL.
I PROBABLY BROUGHT THEIR FATHERS IN TWENTY YEARS AGO.
YOU'RE AS TALKATIVE AS USUAL.
FIVE VICTIMS. MALE.
THREE BLACK, TWO HISPANIC. LATE TEENS. BRICK BOYS.
NO I.D.s, BUT THEY EACH HAVE THE THREE-CIRCLE TATTOO BETWEEN THE THUMB AND FOREFINGER.
WE'VE HAD A RESURGENCE OF THE LORDS ON THE WEST SIDE OF THE HILL.
FIGURES THE TRINITY ARE HERE ON THE EAST NOW, TOO.
NO METAHUMAN INVOLVEMENT.
CRAP.
HERE? NEVER. STRICTLY SMASH-AND-GRAB. CONTRABAND AND BULLETS.
BUT YOU KNOW THAT.
YOU... KNOW THAT.
AND YOU ALSO KNOW THAT SOMEONE WITH THE RANK OF COMMISSIONER--THAT WOULD BE ME--IS ONLY LOOPED IN ON THE WEIRD CALLS.
THE CRAP CALLS.
THAT'S WHY YOU'RE HERE, ISN'T IT?

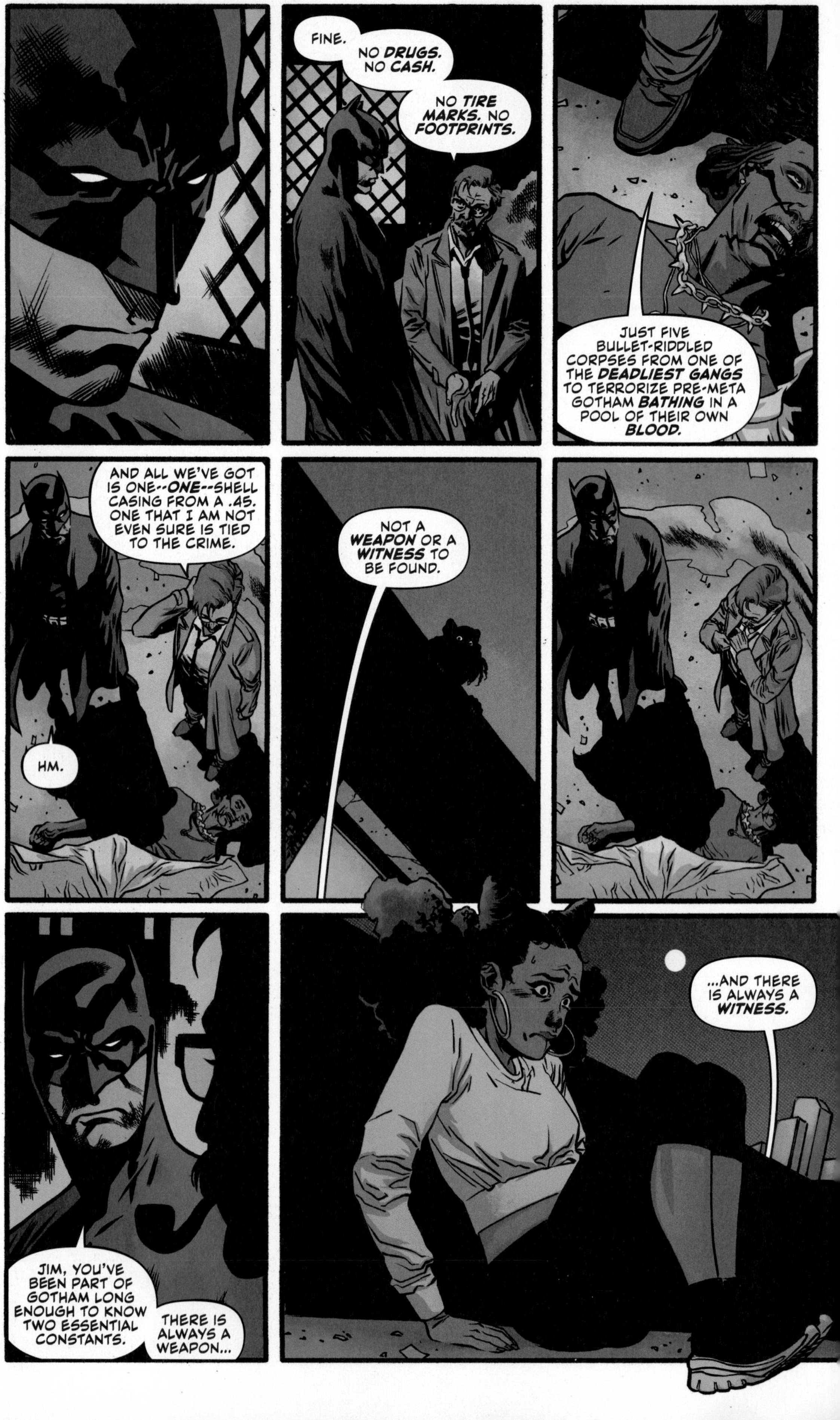
FINE.
NO DRUGS. NO CASH.
NO TIRE MARKS. NO FOOTPRINTS.
JUST FIVE BULLET-RIDDLED CORPSES FROM ONE OF THE DEADLIEST GANGS TO TERRORIZE PRE-META GOTHAM BATHING IN A POOL OF THEIR OWN BLOOD.
AND ALL WE'VE GOT IS ONE--ONE--SHELL CASING FROM A .45. ONE THAT I AM NOT EVEN SURE IS TIED TO THE CRIME.
HM.
NOT A WEAPON OR A WITNESS TO BE FOUND.
JIM, YOU'VE BEEN PART OF GOTHAM LONG ENOUGH TO KNOW TWO ESSENTIAL CONSTANTS.
THERE IS ALWAYS A WEAPON...
...AND THERE IS ALWAYS A WITNESS.

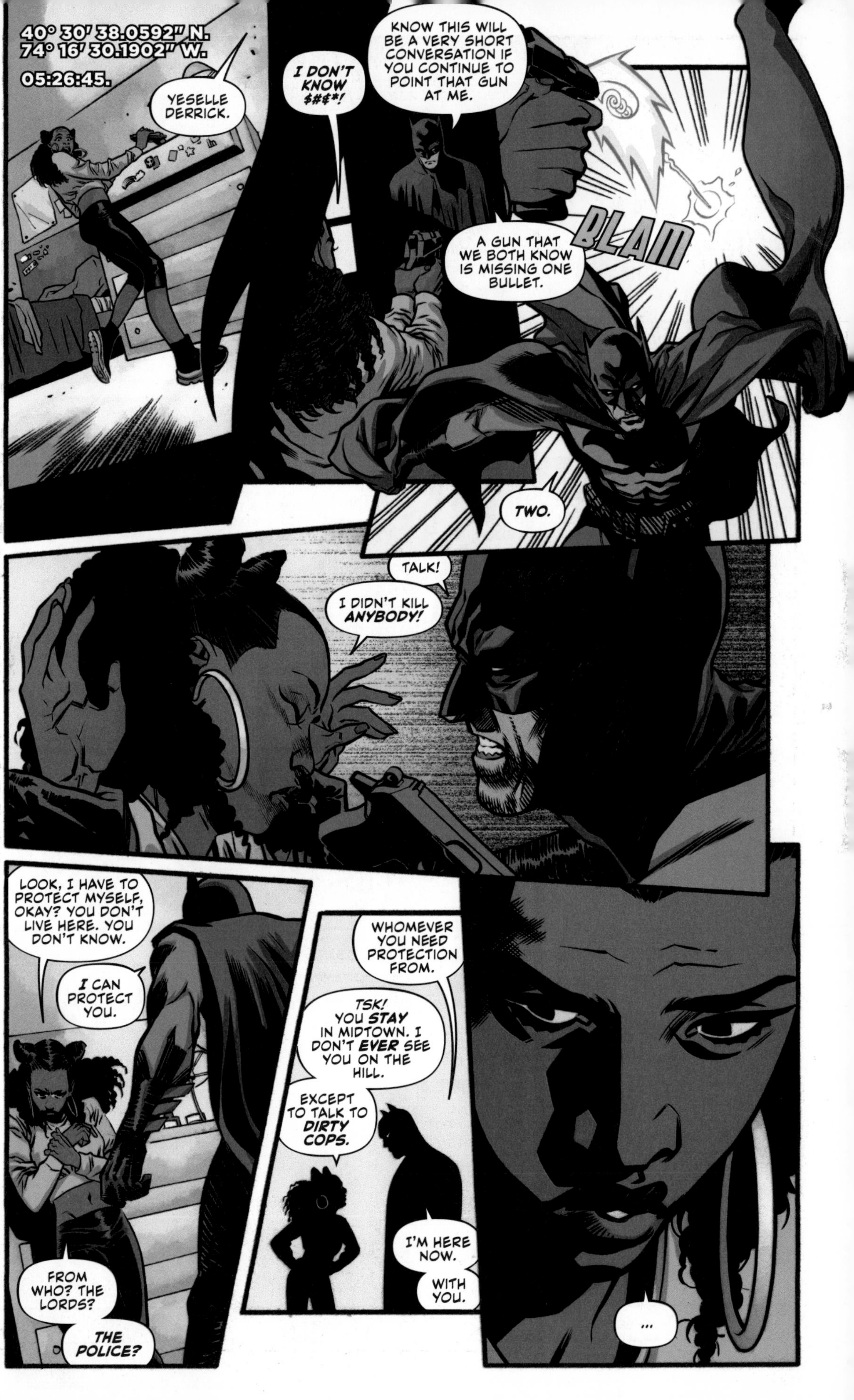
40° 30' 38.0592" N.
74° 16' 30.1902" W.
05:26:45.
YESELLE DERRICK.
I DON'T KNOW $#$*!
KNOW THIS WILL BE A VERY SHORT CONVERSATION IF YOU CONTINUE TO POINT THAT GUN AT ME.
A GUN THAT WE BOTH KNOW IS MISSING ONE BULLET.
BLAM
TWO.
TALK!
I DIDN'T KILL ANYBODY!
LOOK, I HAVE TO PROTECT MYSELF, OKAY? YOU DON'T LIVE HERE. YOU DON'T KNOW.
I CAN PROTECT YOU.
FROM WHO? THE LORDS?
THE POLICE?
WHOMEVER YOU NEED PROTECTION FROM.
TSK! YOU STAY IN MIDTOWN. I DON'T EVER SEE YOU ON THE HILL.
EXCEPT TO TALK TO DIRTY COPS.
I'M HERE NOW.
WITH YOU.
...

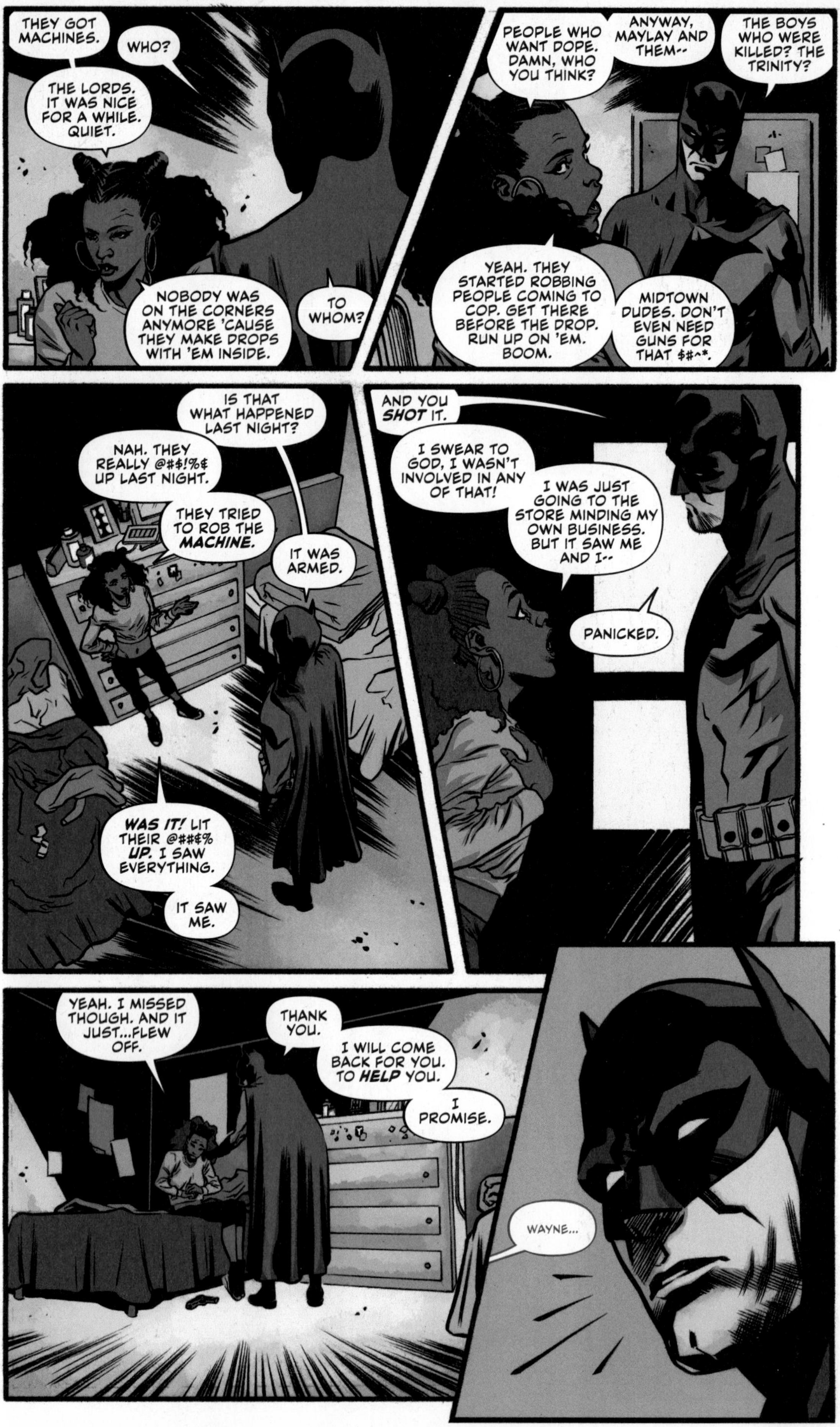
THEY GOT MACHINES.
WHO?
THE LORDS. IT WAS NICE FOR A WHILE. QUIET.
NOBODY WAS ON THE CORNERS ANYMORE 'CAUSE THEY MAKE DROPS WITH 'EM INSIDE.
TO WHOM?
PEOPLE WHO WANT DOPE. DAMN, WHO YOU THINK?
ANYWAY, MAYLAY AND THEM--
THE BOYS WHO WERE KILLED? THE TRINITY?
YEAH. THEY STARTED ROBBING PEOPLE COMING TO COP. GET THERE BEFORE THE DROP. RUN UP ON 'EM. BOOM.
MIDTOWN DUDES. DON'T EVEN NEED GUNS FOR THAT $#^*.
IS THAT WHAT HAPPENED LAST NIGHT?
NAH. THEY REALLY @#$!%$ UP LAST NIGHT.
THEY TRIED TO ROB THE MACHINE.
IT WAS ARMED.
WAS IT! LIT THEIR @##$% UP. I SAW EVERYTHING.
IT SAW ME.
AND YOU SHOT IT.
I SWEAR TO GOD, I WASN'T INVOLVED IN ANY OF THAT!
I WAS JUST GOING TO THE STORE MINDING MY OWN BUSINESS. BUT IT SAW ME AND I--
PANICKED.
YEAH. I MISSED THOUGH. AND IT JUST...FLEW OFF.
THANK YOU.
I WILL COME BACK FOR YOU. TO HELP YOU.
I PROMISE.
WAYNE...

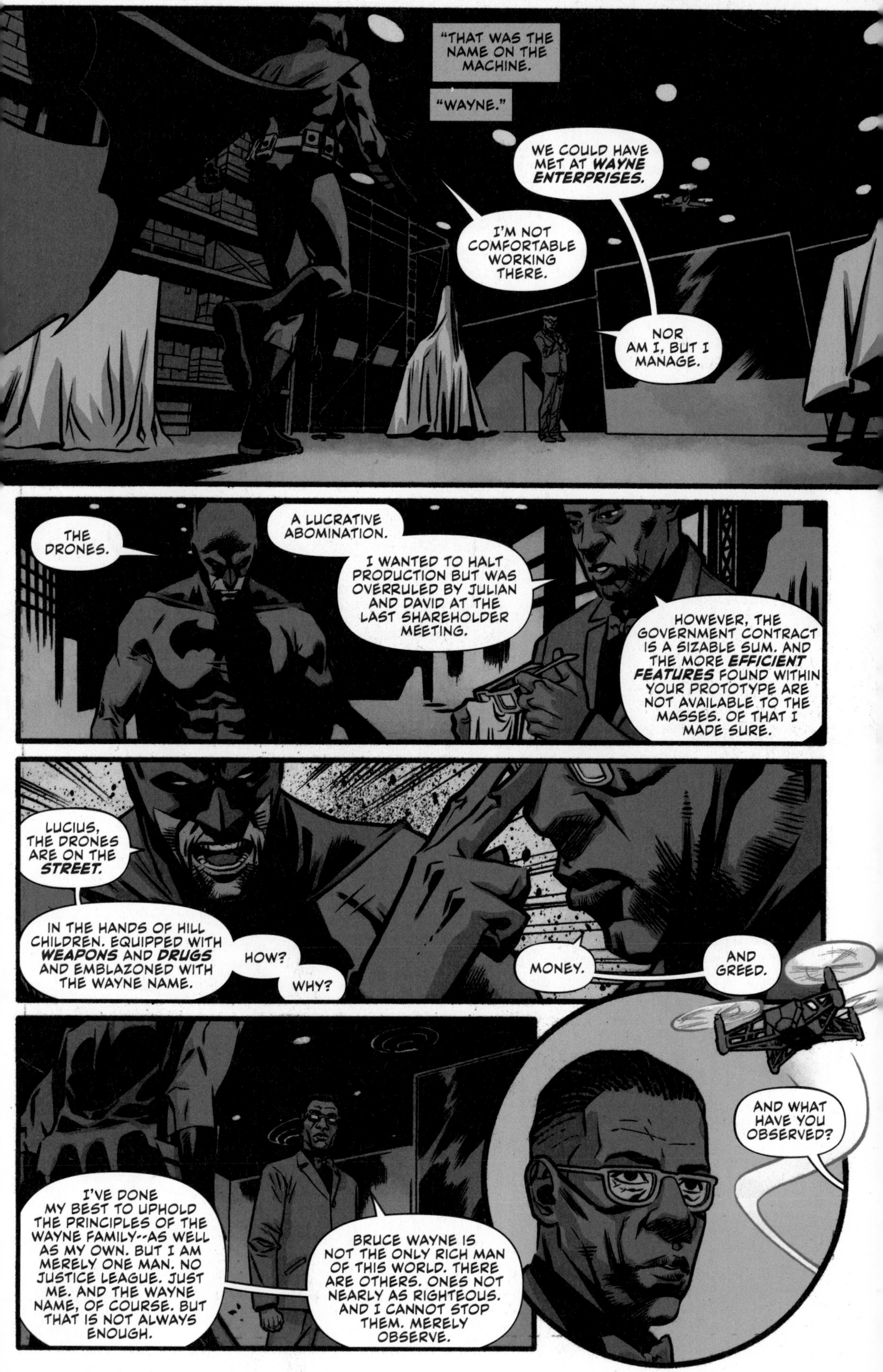
"THAT WAS THE NAME ON THE MACHINE.
"WAYNE."
WE COULD HAVE MET AT WAYNE ENTERPRISES.
I'M NOT COMFORTABLE WORKING THERE.
NOR AM I, BUT I MANAGE.
THE DRONES.
A LUCRATIVE ABOMINATION.
I WANTED TO HALT PRODUCTION BUT WAS OVERRULED BY JULIAN AND DAVID AT THE LAST SHAREHOLDER MEETING.
HOWEVER, THE GOVERNMENT CONTRACT IS A SIZABLE SUM. AND THE MORE EFFICIENT FEATURES FOUND WITHIN YOUR PROTOTYPE ARE NOT AVAILABLE TO THE MASSES. OF THAT I MADE SURE.
LUCIUS, THE DRONES ARE ON THE STREET.
IN THE HANDS OF HILL CHILDREN. EQUIPPED WITH WEAPONS AND DRUGS AND EMBLAZONED WITH THE WAYNE NAME.
HOW?
WHY?
MONEY.
AND GREED.
AND WHAT HAVE YOU OBSERVED?
I'VE DONE MY BEST TO UPHOLD THE PRINCIPLES OF THE WAYNE FAMILY--AS WELL AS MY OWN. BUT I AM MERELY ONE MAN. NO JUSTICE LEAGUE. JUST ME. AND THE WAYNE NAME, OF COURSE. BUT THAT IS NOT ALWAYS ENOUGH.
BRUCE WAYNE IS NOT THE ONLY RICH MAN OF THIS WORLD. THERE ARE OTHERS. ONES NOT NEARLY AS RIGHTEOUS. AND I CANNOT STOP THEM. MERELY OBSERVE.

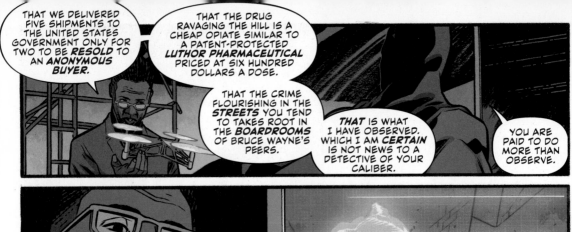

THAT WE DELIVERED FIVE SHIPMENTS TO THE UNITED STATES GOVERNMENT ONLY FOR TWO TO BE **RESOLD** TO AN **ANONYMOUS BUYER.**

THAT THE DRUG RAVAGING THE HILL IS A CHEAP OPIATE SIMILAR TO A PATENT-PROTECTED **LUTHOR PHARMACEUTICAL** PRICED AT SIX HUNDRED DOLLARS A DOSE.

THAT THE CRIME FLOURISHING IN THE **STREETS** YOU TEND TO TAKES ROOT IN THE **BOARDROOMS** OF BRUCE WAYNE'S PEERS.

THAT IS WHAT I HAVE OBSERVED. WHICH I AM **CERTAIN** IS NOT NEWS TO A DETECTIVE OF YOUR CALIBER.

YOU ARE PAID TO DO MORE THAN OBSERVE.

I AM AWARE! I AM ALSO PAID TO INVENT. AND TO BEHAVE AS PARANOID AS YOU IN BRUCE WAYNE'S ABSENCE.

WHICH IS WHY YOUR PROTOTYPE SERVES AS A HUB. YOU CAN RANDOMLY ACCESS THE AUDIO AND VISUAL FEEDS OF ANY MODEL SOLD FROM YOUR OWN.

LIKE SO.

YESELLE!

CLINK

HOW DO I CONTROL THE DRONES?!

LUCIUS!

YOU CAN'T! MERELY MONITOR. EITHER THAT OR SHUT DOWN THE **WHOLE PROGRAM.** THAT WOULD BE **HUNDREDS** OF--

TH-THE **RETINAL SCANNER!** I-IT'LL GRANT YOU ACCESS FOR **DEACTIVATION!**

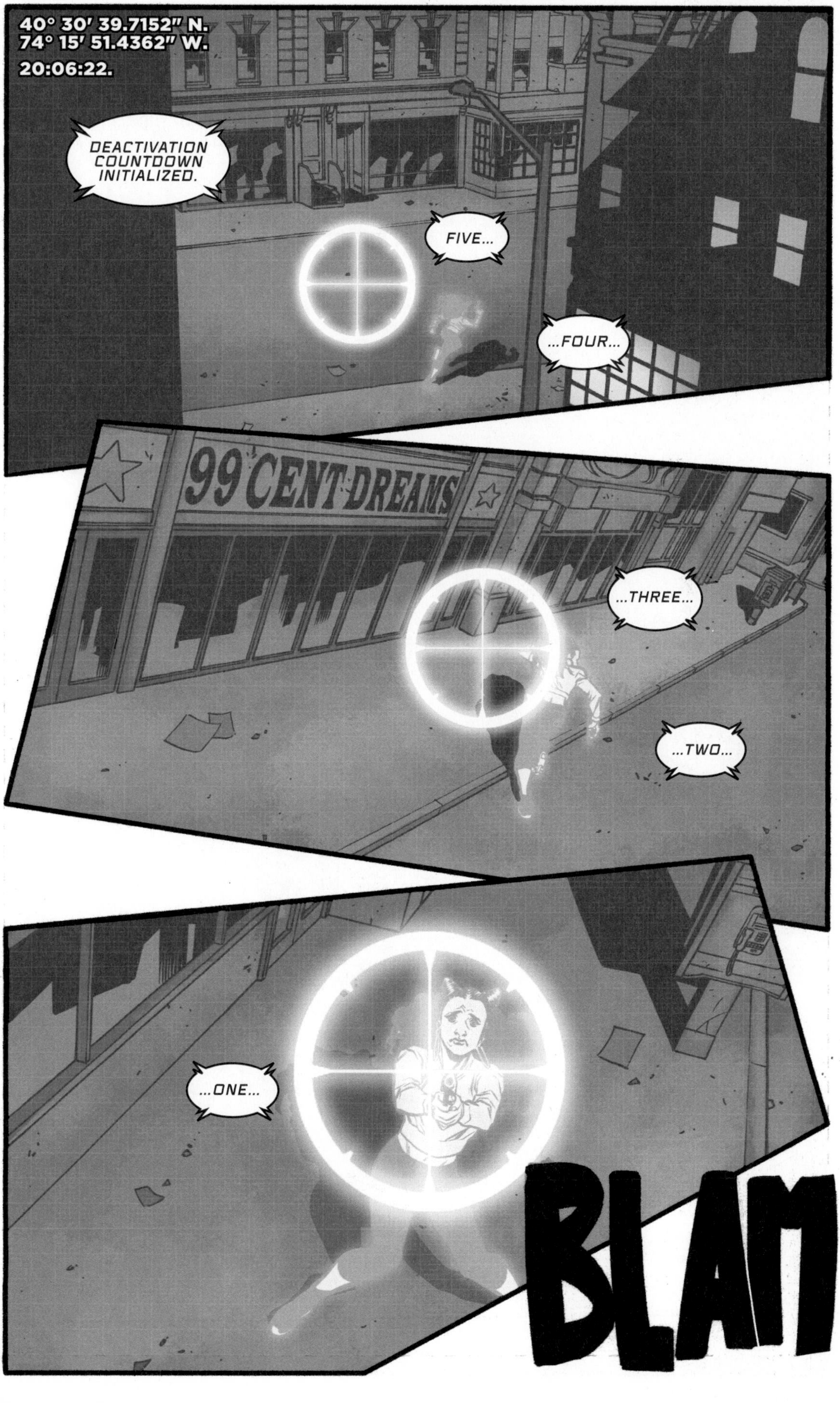

40° 30′ 39.7152″ N.
74° 15′ 51.4362″ W.
20:06:22.
DEACTIVATION COUNTDOWN INITIALIZED.
FIVE...
...FOUR...
99 CENT DREAMS
...THREE...
...TWO...
...ONE...
BLAM

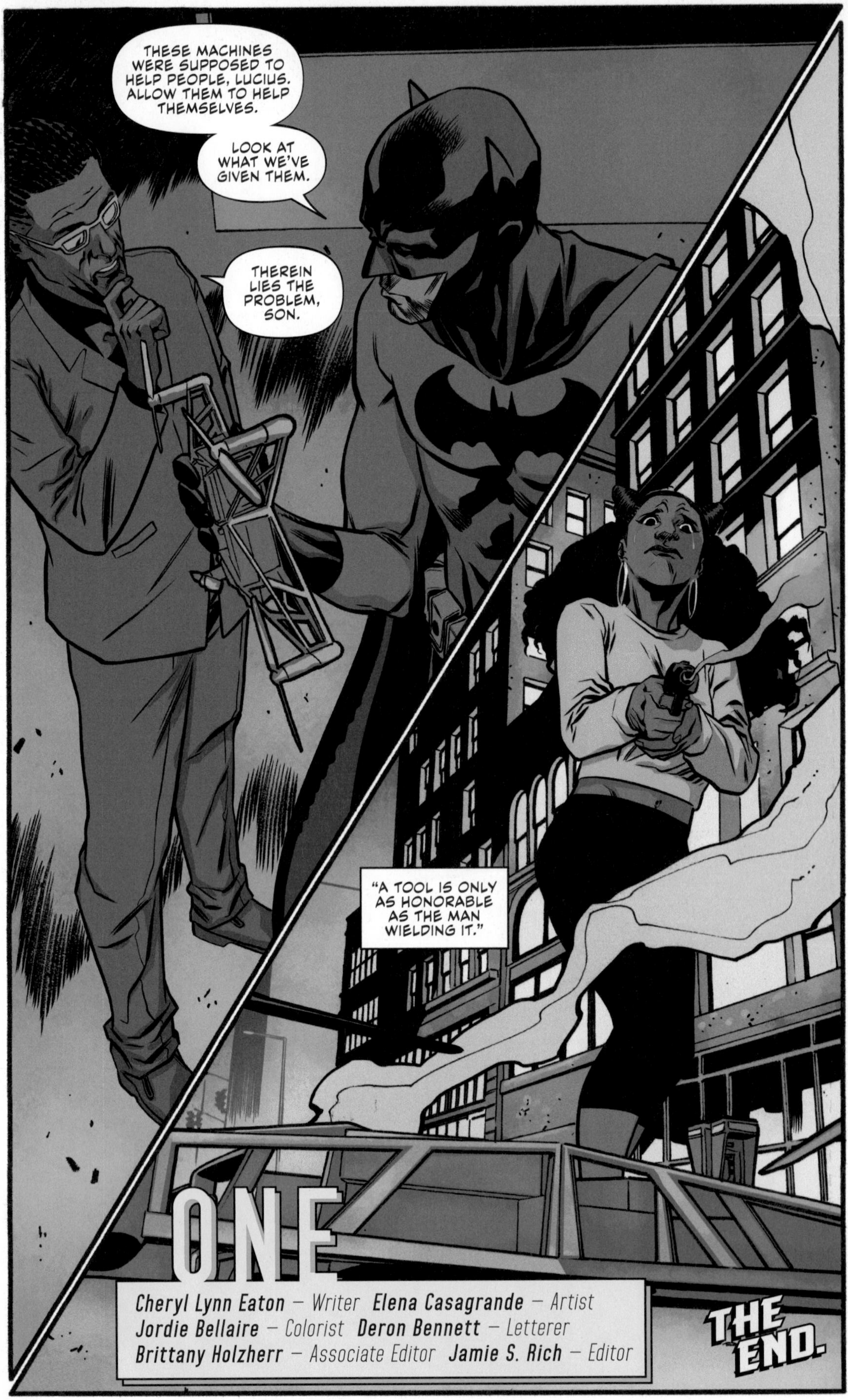
THESE MACHINES WERE SUPPOSED TO HELP PEOPLE, LUCIUS. ALLOW THEM TO HELP THEMSELVES.
LOOK AT WHAT WE'VE GIVEN THEM.
THEREIN LIES THE PROBLEM, SON.
"A TOOL IS ONLY AS HONORABLE AS THE MAN WIELDING IT."
ONE
Cheryl Lynn Eaton – Writer Elena Casagrande – Artist
Jordie Bellaire – Colorist Deron Bennett – Letterer
Brittany Holzherr – Associate Editor Jamie S. Rich – Editor
THE END.

THERE'RE RUMORS THAT SOMEWHERE, IN GOTHAM'S MOST BEAUTIFUL, SNOW-TOPPED MOUNTAINS, A MONSTER IS RUNNING AROUND.

I HAVE A SUSPICION *MAN-BAT* IS BEHIND THE STRANGE ACTIVITY.

MOUNTAIN CLIMBERS LOSING THEIR CAMPS, SKI RESORTS WITH MISSING GUESTS, A STRANGE BEAST BEING SEEN IN THE DARK.

SOMETHING COVERED IN HAIR, SOMETHING REMARKABLY LARGE.

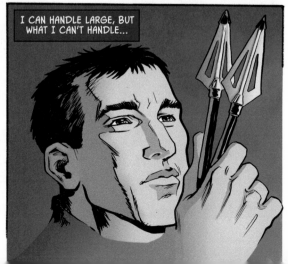

I CAN HANDLE LARGE, BUT WHAT I CAN'T HANDLE...

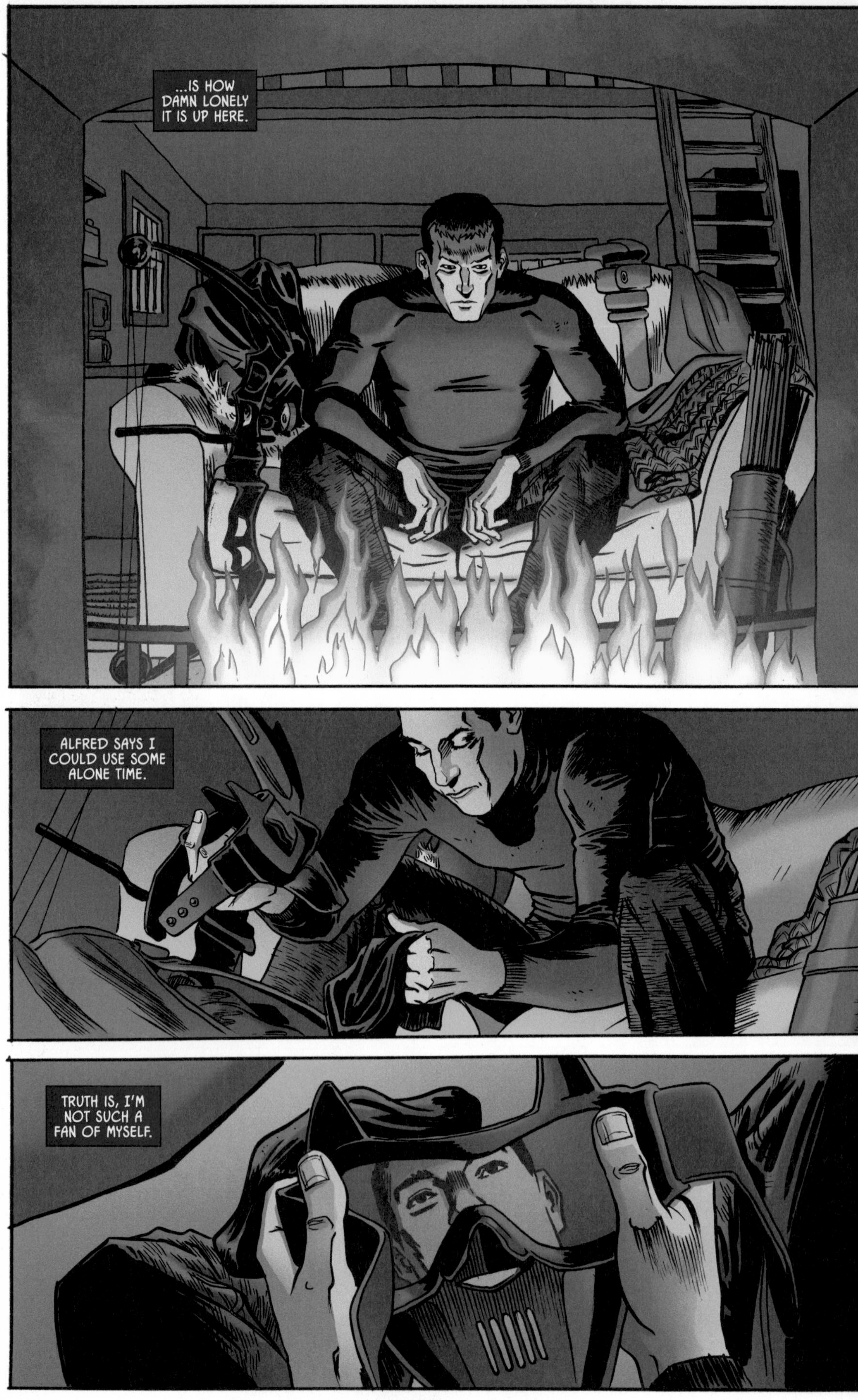
...IS HOW DAMN LONELY IT IS UP HERE.
ALFRED SAYS I COULD USE SOME ALONE TIME.
TRUTH IS, I'M NOT SUCH A FAN OF MYSELF.

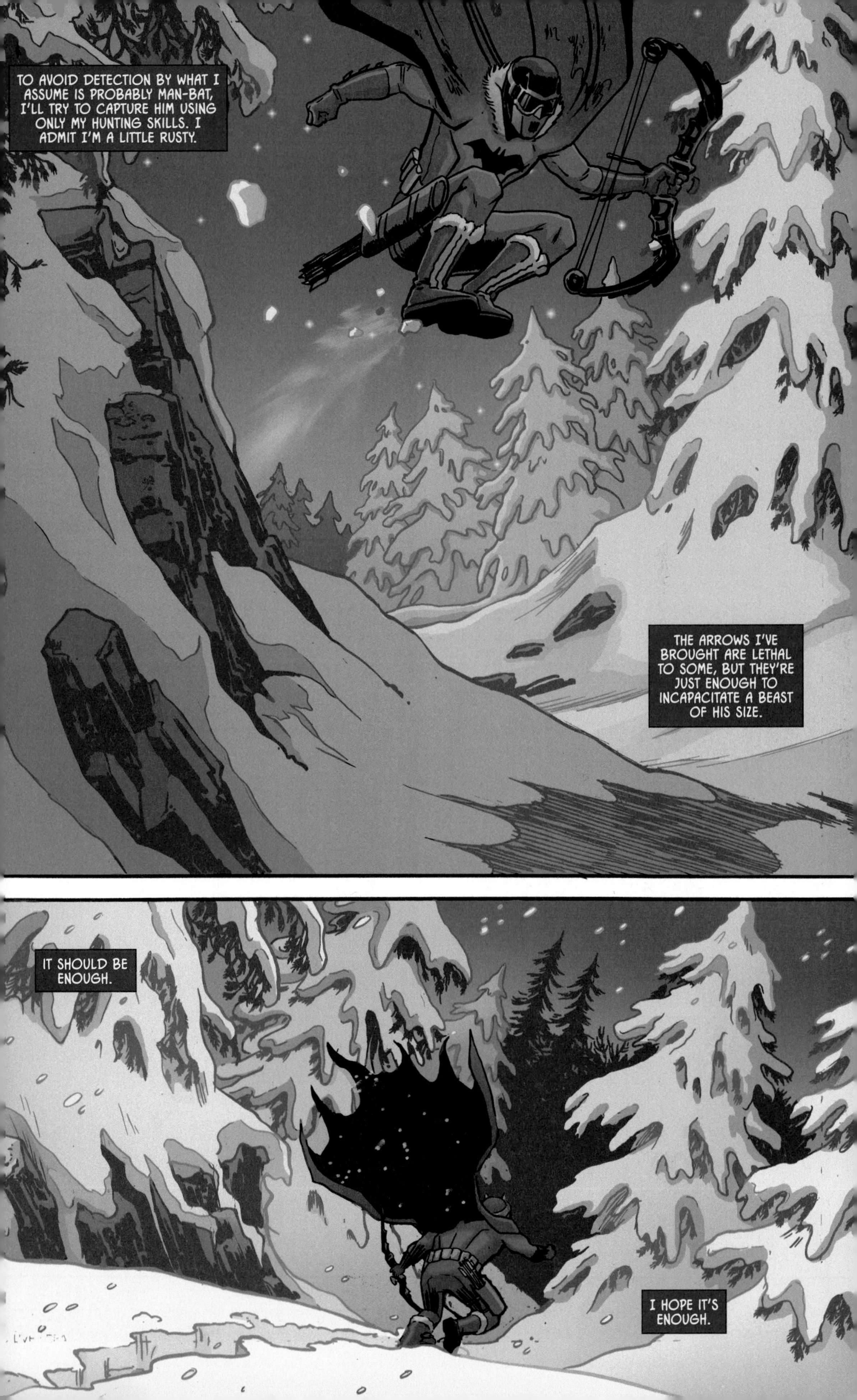

TO AVOID DETECTION BY WHAT I ASSUME IS PROBABLY MAN-BAT, I'LL TRY TO CAPTURE HIM USING ONLY MY HUNTING SKILLS. I ADMIT I'M A LITTLE RUSTY.
THE ARROWS I'VE BROUGHT ARE LETHAL TO SOME, BUT THEY'RE JUST ENOUGH TO INCAPACITATE A BEAST OF HIS SIZE.
IT SHOULD BE ENOUGH.
I HOPE IT'S ENOUGH.

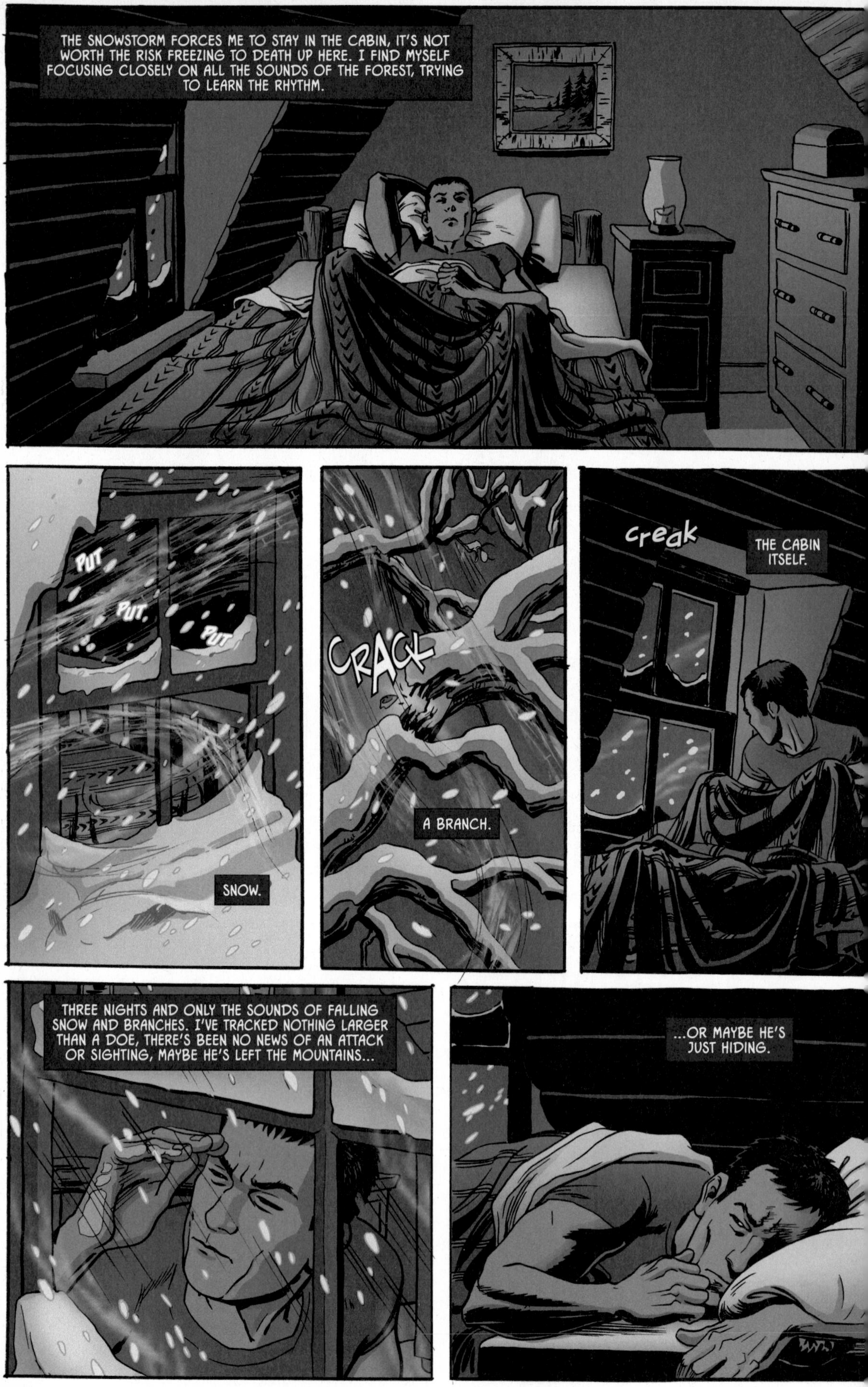
THE SNOWSTORM FORCES ME TO STAY IN THE CABIN, IT'S NOT WORTH THE RISK FREEZING TO DEATH UP HERE. I FIND MYSELF FOCUSING CLOSELY ON ALL THE SOUNDS OF THE FOREST, TRYING TO LEARN THE RHYTHM.
PUT
PUT
PUT
SNOW.
CRACK
A BRANCH.
creak
THE CABIN ITSELF.
THREE NIGHTS AND ONLY THE SOUNDS OF FALLING SNOW AND BRANCHES. I'VE TRACKED NOTHING LARGER THAN A DOE, THERE'S BEEN NO NEWS OF AN ATTACK OR SIGHTING, MAYBE HE'S LEFT THE MOUNTAINS...
...OR MAYBE HE'S JUST HIDING.

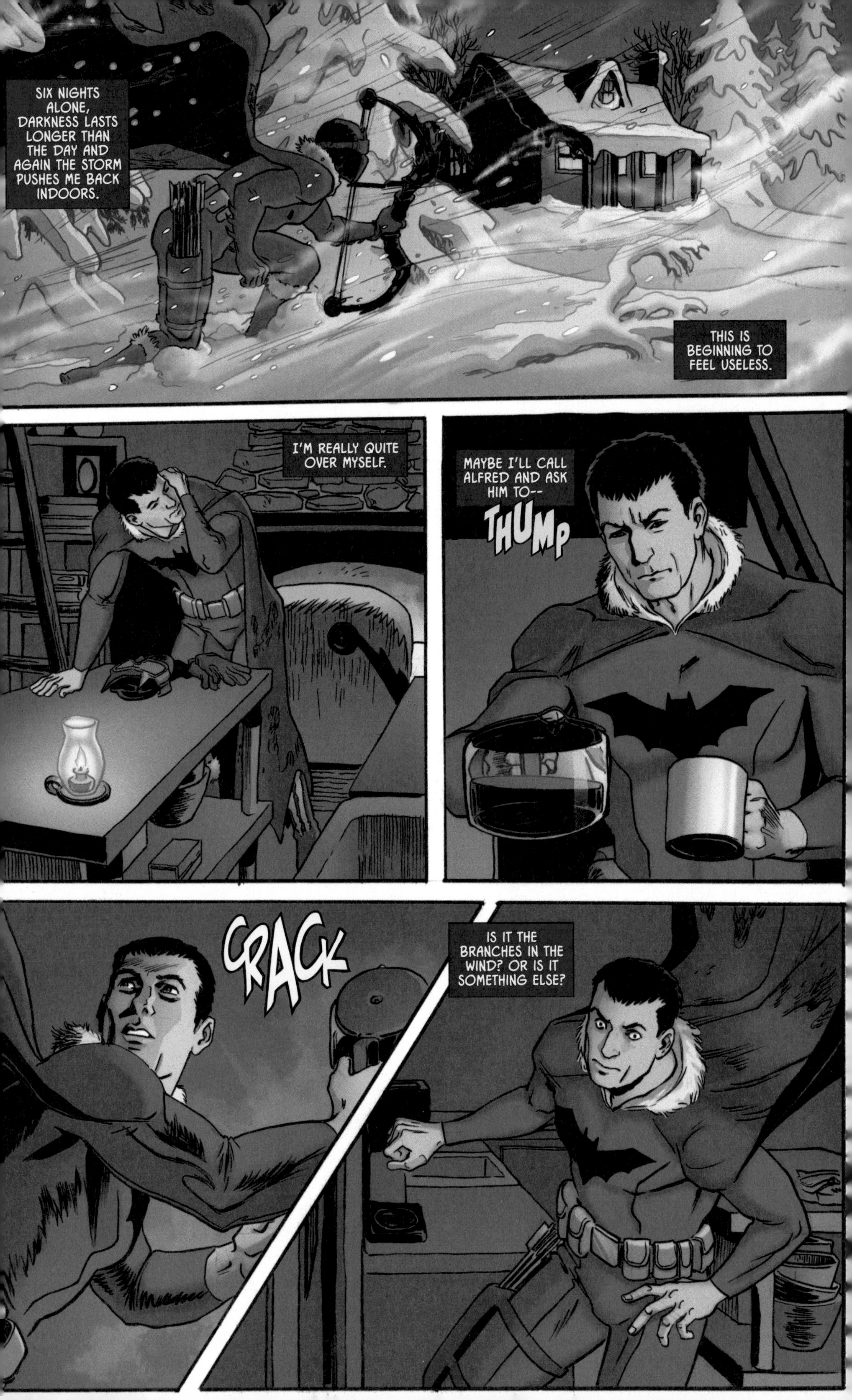
SIX NIGHTS ALONE, DARKNESS LASTS LONGER THAN THE DAY AND AGAIN THE STORM PUSHES ME BACK INDOORS.
THIS IS BEGINNING TO FEEL USELESS.
I'M REALLY QUITE OVER MYSELF.
MAYBE I'LL CALL ALFRED AND ASK HIM TO--
THUMP
CRACK
IS IT THE BRANCHES IN THE WIND? OR IS IT SOMETHING ELSE?

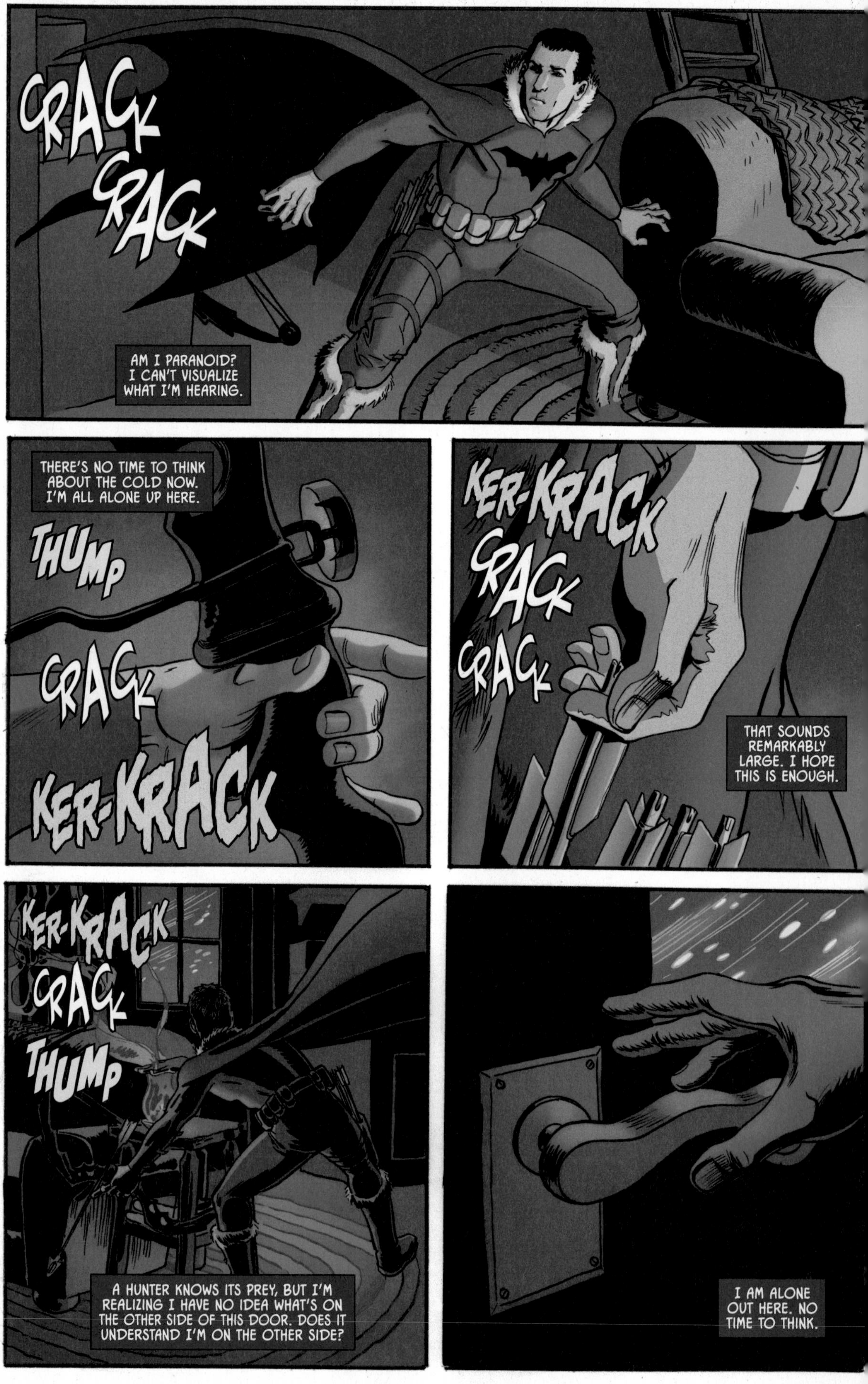
CRACK
CRACK
AM I PARANOID? I CAN'T VISUALIZE WHAT I'M HEARING.
THERE'S NO TIME TO THINK ABOUT THE COLD NOW. I'M ALL ALONE UP HERE.
THUMP
CRACK
KER-KRACK
KER-KRACK
CRACK
CRACK
THAT SOUNDS REMARKABLY LARGE. I HOPE THIS IS ENOUGH.
KER-KRACK
CRACK
THUMP
A HUNTER KNOWS ITS PREY, BUT I'M REALIZING I HAVE NO IDEA WHAT'S ON THE OTHER SIDE OF THIS DOOR. DOES IT UNDERSTAND I'M ON THE OTHER SIDE?
I AM ALONE OUT HERE. NO TIME TO THINK.

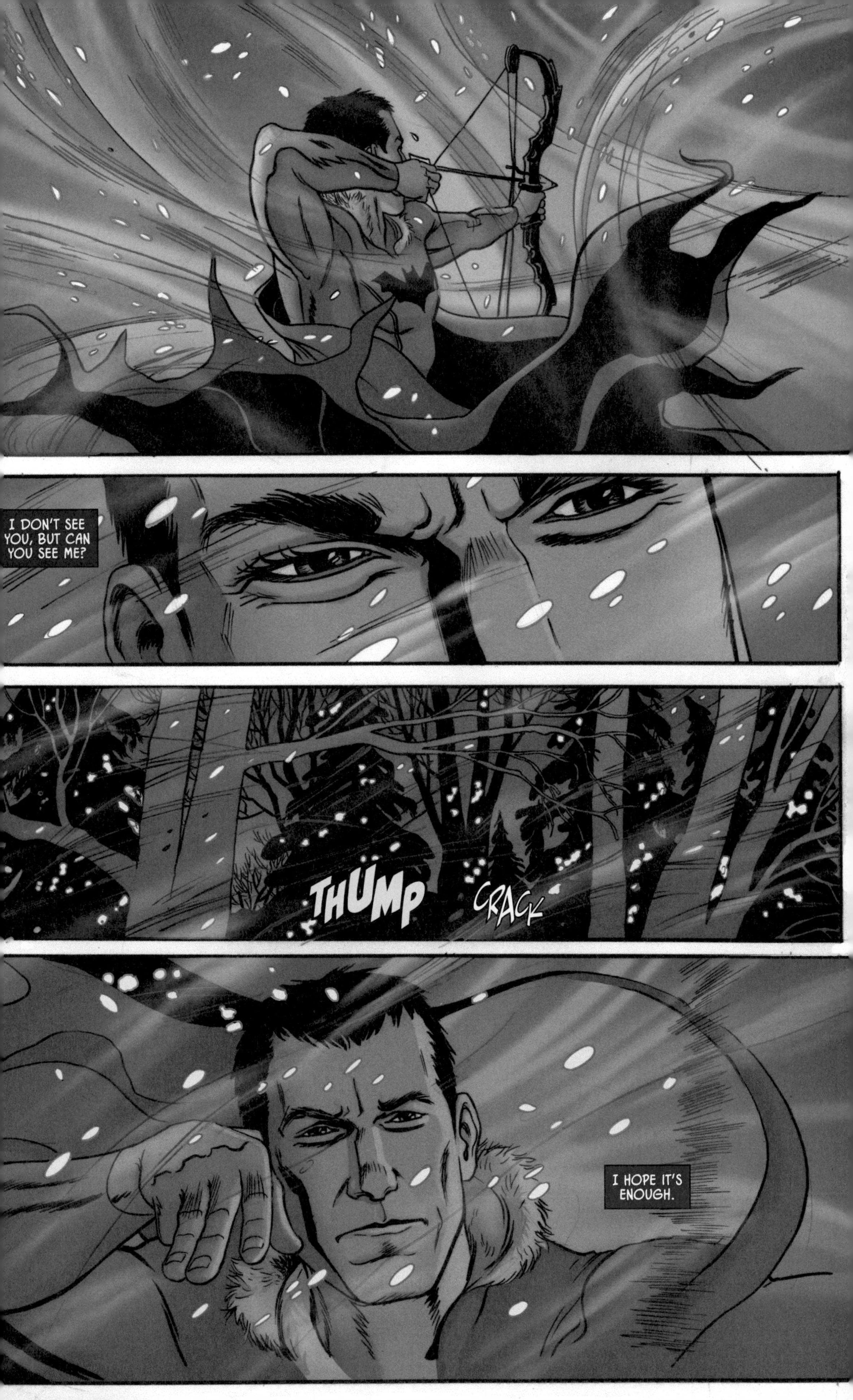
I DON'T SEE YOU, BUT CAN YOU SEE ME?
THUMP
CRACK
I HOPE IT'S ENOUGH.

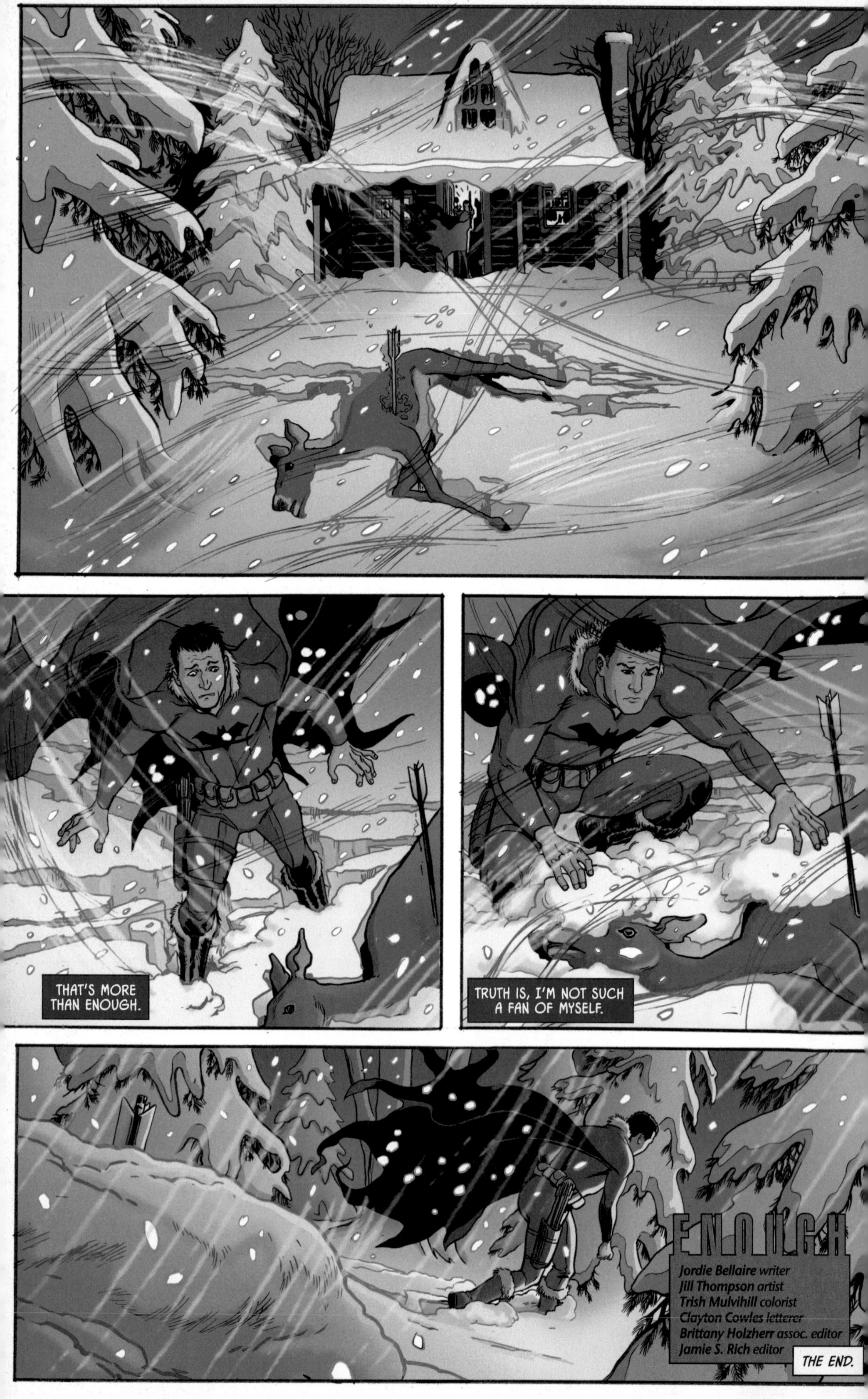
THAT'S MORE THAN ENOUGH.
TRUTH IS, I'M NOT SUCH A FAN OF MYSELF.
ENOUGH
Jordie Bellaire writer
Jill Thompson artist
Trish Mulvihill colorist
Clayton Cowles letterer
Brittany Holzherr assoc. editor
Jamie S. Rich editor
THE END.

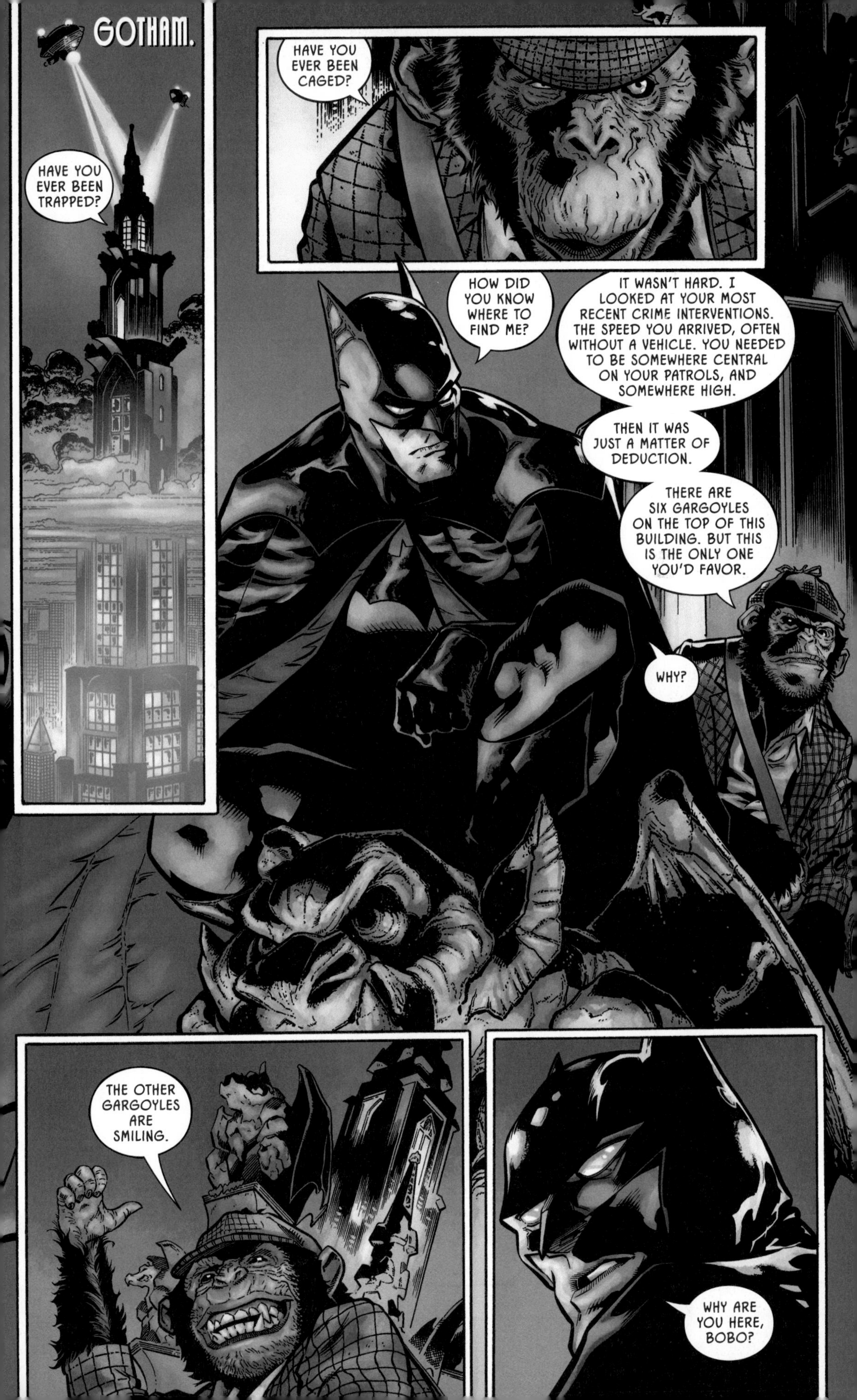
GOTHAM.
HAVE YOU EVER BEEN TRAPPED?
HAVE YOU EVER BEEN CAGED?
HOW DID YOU KNOW WHERE TO FIND ME?
IT WASN'T HARD. I LOOKED AT YOUR MOST RECENT CRIME INTERVENTIONS. THE SPEED YOU ARRIVED, OFTEN WITHOUT A VEHICLE. YOU NEEDED TO BE SOMEWHERE CENTRAL ON YOUR PATROLS, AND SOMEWHERE HIGH.
THEN IT WAS JUST A MATTER OF DEDUCTION.
THERE ARE SIX GARGOYLES ON THE TOP OF THIS BUILDING. BUT THIS IS THE ONLY ONE YOU'D FAVOR.
WHY?
THE OTHER GARGOYLES ARE SMILING.
WHY ARE YOU HERE, BOBO?

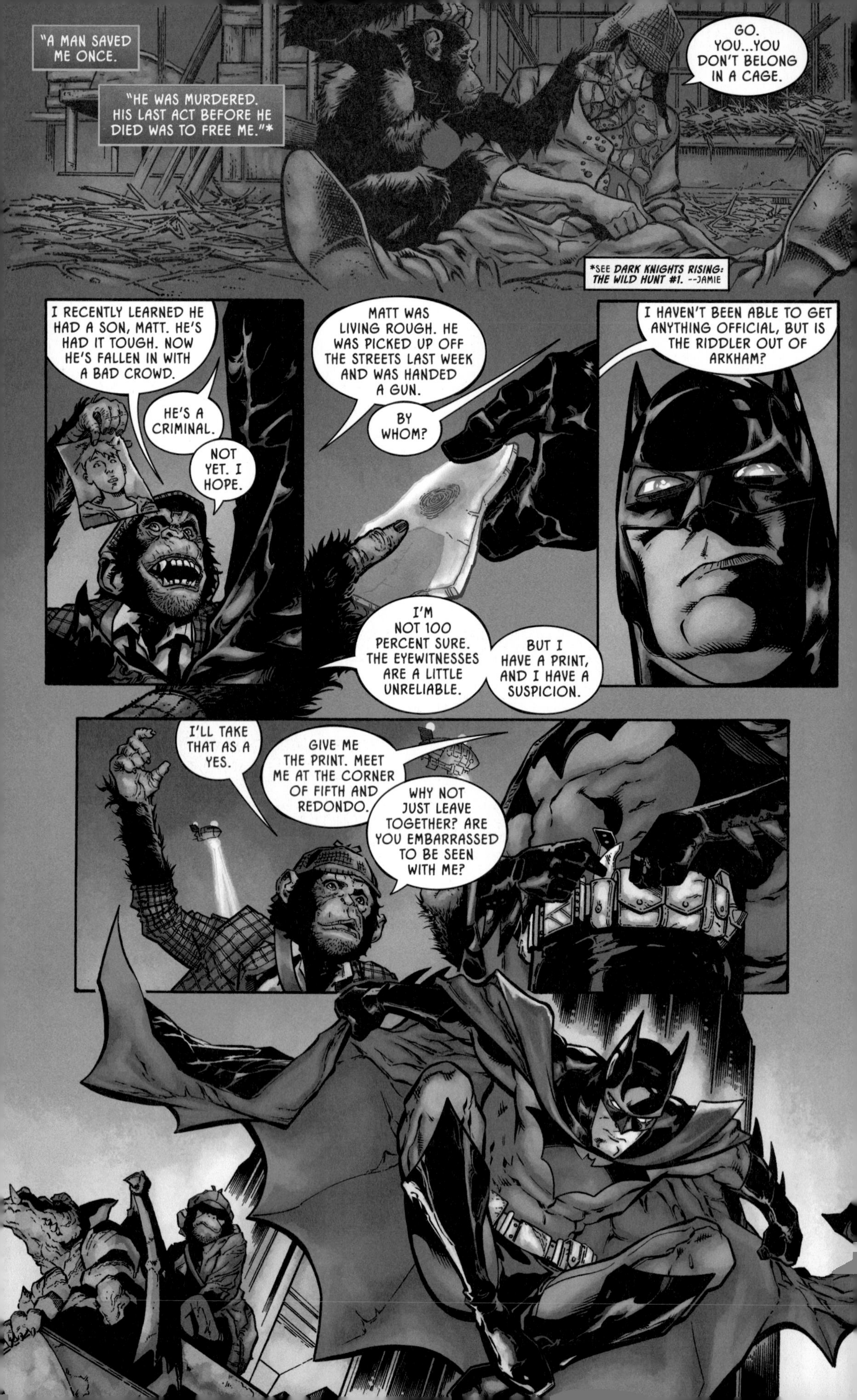
"A MAN SAVED ME ONCE.
"HE WAS MURDERED. HIS LAST ACT BEFORE HE DIED WAS TO FREE ME."*
GO. YOU...YOU DON'T BELONG IN A CAGE.
*SEE DARK KNIGHTS RISING: THE WILD HUNT #1. --JAMIE
I RECENTLY LEARNED HE HAD A SON, MATT. HE'S HAD IT TOUGH. NOW HE'S FALLEN IN WITH A BAD CROWD.
HE'S A CRIMINAL.
NOT YET. I HOPE.
MATT WAS LIVING ROUGH. HE WAS PICKED UP OFF THE STREETS LAST WEEK AND WAS HANDED A GUN.
BY WHOM?
I'M NOT 100 PERCENT SURE. THE EYEWITNESSES ARE A LITTLE UNRELIABLE.
BUT I HAVE A PRINT, AND I HAVE A SUSPICION.
I HAVEN'T BEEN ABLE TO GET ANYTHING OFFICIAL, BUT IS THE RIDDLER OUT OF ARKHAM?
I'LL TAKE THAT AS A YES.
GIVE ME THE PRINT. MEET ME AT THE CORNER OF FIFTH AND REDONDO.
WHY NOT JUST LEAVE TOGETHER? ARE YOU EMBARRASSED TO BE SEEN WITH ME?

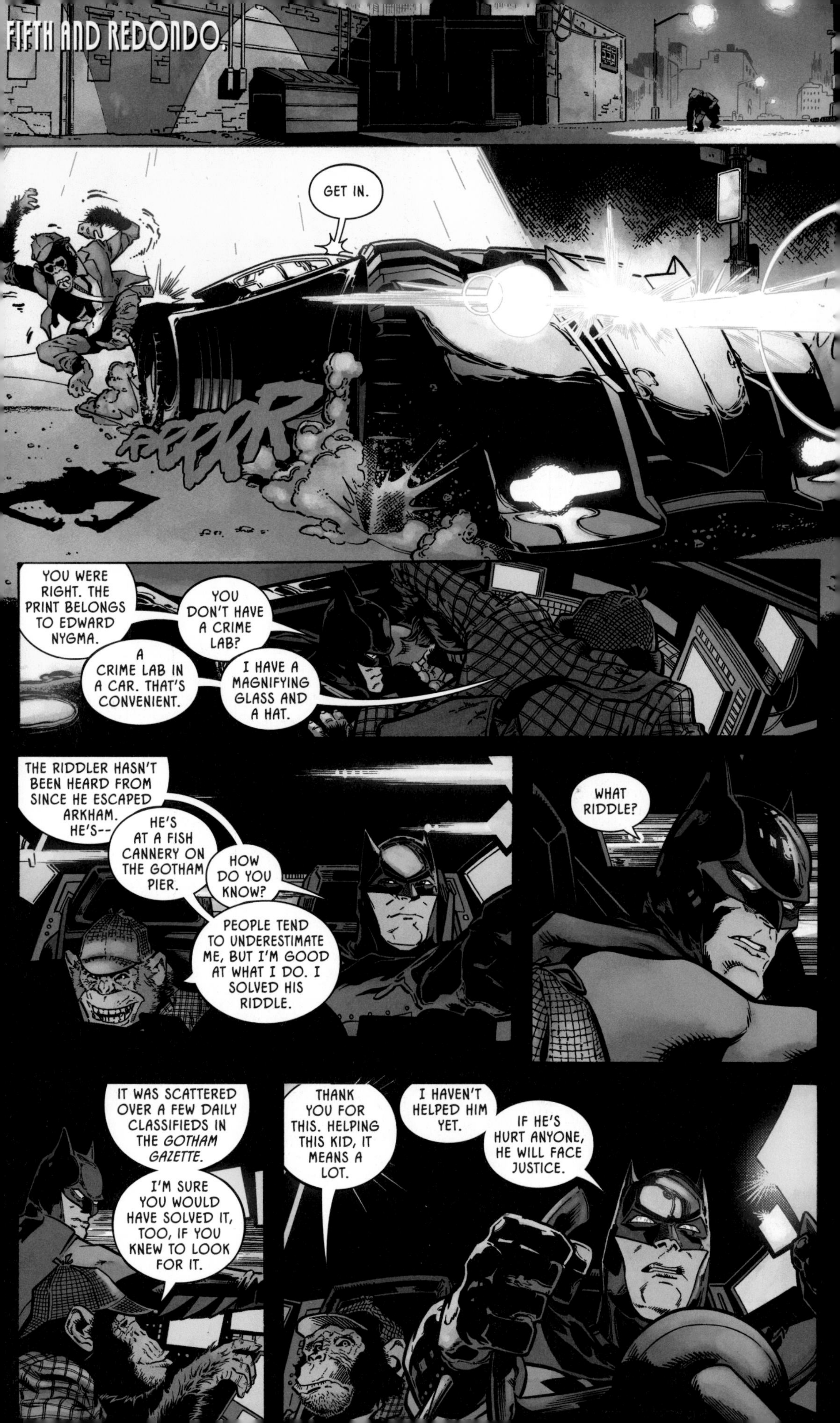
FIFTH AND REDONDO.
GET IN.
RRRRR
YOU WERE RIGHT. THE PRINT BELONGS TO EDWARD NYGMA.
YOU DON'T HAVE A CRIME LAB?
A CRIME LAB IN A CAR. THAT'S CONVENIENT.
I HAVE A MAGNIFYING GLASS AND A HAT.
THE RIDDLER HASN'T BEEN HEARD FROM SINCE HE ESCAPED ARKHAM. HE'S--
HE'S AT A FISH CANNERY ON THE GOTHAM PIER.
HOW DO YOU KNOW?
PEOPLE TEND TO UNDERESTIMATE ME, BUT I'M GOOD AT WHAT I DO. I SOLVED HIS RIDDLE.
WHAT RIDDLE?
IT WAS SCATTERED OVER A FEW DAILY CLASSIFIEDS IN THE *GOTHAM GAZETTE*.
I'M SURE YOU WOULD HAVE SOLVED IT, TOO, IF YOU KNEW TO LOOK FOR IT.
THANK YOU FOR THIS. HELPING THIS KID, IT MEANS A LOT.
I HAVEN'T HELPED HIM YET.
IF HE'S HURT ANYONE, HE WILL FACE JUSTICE.

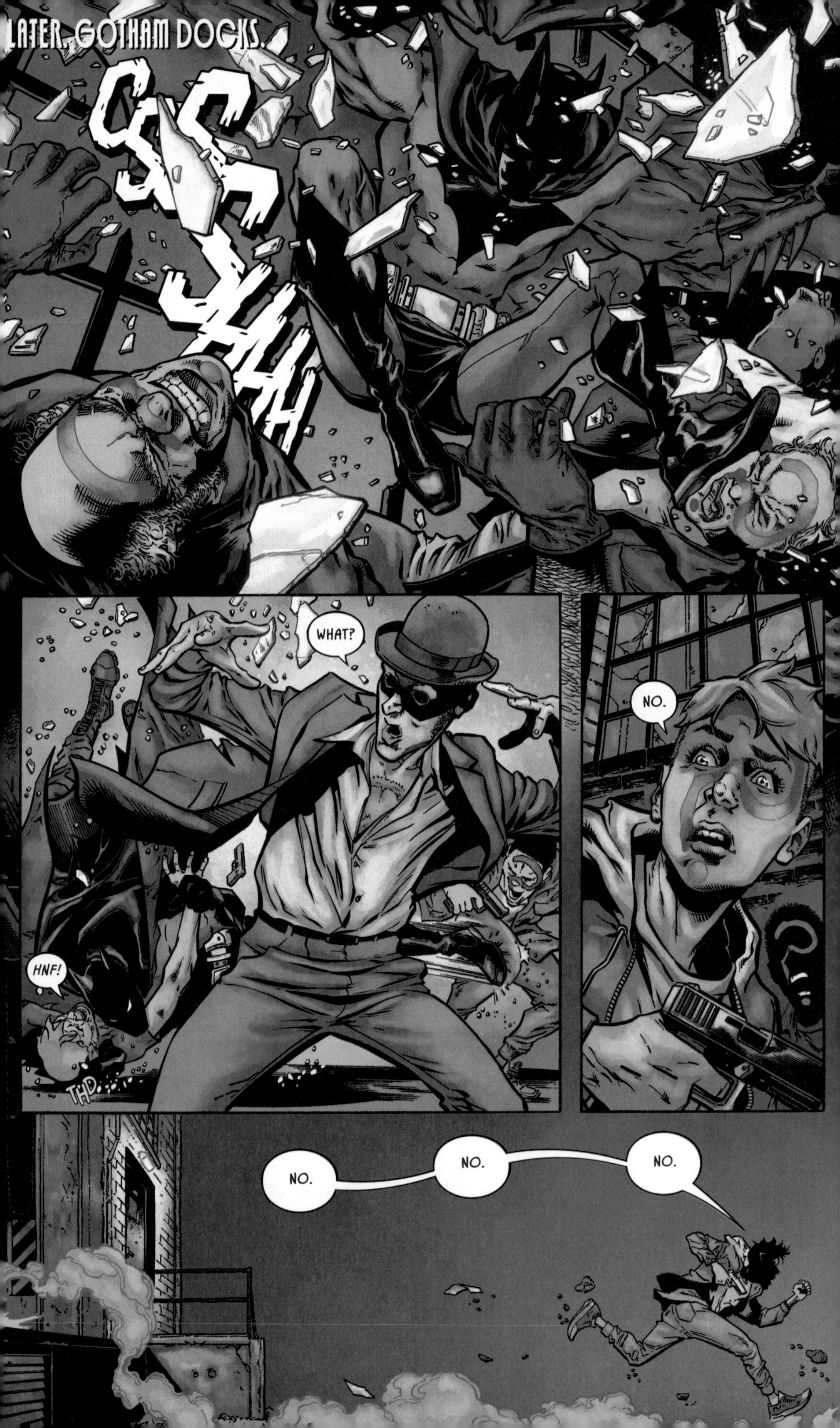
LATER, GOTHAM DOCKS.
CSSHHH
WHAT?
HNF!
THD
NO.
NO.
NO.
NO.

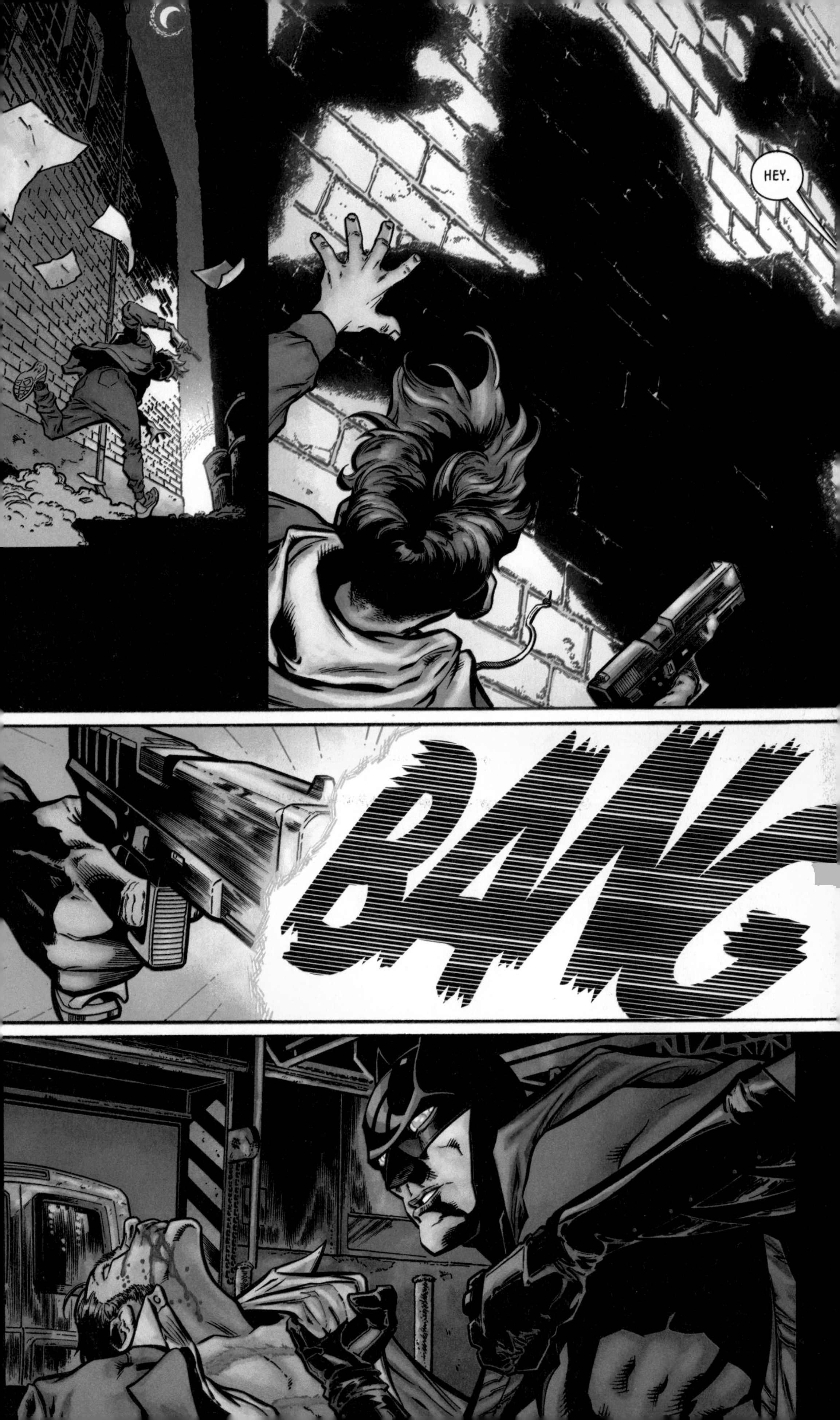
HEY.
BANG

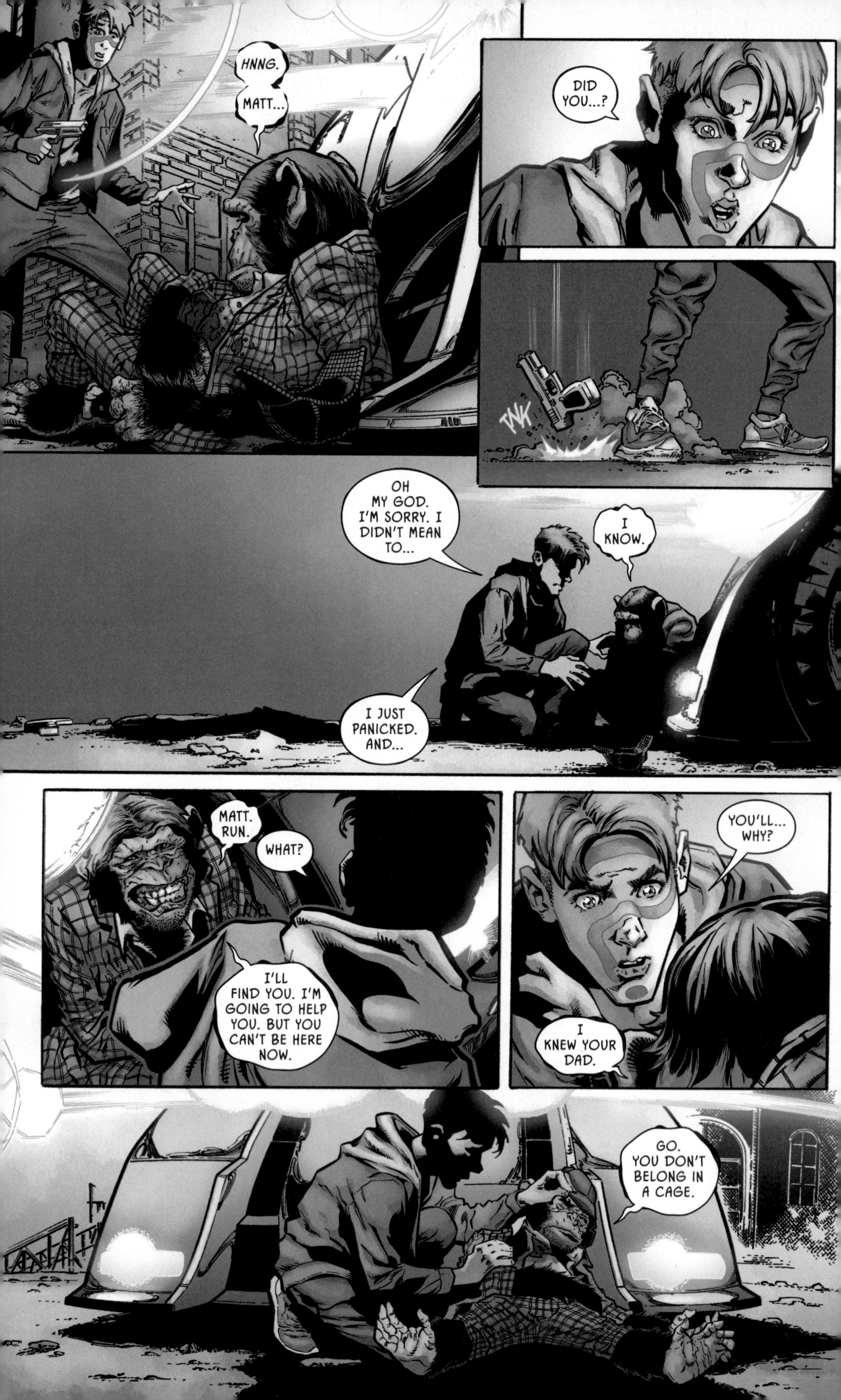
HNNG.
MATT...
DID YOU...?
TNK
OH MY GOD. I'M SORRY. I DIDN'T MEAN TO...
I KNOW.
I JUST PANICKED. AND...
MATT. RUN.
WHAT?
I'LL FIND YOU. I'M GOING TO HELP YOU. BUT YOU CAN'T BE HERE NOW.
YOU'LL... WHY?
I KNEW YOUR DAD.
GO. YOU DON'T BELONG IN A CAGE.

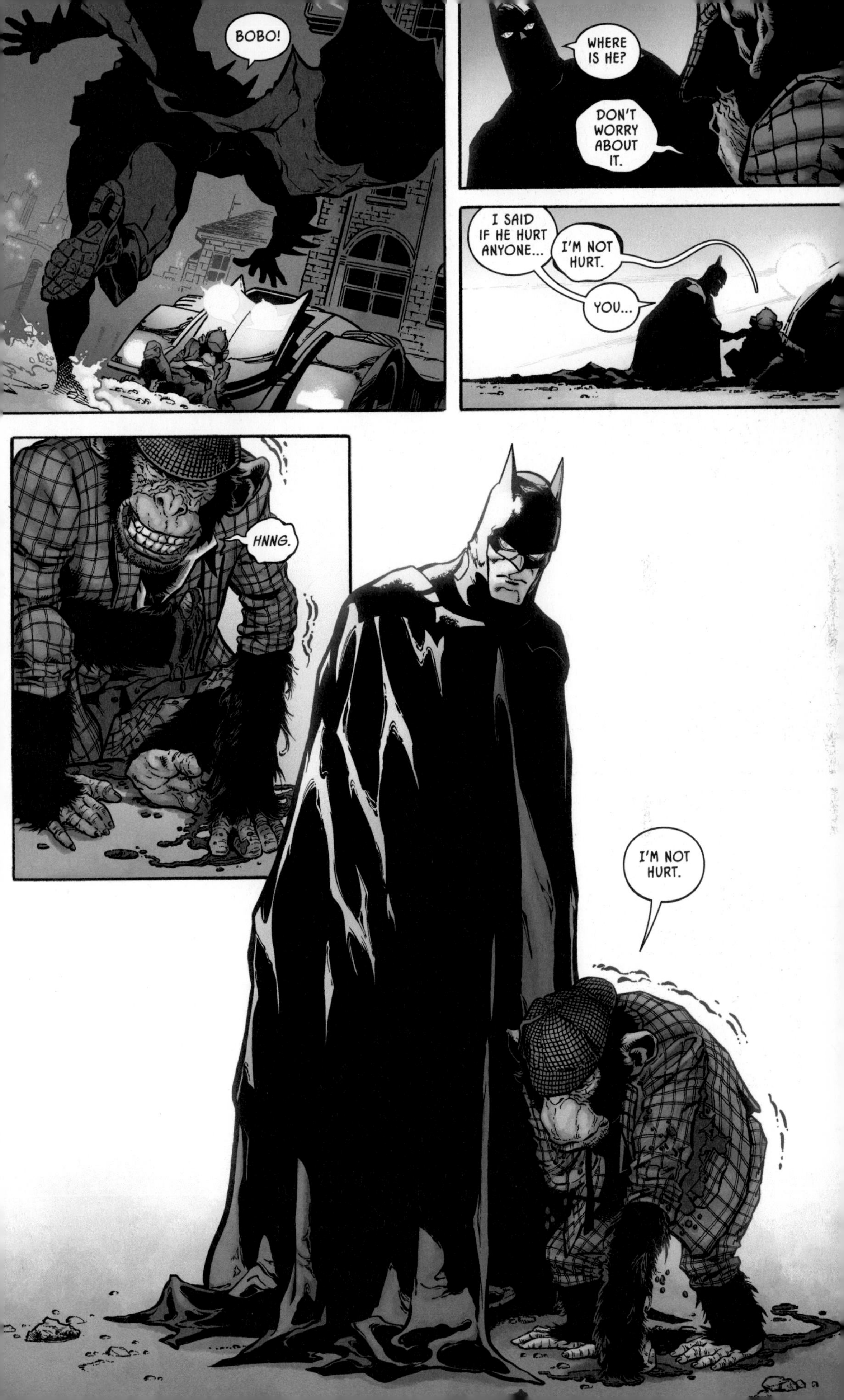
BOBO!
WHERE IS HE?
DON'T WORRY ABOUT IT.
I SAID IF HE HURT ANYONE...
I'M NOT HURT.
YOU...
HNNG.
I'M NOT HURT.

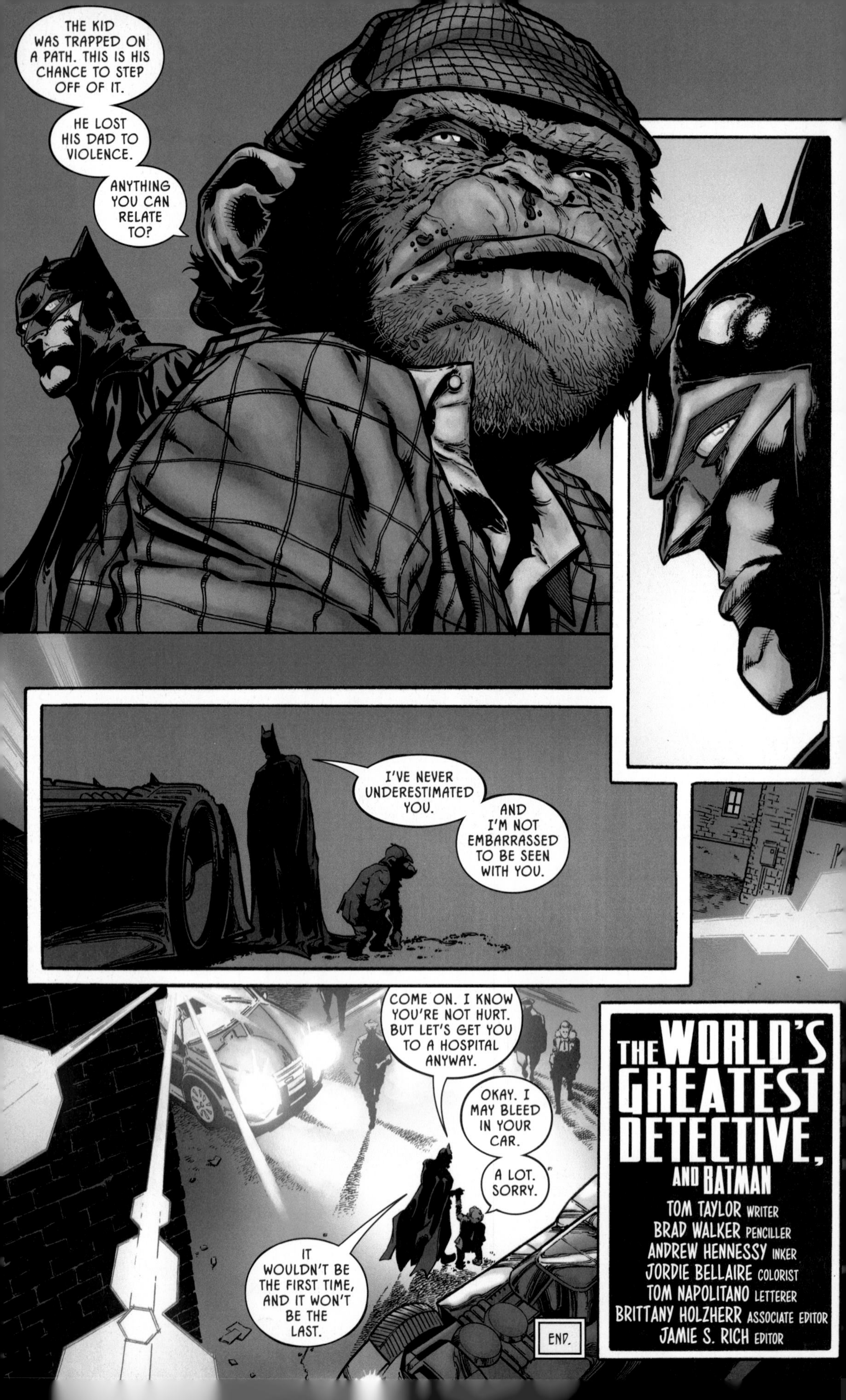
THE KID WAS TRAPPED ON A PATH. THIS IS HIS CHANCE TO STEP OFF OF IT.
HE LOST HIS DAD TO VIOLENCE.
ANYTHING YOU CAN RELATE TO?
I'VE NEVER UNDERESTIMATED YOU.
AND I'M NOT EMBARRASSED TO BE SEEN WITH YOU.
COME ON. I KNOW YOU'RE NOT HURT. BUT LET'S GET YOU TO A HOSPITAL ANYWAY.
OKAY. I MAY BLEED IN YOUR CAR.
A LOT. SORRY.
IT WOULDN'T BE THE FIRST TIME, AND IT WON'T BE THE LAST.
END.
THE WORLD'S GREATEST DETECTIVE, AND BATMAN
TOM TAYLOR WRITER
BRAD WALKER PENCILLER
ANDREW HENNESSY INKER
JORDIE BELLAIRE COLORIST
TOM NAPOLITANO LETTERER
BRITTANY HOLZHERR ASSOCIATE EDITOR
JAMIE S. RICH EDITOR

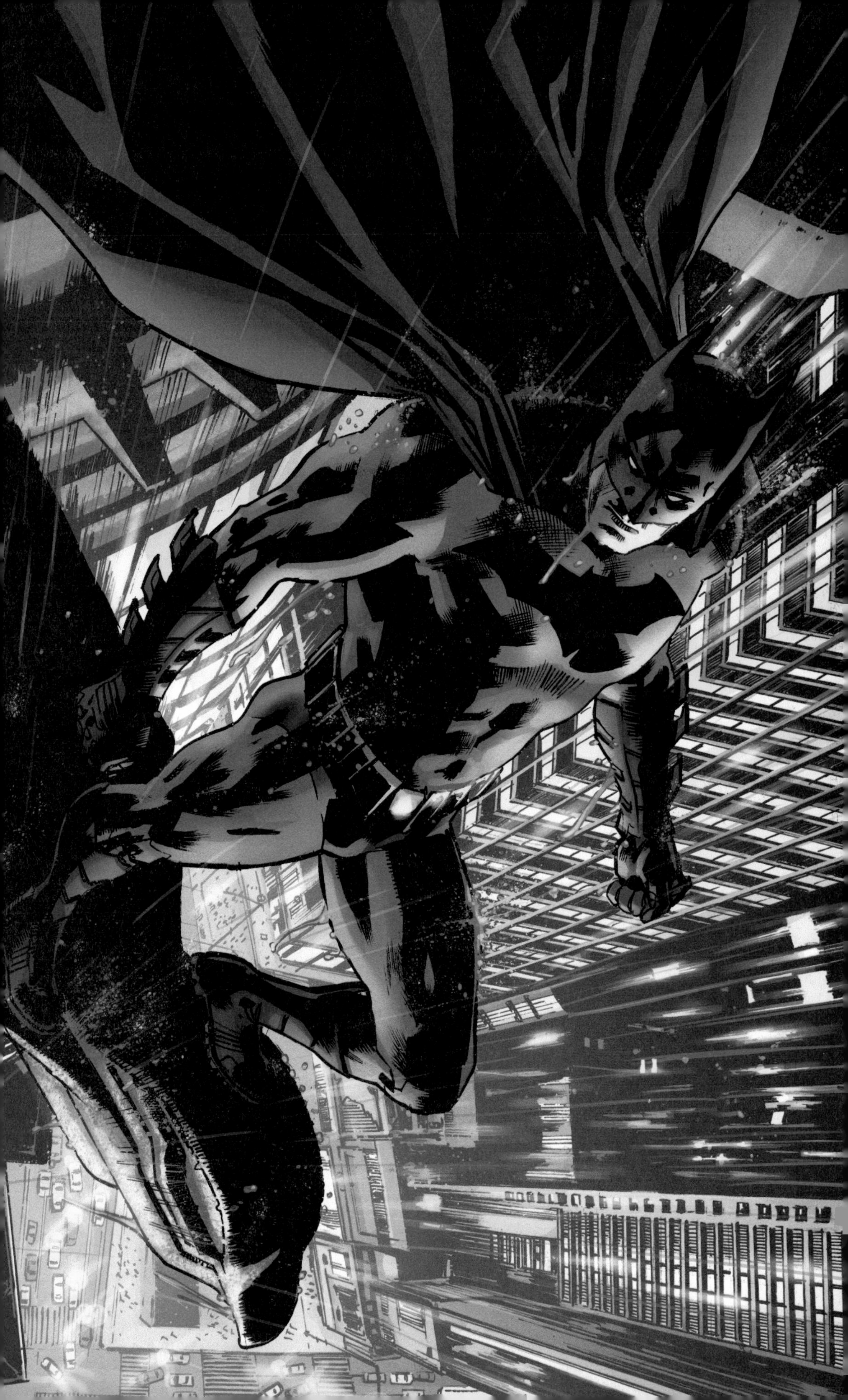

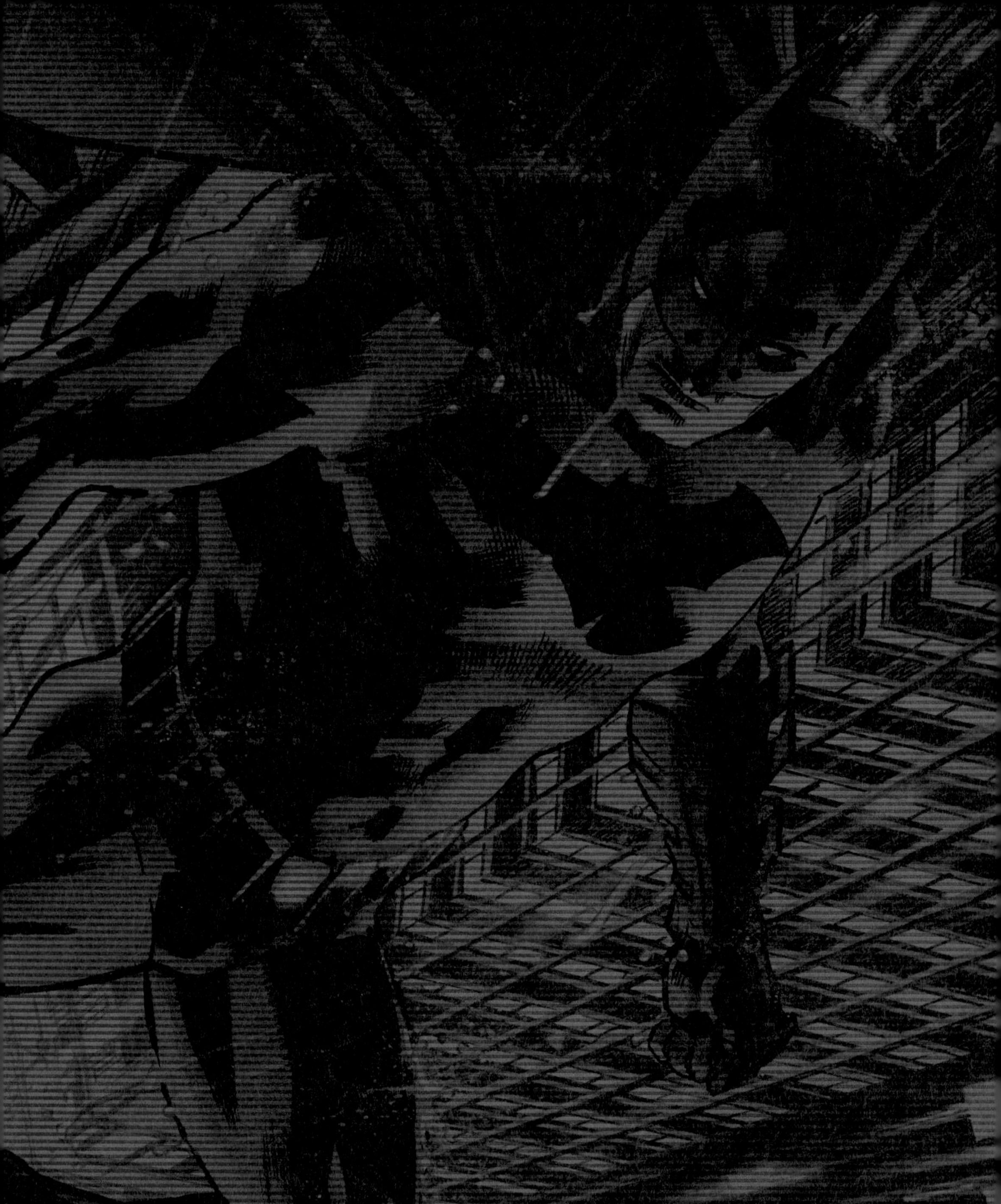

BATMAN
ANNUAL #3

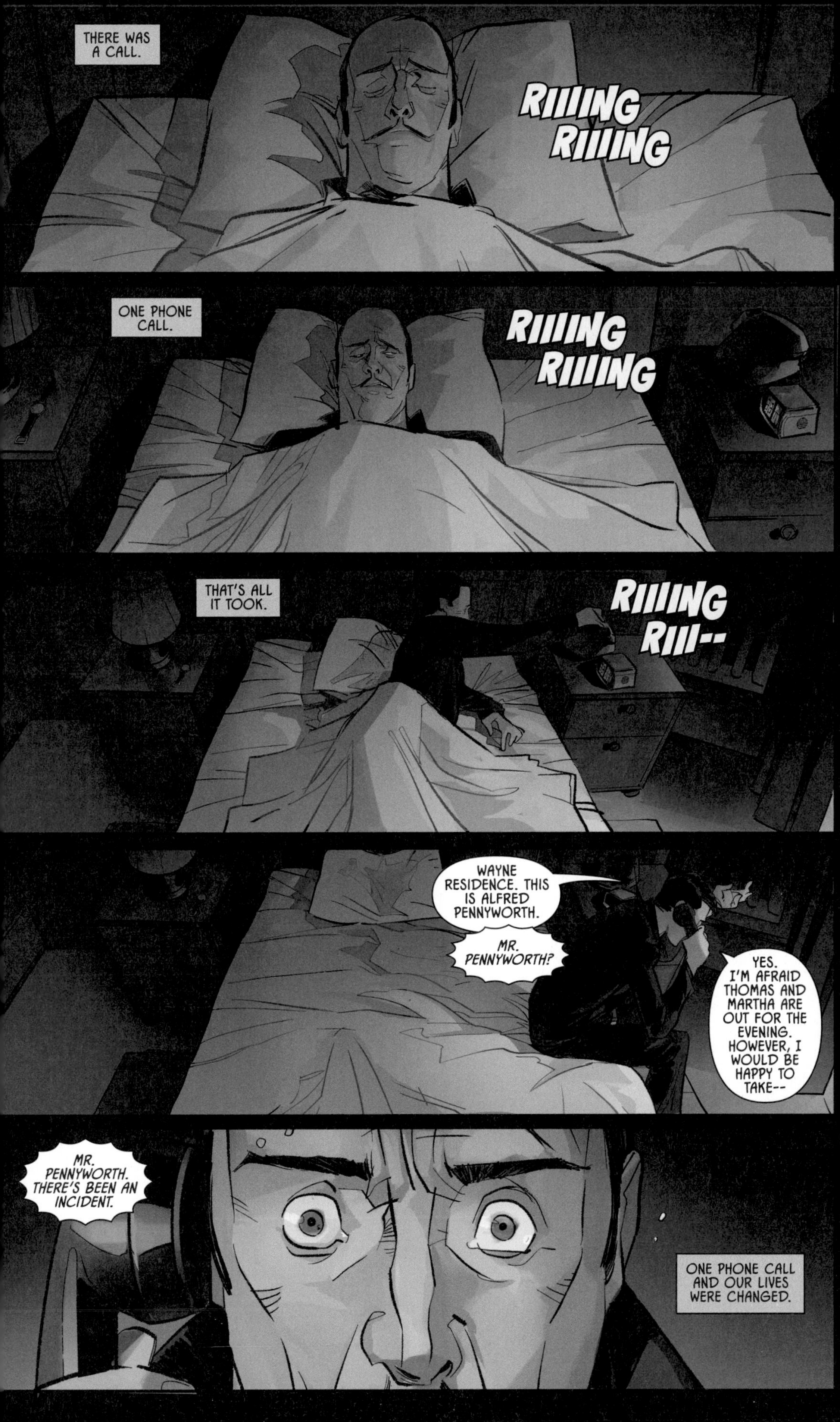
THERE WAS A CALL.
RIIIING RIIIING
ONE PHONE CALL.
RIIIING RIIIING
THAT'S ALL IT TOOK.
RIIIING RIII--
WAYNE RESIDENCE. THIS IS ALFRED PENNYWORTH.
MR. PENNYWORTH?
YES. I'M AFRAID THOMAS AND MARTHA ARE OUT FOR THE EVENING. HOWEVER, I WOULD BE HAPPY TO TAKE--
MR. PENNYWORTH. THERE'S BEEN AN INCIDENT.
ONE PHONE CALL AND OUR LIVES WERE CHANGED.

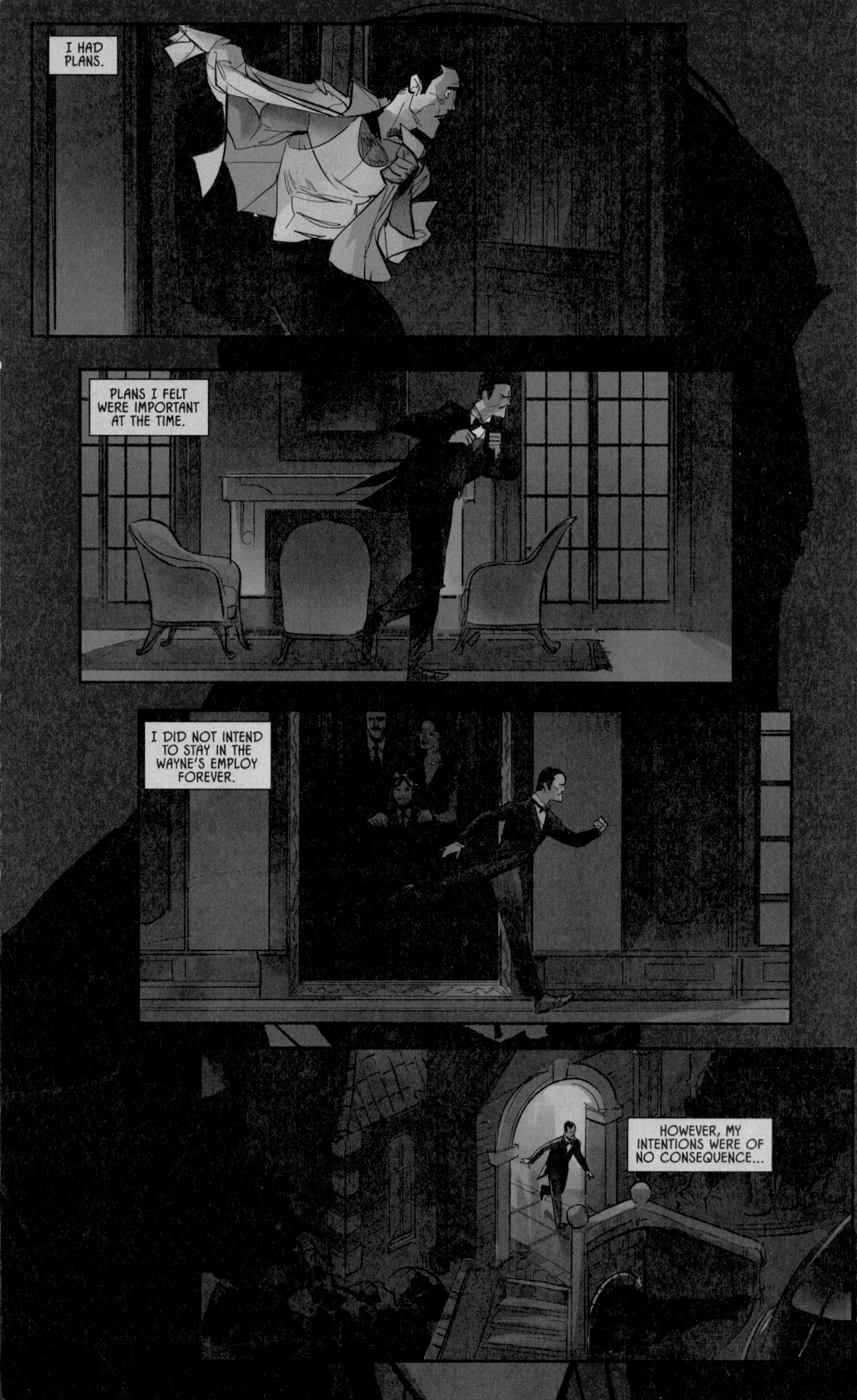
I HAD PLANS.
PLANS I FELT WERE IMPORTANT AT THE TIME.
I DID NOT INTEND TO STAY IN THE WAYNE'S EMPLOY FOREVER.
HOWEVER, MY INTENTIONS WERE OF NO CONSEQUENCE...

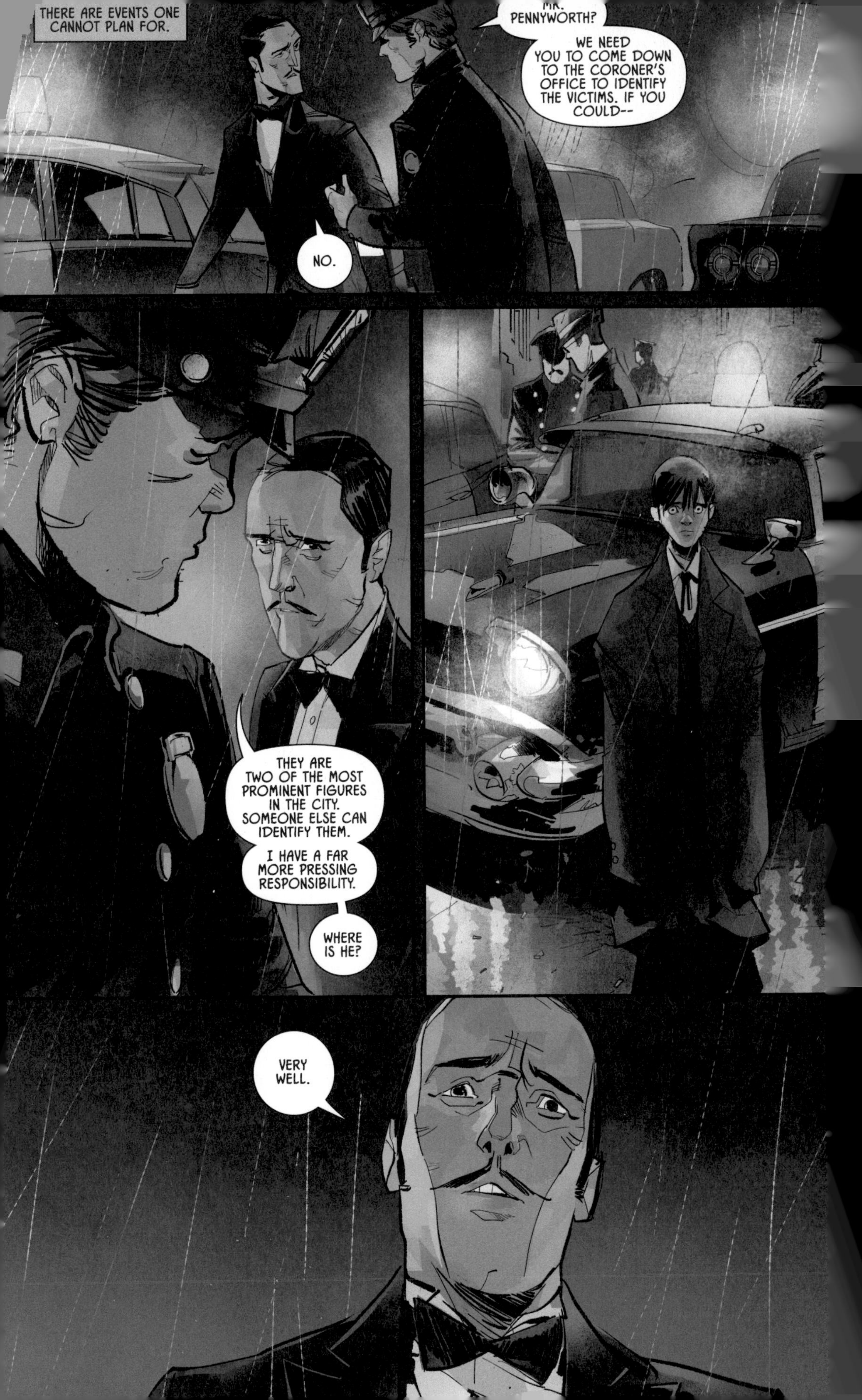
THERE ARE EVENTS ONE CANNOT PLAN FOR.
MR. PENNYWORTH?
WE NEED YOU TO COME DOWN TO THE CORONER'S OFFICE TO IDENTIFY THE VICTIMS. IF YOU COULD--
NO.
THEY ARE TWO OF THE MOST PROMINENT FIGURES IN THE CITY. SOMEONE ELSE CAN IDENTIFY THEM.
I HAVE A FAR MORE PRESSING RESPONSIBILITY.
WHERE IS HE?
VERY WELL.

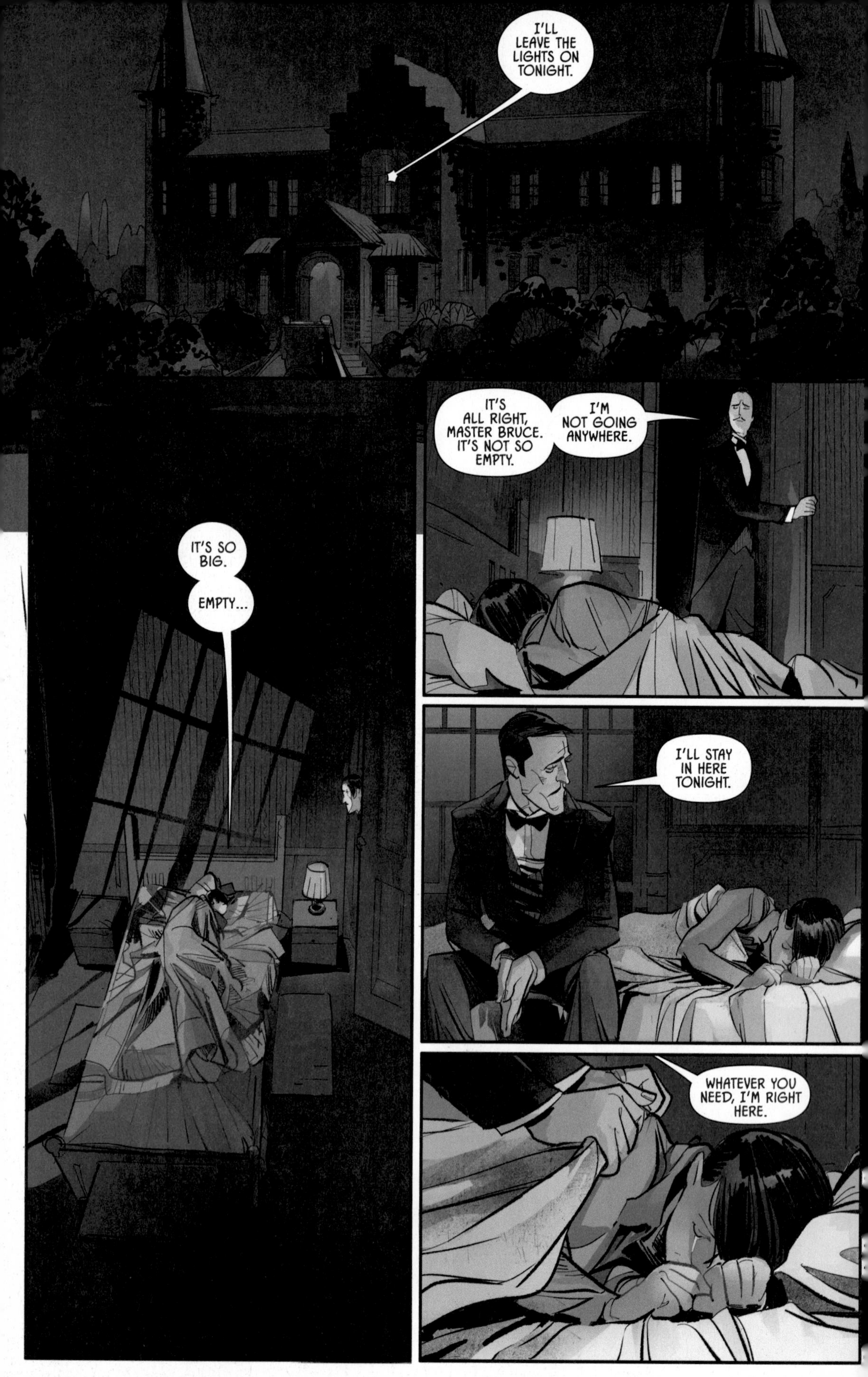
I'LL LEAVE THE LIGHTS ON TONIGHT.
IT'S SO BIG.
EMPTY...
IT'S ALL RIGHT, MASTER BRUCE. IT'S NOT SO EMPTY.
I'M NOT GOING ANYWHERE.
I'LL STAY IN HERE TONIGHT.
WHATEVER YOU NEED, I'M RIGHT HERE.

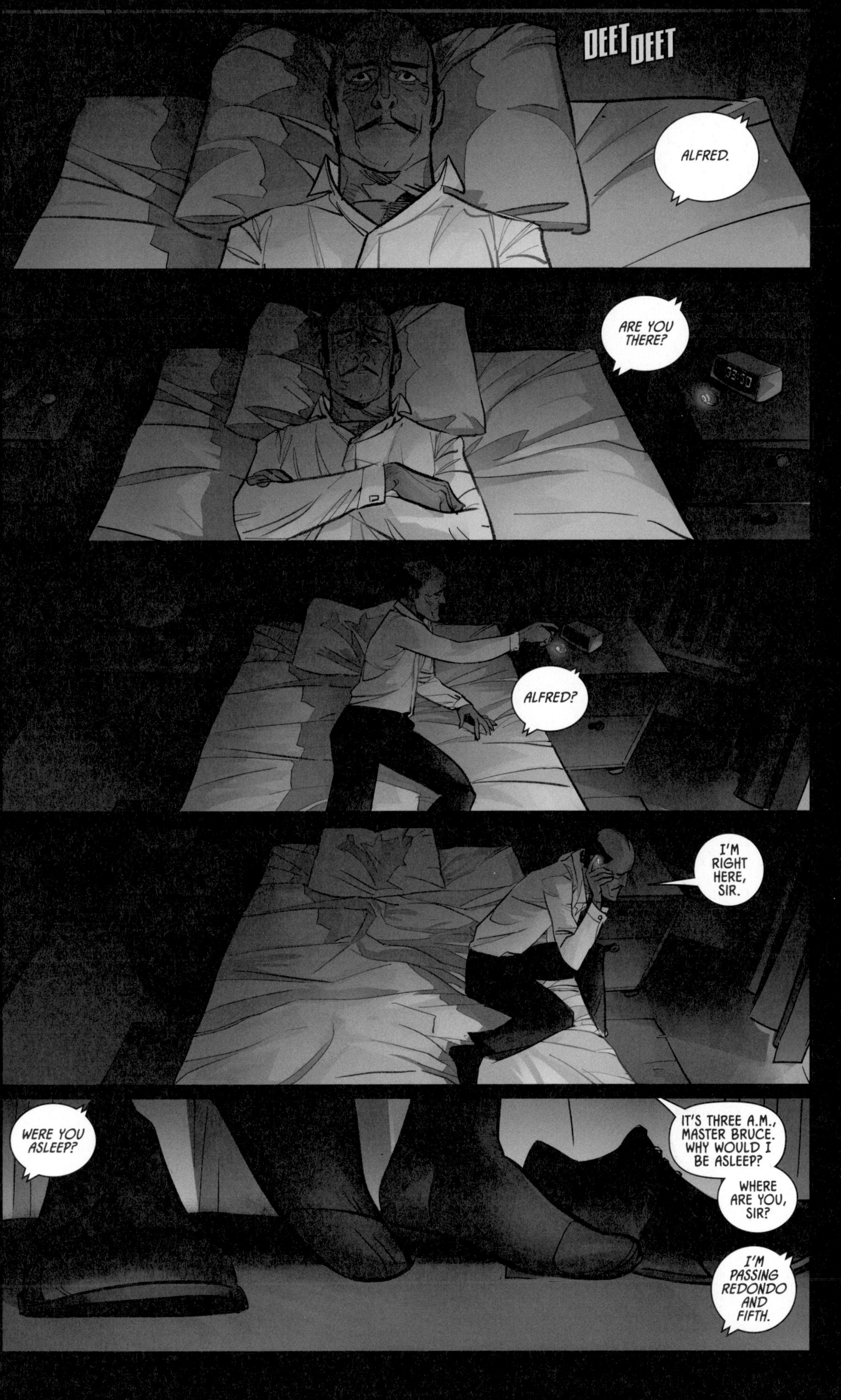
DEET DEET
ALFRED.
ARE YOU THERE?
ALFRED?
I'M RIGHT HERE, SIR.
WERE YOU ASLEEP?
IT'S THREE A.M., MASTER BRUCE. WHY WOULD I BE ASLEEP?
WHERE ARE YOU, SIR?
I'M PASSING REDONDO AND FIFTH.

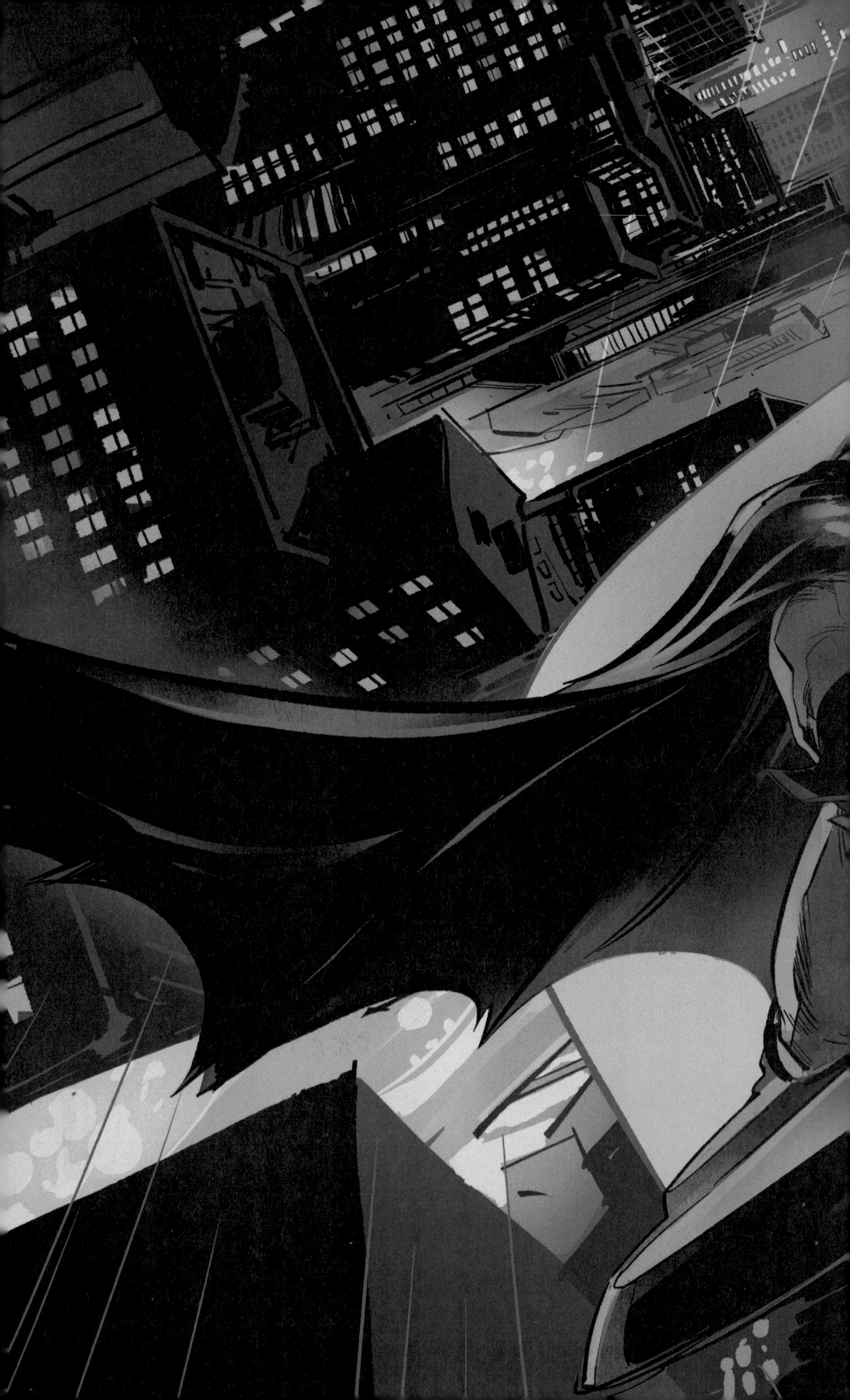

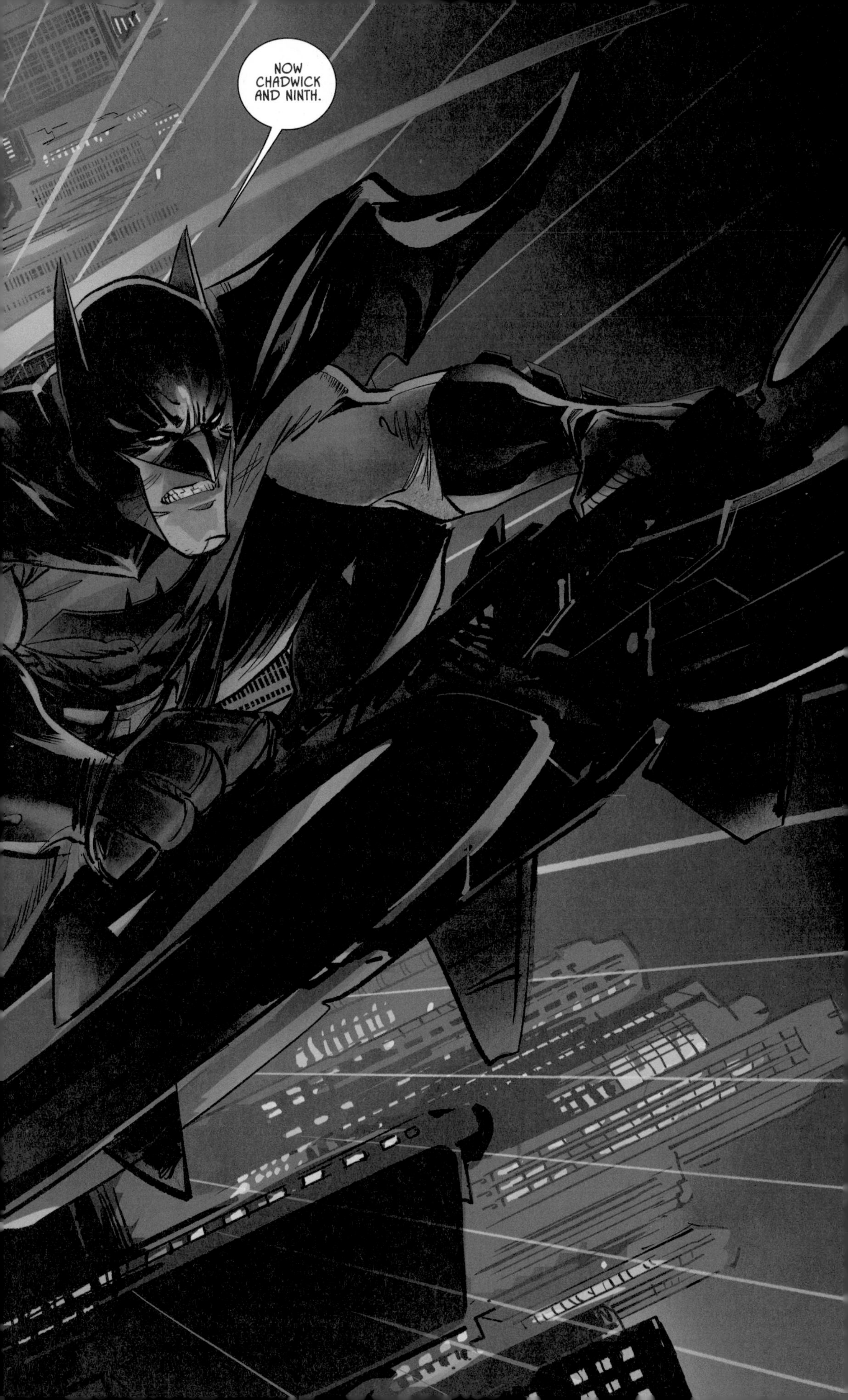
NOW CHADWICK AND NINTH.

YOU MOVED FOUR BLOCKS IN TWO SENTENCES?
I'M STEERING A PREDATOR DRONE AWAY FROM POPULATED AREAS. OUT TO THE HARBOR.
OF COURSE YOU ARE.
DEET
TSHHH

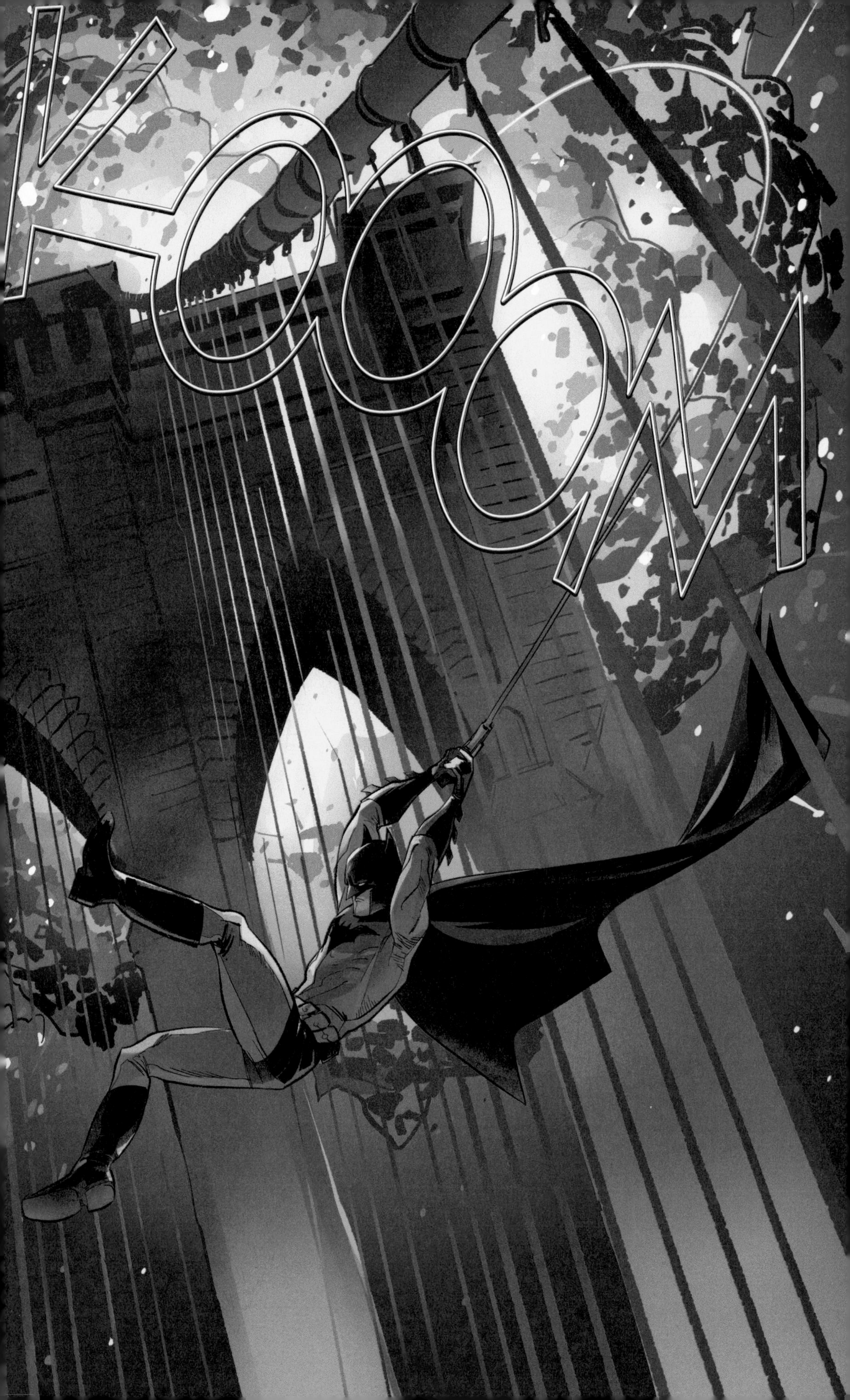
KOOOM

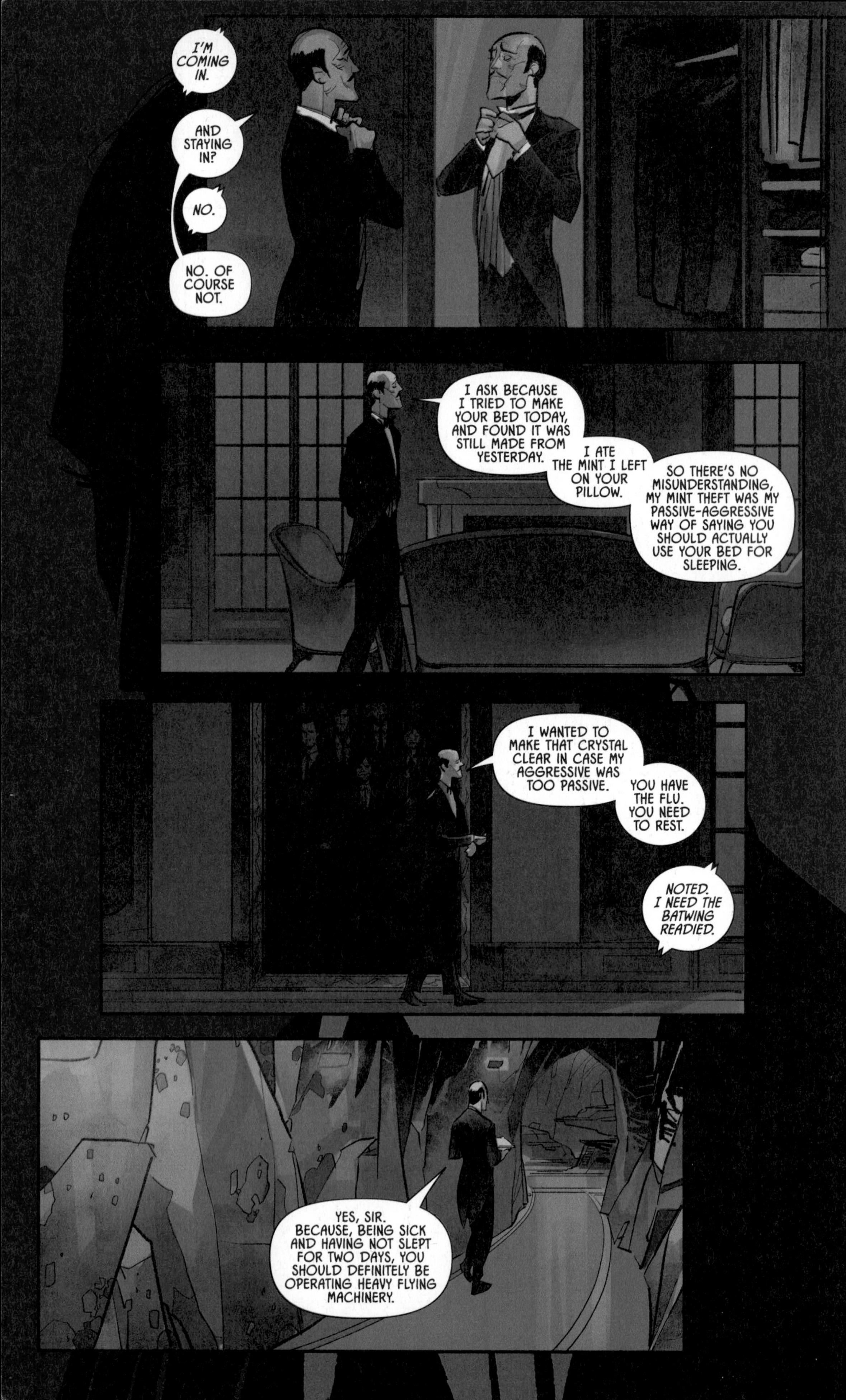
I'M COMING IN.
AND STAYING IN?
NO.
NO. OF COURSE NOT.
I ASK BECAUSE I TRIED TO MAKE YOUR BED TODAY, AND FOUND IT WAS STILL MADE FROM YESTERDAY.
I ATE THE MINT I LEFT ON YOUR PILLOW.
SO THERE'S NO MISUNDERSTANDING, MY MINT THEFT WAS MY PASSIVE-AGGRESSIVE WAY OF SAYING YOU SHOULD ACTUALLY USE YOUR BED FOR SLEEPING.
I WANTED TO MAKE THAT CRYSTAL CLEAR IN CASE MY AGGRESSIVE WAS TOO PASSIVE.
YOU HAVE THE FLU. YOU NEED TO REST.
NOTED. I NEED THE BATWING READIED.
YES, SIR. BECAUSE, BEING SICK AND HAVING NOT SLEPT FOR TWO DAYS, YOU SHOULD DEFINITELY BE OPERATING HEAVY FLYING MACHINERY.

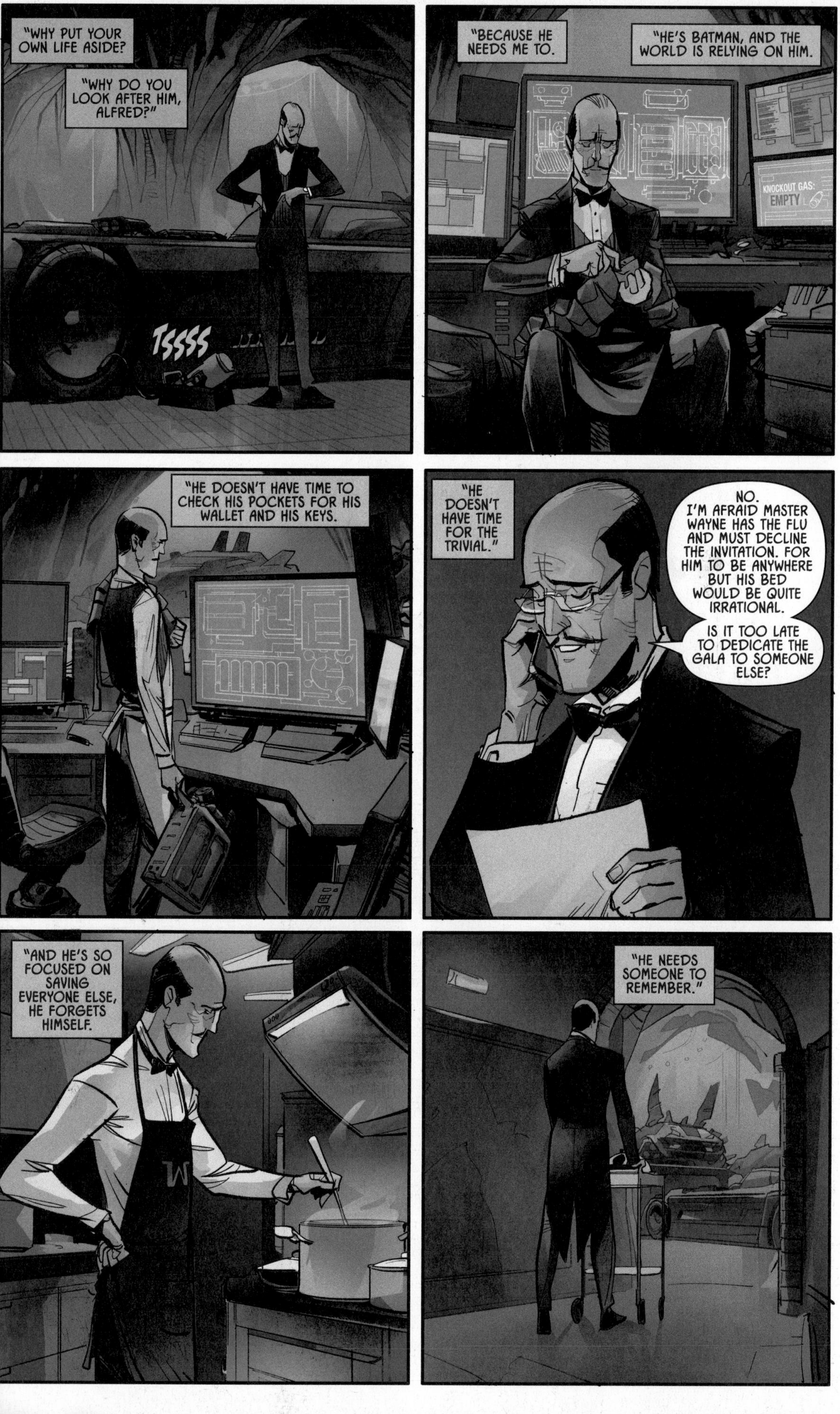
"WHY PUT YOUR OWN LIFE ASIDE?
"WHY DO YOU LOOK AFTER HIM, ALFRED?"
TSSSS
"BECAUSE HE NEEDS ME TO.
"HE'S BATMAN, AND THE WORLD IS RELYING ON HIM.
KNOCKOUT GAS: EMPTY
"HE DOESN'T HAVE TIME TO CHECK HIS POCKETS FOR HIS WALLET AND HIS KEYS.
"HE DOESN'T HAVE TIME FOR THE TRIVIAL."
NO. I'M AFRAID MASTER WAYNE HAS THE FLU AND MUST DECLINE THE INVITATION. FOR HIM TO BE ANYWHERE BUT HIS BED WOULD BE QUITE IRRATIONAL.
IS IT TOO LATE TO DEDICATE THE GALA TO SOMEONE ELSE?
"AND HE'S SO FOCUSED ON SAVING EVERYONE ELSE, HE FORGETS HIMSELF.
"HE NEEDS SOMEONE TO REMEMBER."

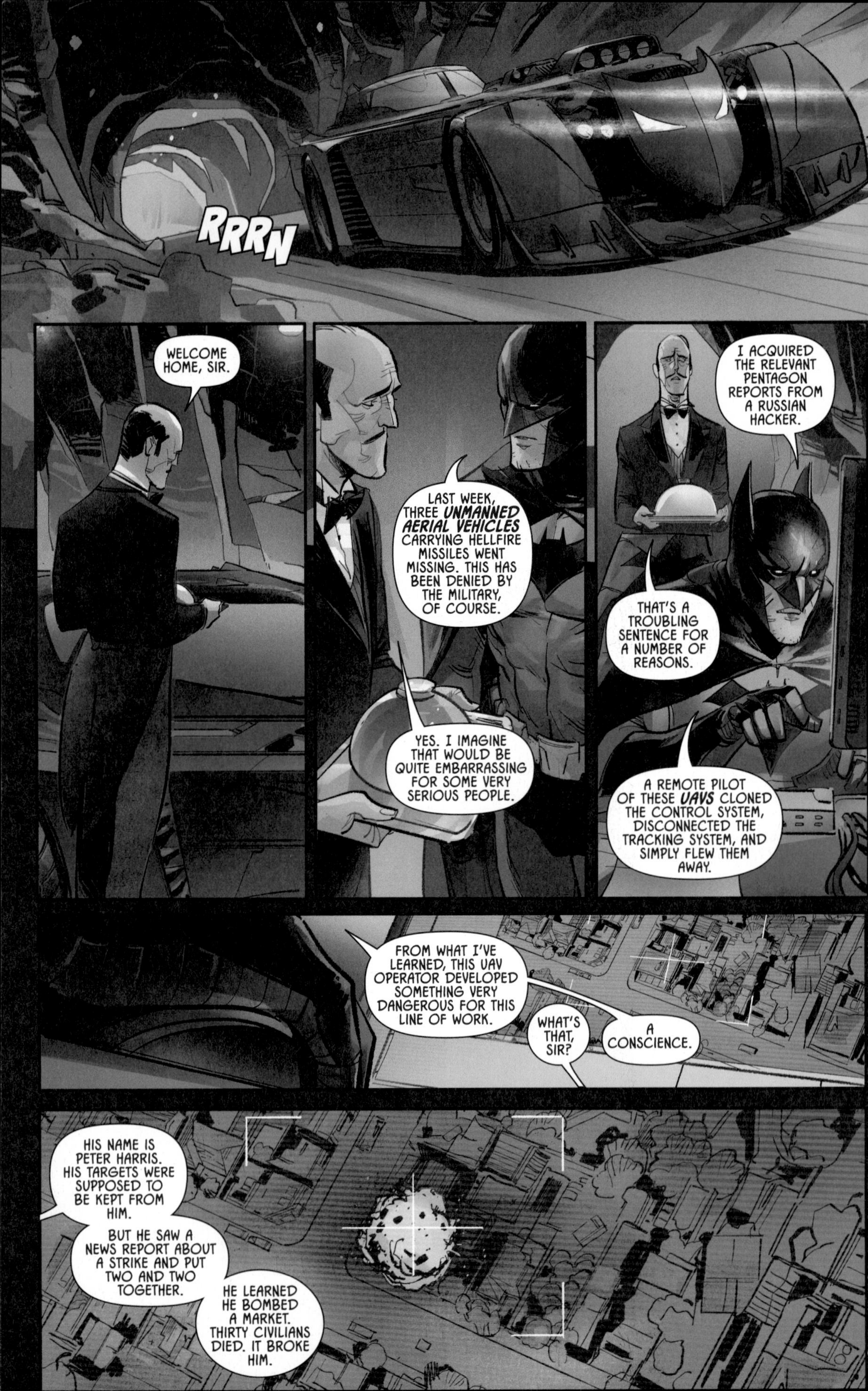
RRRN
WELCOME HOME, SIR.
LAST WEEK, THREE UNMANNED AERIAL VEHICLES CARRYING HELLFIRE MISSILES WENT MISSING. THIS HAS BEEN DENIED BY THE MILITARY, OF COURSE.
YES. I IMAGINE THAT WOULD BE QUITE EMBARRASSING FOR SOME VERY SERIOUS PEOPLE.
I ACQUIRED THE RELEVANT PENTAGON REPORTS FROM A RUSSIAN HACKER.
THAT'S A TROUBLING SENTENCE FOR A NUMBER OF REASONS.
A REMOTE PILOT OF THESE UAVS CLONED THE CONTROL SYSTEM, DISCONNECTED THE TRACKING SYSTEM, AND SIMPLY FLEW THEM AWAY.
FROM WHAT I'VE LEARNED, THIS UAV OPERATOR DEVELOPED SOMETHING VERY DANGEROUS FOR THIS LINE OF WORK.
WHAT'S THAT, SIR?
A CONSCIENCE.
HIS NAME IS PETER HARRIS. HIS TARGETS WERE SUPPOSED TO BE KEPT FROM HIM.
BUT HE SAW A NEWS REPORT ABOUT A STRIKE AND PUT TWO AND TWO TOGETHER.
HE LEARNED HE BOMBED A MARKET. THIRTY CIVILIANS DIED. IT BROKE HIM.

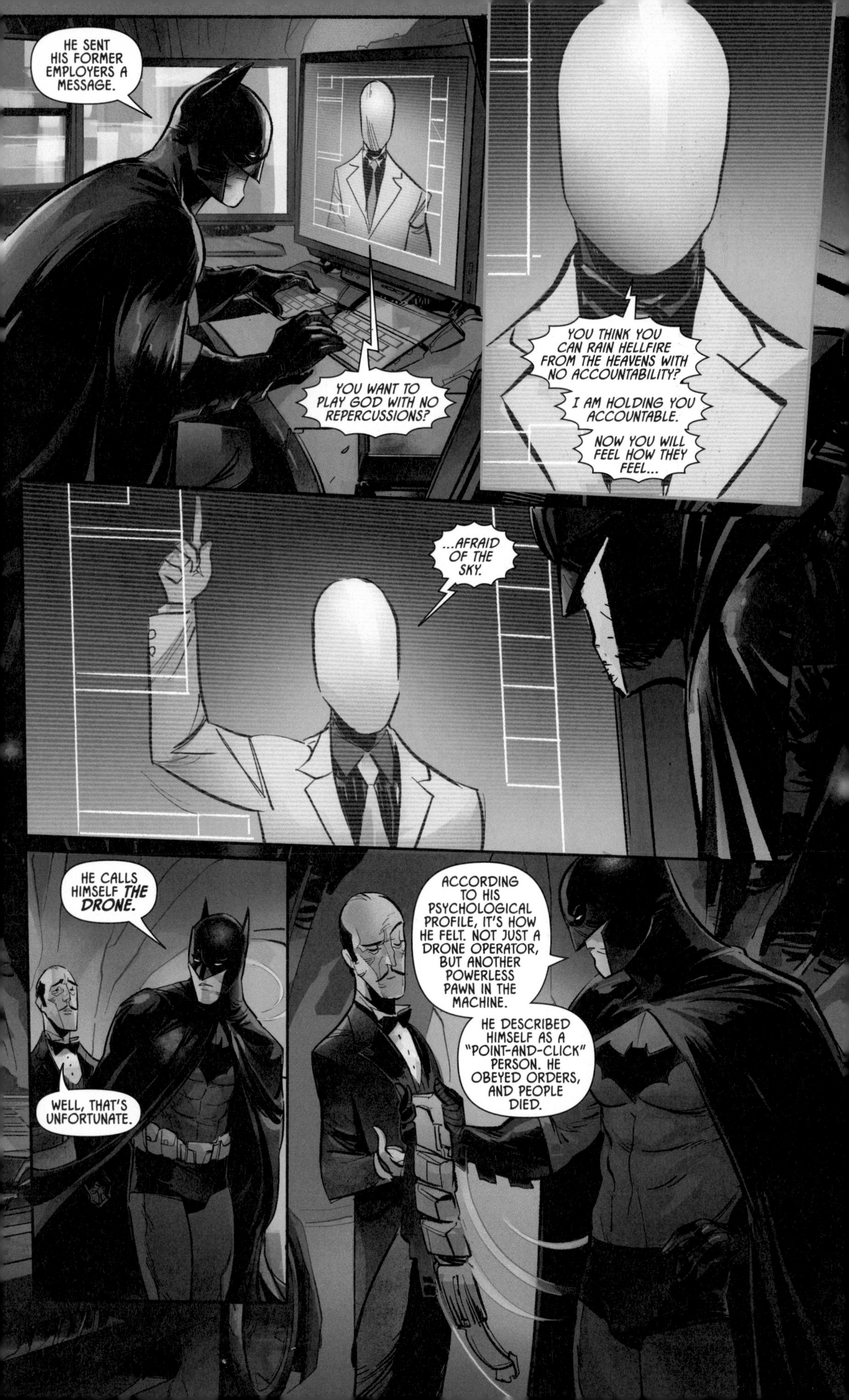
HE SENT HIS FORMER EMPLOYERS A MESSAGE.
YOU WANT TO PLAY GOD WITH NO REPERCUSSIONS?
YOU THINK YOU CAN RAIN HELLFIRE FROM THE HEAVENS WITH NO ACCOUNTABILITY?
I AM HOLDING YOU ACCOUNTABLE.
NOW YOU WILL FEEL HOW THEY FEEL...
...AFRAID OF THE SKY.
HE CALLS HIMSELF ***THE DRONE.***
WELL, THAT'S UNFORTUNATE.
ACCORDING TO HIS PSYCHOLOGICAL PROFILE, IT'S HOW HE FELT. NOT JUST A DRONE OPERATOR, BUT ANOTHER POWERLESS PAWN IN THE MACHINE.
HE DESCRIBED HIMSELF AS A "POINT-AND-CLICK" PERSON. HE OBEYED ORDERS, AND PEOPLE DIED.

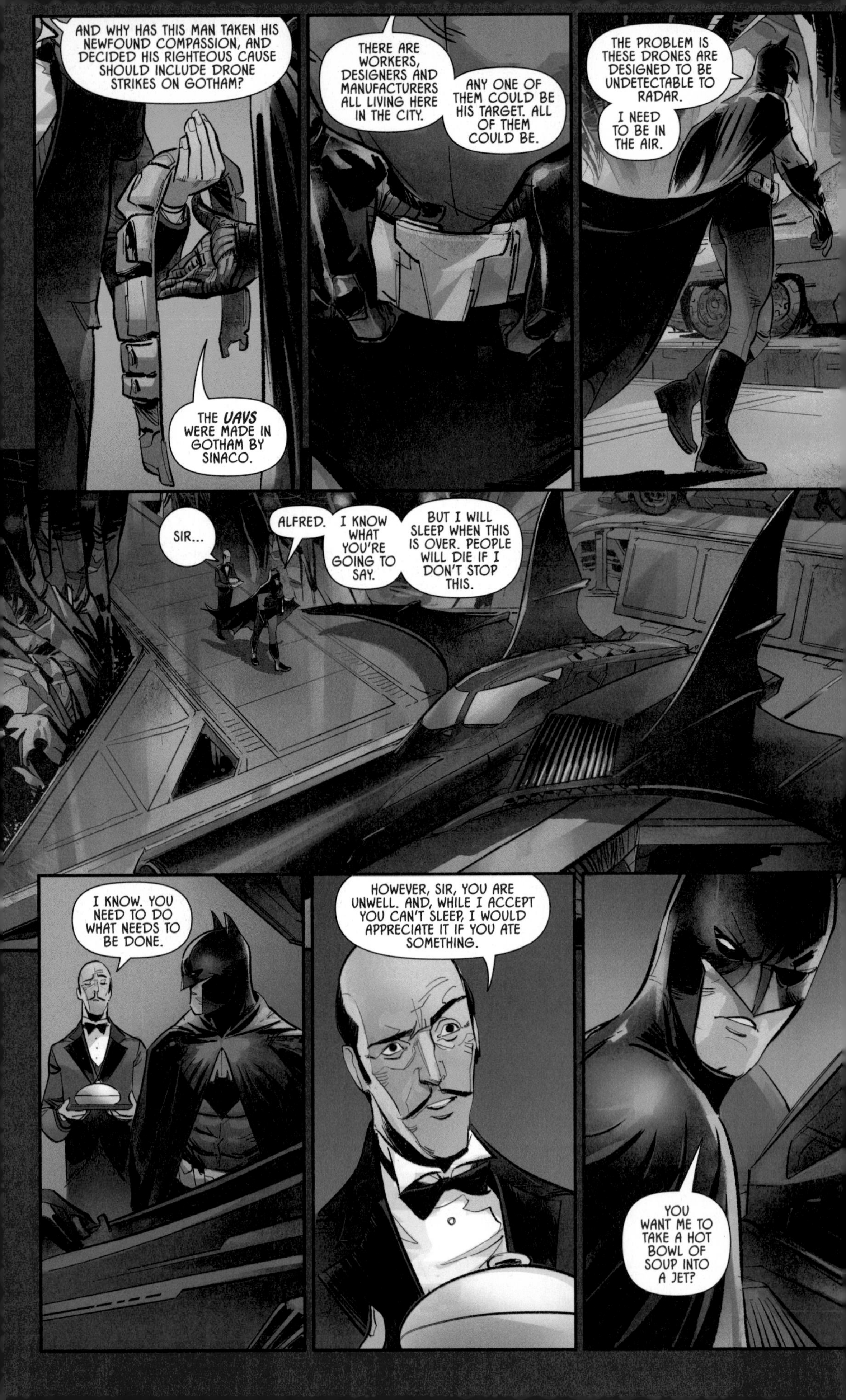
AND WHY HAS THIS MAN TAKEN HIS NEWFOUND COMPASSION, AND DECIDED HIS RIGHTEOUS CAUSE SHOULD INCLUDE DRONE STRIKES ON GOTHAM?
THE UAVS WERE MADE IN GOTHAM BY SINACO.
THERE ARE WORKERS, DESIGNERS AND MANUFACTURERS ALL LIVING HERE IN THE CITY.
ANY ONE OF THEM COULD BE HIS TARGET. ALL OF THEM COULD BE.
THE PROBLEM IS THESE DRONES ARE DESIGNED TO BE UNDETECTABLE TO RADAR.
I NEED TO BE IN THE AIR.
SIR...
ALFRED.
I KNOW WHAT YOU'RE GOING TO SAY.
BUT I WILL SLEEP WHEN THIS IS OVER. PEOPLE WILL DIE IF I DON'T STOP THIS.
I KNOW. YOU NEED TO DO WHAT NEEDS TO BE DONE.
HOWEVER, SIR, YOU ARE UNWELL. AND, WHILE I ACCEPT YOU CAN'T SLEEP, I WOULD APPRECIATE IT IF YOU ATE SOMETHING.
YOU WANT ME TO TAKE A HOT BOWL OF SOUP INTO A JET?

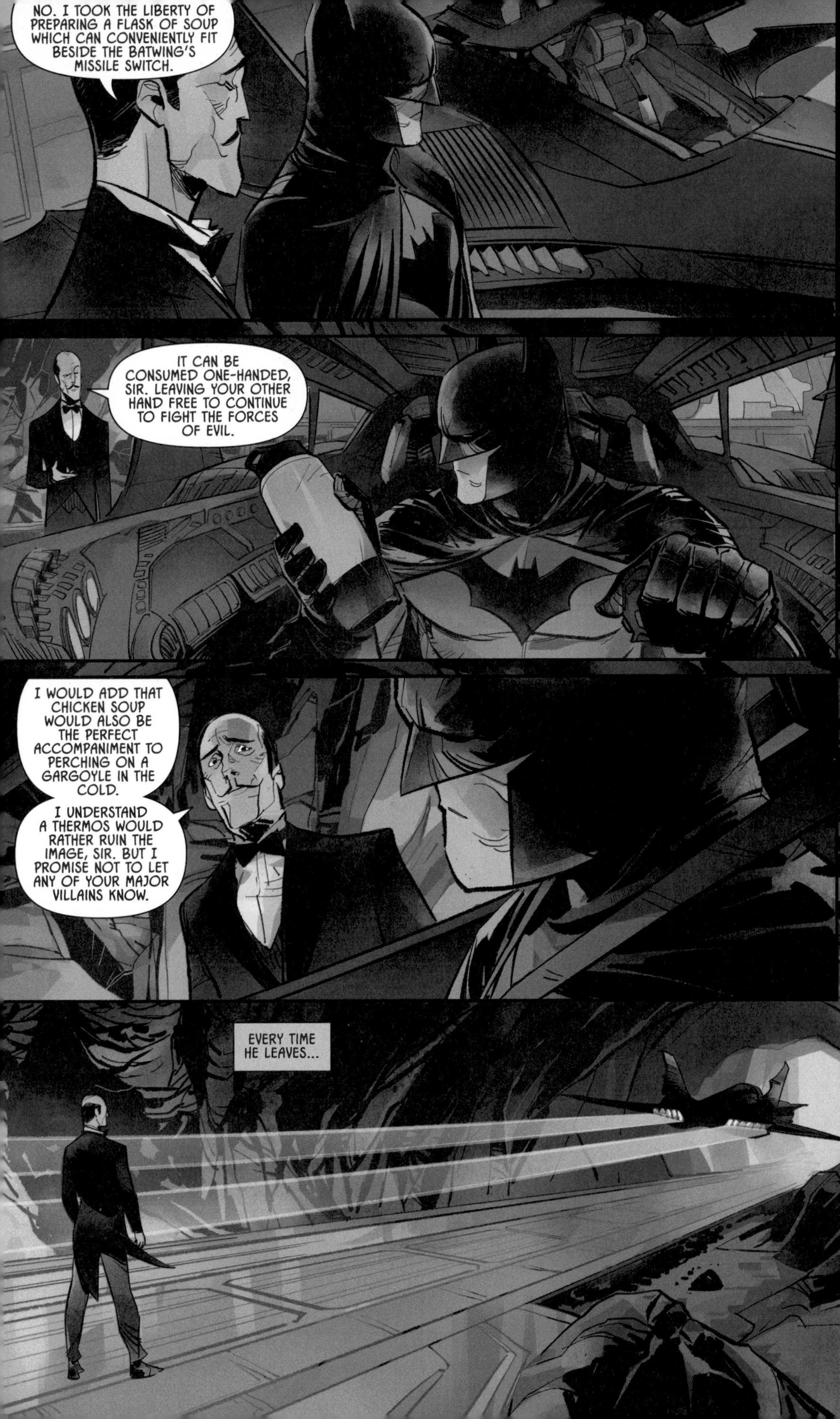
NO. I TOOK THE LIBERTY OF PREPARING A FLASK OF SOUP WHICH CAN CONVENIENTLY FIT BESIDE THE BATWING'S MISSILE SWITCH.
IT CAN BE CONSUMED ONE-HANDED, SIR. LEAVING YOUR OTHER HAND FREE TO CONTINUE TO FIGHT THE FORCES OF EVIL.
I WOULD ADD THAT CHICKEN SOUP WOULD ALSO BE THE PERFECT ACCOMPANIMENT TO PERCHING ON A GARGOYLE IN THE COLD.
I UNDERSTAND A THERMOS WOULD RATHER RUIN THE IMAGE, SIR. BUT I PROMISE NOT TO LET ANY OF YOUR MAJOR VILLAINS KNOW.
EVERY TIME HE LEAVES...

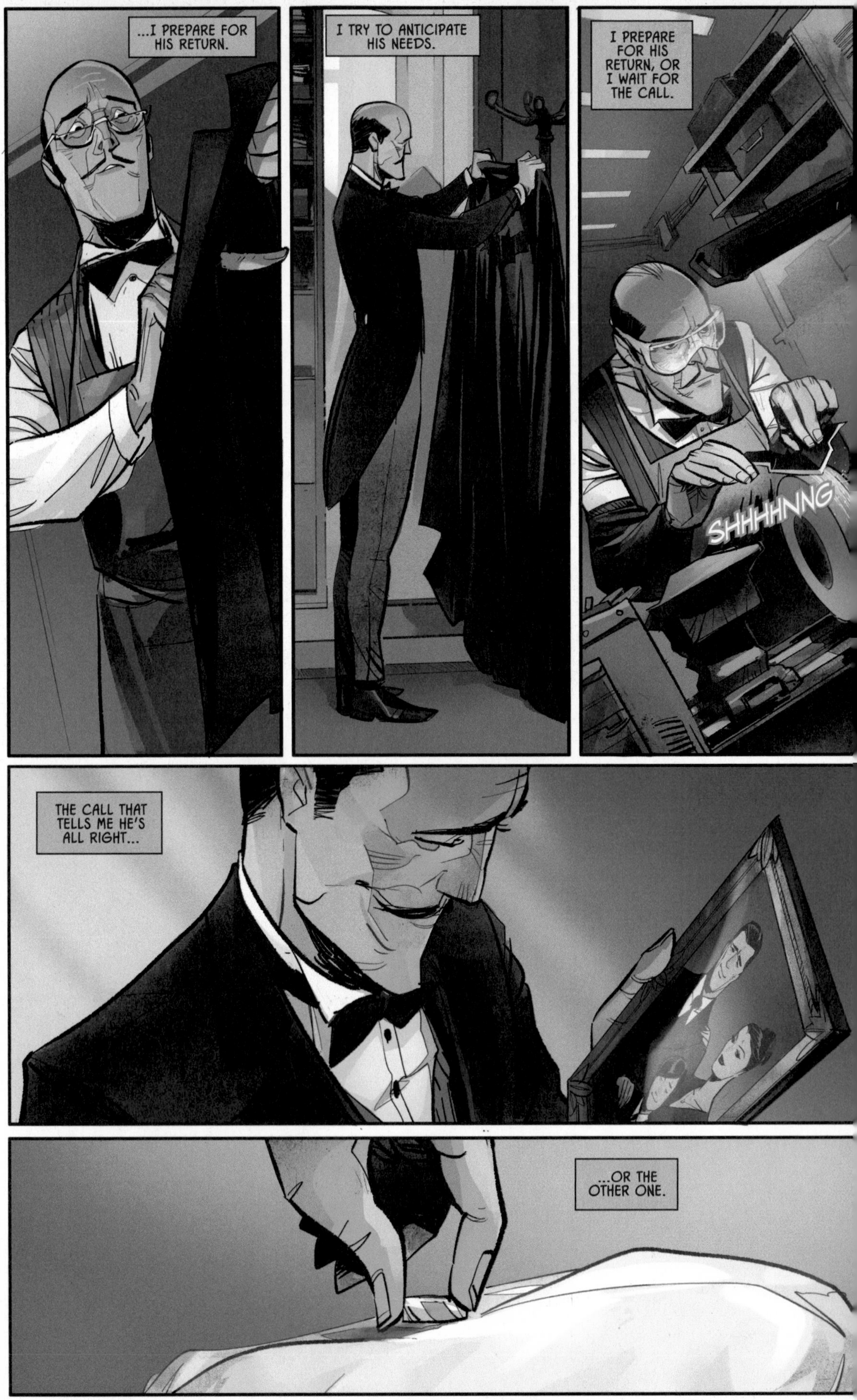
...I PREPARE FOR HIS RETURN.
I TRY TO ANTICIPATE HIS NEEDS.
I PREPARE FOR HIS RETURN, OR I WAIT FOR THE CALL.
SHHHHNNG
THE CALL THAT TELLS ME HE'S ALL RIGHT...
...OR THE OTHER ONE.

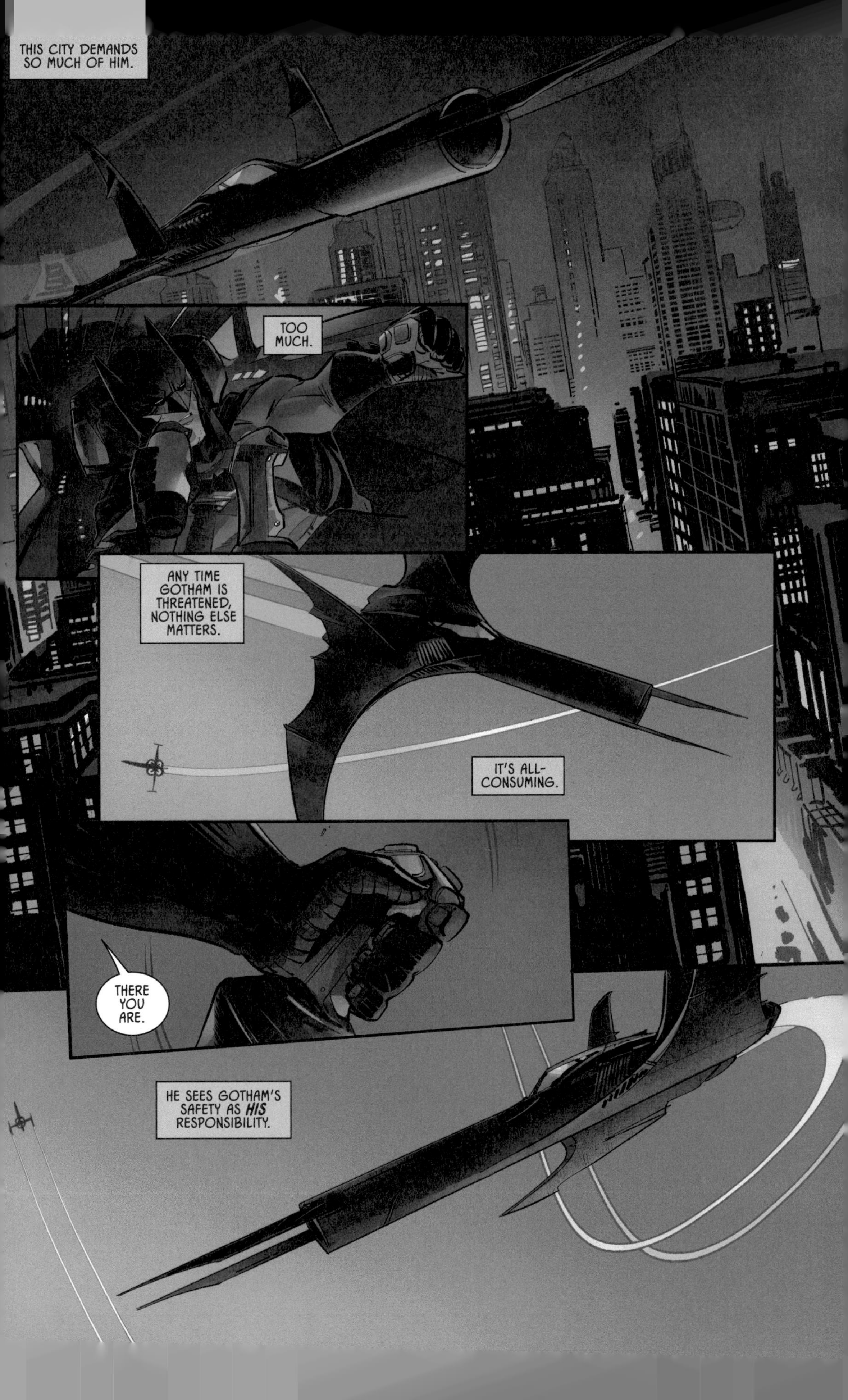
THIS CITY DEMANDS SO MUCH OF HIM.
TOO MUCH.
ANY TIME GOTHAM IS THREATENED, NOTHING ELSE MATTERS.
IT'S ALL-CONSUMING.
THERE YOU ARE.
HE SEES GOTHAM'S SAFETY AS HIS RESPONSIBILITY.

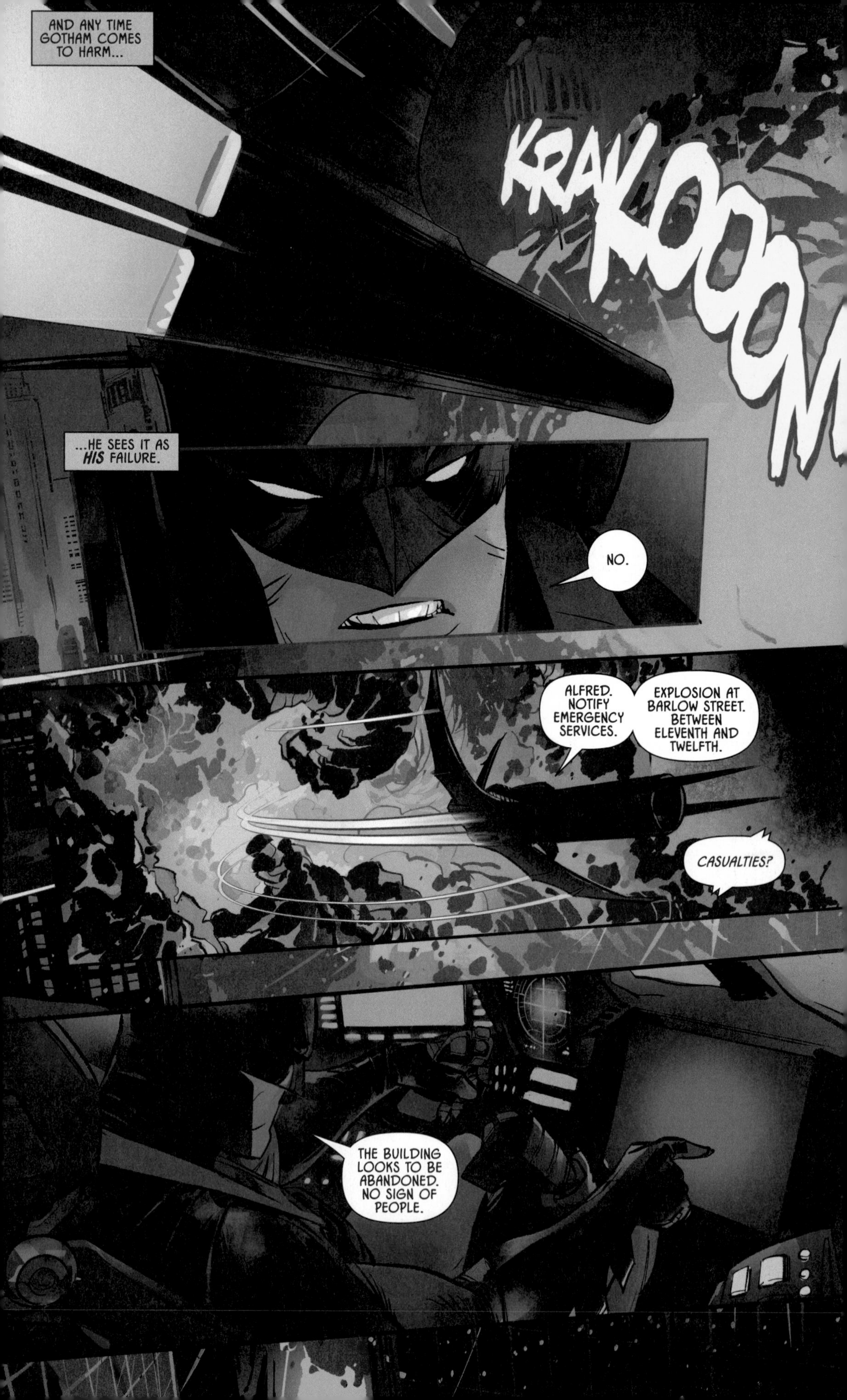
AND ANY TIME GOTHAM COMES TO HARM...
KRAKOOOM
...HE SEES IT AS HIS FAILURE.
NO.
ALFRED. NOTIFY EMERGENCY SERVICES.
EXPLOSION AT BARLOW STREET. BETWEEN ELEVENTH AND TWELFTH.
CASUALTIES?
THE BUILDING LOOKS TO BE ABANDONED. NO SIGN OF PEOPLE.

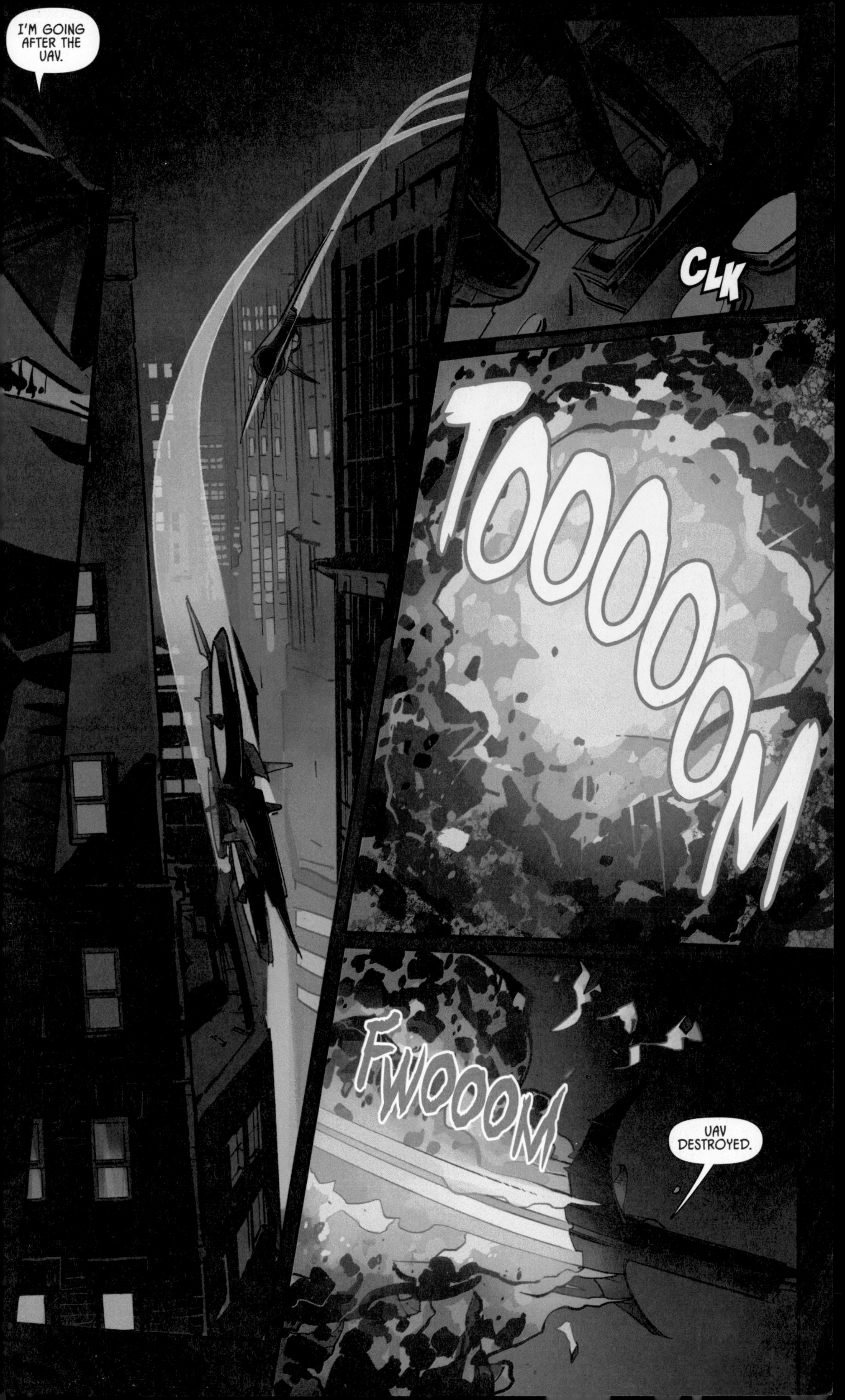
I'M GOING AFTER THE UAV.
CLK
TOOOOOOM
FWOOOM
UAV DESTROYED.

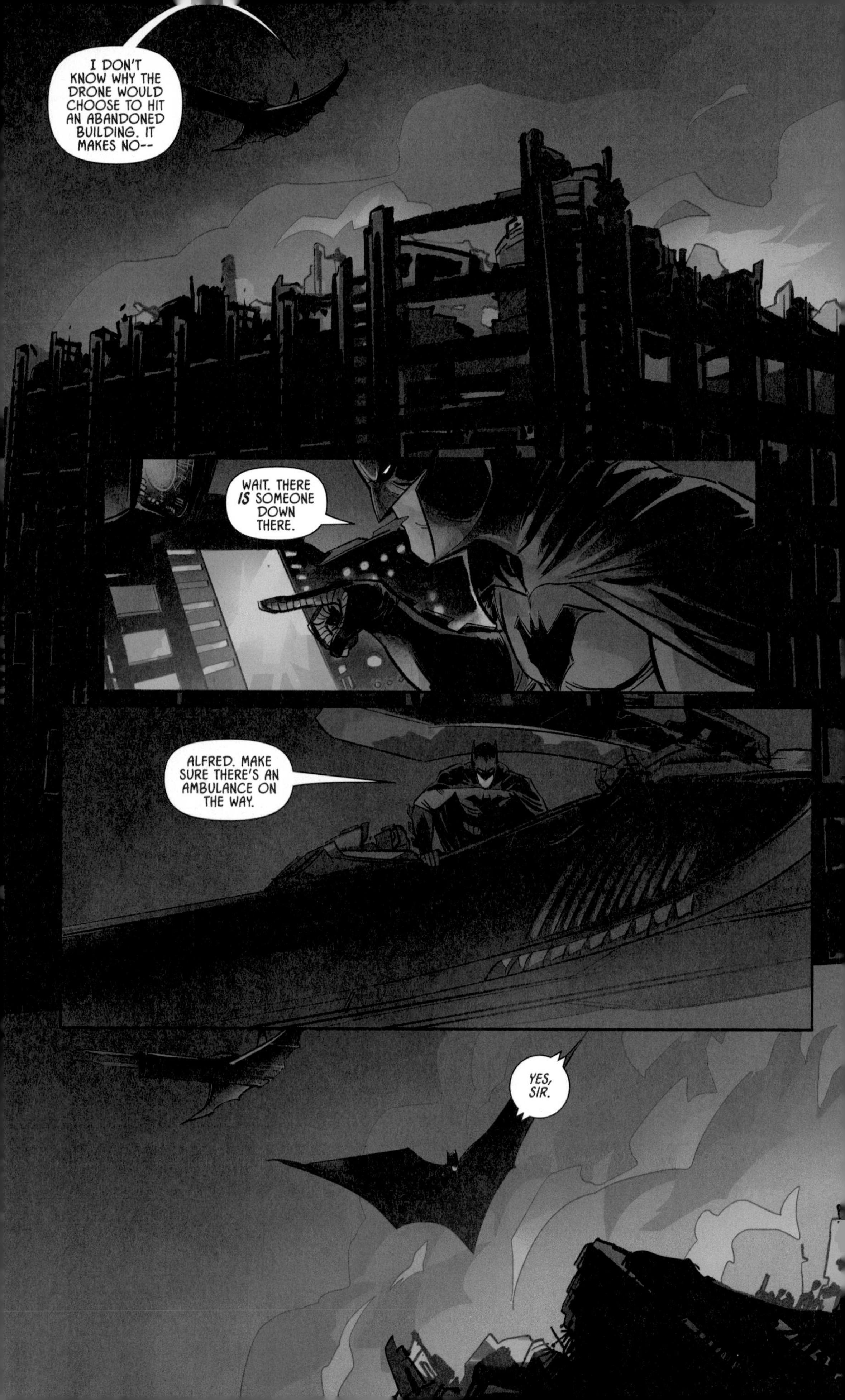
I DON'T KNOW WHY THE DRONE WOULD CHOOSE TO HIT AN ABANDONED BUILDING. IT MAKES NO--
WAIT. THERE *IS* SOMEONE DOWN THERE.
ALFRED. MAKE SURE THERE'S AN AMBULANCE ON THE WAY.
YES, SIR.

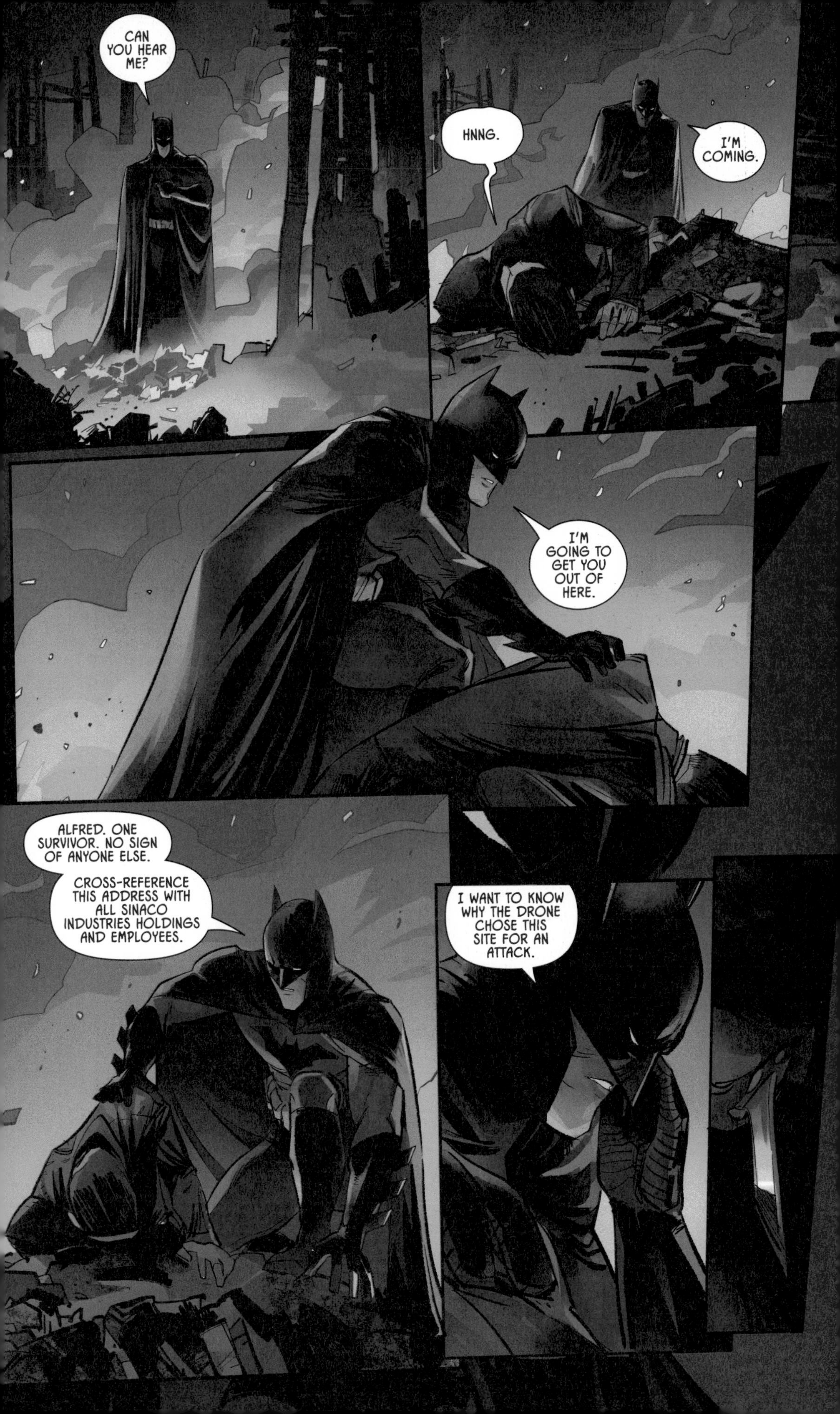
CAN YOU HEAR ME?
HNNG.
I'M COMING.
I'M GOING TO GET YOU OUT OF HERE.
ALFRED. ONE SURVIVOR. NO SIGN OF ANYONE ELSE.
CROSS-REFERENCE THIS ADDRESS WITH ALL SINACO INDUSTRIES HOLDINGS AND EMPLOYEES.
I WANT TO KNOW WHY THE DRONE CHOSE THIS SITE FOR AN ATTACK.

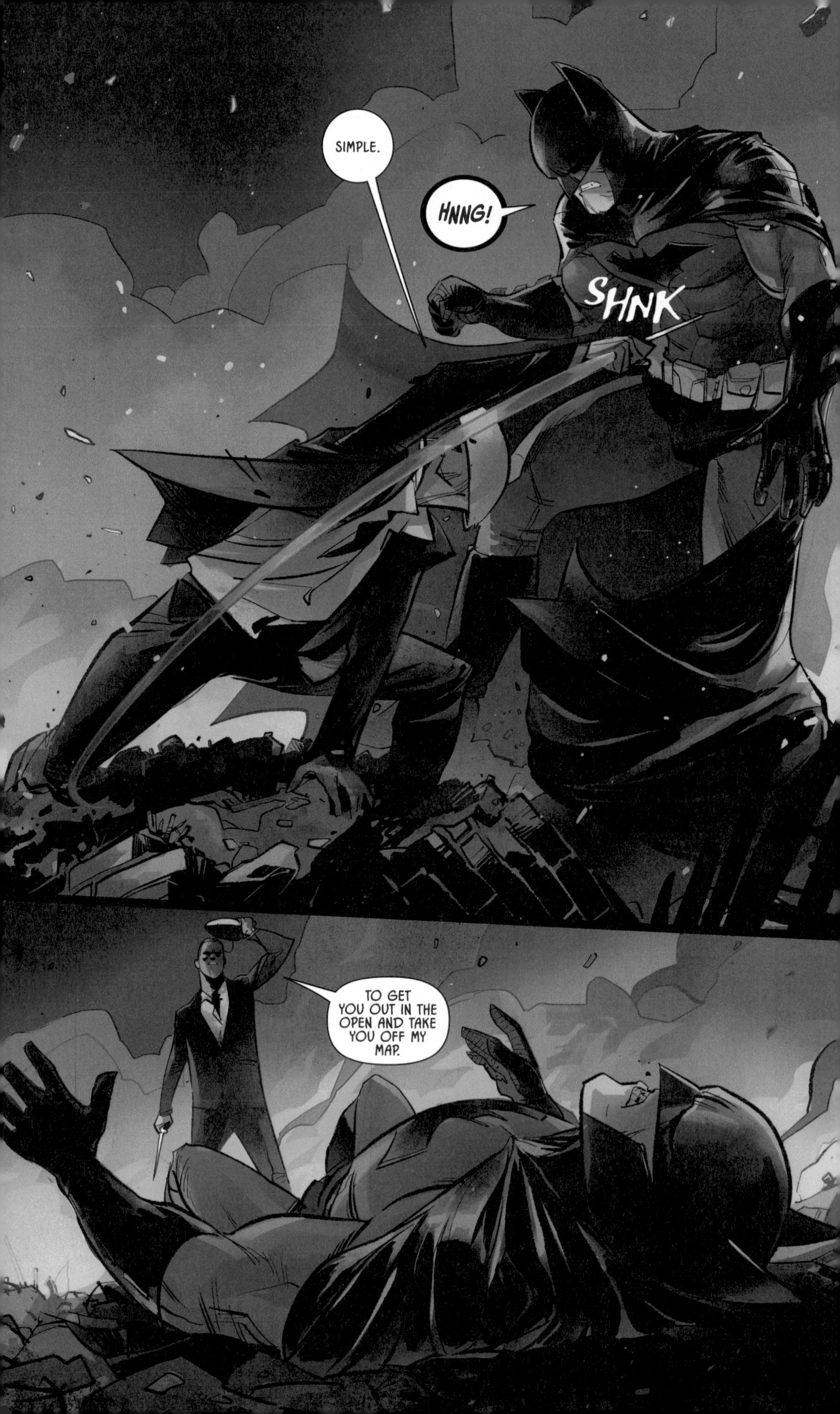
SIMPLE.
HNNG!
SHNK
TO GET YOU OUT IN THE OPEN AND TAKE YOU OFF MY MAP.

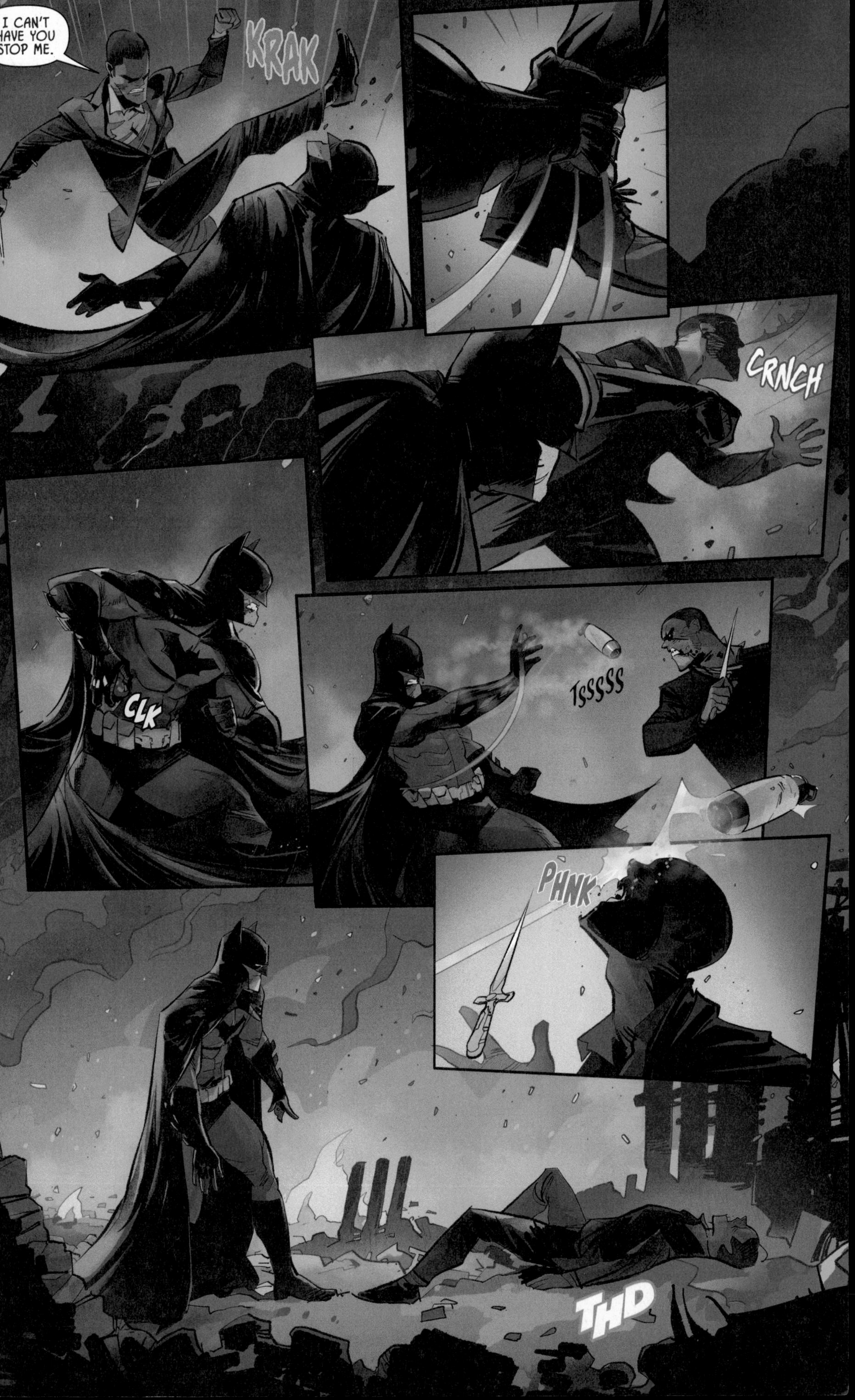
I CAN'T HAVE YOU STOP ME.
KRAK
CRNCH
CLK
TSSSSS
PHNK
THD

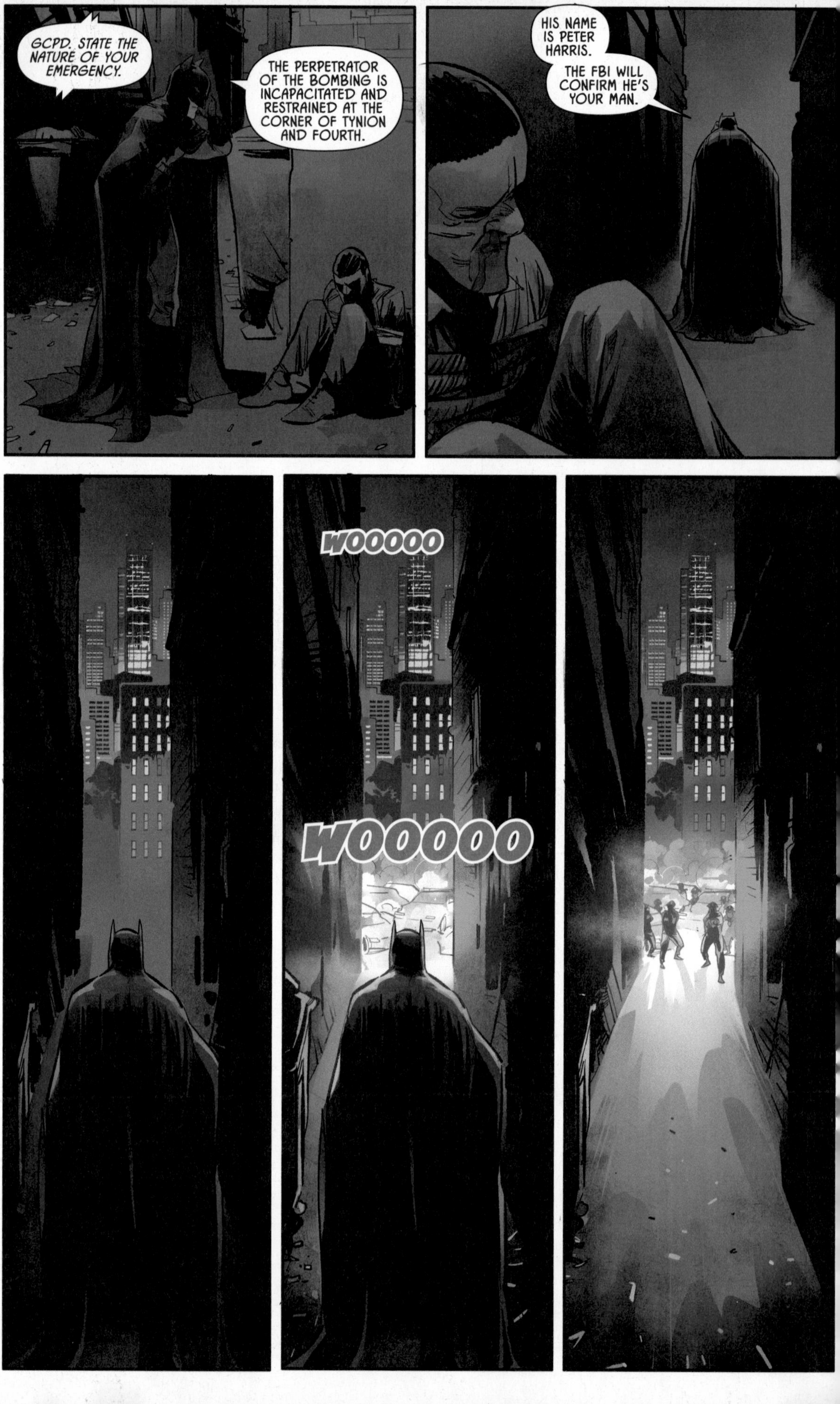
GCPD. STATE THE NATURE OF YOUR EMERGENCY.
THE PERPETRATOR OF THE BOMBING IS INCAPACITATED AND RESTRAINED AT THE CORNER OF TYNION AND FOURTH.
HIS NAME IS PETER HARRIS.
THE FBI WILL CONFIRM HE'S YOUR MAN.
WOOOOO
WOOOOO

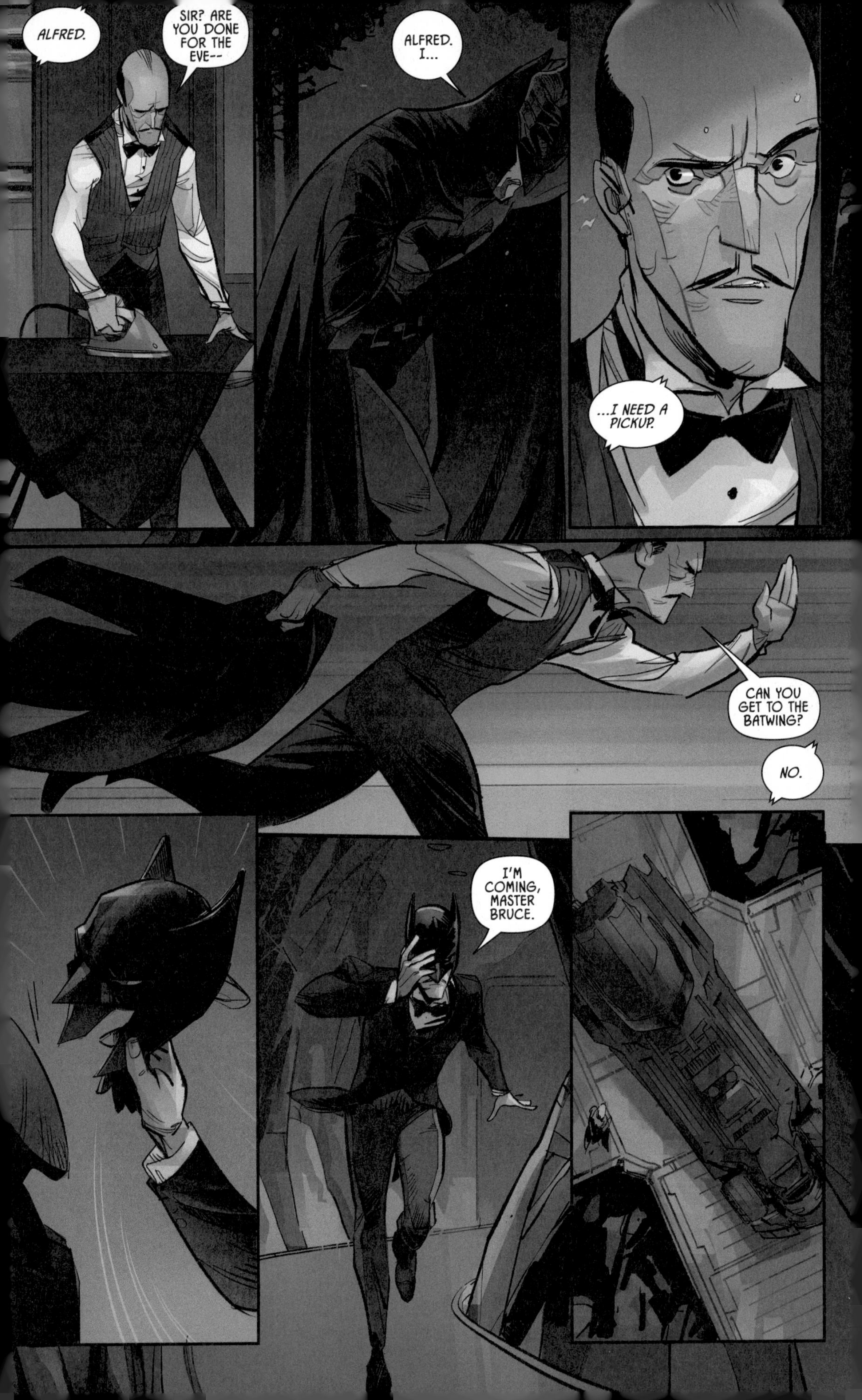
ALFRED.
SIR? ARE YOU DONE FOR THE EVE--
ALFRED. I...
...I NEED A PICKUP.
CAN YOU GET TO THE BATWING?
NO.
I'M COMING, MASTER BRUCE.

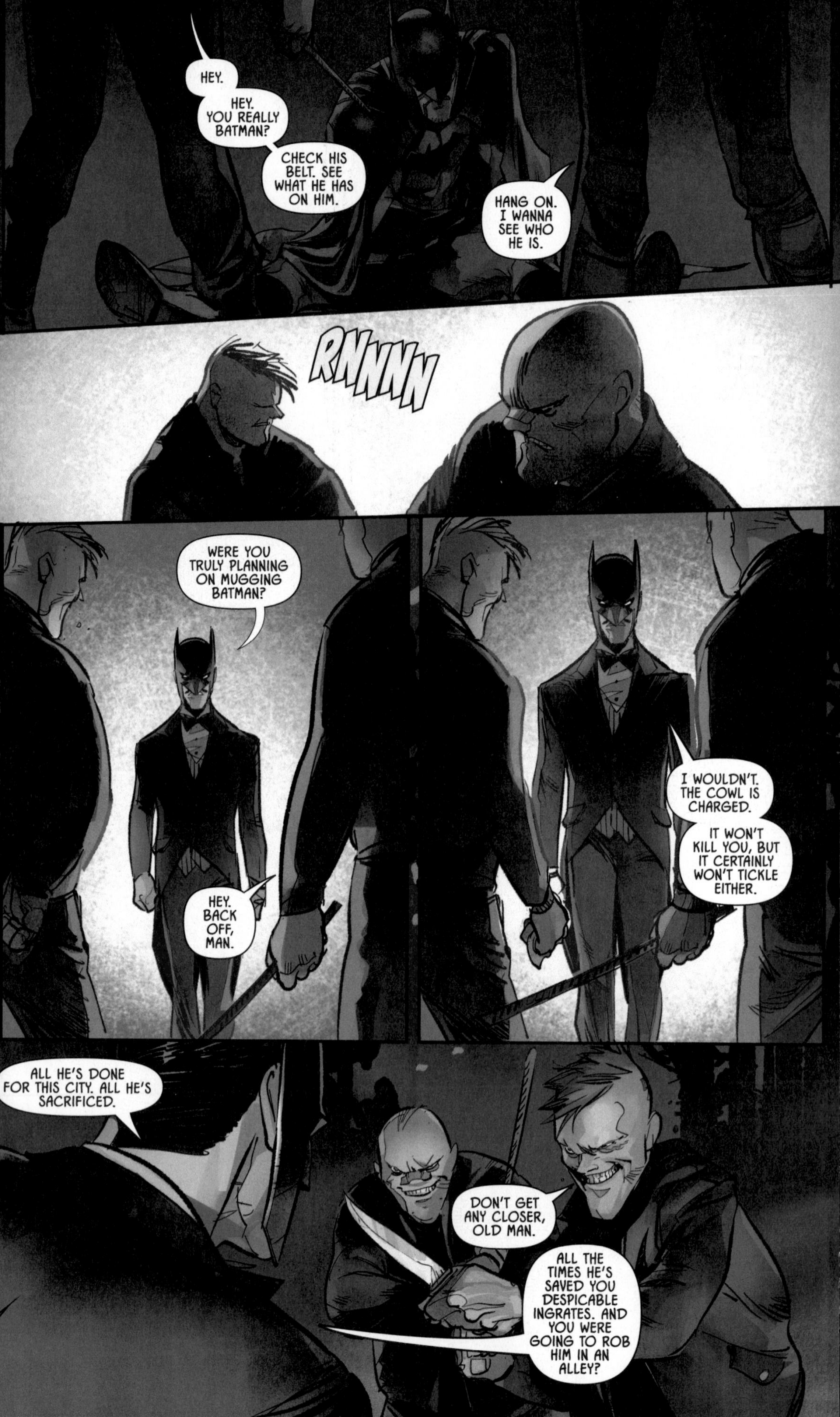
HEY.
HEY. YOU REALLY BATMAN?
CHECK HIS BELT. SEE WHAT HE HAS ON HIM.
HANG ON. I WANNA SEE WHO HE IS.
RNNNN
WERE YOU TRULY PLANNING ON MUGGING BATMAN?
HEY. BACK OFF, MAN.
I WOULDN'T. THE COWL IS CHARGED.
IT WON'T KILL YOU, BUT IT CERTAINLY WON'T TICKLE EITHER.
ALL HE'S DONE FOR THIS CITY. ALL HE'S SACRIFICED.
DON'T GET ANY CLOSER, OLD MAN.
ALL THE TIMES HE'S SAVED YOU DESPICABLE INGRATES. AND YOU WERE GOING TO ROB HIM IN AN ALLEY?

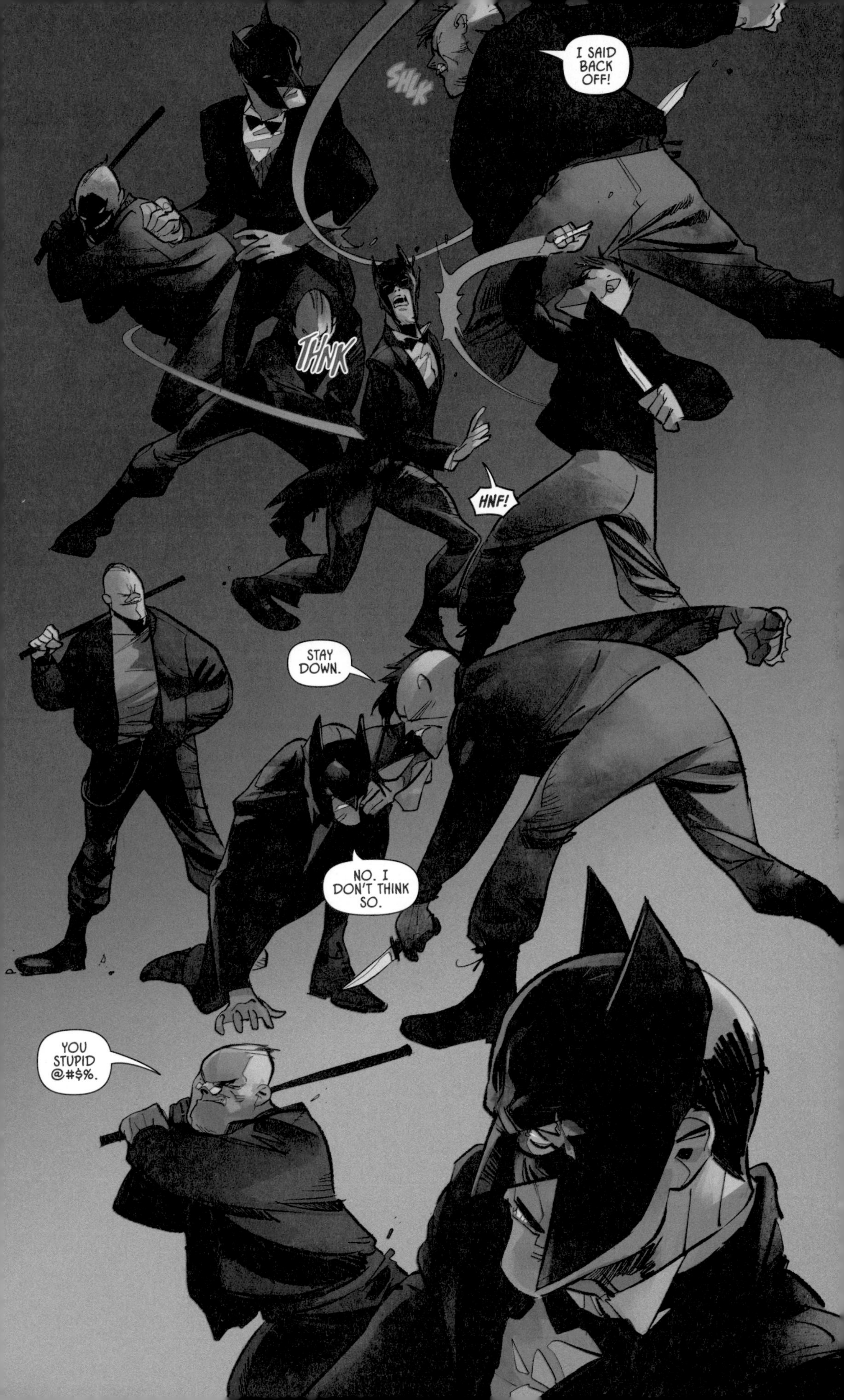
SHLK
I SAID BACK OFF!
THNK
HNF!
STAY DOWN.
NO. I DON'T THINK SO.
YOU STUPID @#$%.

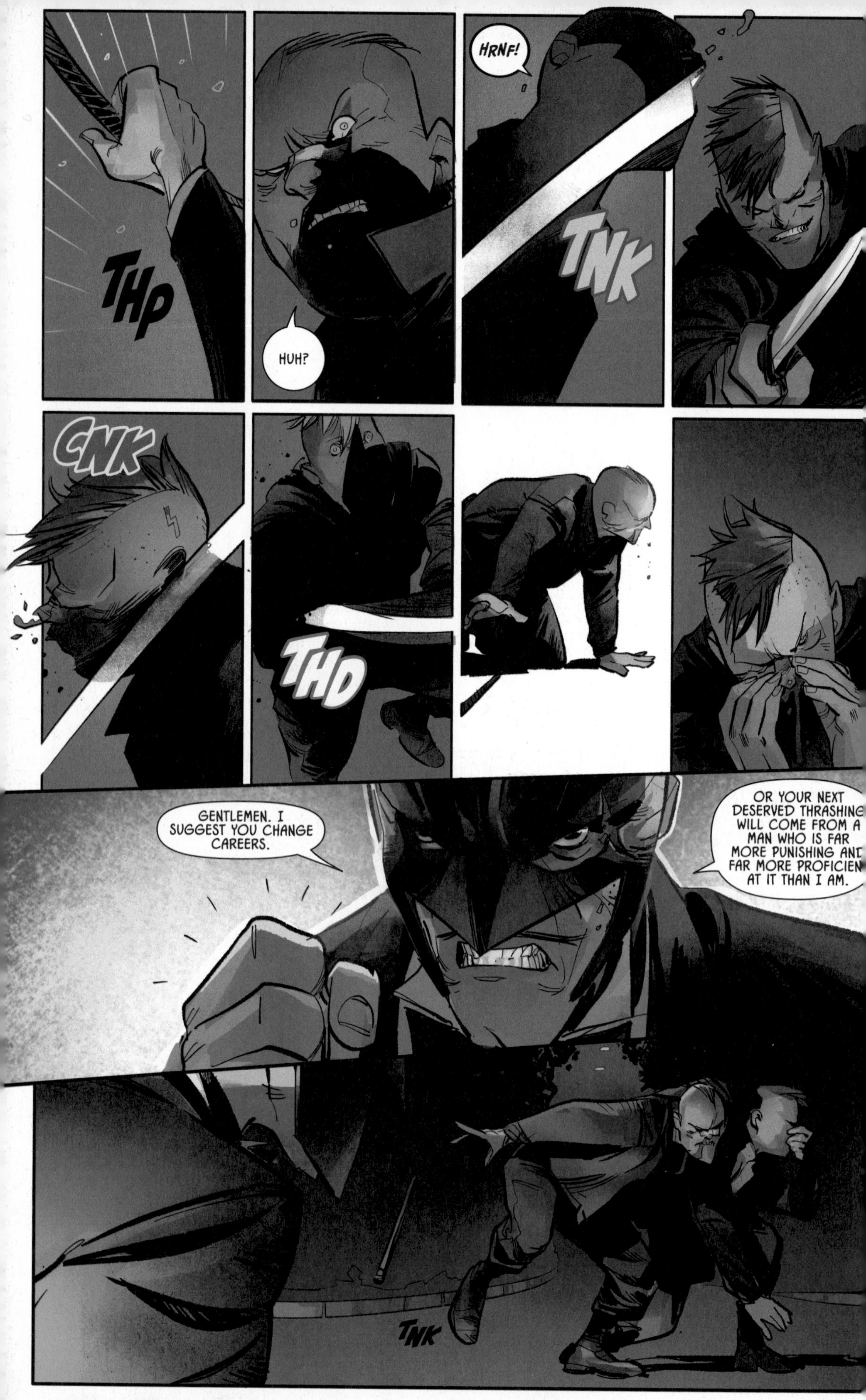
THP
HUH?
HRNF!
TNK
CNK
THD
GENTLEMEN. I SUGGEST YOU CHANGE CAREERS.
OR YOUR NEXT DESERVED THRASHING WILL COME FROM A MAN WHO IS FAR MORE PUNISHING AND FAR MORE PROFICIENT AT IT THAN I AM.
TNK

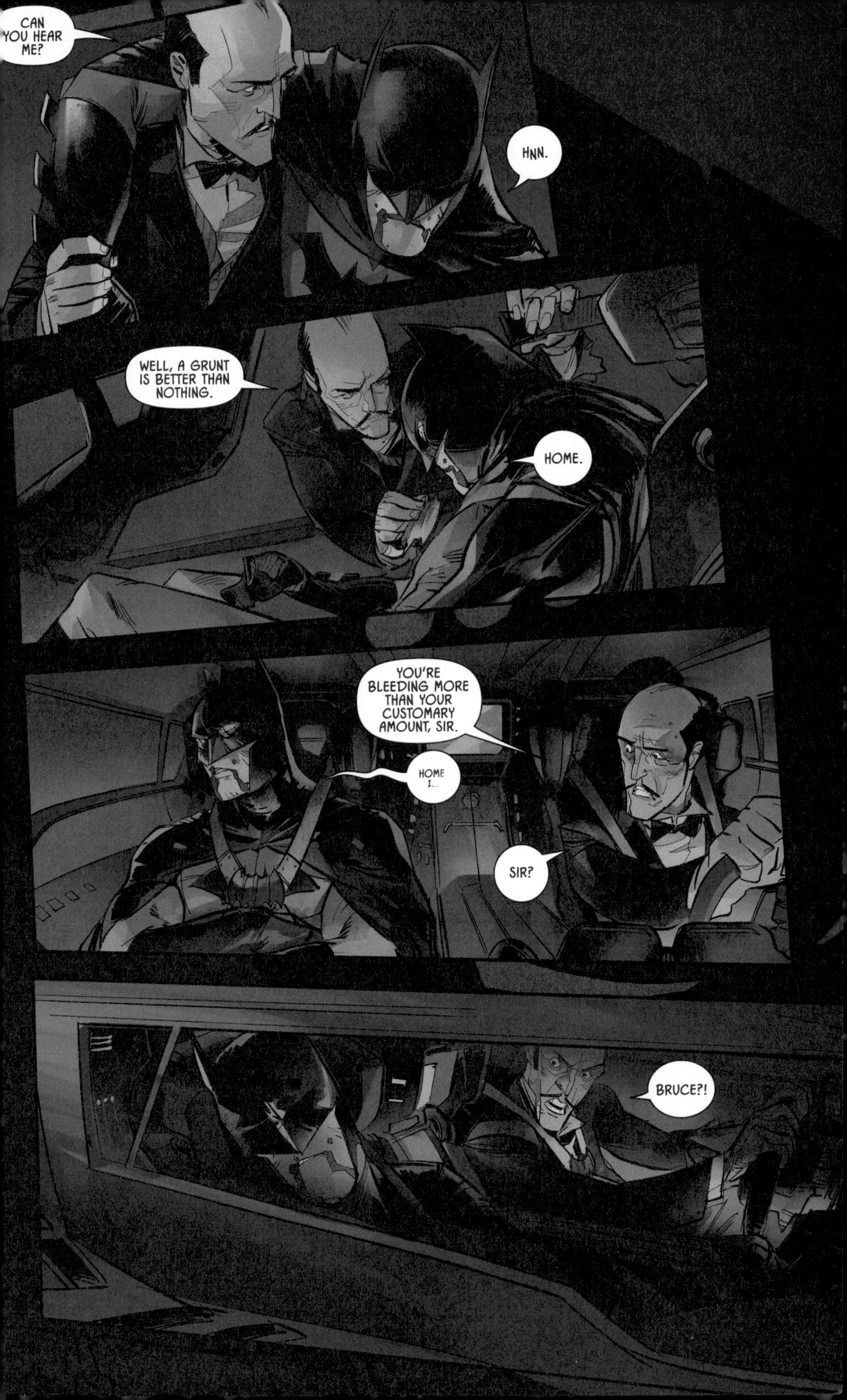
CAN YOU HEAR ME?
HNN.
WELL, A GRUNT IS BETTER THAN NOTHING.
HOME.
YOU'RE BLEEDING MORE THAN YOUR CUSTOMARY AMOUNT, SIR.
HOME. I...
SIR?
BRUCE?!

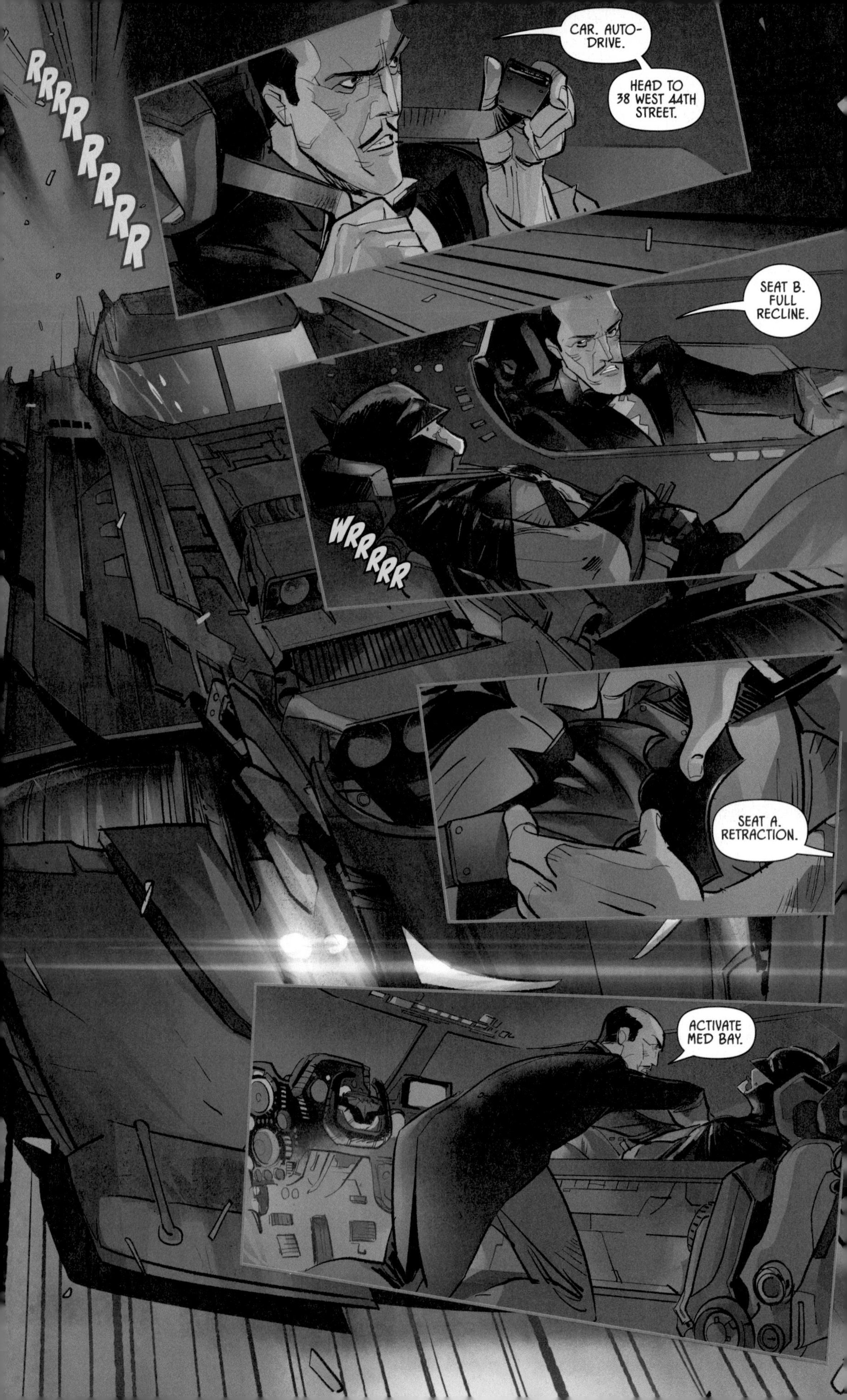
RRRRRRRRR
CAR. AUTO-DRIVE.
HEAD TO 38 WEST 44TH STREET.
SEAT B. FULL RECLINE.
WRRRRR
SEAT A. RETRACTION.
ACTIVATE MED BAY.

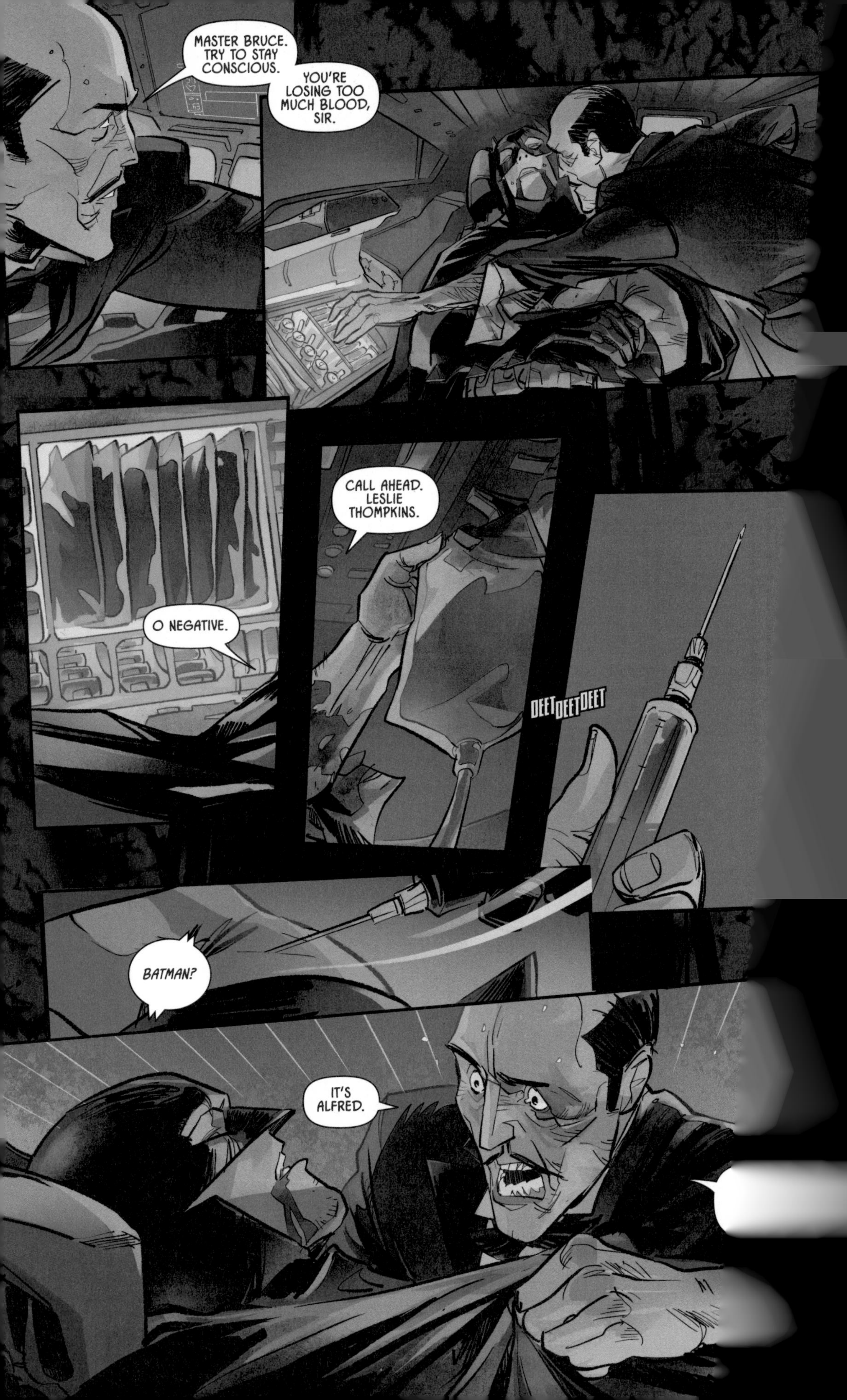
MASTER BRUCE. TRY TO STAY CONSCIOUS.
YOU'RE LOSING TOO MUCH BLOOD, SIR.
O NEGATIVE.
CALL AHEAD. LESLIE THOMPKINS.
DEETDEETDEET
BATMAN?
IT'S ALFRED.

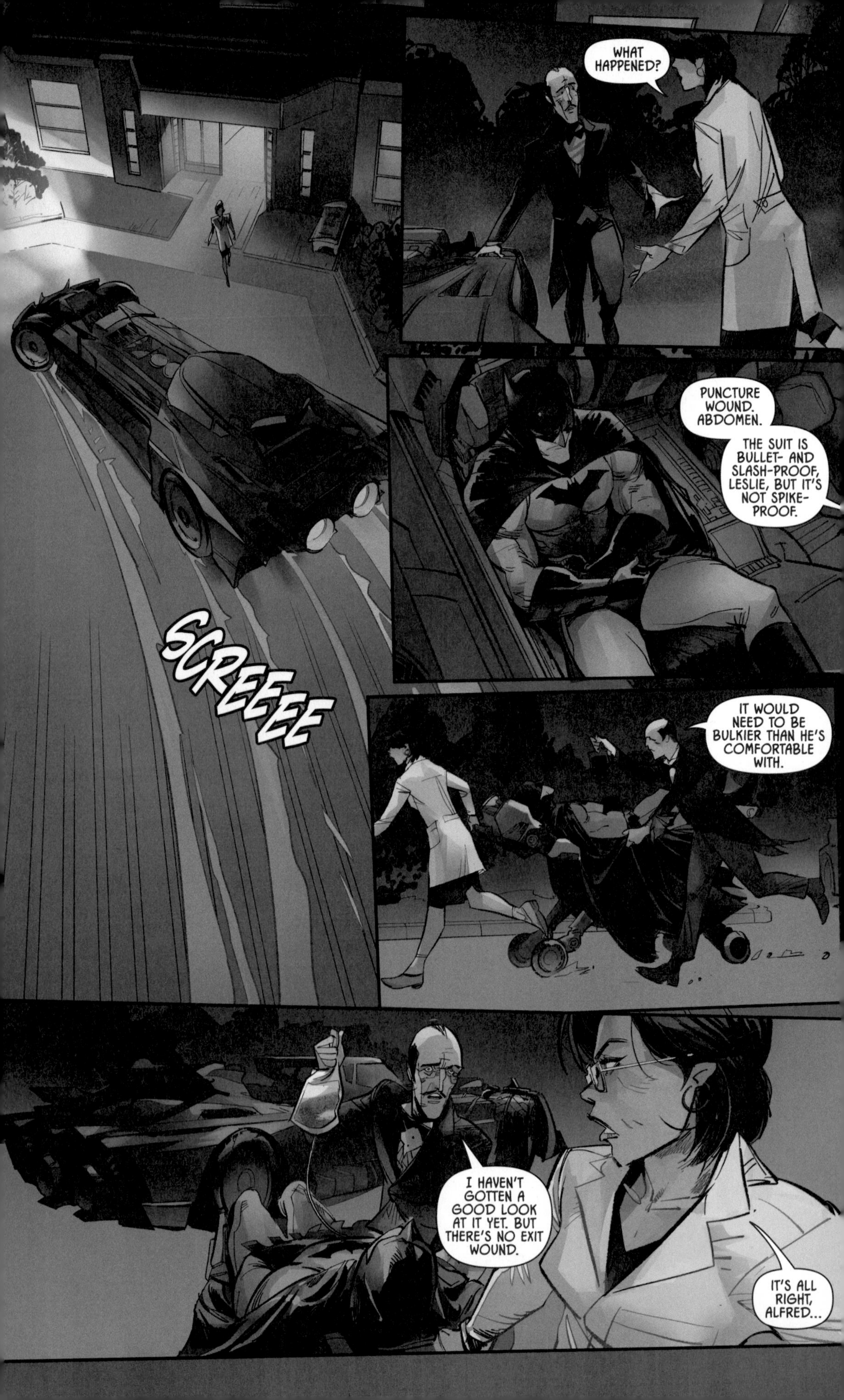
SCREEEEE
WHAT HAPPENED?
PUNCTURE WOUND. ABDOMEN.
THE SUIT IS BULLET- AND SLASH-PROOF, LESLIE, BUT IT'S NOT SPIKE-PROOF.
IT WOULD NEED TO BE BULKIER THAN HE'S COMFORTABLE WITH.
I HAVEN'T GOTTEN A GOOD LOOK AT IT YET. BUT THERE'S NO EXIT WOUND.
IT'S ALL RIGHT, ALFRED...

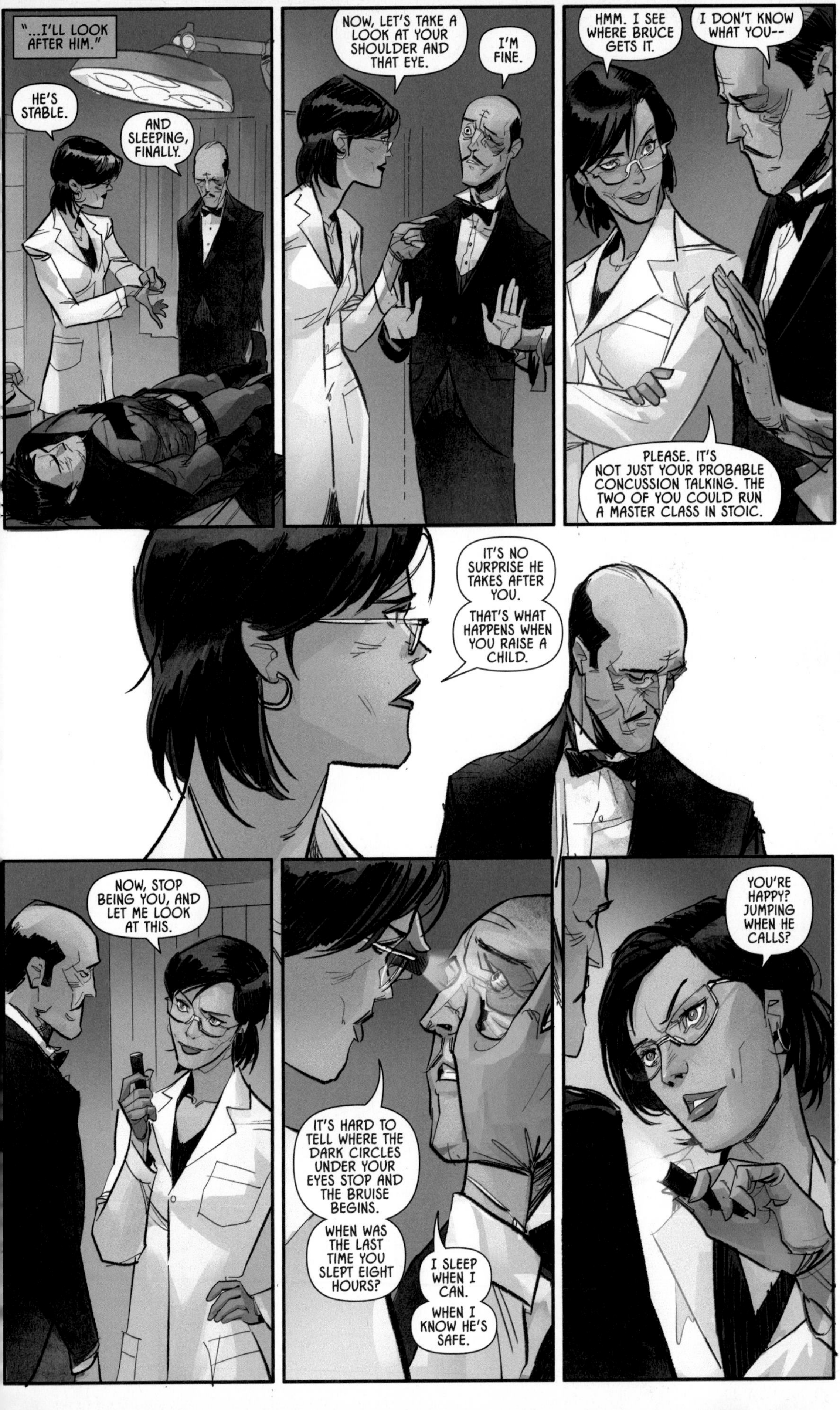
"...I'LL LOOK AFTER HIM."
HE'S STABLE.
AND SLEEPING, FINALLY.
NOW, LET'S TAKE A LOOK AT YOUR SHOULDER AND THAT EYE.
I'M FINE.
HMM. I SEE WHERE BRUCE GETS IT.
I DON'T KNOW WHAT YOU--
PLEASE. IT'S NOT JUST YOUR PROBABLE CONCUSSION TALKING. THE TWO OF YOU COULD RUN A MASTER CLASS IN STOIC.
IT'S NO SURPRISE HE TAKES AFTER YOU.
THAT'S WHAT HAPPENS WHEN YOU RAISE A CHILD.
NOW, STOP BEING YOU, AND LET ME LOOK AT THIS.
IT'S HARD TO TELL WHERE THE DARK CIRCLES UNDER YOUR EYES STOP AND THE BRUISE BEGINS.
WHEN WAS THE LAST TIME YOU SLEPT EIGHT HOURS?
I SLEEP WHEN I CAN.
WHEN I KNOW HE'S SAFE.
YOU'RE HAPPY? JUMPING WHEN HE CALLS?

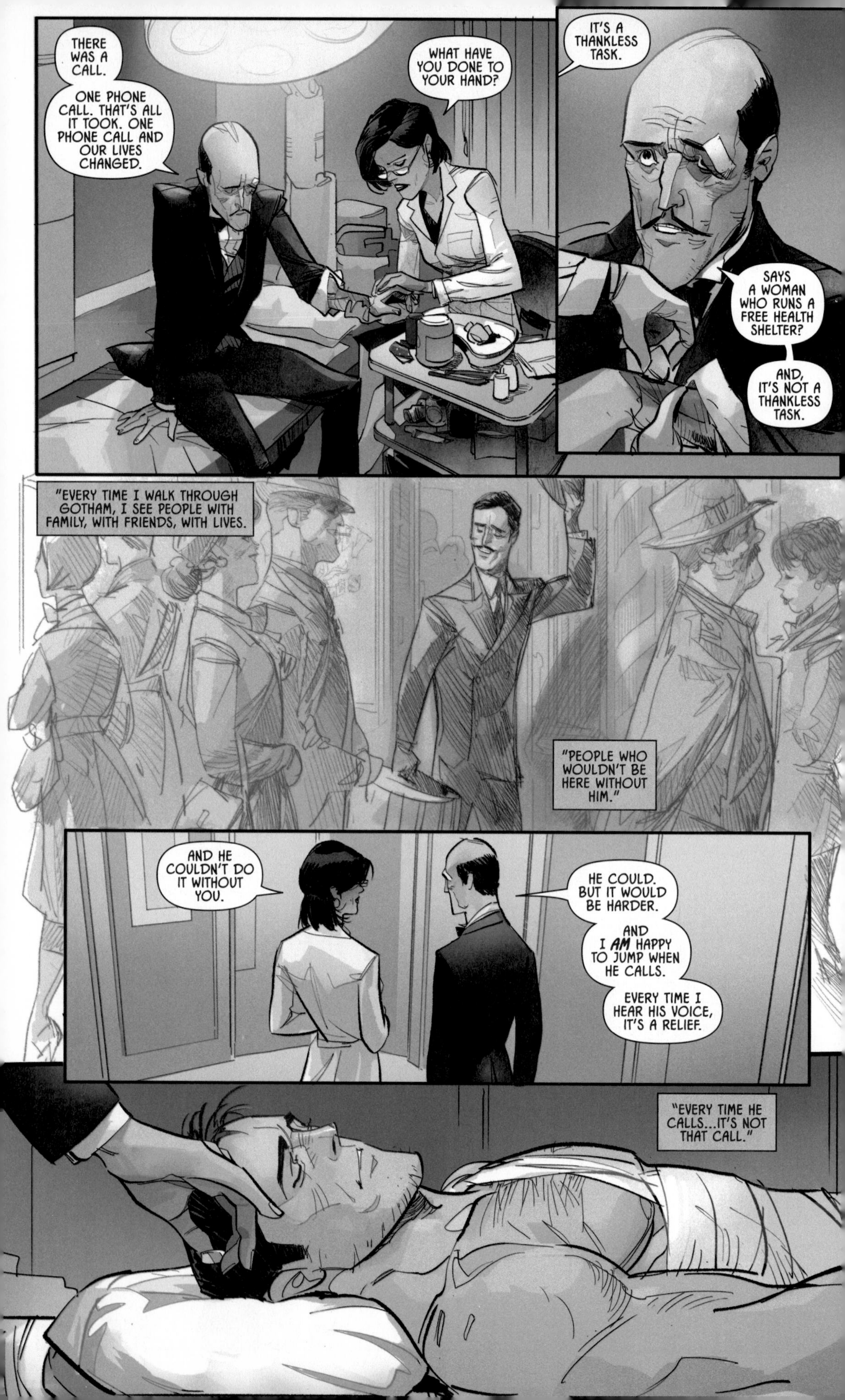
THERE WAS A CALL.
ONE PHONE CALL. THAT'S ALL IT TOOK. ONE PHONE CALL AND OUR LIVES CHANGED.
WHAT HAVE YOU DONE TO YOUR HAND?
IT'S A THANKLESS TASK.
SAYS A WOMAN WHO RUNS A FREE HEALTH SHELTER?
AND, IT'S NOT A THANKLESS TASK.
"EVERY TIME I WALK THROUGH GOTHAM, I SEE PEOPLE WITH FAMILY, WITH FRIENDS, WITH LIVES.
"PEOPLE WHO WOULDN'T BE HERE WITHOUT HIM."
AND HE COULDN'T DO IT WITHOUT YOU.
HE COULD. BUT IT WOULD BE HARDER.
AND I *AM* HAPPY TO JUMP WHEN HE CALLS.
EVERY TIME I HEAR HIS VOICE, IT'S A RELIEF.
"EVERY TIME HE CALLS...IT'S NOT THAT CALL."

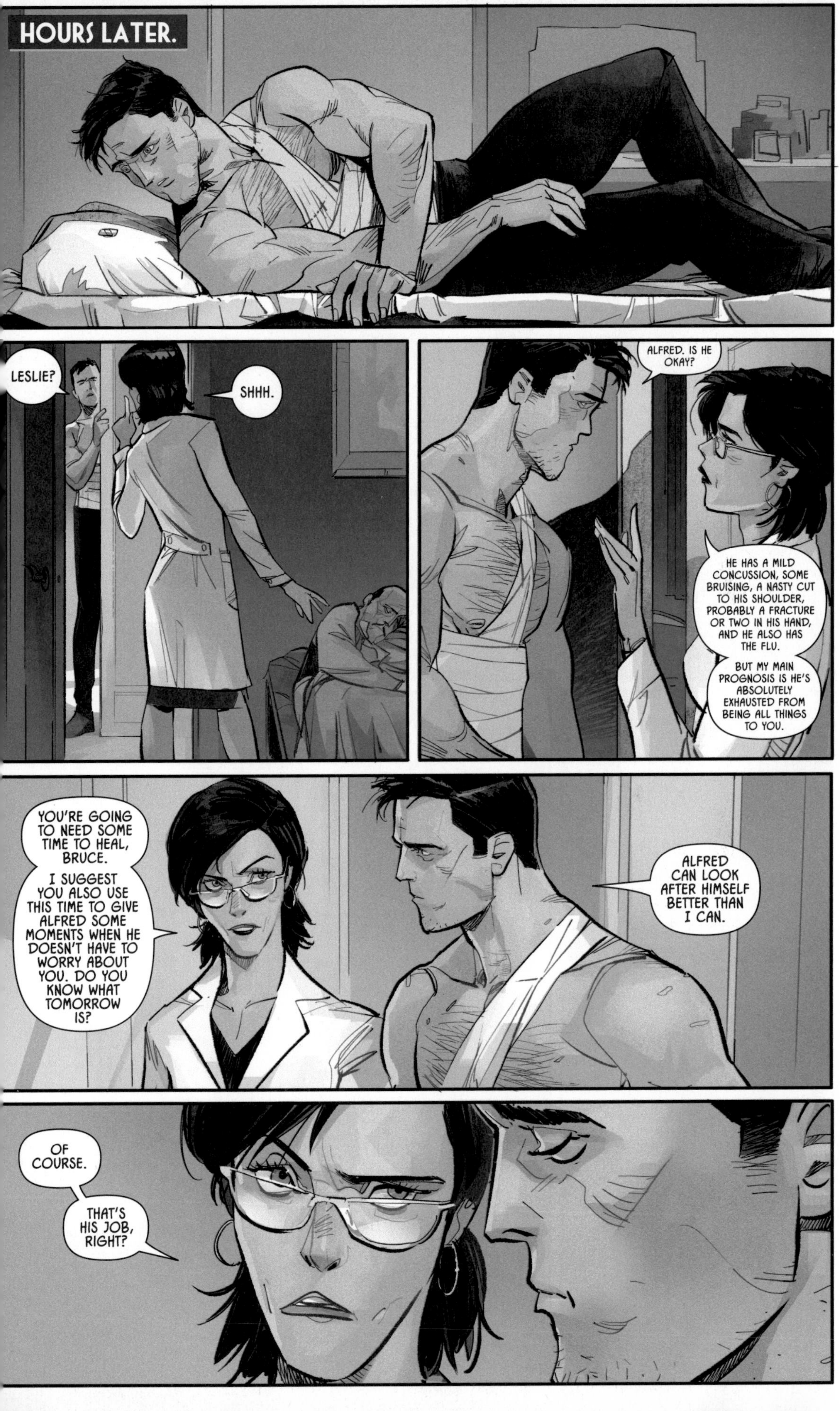
HOURS LATER.
LESLIE?
SHHH.
ALFRED. IS HE OKAY?
HE HAS A MILD CONCUSSION, SOME BRUISING, A NASTY CUT TO HIS SHOULDER, PROBABLY A FRACTURE OR TWO IN HIS HAND, AND HE ALSO HAS THE FLU.
BUT MY MAIN PROGNOSIS IS HE'S ABSOLUTELY EXHAUSTED FROM BEING ALL THINGS TO YOU.
YOU'RE GOING TO NEED SOME TIME TO HEAL, BRUCE.
I SUGGEST YOU ALSO USE THIS TIME TO GIVE ALFRED SOME MOMENTS WHEN HE DOESN'T HAVE TO WORRY ABOUT YOU. DO YOU KNOW WHAT TOMORROW IS?
ALFRED CAN LOOK AFTER HIMSELF BETTER THAN I CAN.
OF COURSE.
THAT'S HIS JOB, RIGHT?

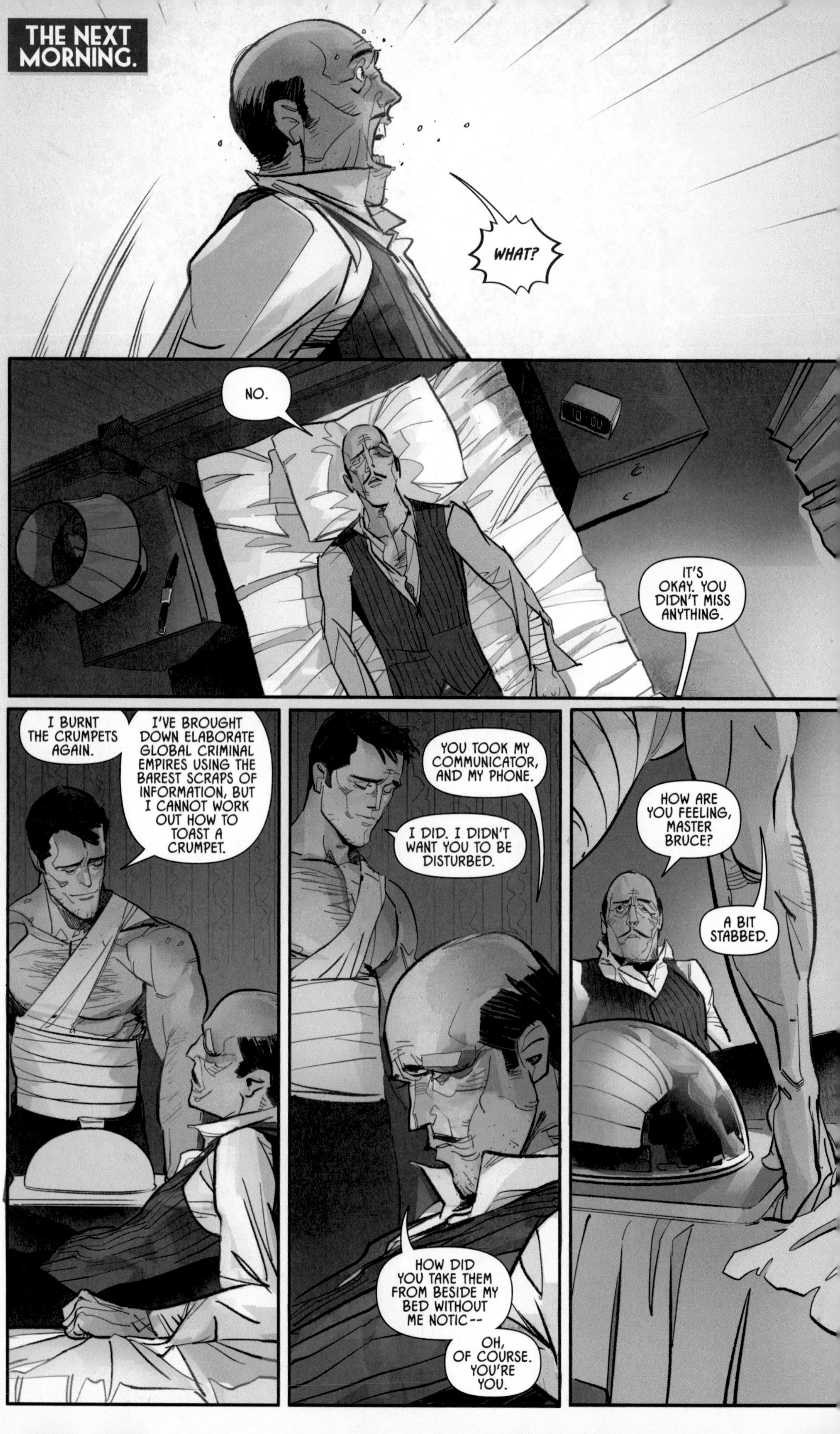

THE NEXT MORNING.
WHAT?
NO.
IT'S OKAY. YOU DIDN'T MISS ANYTHING.
I BURNT THE CRUMPETS AGAIN.
I'VE BROUGHT DOWN ELABORATE GLOBAL CRIMINAL EMPIRES USING THE BAREST SCRAPS OF INFORMATION, BUT I CANNOT WORK OUT HOW TO TOAST A CRUMPET.
YOU TOOK MY COMMUNICATOR, AND MY PHONE.
I DID. I DIDN'T WANT YOU TO BE DISTURBED.
HOW DID YOU TAKE THEM FROM BESIDE MY BED WITHOUT ME NOTIC--
OH, OF COURSE. YOU'RE YOU.
HOW ARE YOU FEELING, MASTER BRUCE?
A BIT STABBED.

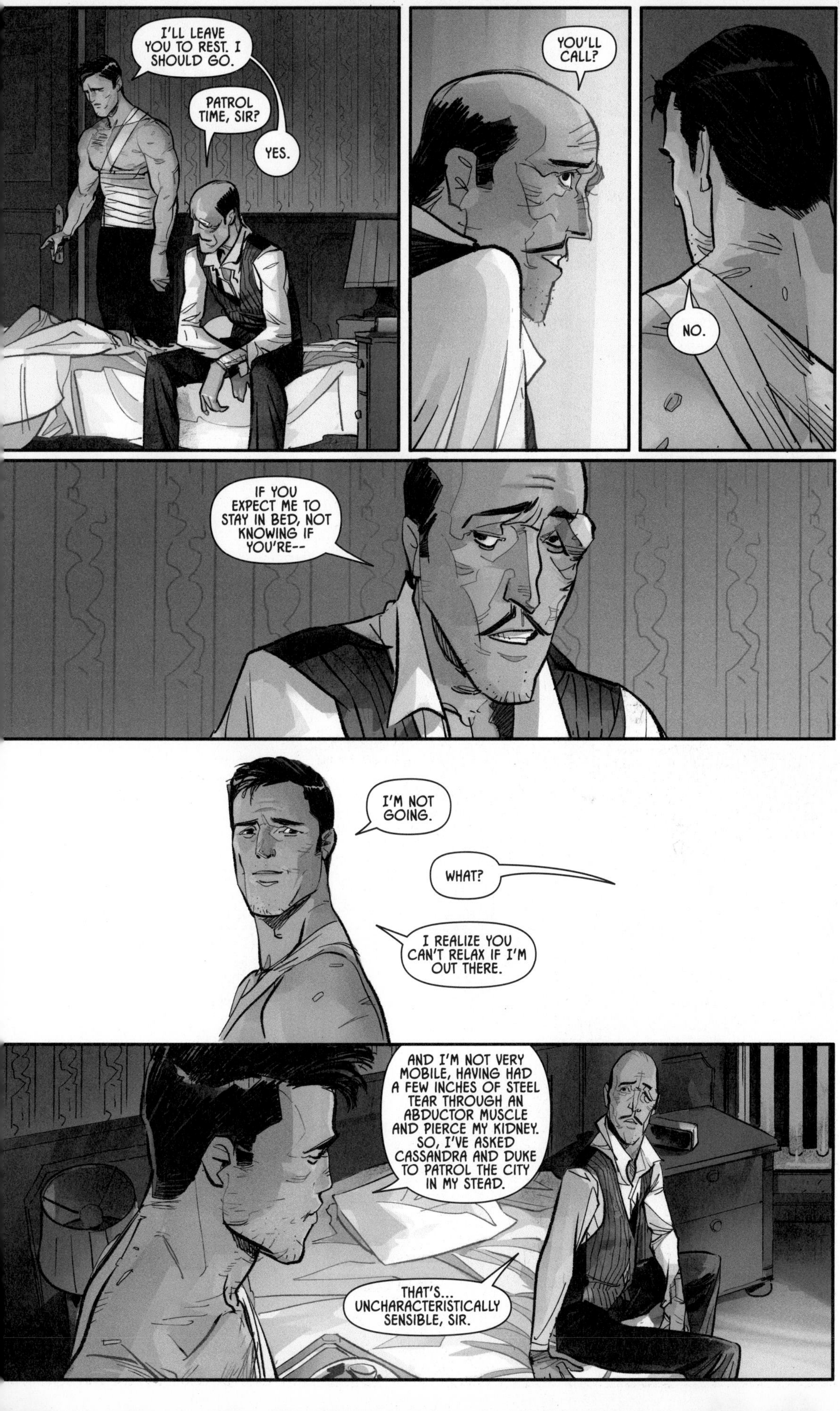
I'LL LEAVE YOU TO REST. I SHOULD GO.
PATROL TIME, SIR?
YES.
YOU'LL CALL?
NO.
IF YOU EXPECT ME TO STAY IN BED, NOT KNOWING IF YOU'RE--
I'M NOT GOING.
WHAT?
I REALIZE YOU CAN'T RELAX IF I'M OUT THERE.
AND I'M NOT VERY MOBILE, HAVING HAD A FEW INCHES OF STEEL TEAR THROUGH AN ABDUCTOR MUSCLE AND PIERCE MY KIDNEY. SO, I'VE ASKED CASSANDRA AND DUKE TO PATROL THE CITY IN MY STEAD.
THAT'S... UNCHARACTERISTICALLY SENSIBLE, SIR.

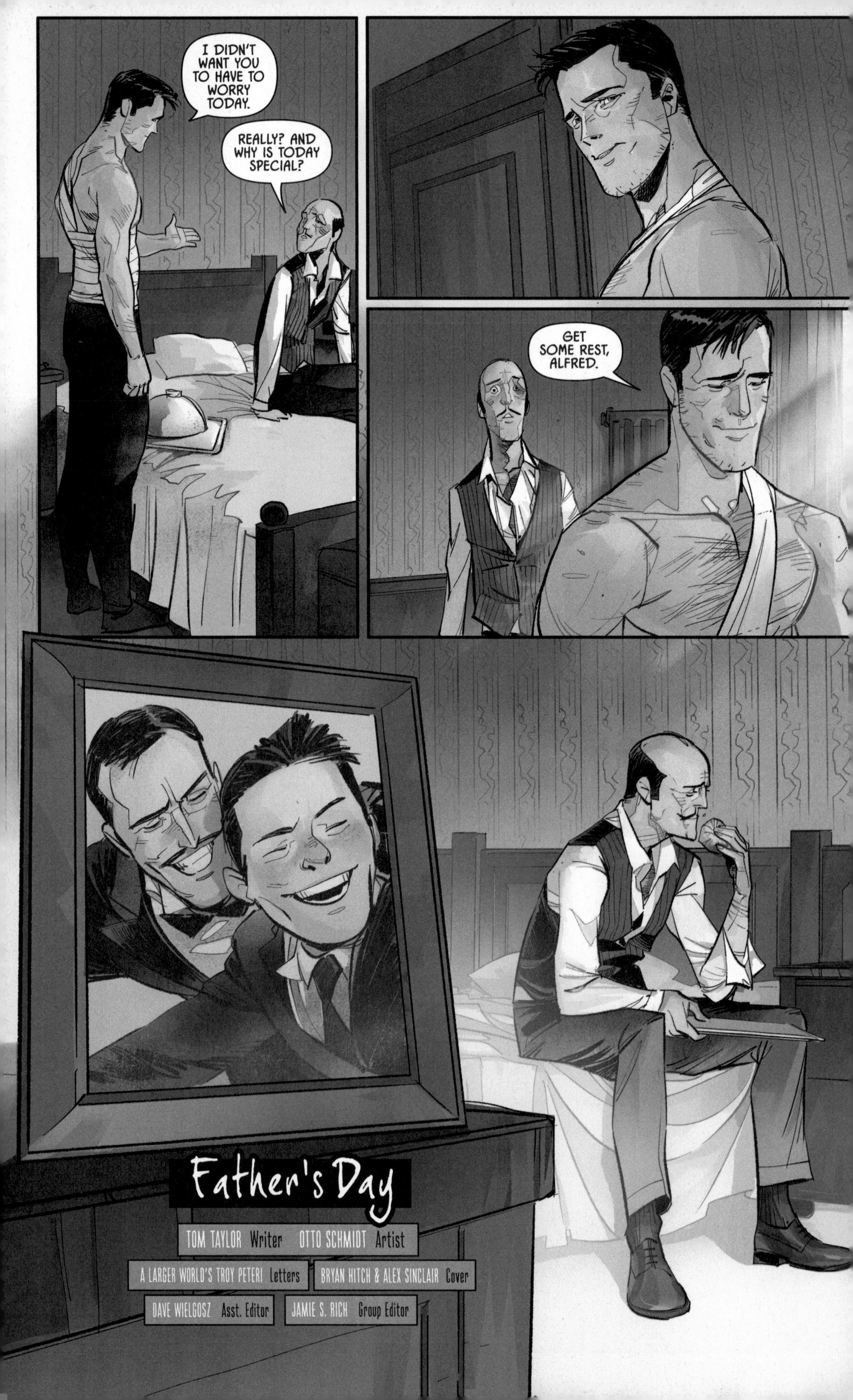
I DIDN'T WANT YOU TO HAVE TO WORRY TODAY.
REALLY? AND WHY IS TODAY SPECIAL?
GET SOME REST, ALFRED.
Father's Day
TOM TAYLOR Writer OTTO SCHMIDT Artist
A LARGER WORLD'S TROY PETERI Letters
BRYAN HITCH & ALEX SINCLAIR Cover
DAVE WIELGOSZ Asst. Editor
JAMIE S. RICH Group Editor

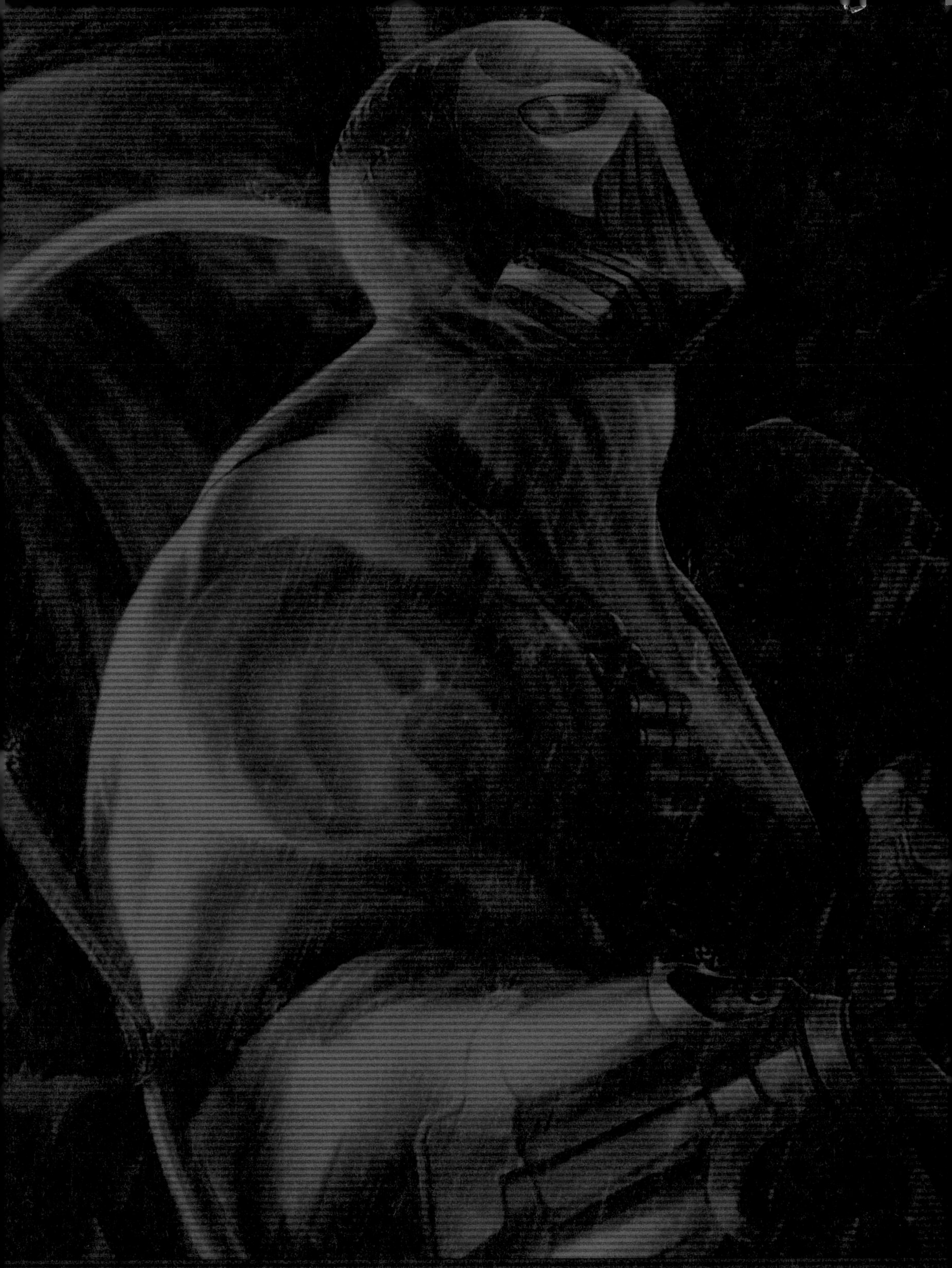

VARIANT COVER GALLERY

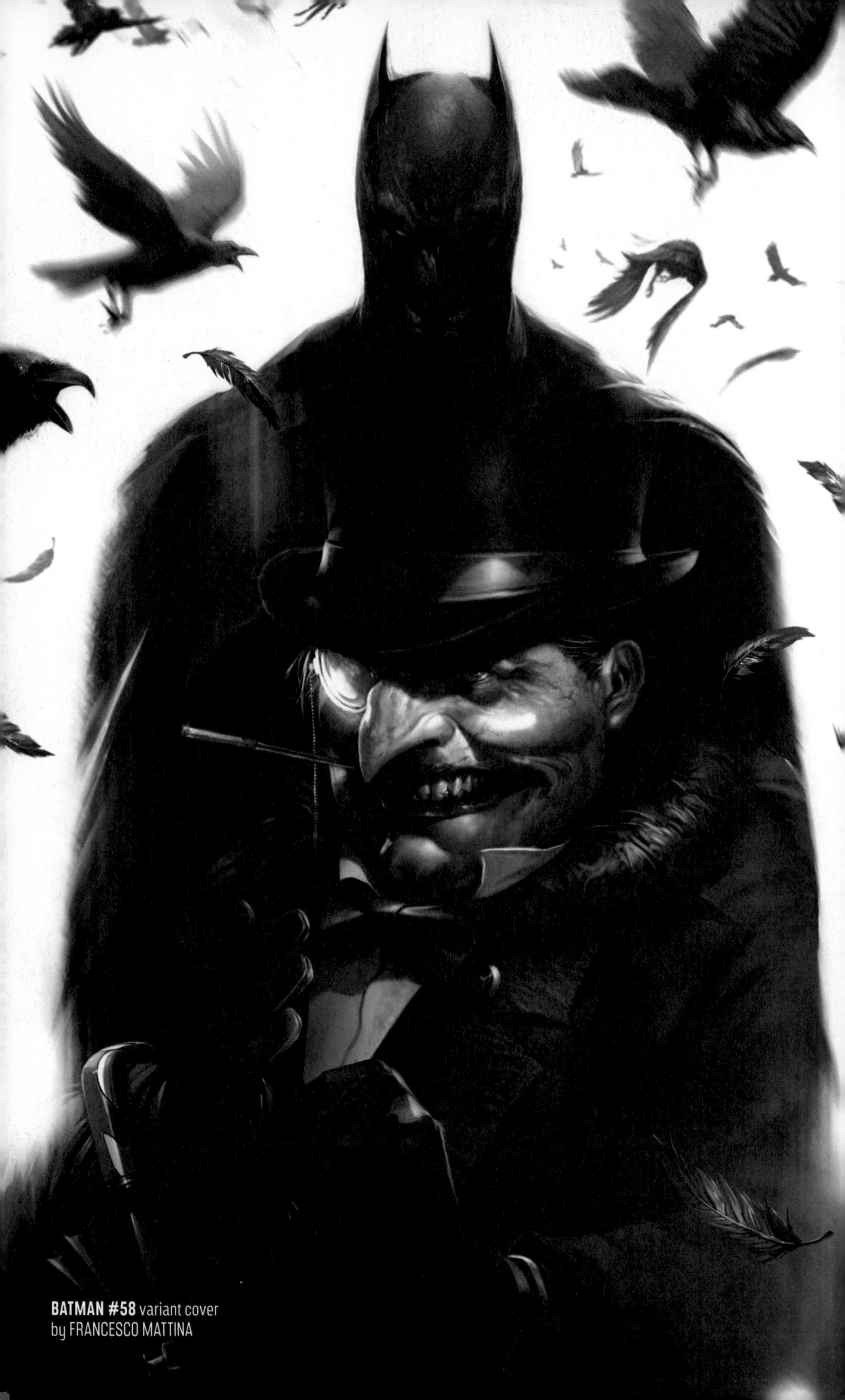

BATMAN #58 variant cover
by FRANCESCO MATTINA

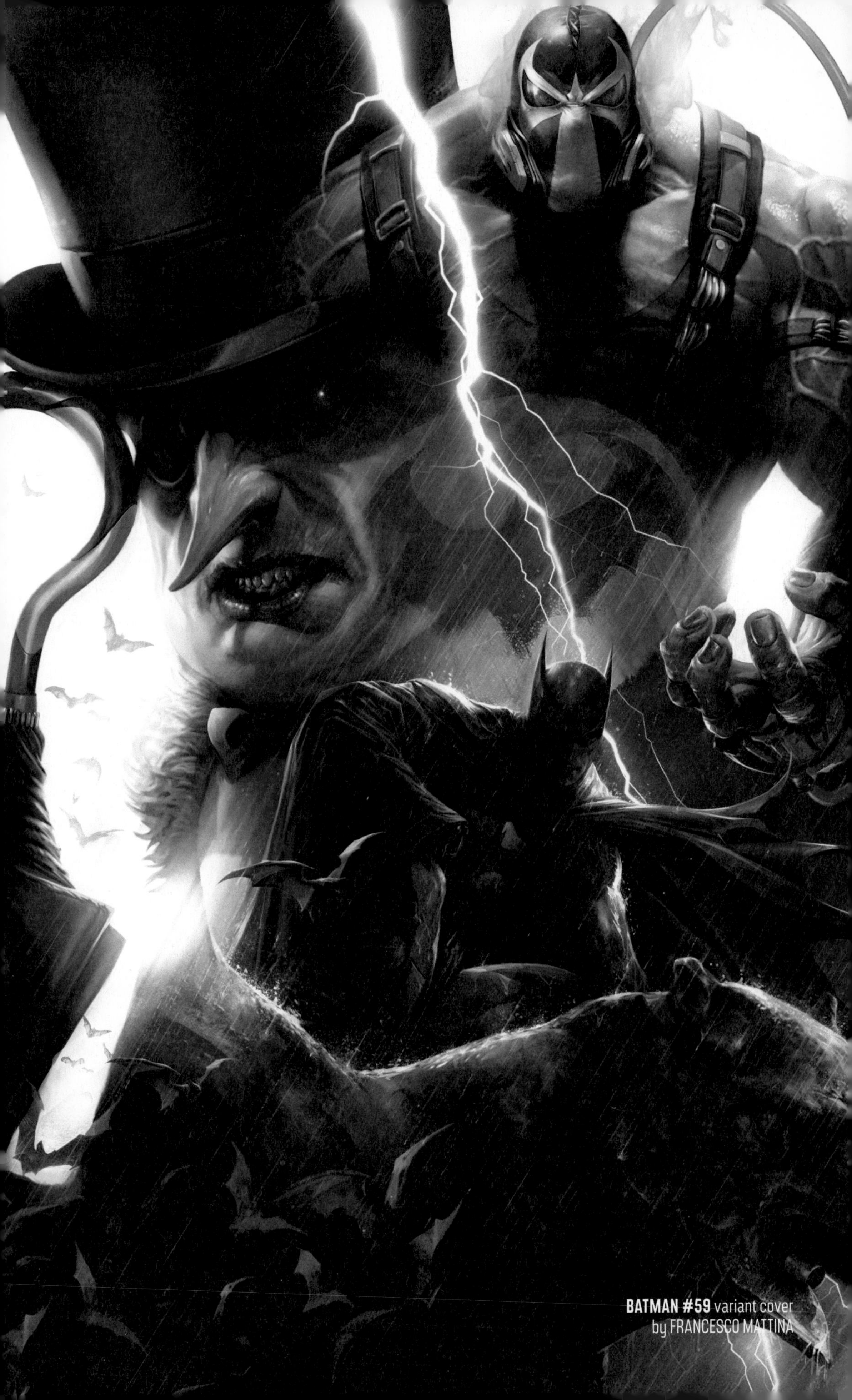

BATMAN #59 variant cover
by FRANCESCO MATTINA

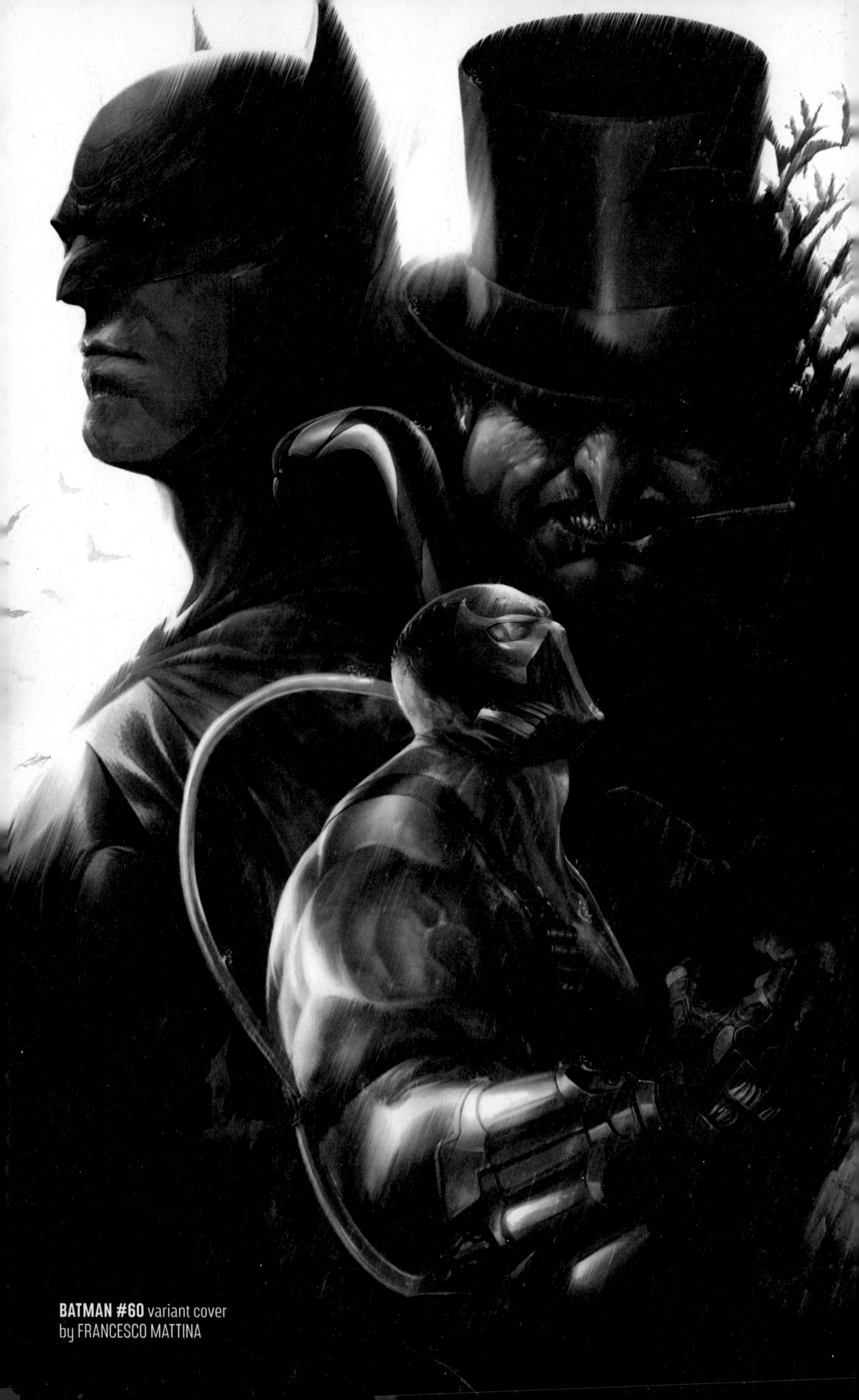

BATMAN #60 variant cover
by FRANCESCO MATTINA